KEATS REVIEWED
BY HIS CONTEMPORARIES

A Collection of Notices
for the Years 1816-1821

by

LEWIS M. SCHWARTZ

The Scarecrow Press, Inc.
Metuchen, N.J.   1973

Library of Congress Cataloging in Publication Data

Schwartz, Lewis M   comp.
  Keats reviewed by his contemporaries.

  Includes bibliographical references.
  1. Keats, John, 1795-1821. I. Title.
PR4837.S33   821'.7   72-12779
ISBN 0-8108-0577-4

Copyright 1973 by Lewis M. Schwartz

For Rona, Marc, and Scott

Acknowledgments and Editorial Notes

The collecting and editing of this material, limited to 1816-1821, was suggested to me by Kenneth Neill Cameron. I am in his debt for the kindness and guidance he has extended to me on many occasions. Arthur A. Houghton, Jr. also has my gratitude for his interest in this project and for his generosity in financing my research in England through the award of a travel grant, which was administered by New York University.

The reviews and notices that follow are arranged chronologically around Keats's three major publications. Chapter Five is a miscellaneous gathering of notices for the years 1820-1821. The sixth chapter deals with notices occasioned by Keats's death and the publication of Adonais. With some exceptions--each noted in the text--the chronological arrangement of the collection is based on the order of J. R. MacGillivray, Keats: A Bibliography and Reference Guide (Toronto, 1949). Material not known to MacGillivray is exactly dated and incorporated at the appropriate points.

Whenever possible, regardless of whether reprints exist, the material in this collection is taken from its original source. The only exceptions to this rule are an article on "Mr. Keats's Endymion" in the Chester Guardian (unavailable), which is reproduced from a reprint in the Examiner of November 1, 1818; and Shelley's Preface to Adonais, which is taken from Thomas Hutchinson's edition of The Complete Poetical Works (Oxford, 1934). In each case the printed texts attempt to reproduce exactly the phrasing, punctuation, and spellings of the original. As for the texts themselves, I have attempted to identify all quotations, references, and allusions by the reviewers. I have also noted instances where I was unable to do so in the hope that others may be able to make the identification.

Serials of the period vary widely in including or omitting the definite article from their titles. For purposes of consistency, I omit the article in all cases.

v

CONTENTS

Chapter | Page

I.   INTRODUCTION | 1

II. KEATS'S RECEPTION THROUGH 1817 | 52

   1. George Felton Mathew's "To A Poetical Friend" in the European Magazine | 52

   2. From Leigh Hunt's "Young Poets" in the Examiner | 54

   3. John Hamilton Reynolds' review of Poems in the Champion | 56

   4. A short review of Poems in the Monthly Magazine | 61

   5. Mathew's review of Poems in the European Magazine | 62

   6. Hunt's review of Poems in the Examiner | 67

   7. From two letters on Keats and Poems by Wilson in the Anti-Gallican Monitor | 77

   8. An exchange on Keats in the Champion | 83

   9. A review of Poems in the Eclectic Review | 84

  10. A review of Poems in the Edinburgh Magazine and Literary Miscellany | 92

III. THE RECEPTION OF ENDYMION AND OTHER NOTICES THROUGH 1820 | 105

   1. A review of Endymion in the Literary Journal | 106

2. Two Letters on Endymion by Benjamin Bailey
   in the Oxford University and City Herald   109

3. A review of Endymion in the Champion   115

4. John Gibson Lockhart's "Cockney School of
   Poetry. No. IV." in Blackwood's Edinburgh
   Magazine   119

5. John Wilson Croker's review of Endymion in
   the Quarterly Review   127

6. A review of Endymion in the British Critic   134

7. Two letters on Endymion in the Morning
   Chronicle   140

8. J. H. Reynolds' "The Quarterly Review--Mr.
   Keats" in the Alfred, West of England
   Journal and General Advertiser   143

9. A short review of Endymion in the Sun   148

10. The Examiner reprints a defense of Keats
    from the Chester Guardian   149

11. Three sonnets to Keats in Hunt's Foliage   151

12. A burlesque of Hunt by "Beppo" in the
    Literary Journal   152

13. Blackwood's "Cockney School of Poetry.
    No. VI."   155

14. John Wilson in Blackwood's alludes to Keats
    in a review of Hunt's Literary Pocketbook
    for 1820   158

15. A review of Endymion in Baldwin's London
    Magazine   159

16. Francis Jeffrey reviews Endymion in the
    Edinburgh Review   173

17. A review of Endymion in the Edinburgh
    Magazine and Literary Miscellany   180

IV.   THE LAMIA VOLUME   201

   1. A review of the Lamia volume in the Monthly
       Review   202

   2. A short review of the Lamia volume in the
       St. James's Chronicle   205

   3. Richard Woodhouse's review of the Lamia
       volume in the Sun   207

   4. Charles Lamb's review of the Lamia volume
       in the New Times   210

   5. A review of the Lamia volume in the Literary
       Chronicle and Weekly Review   213

   6. Hunt's review of the Lamia volume in the
       Indicator   214

   7. A review of the Lamia volume in the
       Guardian   228

   8. A review of the Lamia volume in the Edin-
       burgh Magazine and Literary Miscellany   232

   9. A review of the Lamia volume in Gold's
       London Magazine   236

  10. A short review of the Lamia volume in the
       Monthly Magazine   258

  11. A review of the Lamia volume in the New
       Monthly Magazine   259

  12. A review of the Lamia volume in the
       British Critic   262

  13. A review of the Lamia volume in the
       Eclectic Review   266

  14. John Scott's review of the Lamia volume
       in Baldwin's London Magazine   274

V.   GENERAL AND MISCELLANEOUS COMMEN-
      TARIES 1820-1821   296

1. From a review of Wallace's Prospects of
   Mankind, etc. in the Retrospective Review 296

2. From an article on "Modern Periodical
   Literature" in the New Monthly Magazine 297

3. From an article "On the present State of
   Poetical Talent" in the New Bon Ton
   Magazine 298

4. Three references to Keats in Blackwood's
   for September 1820 299

5. Hunt's farewell to Keats in the Indicator 302

6. A reply to Blackwood's in Baldwin's London
   Magazine 303

7. From an "Essay on Poetry" in Gold's
   London Magazine 306

8. Two references to Keats by Hazlitt 307

VI. KEATS'S DEATH, AFTERMATH, AND THE
    RECEPTION OF ADONAIS THROUGH 1821 312

1. Verses to Keats by "P." in the Literary
   Chronicle and Weekly Review 313

2. "Death of Mr. John Keats" by "L." (B. W.
   Procter?) in Baldwin's London Magazine 314

3. J. W. Dalby's "Remarks on Keats" in the
   Pocket Magazine of Classic and Polite
   Literature 316

4. A reference to Keats in a "Posthumous
   Epistle From the Author of Tristram
   Shandy" in the Gossip 320

5. A sonnet on Keats's death in the Kaleidoscope; or, Literary and Scientific Mirror 320

6. A sonnet on Keats's death in Baldwin's
   London Magazine 321

7. Keats's death is reported in the New Monthly
   Magazine   322

8. "G. V. D. 's" "On Reading Lamia, and Other
   Poems by John Keats" in the Gossip   323

9. J. H. Reynolds alludes to Keats in his
   Preface to The Garden of Florence   324

10. Shelley's Preface to Adonais   325

11. Charles Cowden Clarke's "John Keats, The
    Poet" in the Morning Chronicle   327

12. John Clare's sonnet to Keats in The Village
    Minstrel   330

13. From a review of Adonais in the Literary
    Chronicle and Weekly Review   331

14. From a review of Adonais in the Literary
    Gazette and Journal of Belles Lettres   332

15. From William Maginn's "Remarks on
    Shelley's Adonais" in Blackwood's Edin-
    burgh Magazine   334

APPENDIX: Summary of English Publications in
          Which Keats is Mentioned, 1816-1821   347

Chapter I

INTRODUCTION

There is more than one yardstick for measuring a
poet's contemporary reputation. T. M. Raysor used the
sales of Wordsworth's poetry as an indicator of the poet's
reception.[1] At best, this is a limited guide, for public
acceptance of a writer can lag behind critical recognition
by many years. Our own century provides us with some
good illustrations. When Robert Frost could not find an
audience for his poetry in the United States, Ezra Pound,
already aware of his fellow American's worth, helped him
publish A Boy's Will and North of Boston in England. Wallace Stevens, another example of early public neglect, was
later to confess to Harriet Monroe that he earned only
$6.70 in royalties for Harmonium during the first six
months of 1924, yet among the more knowledgeable critics
and writers of the twenties, Stevens had already gained acceptance as an outstanding poet. Today, one need only
refer to the list of accomplished poets teaching at our major
universities to realize that many are unable to support
themselves on the sales of their verse alone. If Keats were
alive today, it is doubtful that our age would be any more
perceptive than was his.

Keats, of course, received very little income from
his poetry. His three volumes of verse sold poorly, and in
the four years that separated publication of his first and
last volumes, he hardly had the time to make the public
impact that Wordsworth was able to achieve after more than
twenty years of relative neglect. Nevertheless, Keats was
not without critical recognition in his own time. His work
was favorably reviewed by Hunt, Jeffrey, Lamb, and
Reynolds; Hazlitt and Shelley came to his defense; his poetry
was reprinted and reviewed with substantial frequency between 1816-1820; and on the news of his death in 1821,
over fifty notices, obituaries and commemorative poems
appeared in many of England's leading periodicals and newspapers. Such a list of particulars falls short of supporting
a claim for wide public acceptance of the poet, but it does

1

indicate that the informed opinion of knowledgeable critics
and writers is a more fruitful approach to the reputation of
a writer during his lifetime.

Certainly, Keats had his detractors, as every student
of the Romantic period knows. The reviews of Endymion
were so unusually severe that Shelley erroneously cited them
as the main cause of Keats's early death. Untold numbers
of readers since have been duly cautioned about the hysteria
of Adonais, but at the time of Keats's death, Shelley's
charge was repeated by Hazlitt and others. Even those who
did not subscribe to the theory of Keats's literary assassination were convinced that he died, like Chatterton, a neglected
and unappreciated genius. Joseph Severn, who nursed Keats
during his last days in Rome, dutifully reported his friend's
despondency, a despondency that was totally understandable
from one whose lungs were rotting in the terminal stages of
tuberculosis. Nevertheless, Keats's friend, Charles Armitage Brown, continued to believe the tenor, if not the substance, of Shelley's charge, and the impact of Adonais
seized the imagination of the Victorians as well as the Romantics. This impact can still be found today by any
traveler who makes the pilgrimage to the old Protestant
Cemetery in Rome and reads the inscription on Keats's
headstone: "This grave contains all that was mortal of a
young English poet, who, on his death bed in the bitterness
of his heart, at the malicious power of his enemies, desired these words on his tomb stone. 'Here lies one whose
name was writ in water.' "

In the Autumn 1968 issue of The Poetry Review,
George Nevin remarks that "in many ways the attitude of
Adonais has done Keats more harm than has yet been re-
alized; for it did not die with Shelley--later critics have
perpetuated it."[2] Even after Marsh and White's seminal
study of "Keats and the Periodicals of His Time" and Mac-
Gillivray's introductory survey of Keats's reputation,[3] Henri
Peyre maintains as late as 1967 that Keats's contemporary
reception was one of the failures of criticism.[4] Peyre's
opinion, however, is not shared by Keats's biographer,
Robert Gittings, and it is directly contradicted by John A.
Hayden in his study of The Romantic Reviewers (Chicago,
1969).[5]

If the weight of critical opinion today confirms Keats's
generally favorable reception, it still leaves many details of
the story untold. The present collection of sixty-four items

includes thirty-two that are reproduced for the first
time or presented in more detail than in existing reprints.   Five of these sixty-four items are new discov-
eries.   In effect, half of the significant public commentaries on Keats by his English contemporaries have been
unavailable previously to students of the period.   The
complete text, as now known, is presented.

The preliminary essay that follows places Keats's reception within the historical perspective of the Regency
period.   It also includes a reassessment of the role of
Leigh Hunt in Keats's career, and a survey of the reviews,
magazines and newspapers of Keats's time.   Finally, it
deals with the poet's reception, particularly in newspapers
of his day; no poet was ever treated more fairly by the
daily, tri-weekly, and weekly press of England.

I

Keats's earliest known publication, the poem "To
Solitude," appeared in John and Leigh Hunt's Examiner of
May 5, 1816.   On June 30 or July 1, 1820, Taylor and
Hessey published the poet's third and last volume, Lamia,
Isabella, The Eve of St. Agnes, and Other Poems, 6 and
reprints of these and other poems of Keats continued to appear through the latter half of 1820 and through 1821.
During his lifetime, Keats's publications thus spanned the
last four years of the regency of the future George IV and
the first two years of George's reign as King.   It was an
unsettling period in English history.   The country began to
readjust from a war economy which had ended with the de-
feat of Napoleon in 1815, and while doing so, the repres-
sive Tory ministry of Lord Liverpool was challenged by
radical advocates of political reform.   It was at this time
also that Thomas Bowdler published his ten-volume edition
of Shakespeare, expurgating or altering parts which could
not "with propriety be read aloud in a family."   Particulars
such as these were symptomatic of the political, economic,
and social conditions which were shaping English society
and its critical viewpoints from 1816-1821.   These conditions
must be explored in further detail, for they had a direct
effect on Keats's contemporary reception.

Tory ministries dominated the political scene through-

4   Keats Reviewed

out the Regency period. After the assassination of Perceval
in 1812, Lord Liverpool became Prime Minister. He remained in that office until 1827, and although his policies
became more liberal after 1822,[7] his conservatism during
Keats's lifetime was notorious. Political protest was dealt
with harshly by Liverpool's ministry. In 1817 Habeas Corpus was suspended. In August 1819 the Peterloo Massacre
occurred in Manchester: eleven people were killed and
hundreds injured when a force of local yeomanry, attempting
to arrest the radical agitator, Henry Hunt, pushed and
hacked its way through a crowd of 60,000 people.[8] Still in
1819, Parliament passed the "Six Acts" which, among other
things, forbade large public meetings and attempted to suppress the radical press by placing a four pence per copy
stamp tax on all newspapers.[9] The Whigs, of course, denounced the Tories; but the most troublesome opposition
came from William Cobbett and the radical press.

Cobbett was a dangerous opponent, primarily because
his weekly Political Register was a powerful public vehicle
with which to express his radicalism. At two pence a copy,
the Political Register was within the means of the working
class, and in November 1816 circulation "rose to 40,000 or
50,000 copies a week: a figure many times larger than that
of any other newspaper; and ... a single copy frequently
served for scores of auditors."[10] The four penny stamp tax
was aimed directly at Cobbett and forced him to raise the
price of his newspaper;[11] however, at the height of his
power in 1816, Cobbett and his Political Register had enor-
mous influence on the working class.[12]

Where the Tories could not tax hostile newspapers
out of existence, they attempted to jail editor, publisher,
or both. John and Leigh Hunt, convicted of libeling the
Prince Regent in the Examiner, spent February 1813-Febru-
ary 1815 in separate prisons. William Hone, who had published an actionable parody of the Catechism, operated his
Reformist Register and Weekly Commentary from prison
for two months in 1817. In that same year, Richard Carlile,
editor of the Republican, served a sentence in Dorchester
Gaol for publishing Paine's Age of Reason.[13] Although
neither editor nor publisher, "Orator" Henry Hunt received
wide attention in the radical press, and he was also jailed
for two years.

Still another form of Tory retaliation was the minis-
terial-controlled press. On March 15, 1817 the Anti-Cob-

bett addressed the workmen of Manchester in an open letter,
informing them of Cobbett's duplicity. Piety and patriotism
were constantly stressed in this newspaper. "The source
of all good is religion, " it proclaimed in an unsigned letter
reprinted from the Day and New Times. "The fear of the
Lord is the beginning of wisdom. If you fear God, you will
honour the King" (February 22, 1817, col. 40). At Manchester again, the scene of the Peterloo Massacre, the
Patriot proclaimed itself in its subtitle to be "a Periodical
Publication, intending to Arrest Progress of Sedition and
Blasphemous Opinions too Prevalent in the Year 1819/1820. "
Similarly, London publications such as the Loyalist; or Anti-
Radical and John Bull were also propaganda vehicles for
George IV and Liverpool. In part or in whole, the government subsidized at one time or another the Morning Chron-
icle, St. James's Chronicle, Sun, Morning Post, Morning
Herald, Courier, Anti-Gallican Monitor, New Times, Star,
and more than a dozen other newspapers.14 But despite
these friendly voices, there was significant opposition in
the daily and Sunday press.

Essentially, Liverpool made enemies because of his
futile attempt to resurrect the pre-Napoleonic past. To
him, and to others of his party, the rising discontent of the
working class was an aberration which had to be suppressed
by any means necessary, even if it meant employing the
methods of a police state. Political unrest resulted from
economic roots as well; it stemmed from lack of food among
the poor. The price of corn and bread was high during the
Napoleonic Wars, 15 and when peace did come in 1815, when
English goods were no longer in demand by the allies, the
English monopoly of trade ceased to exist. Bankruptcy and
unemployment occurred in the cities; in the country, farmers
who had survived the system of land enclosure were now
also going bankrupt. 16 For the working class, for those to
whom Henry Hunt, Carlile, and Cobbett spoke and wrote,
economic and political redress were still many years away.
Finally, in 1823, Pitt's Combination Acts were repealed and
trade union action was no longer illegal. Even so, the Reform Bill of 1832 left the working and lower-middle classes
still disenfranchised.

Religious and moral attitudes were no less stringent
than the economic and political austerities of the Regency
period. The Critical Review, Annual Review and History
of Literature, British Critic, British Review and London
Critical Journal, and Eclectic Review were all founded under

Church patronage, and the titles of at least fifty more magazines "contain the word 'Christian,' 'theological,' or some
other term which indicates the religious aims of their
founders."17 A certain moral prudishness in these magazines and reviews is understandable, but the same attitude
is also evident in serials without any direct Church affiliation. Blackwood's Edinburgh Magazine attacks the Story of
the Rimini (1816) because of Hunt's "extreme moral depravity" (II [October 1817], 40). It questions "the propriety of
making incest the subject of poetry" (II [November 1817],
194). "There can be no radical distinction allowed between
the private and public character of a poet," Blackwood's
concludes, and therefore any slander whatsoever is justi-
fiable against a man who writes a poem about incest (III
[July 1818], 454).18 Similarly, Shelley's Queen Mab, which
appeared in 1821 in separate pirated editions by William
Clark and William Benbow, is attacked for its atheism in
the Literary Gazette and the Beacon. The review in the
Beacon is characteristic of the more extreme form of
moral contempt with which Queen Mab was greeted.

> A work of the most outrageous blasphemy and
> most loathsome indecency, has just appeared....
> The name of the author prefixed is Percy Bysshe
> Shelley.... This same name ... will be re-
> membered by all who have had the greatest mis-
> fortune of meeting with a dramatic poem entitled
> the 'Cenci,' a sample of the manufacture of hell,
> woven in the tissue of crimes, of which parricide
> is the least....
> It is to be hoped that no such person as Percy
> Bysshe Shelley, the author, exists.... But if
> such be the case, never was a stronger illustra-
> tion of the danger of tampering with the arms of
> Satan, than the publication of Queen Mab presents.19

An attack of this nature also occurred in the second part of
the Investigator, or Quarterly Magazine for 1822. Byron too
was attacked for sceptical and irreverent passages in Childe
Harold and Don Juan. What was singled out for praise was
equally revealing. Of the notorious blue-pencilled Family
Shakespeare (1818), the Edinburgh Review can discern
nothing "of a ... prudish spirit." In fact, Bowdler "has
left many things in the text which, to a delicate taste, must
still appear coarse and reprehensible."20

During the Regency, then, moral posturing and fear

of radical political change became the tonic keys of conservative politician, magazine, and newspaper alike. This
attitude had an effect upon the critical reception of the
second generation of Romantics. The more outrageous attacks on the "radical" and "atheistical" Shelley were the
result of fear rather than critical insensitivity.[21] With the
exception of De Quincey, the younger Romantics were hostile
to the Established Church.[22] Keats, who on his deathbed
received no solace from the Bible,[23] never overtly attacked
either Church or State; but Hunt did, and Keats was identified with the older poet. Reference to Keats's publishing
history and his reception in influential Tory periodicals will
show clearly why hostile critics assumed that this "Cockney
upstart" was simply a literary appendage of his mentor,
Leigh Hunt.

II

On December 1, 1816 an article by Leigh Hunt on
the "Young Poets" appeared in the Examiner. This article
singled out Shelley, Reynolds, and Keats as three young
writers of new poetic promise. Of the three, Keats was
almost a complete unknown. Shelley had recently published
Alastor, and a few readers were familiar with Reynolds as
the author of Safie and the Naiad. John Keats, however,
who had that past July successfully completed his examina-
tions to practice as an apothecary and was still at Guy's
Hospital in the fall of 1816, had published only one short
poem. His sonnet "To Solitude" had appeared in the
Examiner of May 5, 1816. Despite this publication, it was
not until late October that Keats was introduced to Hunt.
A quick friendship followed, and Keats was both to lose and
profit from the relationship.

After the publication of "To Solitude," poems of
Keats appeared in Hunt's Examiner, Literary Pocketbook,
Indicator, and the Months through 1821. By March 1817,
seven poems of Keats had made their first appearance in
the Examiner.[24] Then, in March of that year, Keats's
sonnets "To Leigh Hunt Esq." and "Written on the Day that
Mr. Leigh Hunt left Prison" appeared in his first volume,
Poems. Hunt reviewed the volume favorably in the Examiner
of June 1, 1817 and July 6 and 13, 1817. The identification
between the young poet and his older friend was to continue.
Hunt praised Keats's Lamia volume in the August 2 and 9,
1820 issues of the Indicator. In Foliage (1816) and Amyntas

(1818), Hunt had addressed poems to Keats or alluded to
him in other ways. Hunt, a liberal but no radical, was
nevertheless considered an extremist by Tory critics, and
Keats suffered by his association with the editor of the
Examiner. This fact is known, but the reasons for it and
its nature have not been properly examined or evaluated.

Three of the major Tory publications of the period
were Blackwood's Edinburgh Magazine, the Quarterly Review, and the British Critic. In Blackwood's, Keats's name
is linked with Hunt as early as October 1817. On this date
the first number of the "Cockney School of Poetry" appeared.
In the fourth number of the "Cockney School" series, the
attack shifts from Hunt to Keats.

The readers of the Examiner newspaper were
informed, some time ago, by a solemn paragraph
in Mr. Hunt's best style, of the appearance of two
new stars of glorious magnitude and splendour in
the poetical horizon of the land of Cockaigne. 25
One of these turned out, by and by, to be no other
than Mr. John Keats. This precocious adulation
confirmed the wavering apprentice in his desire to
quit the gallipots, and at the same time excited in his
too susceptible mind a fatal admiration for the
character and talents of the most worthless and
affected of all the versifiers of our time. One of
his first productions was the following sonnet,
"written on the day when Mr. Leigh Hunt left
prison. " It will be recollected, that the cause of
Hunt's confinement was a series of libels against
his sovereign, and that its fruit was the odious
and incestuous "Story of Rimini. " (p. 519, but
paginated erroneously as p. 521.)

Keats's association with Hunt was regarded with equal dis-
favor by the Quarterly Review. The April 1818 edition,
which did not appear until September, contains an unfavorable review of Endymion. The author, John Wilson Croker,
affixes Blackwood's label of "Cockney" to Keats. "Of this
school, Mr. Leigh Hunt, as we observed in a former Number, aspires to be the hierophant.... This author [Keats]
is a copyist of Mr. Hunt, but he is more unintelligible,
almost as rugged, twice as diffuse, and ten time more
tiresome and absurd than his prototype" (XIX, 204-205). In
his Preface to Rimini, Hunt theorized about the superiority
of open couplets and announced his intention of employing

them in his poem. Keats also used open couplets in Endymion "and, being bitten by Mr. Leigh Hunt's insane criticism, [he] more than rivals the insanity of his poetry" (p.
205).

The June 1818 issue of the British Critic appeared in
September, shortly after Croker's review in the Quarterly.
In this High Church and Tory journal's unfavorable review
of Endymion, the link with Hunt is stated at the outset.
"This is the most delicious poem, of its kind, which has
fallen within our notice, and if Mr. Leigh Hunt had never
written, we believe we might have pronounced it to be sui
generis without fear of contradiction" (IX, 649). Despite an
admission of undue severity in its treatment of Endymion,
the Critic finds it difficult to retreat with consistency in its
September 1820 review of the Lamia volume.

> If there be one person in the present day, for
> whom we feel an especial contempt, it is Mr.
> Examiner Hunt; and we confess that it is not easy
> for us to bring our minds to entertain respect for
> any one whose taste, whether in morals, in poetry,
> or politics, is so exceedingly corrupt as that per-
> son's must be supposed to be, who is willing to
> take such a man for his model. It was for this
> reason that Mr. Keats fell under our lash, so
> severely, upon the occasion of his poem of Endy-
> mion. Upon recurring to the poem, we are not un-
> willing to admit, that it possesses more merit,
> than upon a first perusal of it we were able to per-
> ceive, or rather that we were in a frame of mind
> to appreciate. We can hardly doubt as to that
> poem having been corrected by our modern Mal-
> volio, and projected by his advice and under his
> superintendence;--so full was it, of all the pe-
> culiarities of that ingenious gentleman's ideas.
> The effect of this upon Mr. Keats's poetry, was
> like an infusion of ipecacuanha powder in a dish of
> marmalade. It created such a sickness and nausea,
> that the mind felt little inclination to analyze the
> mixture produced, and to consider, whether after
> all, the dose might not have been mixed with some
> ingredients that were in themselves agreeable. In
> the poems before us, the same obstacle to a dis-
> passionate judgment, is still to be encountered--
> not perhaps to so great a degree, as upon the
> former occasion, but still in such a degree, as to

reflect great praise, we think, upon our impartiality for the commendation which we feel willing
to bestow. (XIV, 257-258.)

Equally as revealing as the political and moral attacks in these reviews is the poetic coupling of Keats with
Hunt. Blackwood's and the British Critic detect Hunt's influence, if not his assistance, in Endymion. Hunt's influence, however, was strongest in Poems, 26 and seven months
before Endymion was published, Keats recognized that this
influence was destructive. Hunt had questioned the wisdom
of writing a poem as long as the projected Endymion, Keats
tells Benjamin Bailey in a letter of October 8, 1817. "You
see Bailey how independent my writing has been. Hunt's
discussion was of no avail." Unless he has his "own un-
fettered scope," Keats fears he "shall have the Reputation
of Hunt's élève."27 Ironically, soon after Blackwood's and
the British Critic publicly attacked Keats for associating
with the "immoral" Hunt, Keats was privately attacking the
morality of that same man. "Hunt--who is certainly a
pleasant fellow in the main when you are with him ... in
reality ... is vain, egotistical, and disgusting in matters
of taste and morals."28 Benjamin Haydon, a friend whom
Keats then respected, frequently applied the word "morals"
to religious opinions. 29 Orthodox in his beliefs, Haydon
found Leigh Hunt's deistical ideas repugnant. He warned
other friends about Hunt; Keats was one of them. 30 There
were still other reasons for Keats's disgust with Hunt. He
could not forgive Hunt entirely for turning to Shelley as his
favorite. A coldness on Keats's part also might have
developed because of Hunt's less than enthusiastic response
to the projected Endymion volume. 31 Moreover, Hunt could
be egotistical and vain. The most satisfying explanation is
that Keats's rebellion against the older and inferior poet's
influence was a necessary and healthy expression of independence. In this sense the immediate causes become less
important; they simply hasten the inevitable. Nevertheless,
Keats's attack on Hunt rankles; it seems to echo the very
phrasing of the British Critic. Hunt deserved better.

If his damaging political and prosodic influence on
Keats is obvious, it is also obvious that Hunt did more
than any of Keats's other friends or acquaintances to intro-
duce him to a reading public. In 1816 Keats was an unknown poet in search of a place to publish, and Hunt supplied him with that place. In addition to the seven poems
of Keats published in the Examiner by March 1817, Hunt

was instrumental in presenting Keats's work to the public
eight more times in the next four years. [32] Hunt also published Keats's unsigned review of John Hamilton Reynolds'
Wordsworth lampoon, Peter Bell, a Lyrical Ballad (Examiner, April 25, 1819, p. 270). Moreover, Hunt's personal contacts were valuable. It was through the older and
more established writer that Keats met, among others,
Hazlitt, Haydon, Severn, and Charles Ollier. [33] Keats remained a lifelong admirer of Hazlitt. Haydon introduced
Keats to Reynolds, and Reynolds' friendship proved less
selfish than the former's. It was at Reynolds' request that
Keats wrote three dramatic reviews in two separate issues
of the Champion. [34] Reynolds may also have introduced
Keats to John Taylor, partner in the firm of Taylor and
Hessey, publishers of Endymion and Lamia, etc. [35] Severn,
of course, accompanied Keats to Rome. Ollier published
Keats's first volume, Poems. At each point in Keats's
publishing history, then, Hunt, was of direct or indirect aid.
If this aid was unfortunate for Keats's reputation, it was not
Hunt's fault. To his credit, Keats never publicly disavowed
Hunt. Any resentment he felt toward the man was expressed
in private letters and conversations with friends.

                                    III

       Blackwood's, the Quarterly, and the British Critic
have already been mentioned in regard to Keats criticism.
More will be said about their origin and history below; but
the Edinburgh, one of the most influential reviews of its
time, deserves first attention.

       The Edinburgh Review was founded in October 1802
by Sydney Smith, Francis Jeffrey, and Francis Horner.
Later, Henry Brougham joined them. Although its founders
were Whigs, the review at first was not intended as a narrow partisan organ. During the first years of its existence,
Sir Walter Scott, a staunch Tory, was a frequent contributor.
Under Jeffrey's editorship (1803-1829), however, the Whigism
of the review soon became apparent. When the Tories came
to absolute power in 1807, Jeffrey's colleagues also abandoned any pretense of party neutrality. As editor, Jeffrey
was initially able to attract contributors of talent by offering high remuneration. As the prestige and circulation of
the Edinburgh grew--10,000 copies were sold in 1812;
14,000 in 1818[36]--payment, although still substantial, became a secondary matter. In addition to Scott, Hazlitt and,

later, Macaulay and Carlyle wrote for the Edinburgh.

From the beginning, the Edinburgh's policy was to
review only literary works of significance.[37] The tone of
the review was frequently pontifical; its pronouncements were
made ex cathedra. Jeffrey's review of Southey's Thalaba
is a good case in point. "Poetry has this much, at least,
in common with religion, that its standards were fixed long
ago, by certain inspired writers, whose authorship it is no
longer lawful to call in question" (I [October 1802], 63).
No substantial change in tone is apparent twelve years later
when, of Wordsworth's Excursion, Jeffrey pronounces, "This
will never do" (XXIV [November 1814], 1).

In toto the attitude of the Edinburgh Review was not
favorable to the major Romantic poets. Its unfair treatment
of Wordsworth is notorious; it ridiculed Coleridge's Christabel and found little intelligent in Kubla Kahn; it failed to review any work by Shelley. Jeffrey was not favorably disposed to the innovations of the Romantics. His adherence
to eighteenth century canons of criticism is clearly suggested
in his review of Thalaba. Although he did not find that his
viewpoints were totally accepted, even by his colleagues,
Jeffrey exerted the major influence on the Edinburgh during
his editorship. After its review of Hours of Idleness in
January 1808, the Edinburgh's estimate of Byron was generally favorable. Unlike Wordsworth and Coleridge, Byron
was not a conservative, and although political viewpoints
did not always determine editorial policy, Jeffrey was sometimes less carping with writers who espoused liberal opinions. Ultimately, Jeffrey was forced to condemn Cain and
Don Juan, but his condemnation was grudging and qualified
by a recognition of Byron's poetic powers. In his generally favorable review of Endymion, Jeffrey praises Keats's
"very beautiful imagination" and "great familiarity with the
finest diction of English poetry" (XXIV [August 1820], 213)
but still characteristically censures the poet's "rash attempts
at originality" (p. 203). The Edinburgh had said nothing
about Endymion for more than two years, and although its
silence possibly might have been construed as consistent
with its policy of reviewing only the major literary works
of an author, Keats angrily rejected this explanation.

> The Edinburgh reviewers are afraid to touch upon
> my Poem--They do not know what to make of it--
> they do not like to condemn it[38] and they will not
> praise it for fear.... The fact is they have no

> real taste--they dare not compromise their Judg-
> ments on so puzzling a Question--If on my next
> Publication they should praise me and so lug in
> Endymion--I will address them in a manner they
> will not at all relish--The Cowardliness of the
> Edinburgh is worse than the abuse of the Quarter-
> ly. [39]

Illness, as Rollins observed, prevented Keats from carrying
out his threat, and probably he would have done nothing even
if his health had permitted it. [40]

   The Quarterly Review was started in 1809 to offset
the Whig influence of the Edinburgh. Although it is difficult
to determine with absolute accuracy the individual who first
conceived of the plan, George and Stratford Canning, repre-
senting the Tory administration, John Murray, future publisher of the review, and Scott and Robert Southey all had a
hand in it. [41] The format of the Quarterly was essentially
the same as that of the Edinburgh. From its inception,
however, the Quarterly was intended as a party organ, and
its Tory viewpoint was more narrowly partisan than its
Whig counterpart. Both reviews had the interests of the
landed aristocracy in mind and were not sympathetic toward
parliamentary reform, but the Quarterly's opposition was
more extreme. It opposed Catholic emancipation and all
forms of protest against the ruling Tory establishment; it
was the champion of the Anglican Church. In terms of
influence and circulation, the Quarterly rivaled and, during
the period when Keats wrote, surpassed the Edinburgh. In
addition to Scott and Southey, the Quarterly attracted Charles
Lamb and Washington Irving as contributors. William Gifford, John Gibson Lockhart, and John Wilson did most of
the reviewing.

   Gifford, former editor of the Tory Anti-Jacobin,
author of some minor satires, [42] translator of Juvenal (1803)
and, later, of Persius (1821), was selected as the first
editor of the Quarterly after Scott had refused the position.
He was not an outstanding critic, and certainly was not the
equal of Jeffrey as an editor. Although he wrote perhaps
only eight complete papers himself, he frequently revised
material submitted by contributors. [43] Gifford's alterations
in Lamb's review of the Excursion resulted in a letter of
disavowal from Lamb to Wordsworth.

> I told you my Review was a very imperfect one.
> But what you will see in the Quarterly is a spuri-
> ous one which Mr. Baviad Gifford has palm'd upon
> it for mine. I never felt more vexd in my life
> than when I read it.... The language he has al-
> tered throughout ... more than a third of the sub-
> stance is cut away....
> They had a right to do it, as no name appears
> to it, and ... Gifford I suppose never waived a
> right he had since he commenced author. God
> confound him and all caitiffs. 44

In this way, Gifford exercised control of the review. He
could be, and frequently was, politically prejudiced. Much
more so than Jeffrey, who was not entirely free of showing
favoritism himself, Gifford indulged his biases. Although
Gifford wrote only one unfavorable review of Hazlitt, 45 the
Quarterly usually condemned any writer who it suspected had
liberal views. Hunt, Shelley, and Keats, as well as Hazlitt,
were consistently attacked by this review.

Lockhart and Croker received notoriety for their unfair treatment of the first three poets. Lockhart's attacks
on Hunt and Keats belong more to the history of Blackwood's
than to the Quarterly, but he did some reviewing for the
Quarterly also and became its editor from 1825-1853.
Croker is identified as the author of the Quarterly's unfavorable review of Endymion. 46 This is the review cited
most frequently by Keats's defenders as destroying the
poet's critical reputation, and more will be said of this
charge later, but it may be observed here that Croker's
strictures against the diction and affected versification of
Endymion were not totally invalid. 47 Croker's other contributions to the review include one or possible two unfavorable reviews of Leigh Hunt. 48 A reading of this material shows that Croker was not a gifted critic.

Despite its dislike of Hazlitt, Hunt, Shelley, and
Keats, the Quarterly extolled the merit of Lord Byron.
Byron, of course, was a nobleman; and Murray was his publisher as well as the publisher of the Quarterly. The reviews of the poet were both favorable and perceptive until
the publication of Don Juan in 1819. Then the Quarterly
remained silent until 1822--by this time Murray had severed
his connection with Byron--when it began to find fault. 49
The views of Wordsworth were more consistent with those
of the Tories, and he was singled out for high praise.

Coleridge too was praised by the review, but it failed to
notice Christabel in 1816. Generally, the first generation
of Romantic poets, Sir Walter Scott and Southey included,
were greeted favorably by the Quarterly. Paradoxically,
the politically reactionary Quarterly was more liberal toward
the new Romantic poetry and its innovations than the Whig
Edinburgh. [50] "For ourselves," a Quarterly reviewer tells
us in an October 1811 critique of Scott's The Vision of Don
Roderick, "we have not been among those ... who 'shake the
head, and whisper much, and change the countenance' at
every little instance of departure from a classical model;
who gravely admonish him [Scott] to revert in good time to
the old established trammels of poetry; and cry out against
the heinous offence of delighting the world in an unusual
way" (VI, 222). [51]

In October 1817, after the sixth number of the undistinguished Edinburgh Monthly Magazine, John Wilson,
James Hogg, and John Gibson Lockhart assumed joint editorial responsibilities, and the magazine was renamed for
its publisher, William Blackwood. Shortly thereafter,
William Maginn, future co-founder of Fraser's Magazine,
joined them. Blackwood's Edinburgh Magazine was founded
with a major objective in mind. In a lighter, less ponder-
ous manner than the Quarterly, it was to offer a Tory alternative to the Edinburgh Review. Consistent with the
literal meaning of a magazine as an omnibus of new literature, Blackwood's published, in addition to literary reviews,
original poetry, short stories, and serialized fiction.

Hogg conceived the idea of a rather vicious satire of
well-known local figures, which purported to be a "Translation from an Ancient Chaldee Manuscript"; Lockhart and
Wilson did most of the writing. Blackwood's achieved instant literary notoriety as a result of the bad taste of the
Chaldee article; but of more importance to its editors and
publisher, the magazine began to sell. The history of
Blackwood's through Keats's lifetime was one of general
critical irresponsibility. Maga, as it was popularly known,
indulged in wholesale slanders and was constantly involved
in libel suits. Under the signature "Z," Wilson and Lockhart had initiated attacks against Hunt, Hazlitt, and Keats.
Hunt twice threatened actions--once in 1817 and again in
1823. [52] Hazlitt also threatened to sue in 1818 and 1823,
settling out of court in 1818. [53]

Less influential than the two giant reviews, but still

one of the most important magazines of its time, Blackwood's
assumes a central place in Keats criticism.   Keats's name
appears in the magazine as early as the October 1817 number, and he continues to receive unfavorable notice through
December 1821, the date at which this collection terminates.
During this time, twenty-three references to Keats occur in
eighteen separate issues of Blackwood's.   Lockhart's "Cockney School of Poetry. No. IV." is devoted entirely to the
poet. [54]   This article, far more offensive than Croker's review in the Quarterly, is a personal attack on Keats as well
as on his poetry.   Lockhart refers to Keats's former ap-
prenticeship to an apothecary and sneeringly suggests that
he return to the shop. [55]   Despite the greater influence of
the Quarterly and the belief of Hazlitt, Shelley, and others
that Croker's review did the most damage to Keats's reputation, a stronger case can be made for Blackwood's. [56]
The Quarterly attacked only Endymion; it said nothing of
Keats's last volume.   Consistently, Blackwood's attacked
every volume that Keats wrote.   Moreover, by applying the
label "Cockney" to Hunt and, by association, to Keats, it
was the first to charge that Keats's poetry was vulgar.
Keats's defenders smarted from the Quarterly article because it seemed to them that it lent respectability to the
disreputable attacks of Blackwood's, but the critical irresponsibility was primarily that of Maga, which had initiated
the charges.

         In regard to other Romantics, however, Blackwood's
was by no means imperceptive.   It attacked Coleridge[57] but
was aware of Shelley's genius, though it condemned his
philosophy. [58]   Neither was it unaware of Byron's great
ability, despite its moral condemnation of Don Juan. [59]   In
contrast to Jeffrey's attack on the Excursion in the Edinburgh, it championed Wordsworth.   Perhaps its most dis-
cerning observations can be found in the second article on
the "Lake School of Poetry."   In Wordsworth's knowledge
of universal moral laws and all the beauties of human affection, "in both of these things," a reviewer explains, "he
has scarcely any precursors, either among the poets or
philosophers of his country" (IV [December 1818], 2).

         Baldwin's London Magazine was founded in 1820 as
a rival to Blackwood's.   It was edited by John Scott until
his death on February 27, 1821. [60]   In July 1821, Keats's
publishers, Taylor and Hessey, purchased the magazine,
and Taylor became the editor.   Between 1820 and 1822,
Lamb's Essays of Elia (1820-1822), DeQuincey's Confessions

of an English Opium Eater (1821), and Hazlitt's Table Talk
(1821) appeared as original contributions. Under Scott, and
shortly thereafter, the London Magazine was probably the
finest literary periodical of its time. 61

    As the former editor of the Champion newspaper,
Scott had a reputation as a superior journalist when he
took charge of Baldwin's magazine. The magazine adopted
an urban, London viewpoint as a counter to the regionalism
of Blackwood's. Unlike the editors of the Edinburgh,
Quarterly, and Blackwood's, Scott never allowed politics to
influence his critical judgment: the London Magazine had no
party affiliation, nor was it an organ of the Cockney School,
as the Tory press frequently charged. It could, and did,
indicate faults in the poetry of Hunt, Shelley, and Keats.
The literary criticism of the London Magazine was outstanding. 62 It discerningly praised Wordsworth. Despite a
favorable review of Hunt, 63 several other comments under-
scored his prosodic weaknesses. In no instance, however,
did the magazine equate these weaknesses with Hunt's political
beliefs. If sometimes critical, its judgments on Byron were
usually sound. Although it did not approve of Shelley's
morality, it recognized his greatness as a poet. Its reviews
of Keats's Endymion and the Lamia volume were honest, intelligent, and favorable.

    These were the four major reviews and magazines
during Keats's lifetime; and criticism, here and in all other
serials, was unsigned. (The names of reviewers already
given are attributions.) There was nothing unusual about
this practice. Anonymity had been the rule since the first
English serials in the seventeenth century. It was as late
as 1912, for instance, before the Edinburgh abandoned the
practice, 64 and even today, criticism in the Times Literary
Supplement is still anonymous. Unsigned criticism contributed to the oracular reputation of such reviews as the Edinburgh and the Quarterly; it created the impression that their
critical judgments emanated from a single, infallible voice.
In an attempt to combat this practice, the playwright Richard
Cumberland announced in 1809 that all articles in his London
Review would be signed. 65 The gesture was made with a
flourish; but, unfortunately, it proved unsuccessful. The
review lasted only ten months. The major objection to unsigned criticism was the free license it gave to the unnamed
reviewer to indulge his political, moral, or personal prejudices without need of assuming responsibility for his statements. In the less scrupulous publications, it resulted in

some of the most notorious reviews in literary history.

John Scott exposed the excesses of Blackwood's in
two articles that eventually cost him his life. "The first
article of their first number [actually No. VII, as Scott indicates in a footnote] was an evidently nefarious assault on
Coleridge, in the course of which all bounds of legitimate
criticism were overpassed, and the defects of the author
made the ground of slander against the man.... "66 In his
next article, Scott defended Hazlitt and Keats from the "foul
mouthed allusions" of Blackwood's, "heartless, impudent,
unfounded insults grossly and ridiculously inapplicable to the
persons they pretended to describe. "67 The victims of
Blackwood's also counterattacked. As a result of "The
Cockney School of Poetry. No. 1, " Hunt irately accused Z
of cowardice and challenged him to reveal his identity, but
Z continued to hide behind his anonymity: "you will permit
me to observe, that you invited Z to disclose his name, in
terms which argued no very chivalrous intentions on your
part. "68 In his "Table Talk" articles in the London Magazine, Hazlitt also defended himself against the anonymous
attacks of Blackwood's and the Quarterly. Writing for the
Edinburgh in May 1823, Hazlitt once more exposed the
prejudices of Tory periodical press in England. Nevertheless, the trend against unsigned criticism, a trend which
Cumberland had anticipated, was not clearly established
until the latter half of the nineteenth century. Writing in
the Contemporary Review in July 1867, J. Boyd Kinnear
attacked the custom of anonymity: "secrecy is said to be
necessary ... to admit the unrestricted treatment of public
events... " (p. 326). "This can be so only in an objectionable sense. It may well be that a writer may indulge in
personalities to which he would be either afraid or ashamed
to put his name. But are these to be encouraged?" (p. 329).
The question was reasonable, but fifty years before it would
have been dismissed as summarily as was Cumberland's
London Review. Of the serials discussed to this point, the
London Magazine was the only publication that did not abuse
the practice of unsigned criticism.

Although the political and moral biases of the Tories
resulted in unfavorable treatment of Keats, this does not
mean that criticism in these reviews and magazines was
incompetent. Even in the unremitting attacks of Blackwood's
in almost a score of separate issues, recognition of Keats's
abilities was not completely lacking. 69 The Quarterly, in
particular, was capable of sound criticism, as its reviews

of Wordsworth indicate.   With Keats it simply allowed
political concerns to override its literary judgment.   Conservative literary standards also account for some perverse
opinions in other serials of the period.   Jeffrey, Gifford,
and other editors were nurtured on the neoclassical values
of the eighteenth century, and Keats's mythological framework in Endymion, Hyperion, and other poems seemed out of
place to men who had been taught to leave mythology to the
Ancients in all instances save the mock heroic.   Even in
his essentially favorable review, Jeffrey advises Keats not
to complete the mythological fragment of Hyperion: "the subject is too far removed from all sources of human interest
to be successfully treated by any modern author" (p. 213).
Finally, the rivalry between various reviews and magazines
affected the direction of some Keats criticism.   Jeffrey's
favorable review in the Edinburgh (August 1820), for instance, might have been motivated in part by the attack on
Keats of the Quarterly.   Similarly, as a result of its
rivalry with Baldwin's, Gold's London Magazine (mentioned
below) was to assume a confusing attitude toward Keats.

There were still nine other quarterlies and monthlies
which published ten reviews and three significant notices
of Keats.   The British Critic's unfavorable estimates of
Endymion and the Lamia volume have been cited.   The
Critic, a monthly organized in 1793 as an instrument of the
Crown, was under the joint editorship of T. F. Middleton,
W. R. Lyall and others during the period when Keats wrote.
Its religious and moral concerns--Middleton later became
Bishop of Calcutta--are clear from its hostile treatment of
Shelley as well as Keats.   As the British Critic was a nar-
row-minded organ of the Established Church, the Eclectic
Review was an equally parochial organ of the Dissenters.
Founded in 1805 and edited by S. Greathead, T. Parker,
and T. Williams, it was a conservative quarterly of scant
literary merit.   Its two reviews of Keats are undistinguished;
its unfavorable review of Poems indicates some awareness
of Keats's promise, but the reviewer of the Lamia volume
concludes that Keats's talent is still misdirected.

Three monthlies may be mentioned here.   The
Monthly Review, or Literary Journal, founded by Ralph
Griffiths, dates back to 1749.   Its major importance is to
the eighteenth century: Sheridan, William Gilpin, Charles
Burney, and Goldsmith were contributors.   Although an intelligent, liberal-minded, dissenting journal, its literary
judgments were conservative.   From 1803-1825, Griffith's

son served as editor.   A mixed review of Keats's Lamia
volume appears in the July 1820 issue (XCII, 305-310).
Despite the reviewer's censure of Keats for obscurity and
failure "to concede something to established tastes, " he
realizes that the volume "displays the ore of true poetic
genius" (p. 305).

A second journal was the Monthly Magazine and
British Register.   Established in 1794 as a dissenting organ,
it was regarded by the Tories as a radical publication.
William Godwin was one of its contributors.   Its founder
and publisher, Richard Phillips, was accused of being a
Jacobin, and the charge was not without some foundation:
during the war years his magazine had shown partiality for
Napoleon. 70   A short, favorable review of Poems appeared
in the magazine for April 1, 1817 (XLIII, 43).   Of particular
interest in the Monthly Magazine's review of the Lamia volume is the favorable, rather than unfavorable, linking of
Keats's name with Leigh Hunt.   "There is a boldness of
fancy and a classical expression of language in the poetry
of this gentleman, which, we think, entitles him to stand
equally high in the estimation of poetic opinion, as the
author of Rimini..." (L [September 1820], 166).   The reviewer has no intention of being ironic.   Evidently, if the
Tories disapproved of Keats's friendship with Hunt, the
Radicals accepted it as prima facie evidence of the younger
poet's talent.

The third journal, the New Monthly Magazine and
Universal Register, was organized in 1814 by Henry Colburn
as a foil to the Monthly Magazine and the Jacobinism of
Richard Phillips.   Under Thomas Campbell's editorship in
1821, the magazine toned down its political diatribe against
the Monthly and assumed more of a literary character:
Universal Register was dropped from the subtitle and Literary Journal was substituted.   In September 1820, a favorable review of the Lamia volume concludes optimistically.
"We now take leave of Mr. Keats with wonder at the gigantic stride which he has taken, and with good hope that,
if he proceeds in the high and pure style he has now chosen,
he will attain an exalted and lasting station among English
poets" (XIV, 248).   In May 1821, a death notice extolling
Keats's genius appeared; it was reprinted in the New Annual
Register for 1821.

Three more monthlies that published reviews of
Keats were the Edinburgh Magazine and Literary Miscellany,

the European Magazine, and Gold's London Magazine. Despite a lukewarm attitude toward Hyperion, the Edinburgh
Magazine published favorable reviews of each of Keats's
three volumes. It was founded as the Scot's Magazine in
1739; Boswell was one of its more famous eighteenth century
contributors. Archibald Constable, publisher of the Edinburgh Review, assumed control of the magazine in 1817 and
changed its title. The new series of issues had a literary
emphasis, and the magazine was ably conducted. The Edinburgh Magazine contained some of the most intelligent reviews of Keats in the period. It recognized the potential
of Poems; it saw in the author of Endymion "a poet of high
and undoubted powers." The review of Endymion was perceptive in recognizing that the excessive praise of Keats's
friends was of as little value to the poet's reputation as the
unthinking censure of his enemies.

> He has evident peculiarities, which some of the
> London critics, who are adverse to his style, have
> seized upon and produced as fair specimens of his
> writings; and this has operated, of course, to his
> disadvantage with the public, who have scarcely had
> an opportunity of judging what his powers really
> are. Some of his friends, indeed, have put in a
> word or two of praise, but it has been nearly un-
> qualified; and this, when viewed at the same time
> with the criticism viewed in an opposite spirit,
> has tended very much to confirm the objections
> made to his poetry. (n. s. VII [August 1820], 107-
> 108)

The review of the Lamia volume concludes with the observation that Keats's works contain "as much absolute poetry as
the works of almost any contemporary writer" (n. s. VII
[October 1820], 316).

The European Magazine, a conservative monthly
founded in 1782 by the Philological Society of London, contains material relating to Keats. In the issue of October
1816, George Felton Mathew published a wretched poem
addressed "To A Poetical Friend"--the friend was Keats.
In May of the next year, Mathew's carping estimate of
Poems appeared. He had intended to write a generally
favorable review but, resentful of Keats's closeness with
Hunt and of recent praise of Keats's first volume by
Reynolds, Mathew singled out the weakest poems for approval, the poems Keats wrote during their friendship in

1815.[71] Of the poems written after that date, "Calidore,"
he explains, "savours too much of the affectation of Leigh
Hunt" (LXXI, 436); "Chapman's Homer," although a fair
specimen of a sonnet, suffers from absurd application and
broken metaphor. The magazine was of a higher quality
than Mathew's review would indicate. From 1820 until it
merged with the Monthly Magazine in 1825, the European
devoted itself primarily to literature; during this time its
political viewpoint became more liberal.

Gold's London Magazine, prefixed with the name of
its publisher to distinguish it from Baldwin's, was founded
in 1820. A Whig publication, the magazine attempted to
convey the impression of liberality in its literary views;
there is, however, an aspish quality to some of its criticism.
In a review of the Lamia volume in August 1820, Gold's
London Magazine defends Keats against his attackers; but
it continually gibes at Baldwin's in the course of the article.
Its rivalry with Baldwin's is petty; so are some curiously
myopic judgments of Keats in what was intended as a mixed
but not entirely unfavorable review. "We are sure," the
reviewer tells us, that "Leigh Hunt never corrected his
exercises in Lamia or the Basil Pot, or else they would
have appeared to more advantage" (II, 161). The reviewer
had heard of Keats's declining health from Hunt's review of
the Lamia volume in the Indicator of August 9, 1820, and
the recommendation that follows may be sincere; but it
contains the suggestion that Keats's poetry is also ailing.
"We shall now proceed to give some account of the work
before us; and shall be the more extended, inasmuch as we
wish to deal fairly by a clever young man, to whom we would
recommend a little country air, to strengthen his nerves;
and a change of diet, as necessary to the preservation of
his health" (p. 161). Lymington and York are then proposed as possible health spas. If we are to take the reviewer seriously, there is an unintended irony in these
statements. It is more likely, however, that the irony is
intended, and that in employing it, the reviewer is attempting
to disassociate Gold's from the more enthusiastic praise of
Baldwin's. There is less chance of misinterpreting the introductory remarks about Isabella that follow: "The story
is told in about two hundred and fifty lines; but as many of
our readers may fear to undertake the task of wading through
it, we shall epitomize it for their edification" (p. 167). No
tonal lapse occurs here; it is reminiscent of the attacks upon
Endymion which resort to counting lines (British Critic) or
suggest that Keats's work will go unread (Quarterly).

Eleven weekly serials account for ten reviews and several significant notices of Keats. Of the eleven, there were one London and three Provincial newspapers; the remaining seven serials may be rather loosely classified as journals of belles lettres. The prestige of these journals never rivaled the Edinburgh or the Quarterly, but several were publications of literary merit. In general, the weekly press reached a reasonably substantial and varied audience.

The Examiner of John and Leigh Hunt was, strictly speaking, a Sunday newspaper. It was conceived in 1808 as a politically independent but liberal publication, interested in the cause of reform. A section of the newspaper was devoted to the theater, and Leigh Hunt occasionally wrote essays on belles lettres; but it was not until Hunt began to attack the critics of Shelley and Keats that the journal assumed an unmistakably literary character. [72] Under Leigh Hunt's editorship (1808-1821), it became the best weekly of Keats's time, despite constant Tory attacks upon the two brothers, convicted libelers of the Prince Regent. The Examiner's estimate of the second generation of Romantics was intelligent and sympathetic. Leigh Hunt was also the founder of the Indicator (1819-1821), a short lived but ably conducted weekly of reviews, original poetry, and miscellaneous essays. Specifically, more favorable Keats material appeared in the Examiner and the Indicator than in any other serials of the time. Hazlitt, Shelley, and Keats made important original contributions to both of Hunt's publications.

Like the Examiner, the Champion was a liberal Sunday newspaper which contained theatrical notices and a substantial amount of literary material. A continuation of Drakard's Paper (1813), the numbers now known to exist span the years 1814-1822. Under the able editorship of John Scott, both Shelley and Keats received attention. Reynolds was the dramatic critic for the newspaper in 1817 and part of 1818, and on two occasions Keats substituted for his friend in this capacity. Reynolds' favorable review of Poems appears on March 9, 1817. A favorable review of Endymion on June 7, 1818 unsuccessfully urges fair treatment of Keats in the influential quarterly reviews.

The Literary Gazette, Literary Journal and General Miscellany of Science, Arts, History, Politics, etc. and Literary Chronicle and Weekly Review were clearly intended as journals of belles lettres. "Under the leadership of the Examiner, the form ... became standardized. This type of

periodical was, with few exceptions, a sixteen page folio,
issued on Saturdays and containing reviews of various lengths,
poetry, letters of contributors, and gossip of books and
authors."[73] The Literary Gazette was the first and most
influential of such reviews. From its inception in 1817
until 1850, it was edited by William Jerdan, a journalist
who later wrote about his life and contacts in his Autobiography (4 vols., 1852-1853) and in Men I Have Known
(1866). William Maginn, a contributor to Blackwood's,
wrote for the Gazette in the early 1820's. In its pages are
found unfavorable reviews of Shelley, as well as a short,
noncommittal notice of the Lamia volume which reprinted
three of Keats's poems. The Gazette was a generally liberal weekly, which attempted to avoid politics, but it ex-
coriated radicals and atheists with great religious zeal. In
a severe review of Adonais on December 8, 1821, Keats is
alluded to unfavorably.

Although not as influential as the Gazette, the Liter-
erary Journal (1818-1819) was critically superior. Published by A. Christie, it was a Sunday weekly that ran to
only fifty-nine numbers.[71] Nevertheless, articles and reviews of Wordsworth, Lamb, Scott, Byron, and Keats appeared in the relatively short fourteen months of its existence. Endymion is favorably reviewed on May 17 and 24,
1818 (pp. 114-115, 131). "With the exception of two passages," the reviewer concludes, "we are induced to give our
most unqualified approbation of this poem.... And ... we
feel persuaded, that genius, like that possessed by Mr. K.,
may with safety venture in the highest walk of poetry" (p.
131). The Literary Chronicle, a moderately liberal Saturday weekly founded in 1819, merged with the Athenáeum in
1828. During the Regency Period, it published readable
but imperceptive reviews of Byron, Shelley, and Keats. A
generally unfavorable review of the Lamia volume appears
on July 29, 1820.

The Guardian, or Historical and Literary Recorder
(1819-1824) also might have been intended as a journal of
belles lettres, but it was a publication of scant literary
merit. It was a Sunday weekly, published and printed by
William Adams. The Prospectus of December 12, 1819,
proclaiming its support for "God and Our Country," gives
a clear indication of its Tory leanings. "We will not seek
a guilty profit, or a guiltier popularity, by reviling our holy
Religion, by libeling established authorities, by calumniating
magistrates, by puffing every bad poet ... by insulting pub-

lic decency.... We believe the present ministers to be the fittest men to conduct the affairs of the country...." In a scoffing review of August 6, 1820, the Guardian mocks the obscurity of the Lamia volume.

Commentary on Keats also appeared in the Anti-Gallican Monitor (1811-1818), a second-rate London weekly. Published and edited by Lewis Goldsmith, who was in Liverpool's pay, this Sunday newspaper was staunchly Tory and anti-Jacobin. It championed the English cause during the Napoleonic Wars. On June 8 and July 6, 1817 two letters, signed "Observator," appear under the heading "Original Compositions." They were written by John Wilson. [75] The first letter includes a personal attack on Keats.

> Keats is an original, but of the Eristotratus species. [76] I hear, while quoting him, that his dress is made by a great grand-child of Milton, after the Poet's mode; and that the white crape in his button-hole, a token of grief for the loss of his liberty, is on the ground of Milton's political principles--Poor youth! The suspenders of the Habeas Corpus Act, (his loss of liberty) would do well to suspend him in Bedlam. His poems, just published, are the echo of Mr. Hunt's: his style in every respect--faulty or not.

The Oxford University and City Herald (1806-1830) was one of three Provincial newspapers to print significant matter relating to Keats. It was a Saturday weekly, published by Munday and Slatter of Oxford. Benjamin Bailey, Keats's friend, wrote letters praising Endymion in the May 30 and June 6, 1818 issues. [77] Both letters may be considered as a single favorable review. A second such weekly, the Alfred, West of England Journal, and General Advertiser (1815-1831), was published in Exeter by R. Cullum. It was a liberal-minded but somewhat pious publication. Reynolds defends Keats against the attack of the Quarterly in the October 6, 1818 issue, [78] and his defense is reprinted in the Examiner on October 12. Almost nothing is known of the Chester Guardian. Only the April 25, 1822 number is now extant. An article defending Endymion in a lost issue of the newspaper was reprinted in the Examiner of November 1, 1818.

Three reviews, one notice, and three letters concerning Keats appeared in one London tri-weekly and three

London dailies. The St. James's Chronicle (1761-1866),
published by Charles Batowin every Tuesday, Thursday, and
Saturday evening, devoted space to literary and dramatic
reviewing in the period contemporary with Keats. Originally
an independent Whig newspaper, it evolved into a Tory
journal which attacked Cobbett and disapproved of the Manchester unrest before the massacre. But despite its conservatism, the St. James's Chronicle refused to attack the
standard literary targets of the Tories. It printed poems of
Hunt and Keats, as well as favorable reviews of Hunt and
Hazlitt. A favorable, but not perceptive, review of The
Pot of Basil is found in the July 1-4, 1820 issue. (The review is noted here for the first time.) Although "an affected peculiarity of expression" hurts Keats's smaller pieces,
it "is indeed, soon lost sight of amid the lively painting and
exquisite tenderness with which his larger poems abound."

        During Keats's time, the Morning Chronicle (1769-
1862) was a newspaper second in importance and influence
only to the Times.[79] From 1780, this Whig journal was
edited by its owner, James Perry. With Perry as over-
seer, John Black became editor in 1817.[80]   Black, an
advocate of reform, nevertheless denounced the victims of
Peterloo.[81]   The Chronicle published some early radical
poems of Coleridge; Lamb and Moore were among its contributors; Hazlitt wrote on politics and later did dramatic
criticism. Three letters in defense of Keats are found in
this newspaper. A letter signed "J. S." (possibly John
Scott) in the October 3, 1818 issue clearly recognizes Keats's
potential: "Mr. K. is capable of producing a poem that shall
challenge the admiration of every reader of true taste and
feeling...." The letter of "R. B." on October 8, 1818 is
minor, and nothing further need be said about it. In the
July 27, 1821 issue of the Chronicle a letter appears in
praise of Keats by "Y., " who later identifies himself as a
friend and former school-fellow. In all likelihood, the
author is Charles Cowden Clarke. Although he realizes
that Keats died of tuberculosis contracted while the poet
nursed his younger brother, Thomas, Clarke puts somewhat too much emphasis on the unfavorable reviews of
Blackwood's and the Quarterly as a contributory cause of
Keats's illness.

        The Sun (1793-1876) and the New Times (1817-1828)
were Tory dailies. For many years the Sun had a disreputable Tory reputation. In 1811, William Jerdan, future
editor of the Literary Gazette, and John Taylor, poet, play-

wright, and editor, became co-owners of the newspaper. [82]
The Sun continued to be staunchly Tory, but it printed a
favorable review of Endymion (October 21, 1818) and Richard
Woodhouse's[83] favorable review of the Lamia volume (July
10, 1820). [84] Woodhouse devotes himself almost entirely to
Hyperion. "It certainly, even in its present unfinished state,
is the greatest effort of Mr. Keats's genius, and gives us
reason to hope for something great from his pen. " The New
Times, edited until 1876 by John Stoddart, a friend of
Coleridge and Lamb's and the brother-in-law of Hazlitt, was
organized in 1817 as a rival to the Times. Stoddart was a
Tory who supported the suspension of Habeas Corpus in 1817.
Nevertheless, he "affected an impartiality and a dignity that
offended the Tories as much as the Whigs. "[85] It is in the
New Times of July 19, 1820 that Charles Lamb's favorable
review of the Lamia volume appears. [86] Lamb enthusiastically approves of the rich, "Chaucer-like" description of
The Eve of St. Agnes "with which this poet illumes every
subject he touches. " Isabella, he concludes, is the "finest
thing in the volume. "

IV

The preceding summary shows that Keats was not
neglected by his contemporaries. His three volumes were
published in the course of little more than three years.
During this time, twenty-seven reviews and seven important
estimates of his work appeared, an average of more than
ten per year. If all the significant allusions during Keats's
lifetime and all the significant tributes in verse and prose
occasioned by the poet's death are included, the total between
1816-1821 reaches seventy-two, and most of these items
were favorable. Those who have studied the reviews and
notices of Keats in detail agree that the poet's reception was
much better than Hazlitt, Shelley, and Keats's friends generally assumed;[87] however, the extent of Keats's sympathetic
reception in the press has not been sufficiently emphasized.

Three newspapers that championed Keats in particular
were the St. James's Chronicle, the Sun, and the Star. In
addition to its review of Isabella, the St. James's Chronicle
reprinted "The Floure and the Lefe" (March 15-18, 1817)
and "A Dream after Reading Dante's Episode of Paolo and
Francesca" (October 30-November 1, 1821). Besides its
review of Keats's second and third volumes, the Sun reprinted
a lengthy excerpt from Endymion on October 5, 1818. An

obituary of Keats appeared in this newspaper on March 22,
1821. The Star, London's first Whig daily, also reprinted
Keats's poem on Chaucer's tale (April 4, 1817), as well
as "To Autumn" (July 22, 1820) and "Ode to a Nightingale"
(July 27, 1820). The last two poems were prefaced with
a brief note of commendation. "We copy the Following
beautiful Stanzas from ... Mr. Keats's New Volume of
Poems, just published."

All of these items, with the exception of Woodhouse's
review of the Lamia volume in the Sun, are new discover-
ies, and there is still more new material. Keats's "To
Autumn" appeared in the General Evening Post (September
14-16, 1820), Morning Herald (September 16, 1820), and
Public Ledger and Daily Advertiser (September 19, 1820).
Obituaries of Keats also appeared in these publications, in
the Times, and in over twenty other London newspapers.
The list of first publications and reprints is still larger,
for Keats's poems also can be found in such diverse London
and Provincial journals as the Alfred, West of England
Journal and General Advertiser, the Champion, the Indicator,
the London Chronicle, and the Yellow Dwarf. We can add
to this list some of the more well-known material: Lamb's
review of the Lamia volume in the New Times; a reprint of
"To Autumn" and excerpts from "Ode to a Nightingale" and
Hyperion (New Times, July 21, 1821); reviews in the Champion, Examiner, and Indicator; letters in the Morning Chronicle from "J. S. ," "R. B. ," and Clarke; letters in defense of
Keats in the Oxford Herald by Bailey, in the Alfred by
Reynolds, and in the Chester Guardian.

The collective weight and number of these references
is significant. The press reached a wider public than the
combined reading audience of the more prestigious quarterly
and monthly literary reviews, [89] and because of its mass
circulation it exerted an important influence on public opinion. At the same time that Keats's poetry was under attack
in Blackwood's, the British Critic, and the Quarterly, it
was being reprinted in most of the newspapers of his day.
Certainly some of these reprints resulted from the good
offices of friends, but they hardly could have produced such
a wide-spread response by themselves. There must have
been a significant number of impartial observers in the press
who refused to accept the oracular judgments of the major
Tory reviews. In fact, it was the press in large part which
turned the tide in Keats's favor after Endymion had been attacked in 1818. Were it not for the steady stream of favor-

able material in newspapers between 1818-1820, Jeffrey, who
was cautious enough to wait two years in any case, might
never have come to Keats's defense in the Edinburgh. By
1820, Keats's reputation had survived the Tory assault on
Endymion, and mainly as a result of a vast body of favorable newspaper material which generally has gone unnoticed.

The discussion to this point has necessarily cut across
chronological lines. What remains to be done is to chart the
course of Keats's reputation from the beginning. On March
3, 1817, the Olliers published a small volume, entitled
Poems. The book had so little advance sale and publicity
that the author's brother, George Keats, mistakenly accused
the publishers of withholding the volume. The Olliers
angrily replied on April 29: "We regret that your brother
ever requested us to publish it."90 Surely they were naïve
if they had expected the book to be a financial success.
Keats was a fledgling poet whose first efforts only had recently appeared in the Examiner. Hunt's mention of him in
his article, "Young Poets," helped; but it did not make him
widely known. In March 1816, George Felton Mathew had
published "To A Poetical Friend" in the European Magazine,
but no one outside of Keats's immediate circle could have
realized that this poem was addressed to him. In such instances a young poet usually hopes for a critical success
and relies on the good offices of his friends. If these
were Keats's expectations, he was not to be disappointed.

Of the five reviews of Poems published in 1817,
three were written by friends. Outside of Mathew in the
European Magazine, Hunt in the Examiner, and Reynolds
in the Champion, the Eclectic Review and the Edinburgh
Magazine reviewed the volume. All of these articles, with
the exception of the review in the Eclectic, were favorable
in intent, and even the censure of the Eclectic was not unreasonable. It criticized the meager subject matter and
obscurity of Poems, faults which Hunt, Reynolds, and the
Edinburgh Magazine had recognized but dismissed as minor
weaknesses, stemming from the poet's youth. The Eclectic
realized, as did the more favorable reviews, that Keats
was "capable of writing good poetry" (s. 2 VIII [September
1817], 270). Overall, Keats's first volume was given a
good reception, although it did not bring the young poet to
significant literary attention. This was understandable.
With the exception of his sonnet, "Chapman's Homer," and
one or two other poems, the volume gave little indication of
what Keats was to achieve three years later.

The reviews of Endymion in 1818 did bring Keats to
public attention, but the poem was received unfavorably.
Charges of obscure and unfit subject matter, language, and
versification, already alluded to in the reviews of Poems,
were to recur throughout Keats's career, particularly in the
reviews of his second volume. Blackwood's, for instance,
puts repeated emphasis on Keats's inappropriate language.
If this weakness exists, it is nevertheless exaggerated. In
Poems, Keats included an expansion of an inferior but harmless valentine originally written for his brother, George, to
be sent to Mary Frogley, a mutual friend. Blackwood's
characterizes these lines as "prurient" and "vulgar," meant
to extoll the virtues of a Cheapside prostitute. Italics call
attention to the Cockney rhymes of "higher" and "Thalia."
The subject matter and versification of Endymion are no
better. "From his prototype Hunt, John Keats has acquired
a sort of vague idea, that the Greeks were a most tasteful
people, and that no mythology can be so finely adopted for
the purposes of poetry as theirs. It is amusing to see what
a hand the two Cockneys make of their mythology, the one
confesses that he never read the Greek Tragedians, and the
other knows Homer only from Chapman..." (III [August 1818],
522). Endymion, we are then informed, "is meant [italics
mine] to be written in English heroic rhyme...."

Croker's less personal attack in the Quarterly also
concentrates upon this same area. Only the first of four
books has been read, the reviewer confesses, and "we are
no better acquainted with the meaning of the book through
which we have so painfully toiled, than we are with the three
which we have not looked into" (XIX [April 1818], 204).
Keats wearies his reader by composing verses to given
rhymes which sacrifice meaning to sound: "the work is
composed of hemistichs which, it is quite evident, have
forced themselves upon the author by the mere force of
the catchwords on which they turn" (p. 206).

The attack on Keats in the British Critic is similar.
The reviewer's summary of Endymion indicates his distaste
for the poet's subject matter. He is no more pleased with
the versification of the poem. "We think it necessary to
add that it is all written in rhyme, and, for the most part,
(when there are syllables enough) in the heroic couplet" (IX
[June 1818], 654). The British Critic, like Blackwood's
and the Quarterly, was hostile to Keats, but even in essentially friendly publications, the poet was censured for his
obscurity;91 and he was not the only one who was victimized.

Shelley was also attacked for the same thing.

Two examples from the Literary Gazette will be
sufficient. On September 9, 1820 the Gazette calls Prometheus Unbound "little else but absolute raving; and were we
not assured to the contrary, we should take it for granted
that the author was a lunatic ... his poetry a mélange of
nonsense" (p. 580). A review of Adonais in the Gazette of
December 8, 1821 condemns Shelley's prosody. "The
poetry of the work is contemptible--a mere collection of
bloated words heaped on each other without order, harmony,
or meaning; the refuse of a schoolboy's common-place book,
full of the vulgarisms of pastoral poetry, yellow gems and
blue stars, bright Phoebus and rosy-fingered Aurora, and
of this stuff is Keats's wretched Elegy compiled...." (p.
773). As a Tory weekly the Gazette was outraged, of
course, at Shelley's impiety; but these remarks also show
a critical inability to comprehend his poetry. When Blackwood's applied the label of "Cockney" to Hunt and Keats, it
suggested that their poetry was as unintelligible as the speech
of London's semi-literate lower class. Although he was
treated more favorably by Blackwood's, Shelley was not
entirely exempt from this charge. He was, after all, a
friend of Hunt's and, thus, a member of the Cockney School
too.

In dealing with Keats, MacGillivray discusses these
"signs of perplexity or distaste which seem strange to the
modern reader" (p. xxviii), but he fails to suggest a reason
for them. To the extent that Keats's use of language was
original, Coleridge's observation, repeated by Wordsworth
in a letter of May 21, 1807 to Lady Beaumont, is close to
the root of this critical dissatisfaction: "every great and
original writer, in proportion as he is great or original,
must himself create the taste by which he is relished."[92]
Except for the best and most perceptive critics, the literary
authorities of any period can be blinded by attempts at
originality of language. With Endymion (and this applies to
the poems of Shelley as well), hostile critics seized upon
real and imaginary weaknesses in the poem, and concluded
too hastily that all of Keats's poetry was obscure.

Defenses, notices, and favorable reviews of Endymion appeared in five newspapers in 1818, but Bailey's review in the Oxford University and City Herald, Reynolds'
letter in the Alfred, West of England Journal, and a defense

in the Chester Guardian were written for Provincial journals
of little literary influence. Hunt reprinted Reynolds' letter
and the Chester Guardian defense in the Examiner, but these
intelligent replies to the Quarterly's attack hardly countered
the influence of that giant Tory review. Even the more influential praise of the Morning Chronicle and the Sun, along
with favorable reviews in the Champion and the Literary
Chronicle, could not fully offset the attacks of the three Tory
journals. By the close of the year 1818 and through 1819,
Keats's reputation was at its lowest ebb; but it significantly
improved in 1820.

        The reviews of 1818 give only a partial picture of
Endymion's reception. In 1820 significant commentaries on
the poem appeared in Baldwin's London Magazine, the Edinburgh Review, and the Edinburgh Magazine. Although these
were written two years after the publication of Keats's poem,
they acted as a counterbalance to the attack of the Tory
quarterlies. The London Magazine and the Edinburgh Review,
the two most influential of the three journals, refer to the
Tory attack of 1818. The London Magazine specifically cites
the unfairness of the Quarterly. The Edinburgh Review, although more restrained in its praise than the London, alludes
to the Quarterly's lack of taste when it observes of Endymion
that "he who does not find a great deal in it to admire and to
give delight, cannot ... find any great pleasure in some of
the finest creations of Milton and Shakespeare" (XXXIV
[August 1820], 205). The Edinburgh Magazine, a monthly
not without influence, approvingly cites lines of Keats which
the Quarterly had condemned. The critical estimates of
Endymion had now turned in Keats's favor; the pattern was
to continue in clear-cut approval of the Lamia volume.

        Perhaps the most remarkable fact about the reception
of Keats's last volume is that the tone of vilification, apparent in the Tory reviews of 1818, is almost completely
lacking in 1820. Only the scoffing review of the Guardian
is completely hostile. The British Critic, which found fault
with these poems, attempted to retract its earlier severity
toward Endymion as best it could. The Quarterly remained
silent. Blackwood's continued to sneer at Keats in incidental notices, but the magazine did not review the volume.
William Blackwood, as recounted by Taylor in an unmailed
letter or memorandum of August 31, 1820 to Hessey, paid
Taylor a visit and announced his intention of speaking favorably of Keats in his magazine. 93 The discussion that ensued might/have dissuaded Blackwood. 94 Nevertheless, a

notice in the September 1820 issue admits that Keats "is evidently possessed of talents" and that "there is much merit in some of the stanzas of Mr. Keats' last volume ..." (VII, 665). Of the less than completely enthusiastic reviews of the non-Tory publications, the Eclectic praises "To Autumn, " "Fancy, " and Lamia; the Literary Chronicle quotes with approval "Ode on a Grecian Urn" and "Bards of Passion"; and Gold's London Magazine admits that Keats's poetical merits have not been duly estimated.

Nine other reviews were essentially favorable. In the same review in which Jeffrey had defended Endymion, he also praised the Lamia volume as much as his neoclassic tastes would permit. Baldwin's London Magazine called attention once more to the injustice done to Keats by the Tory reviewers. The excellence of "Ode to a Nightingale" and The Eve of St. Agnes were recognized. Hyperion was called "one of the most extraordinary creations of any modern imagination" (II [September 1820], 319). Lamb's perceptive review in the New Times, later reprinted in the Examiner, begins by enthusiastically quoting from Keats's description of Madeline's casement window and her preparations for the bedchamber. "We have, " Lamb concludes, "scarcely anything like it in modern description" (July 19, 1820). The Tory Sun and the New Monthly Magazine, like the Tory New Times, also praised Keats. The unqualified commendation of these Tory journals is a clear indication that Keats had survived the association with Hunt which had precipitated the assault of Blackwood's, the Quarterly, and the British Critic. Favorable reviews appeared also in Hunt's Indicator, the Monthly Magazine, the Edinburgh Magazine, and the St. James's Chronicle; as previously indicated, poems of Keats appeared in more than a dozen newspapers. Other incidental notices and allusions occurred in 1820, some of which were unfavorable, but they were not reviews, nor did they appear in particularly important journals. 95 Despite some occasional criticism, Keats was now receiving favorable attention in most of the influential reviews, magazines and newspapers of his day.

The trend continued through 1821, the year of Keats's death. Tributes in verse and prose, obituaries, and longer death notices total well over fifty for this year alone, and they appear in magazines and newspapers published throughout the British Isles. Obituaries are found in a substantial number of influential serials and in such unlikely sources as the Military Register and the British Freeholder. Hunt's

farewell to Keats on his departure for Italy was published in
the Indicator for September 1820.   Keats died on February
13 of the next year, but notice of his death did not reach
England until one month later.   Three poems on Keats's
death--one possibly by his publisher, John Taylor--and a
poem "On Reading Lamia" appeared between March and
May. 96   Favorable notices of substance concerning Keats's
death appeared in Baldwin's London Magazine, the New
Monthly and Pocket magazines, as well as in the New Annual
Register.   (The notice in the New Monthly was reprinted in
the New Annual Register.)

Shelley's Adonais, published in Pisa on July 13, 1821
was the most important tribute to Keats.   Shelley introduced
his elegy with an enthusiastic, if mistaken, Preface which
accused the Quarterly of having caused Keats's death.   "I
consider the fragment of Hyperion, " he states, "as second
to nothing that was ever produced by a writer of the same
years. "97   A sympathetic review of Adonais appeared in the
Literary Chronicle and Weekly Review and, in incidental
comments, Keats was called "a youthful poet of considerable
promise" (December 1, 1821, p. 751).   The censure of the
Literary Gazette has already been noticed; its disapproval
of Adonais resulted in incidental sneers against Keats.
Praise by Shelley was to have the same consequences to
Keats in Blackwood's as Hunt's earlier approval.   The
magazine's displeasure with the poem and the Preface is
understandable, for Shelley's accusation against the Quarterly
might have been more easily leveled against William Blackwood's publication, and Blackwood knew this. 98   It was inevitable that the attack against Shelley also attempt to dis-
credit Keats.   Hunt's review in the Examiner (July 7, 1822)
and an anonymous review in the European Magazine (April
1825) eventually redressed the balance in favor of Shelley
and Keats.

The controversy concerning Adonais should not obscure the favorable reception of the Lamia volume.   It is
significant that of the fourteen reviews in Chapter Four which
deal with Keats's last volume, nine are reproduced
for the first time.   This is a surprising statistic.   Keats's
work received far greater attention in 1820 than many have
realized, and the general tenor of most of this commentary
was clearly sympathetic.   Neither in weight nor in numbers
can it be said that the poet was reviewed unfavorably during
the last two years of his life.   Admittedly, this was not the
opinion of Keats's defenders.   Even before Adonais was pub-

lished in July 1821, the notices of Keats's death for that
year emphasized the poet's neglect.   Like Chatterton and
White, Keats died at a young age.   Moreover, there was
the touching instance of his last days with Severn when he
coined the epitaph of his neglect that was to appear on his
tombstone.   With Keats's words in mind, "L." reports in
Baldwin's London Magazine that the poet "has been suffered
to rise and pass away almost without a notice..." (III April
1821, 426).   In his Preface to Adonais, Shelley not only
repeats this claim but charges that Keats's death resulted
from such neglect: "I am given to understand that the wound
which his sensitive spirit had received from the criticism of
Endymion was exasperated by the bitter sense of unrequited
benefits; the poor fellow seems to have been hooted from
the stage of life...."99   However, Keats contradicted himself, Baldwin's, and Shelley the year before when he wrote
to Charles Armitage Brown that the Lamia volume "has good
success among literary people, and, I believe, has a moderate sale."100   This was in August 1820; favorable reviews
were still to appear through September and October; but
Keats, who was already ill and was to set out for Italy on
September 17, may not have seen them.   Nevertheless, the
opinion persisted among his contemporaries that he had been
poorly received, and Shelley and Hazlitt helped to perpetuate
this opinion.

        Shelley's viewpoint was the most extreme.   The
earliest private reference to his charge of death by derision
in Adonais occurs in a letter to Byron on April 16 or 17,
1821.   Shelley wrote to Byron that Keats's death resulted
from "the contemptuous attack on his book in the Quarterly
Review."101   Subsequently, Byron, experienced in the art
of derision himself, was to allude caustically to Keats's
death in his "fiery particle" couplet in Don Juan.102   But
despite his incredulousness, Byron seemed to accept Shelley's charge, and some of Keats's friends also concurred
with Shelley's misinformed judgment, Brown and Haydon
being among them.   Hazlitt, an acquaintance whom Keats
admired but not a close friend, used the accusation as a
club against the Tories.   In "The Periodical Press" (Edinburgh Review, XXXVII [May 1823], 203-213), Hazlitt attacks
Keats's Tory critics, with whom he links the poet's death,
and repeats his attack in a review of Shelley's Posthumous
Poems (Edinburgh Review, XL [July 1824], 494-514), as
well as in his attack upon Gifford in The Spirit of the Age
(London, 1825) and in his earlier observations "On Living
to One's-Self" in Table Talk (London, 1821).   In these

reviews and essays, Hazlitt deliberately overemphasized the
case of Keats as a martyred poet, and for understandable
reasons.   Hazlitt was no more favorably responsive to the
Tory reviewers than Shelley was: both men had been victimized by the Tory press.

      Because the Quarterly had been far more abusive to
Shelley than Blackwood's, it was singled out as the villain
of Adonais.   Although Shelley may not have been fully conscious of his motivation, his vindication of Keats was also
a defense of himself.

> Previous to its [Adonais] composition Shelley was
> by no means an unqualified admirer of Keats'
> poetry.   His personal connection with Keats was
> rather slight.   Although Shelley's hatred of oppres-
> sion was so great that the conception of Keats as
> a victim of tyranny would undoubtedly have been
> sufficient to account for the poem, yet there seems
> to be a personal feeling in it not quite explicable
> on this basis alone.   The explanation is not so
> difficult....   Shelley himself was a victim of
> critical oppression, as Keats had been.   For him-
> self, he sedulously professed an indifference which
> he tried vainly to experience.   Hatred and revenge
> were contrary to his avowed creed; hence he could
> not retaliate....   But for Keats, he could speak
> feelings otherwise suppressed.   Temporary identi-
> fication with Keats would have been practically
> inevitable under the circumstances.   In the sig-
> nificantly long passage on himself he even de-
> scribes himself as a pathetic poet overcome by the
> weight of the superincumbent hour "who in another's
> fate now wept his own."[103]

Similarly, Hazlitt had been attacked both by Blackwood's
and the Quarterly.   The attack of Blackwood's, primarily
because it was personal and unexpected (it contradicted the
magazine's former favorable notices of his "Lectures on
English Poetry"), irritated Hazlitt in particular.   Blackwood's Rhymed Notices of March 1818 refer to "pimpled
Hazlitt's coxcomb" lectures, and the term "pimpled Hazlitt"
soon became a catchphrase in the magazine.   Hazlitt was
furious.   "Sir, you call me as a nickname 'pimpled Hazlitt.'
And I am not pimpled, but remarkably pale and sallow.   You
were told of this as a false fact, and you repeated and still
repeat it...."[104]   The Quarterly was equally hostile.   Be-

tween 1817 and 1821 unfavorable reviews of five of Hazlitt's
works appeared in this journal. [105]

Hazlitt's premature eulogy of Keats in January 1821
is particularly revealing. (Keats was still alive at the time,
although Hazlitt knew that he was seriously ill and probably
dying in Italy.) "A crew of mischievous critics at Edinburgh ... affixed the epithet of the Cockney School to one
or two writers born in the metropolis.... This epithet
proved too much for one of the writers in question, and
stuck like a barbed arrow in his heart. Poor Keats! What
was sport to the town, was death to him. Young, sensitive,
delicate, he ... withdrew to sigh his last breath in foreign
climes."[106] The reference here is to Blackwood's, but the
context of the essay indicates that Hazlitt assigns equal
blame to the Quarterly, and he clearly establishes his personal motive for doing so in a sentence that precedes this
defense. "Taylor and Hessey told me that they had sold
nearly two editions of the Characters of Shakespear's Plays
in about three months, but that after the Quarterly Review
of them came out, they never sold another copy."[107] This
pattern is repeated after Keats's death in The Spirit of the
Age. Hazlitt charges that as a result of Gifford and the
Quarterly, "Mr. Keats was hooted out of the world, and his
fine talents and wounded sensibilities consigned to an early
grave" (p. 305), but in the same paragraph he also pointed-
ly refers to the Quarterly's attacks upon his own works. As
his biographer observes of Hazlitt, "when he wrote of Keats
it was almost always to denounce those writers of the
Quarterly Review and Blackwood's Magazine who had damned
them both as the Cockney friends of Hunt."[108]

Around the charges of Shelley, Hazlitt, and some of
Keats's friends, the myth of the poet's death grew, and although there were others who repudiated it--Hunt and Clarke
in particular--they accepted the assumption on which it grew,
that Keats had been reviewed badly by the periodical press. [109]
Baldwin's London Magazine did no more than repeat these
charges. By concentrating upon the Tory reviews of 1818,
Keats's friends and defenders put undue emphasis upon the
poet's early unfavorable reception; they neglected the friendly
reviews of 1820. Although he was never given the acclaim
he deserved, Keats was generally well-received toward the
end of his life. If he did not gain the recognition in his
lifetime that came to Wordsworth, for instance, the reason
was obvious. Wordsworth's fame was not immediate; it
was perhaps as late as 1827, twenty-nine years after the

Lyrical Ballads, before he began to receive wide popular
recognition. 110 Keats's career, from the time "To Solitude"
first appeared in print until his last volume, was little more
than four years.   Moreover, his only published volume of
unquestioned greatness was his last one.   He was dead
seven months later: there was hardly enough time for his
reputation to grow as Wordsworth's did.

Notes

1. "The Establishment of Wordsworth's Reputation," JEGP,
   LIV (1944), 61-71.

2. LIX, 202.

3. George L. Marsh and Newman I. White, "Keats and
   the Periodicals of His Time," MP, XXXII (August
   1934), 37-53; J. R. MacGillivray, Keats: A Bibliography and Reference Guide (Toronto 1949).

4. The Failures of Criticism (Ithaca; rev. ed., 1967).

5. See pp. 190-204.

6. In John Keats (New York, 1966), Walter J. Bate states
   that this volume was published on either "Saturday,
   July 1, or Monday, July 3" (p. 650).   However,
   publication notices in the Sun of June 30 and the
   Star of July 1 both state that the Lamia volume
   was published "This Day."

7. G. M. Treveylan, History of England (New York; revised Anchor Edition, 1952), III, 305.

8. In protest against the government's brutal suppression
   of this meeting, Shelley wrote the Masque of
   Anarchy.

9. G. M. Trevelyan. British History in the Nineteenth
   Century and After (New York, 1938), pp. 190-191.

10. A. Aspinall, Politics and The Press, c. 1780-1850
    (London 1949), p. 30.

11. Until this time Cobbett had evaded former newspaper
    duties "by omitting news and writing his Political

Register in the form of Open Letters addressed
to certain people, so claiming that his newspaper
was really a pamphlet, on which the nominal duty
of 3 s. per edition was payable." (Politics and
The Press, p. 57.) The four pence stamp tax
smashed Cobbett's practice by extending the defini-
tion of a newspaper.

12. There were, of course, many other reformist news-
papers--John Hunt's Yellow Dwarf; T. J. Wooler's
three newspapers, the Black Dwarf, Manchester
Observer, and British Gazette; the Cap of Liberty,
Medusa; or, Penny Politician; Cobbett's Evening
Post--but none were as successful as the Political
Register.

13. Carlile's wife was sent to prison for repeating her
husband's offense. As a result of a series of con-
victions between 1817 and 1834, Carlile spent almost ten years in jail. (Newman I. White, The
Unextinguished Hearth [Durham, 1938], p. 9.)

14. For a complete list and discussion see Aspinall,
Politics and The Press, pp. 66-102.

15. G. M. Trevelyan, English Social History (New York,
1942), p. 465.

16. Trevelyan, British History, pp. 187-188.

17. William S. Ward, "Some Aspects of the Conservative
Attitude Toward Poetry in English Criticism, 1798-
1820," PMLA, LX (1945), 390 and note.

18. Of course, Blackwood's attacks on Hunt were political
rather than moral, but it is significant that the
excuse for these slanders was rooted in moral
grounds. Such attacks were hypocritical but cunning; they appealed to the moral biases of the age.

19. June 2, 1821, p. 174.

20. XXXVI (October 1817), 53.

21. White, Hearth, pp. 20-21.

22. Ian Jack, English Literature, 1815-1832 (Oxford 1962),
p. 6.

23. *Letters of John Keats*, ed. Hyder E. Rollins (Cam-
     bridge, Mass., 1958), II, 368.

24. "To Solitude" (May 5, 1816, p. 282), "Chapman's
     Homer" (December 1, 1816, p. 76), "To Koscius-
     ko" (February 16, 1817, p. 107), "After Dark
     Vapours" (February 23, 1817, p. 124), "On Seeing
     the Elgin Marbles" and "To Haydon" (March 9,
     1817, p. 155), On "The Floure and the Lefe"
     (March 16, 1817, p. 173).

25. Shelley and Keats.

26. "On y trouve," Louis Landré explains, "des tournures
     familières, une accumulation d'épithètes, de nom-
     breuses descriptions, une façon affectée de parler
     des femmes qui sont tout à fait dans la manière
     de Hunt" (*Leigh Hunt: contribution à l'histoire du
     Romantisme anglais* [Paris, 1935], I, 122).

27. *Letters of Keats*, I, 170.

28. To George and Georgiana Keats, December 16, 1818-
     January 4, 1819 in *Letters of Keats*, II, 71.

29. Rollins, *Letters of Keats*, II, 71 n.

30. Edmund Blunden, *Leigh Hunt* (London, 1930), p. 116.

31. Writing of Hunt's unfavorable opinion of Book I of
     Endymion, Keats remarks that "the fact is he and
     Shelley are hurt and perhaps justly, at my not
     having showed them the affair officiously--and from
     several hints I have had they appear much disposed
     to dissect and anatomize any trip or slip I might
     have made" (To George and Thomas Keats, Jan-
     uary 23, 1818 in *Letters of Keats*, I, 214).

32. "On the Grasshopper and Cricket," *Examiner* (Septem-
     ber 21, 1817, p. 599); "The Human Seasons" and
     "To Ailsa Rock," Hunt's *Literary Pocketbook*
     (1819); "La Belle Dame sans Merci," *Indicator*
     (May 10, 1820, p. 248); "A Dream, after Reading
     Dante's Episode of Paolo and Francesca," *Indi-
     cator* (June 21, 1820, p. 304); "Cap and Bells"
     (excerpt) in an article by Hunt on "Coaches,"
     Indicator (August 23, 1820, pp. 367-368); "Grass-

hopper and Cricket" and "Ode to Autumn" (excerpts)
in Hunt's the Months (1821).

33. Landré, I, 122.

34. "Mr. Kean," December 21, 1817, p. 405; review of
     Retribution and Harlequin's Vision (mistitled Don
     Giovanni), January 4, 1818, pp. 10-11. Leonidas
     M. Jones proves that a December 26 review of
     "Richard, Duke of York," generally attributed to
     Keats, is in fact Reynolds' ("Keats's Theatrical
     Reviews in the Champion," K-SJ, III [1954], 54-
     65).

35. Bate, Keats, p. 118.

36. Walter Graham, English Literary Periodicals (New
     York, 1930), p. 236.

37. The Advertisement in its first volume emphasizes
     selection rather than number of articles.

38. A reference to the tendency of the Edinburgh to take
     the opposite view of the Tory Quarterly, which
     had condemned the poem.

39. To George and Georgiana Keats, September 17-27,
     1819 in Letters of Keats, II, 200.

40. Letters of Keats, II, 200 n.

41. Graham dismisses Southey's claim and suggests that
     the plan was first conceived by either George
     Canning or Murray (Periodicals, pp. 241-242).

42. The Baviad (1794) and Maeviad (1795).

43. H. and H. C. Shine, The Quarterly Review Under
     Gifford: Identification of Contributors, 1809-1824
     (Chapel Hill, 1949), indicate that in addition to
     his eight articles there are "thirty-nine others in
     which he took some hand" (p. xvii).

44. Letter of January 1815 in E. V. Lucas, The Letters
     of Charles and Mary Lamb (New Haven, 1935), II,
     148-149.

45. Review of Political Essays, XXII (July 1820), 158-163.
    The attribution is made by Walter Graham (Tory
    Criticism in the Quarterly Review, 1809-1853 [New
    York, 1921], p. 47) and by H. and H. C. Shine
    (p. 67). Graham misdates the review as Novem-
    ber 1820, but the Shines correct him.

46. Graham, Tory Criticism, p. 48; H. and H. C. Shine,
    p. 61.

47. See M. F. Brightfield, John Wilson Croker (Berkeley,
    1940), pp. 348-349, and J. R. MacGillivray, p.
    xxv.

48. Review of The Story of the Rimini, XIV (January 1816),
    473-481; review of Foliage, XVIII (January 1818),
    324-335. See Graham, Tory Criticism (p. 47) for
    both Croker attributions. H. and H. C. Shine (p.
    51) list Gifford as the possible reviewer of Foli-
    age but indicate that Croker is the more likely
    choice. Again, the Shines correct Graham, who
    dated the Foliage review May 1818.

49. The Quarterly's review of Byron's Dramas, XXVII
    (July 1822), 476-524 is more critical than any of
    its previous evaluations of Byron's poetry.

50. Graham, Periodicals, pp. 244-245.

51. As Welker observes, the Quarterly's approval of innova-
    tion is a "tendency rather than a clearly defined
    attitude." ("The Position of the Quarterlies on
    Some Classical Dogmas," SP, XXXVII [1940], 551.)
    His conclusion "that the triumph of the Romantic
    Movement lies quite as much with the Quarterly
    Review as with the Romantic authors themselves"
    (p. 562) is exaggerated.

52. Margaret Oliphant, Annals of a Publishing House:
    William Blackwood and His Sons (London, 1897),
    I, 133-140, 274-275.

53. Hazlitt's suits are mentioned by Oliphant, but the fullest
    discussion of his relations with Blackwood's is in
    Herschel Baker's William Hazlitt (Cambridge, Mass.,
    1962), pp. 370-381. Further information may also
    be found in Theodore Besterman's "Hazlitt and

Maga, " TLS, August 22, 1935, p. 525; Alan Lang
Strout's "Hunt, Hazlitt, and Maga, " ELH, IV
(1937), 151-159; and Ralph M. Wardle's "Outwitting
Hazlitt, " MLN, XVII (1942), 459-462.

54. Among others, this attribution is given by MacGillivray,
p. xviii n. It is possible, as Carl R. Woodring
indicates (Prose of the Romantic Period [Cambridge,
Mass., 1961], p. 597), that Wilson might have had
some small hand in the article; but it is essentially,
if not entirely, Lockhart's review.

55. Andrew Lang, Life and Letters of John Gibson Lockhart (London, 1897), I, 198-199, and Gilbert
Macbeth, John Gibson Lockhart: A Critical Study
(Urbana, 1935) p. 115, discuss Lockhart's sources
of information. John Christie, who wished Keats
well, and the poet's friends, Benjamin Bailey and
John Hamilton Reynolds, unwittingly supplied Lockhart with enough information about Keats to allow
"the scorpion, " as he was then called, to launch
a personal attack against the poet.

56. MacGillivray, pp. xxv-xxvi, was the first to make this
observation.

57. Walter Graham, "Contemporary Critics of Coleridge,
The Poet, " PMLA, XXXVII (1928), 283.

58. White, Hearth, pp. 21-23.

59. Blackwood's was impressed by the power of Manfred
(I [June 1817], 289-295), and although Byron
answered its moral censure of Don Juan (VI
[August 1819], 512-522) in his posthumously
published "Reply, " Blackwood's still perceived
that Byron's poem was a great work of genius.

60. Scott died by the hand of John Christie as the result
of a wound suffered in a duel at Chalk Farm. Although Christie was one of the men who had hoped
to dissuade Lockhart from attacking Keats,
he was loyal to Blackwood's. The duel
grew out of a quarrel brought on by Scott's attacks on Blackwood's in defense of Keats. Complete details are given by Josephine Bauer, The
London Magazine (Copenhagen, 1953), pp. 75-80.

Bauer's book is the standard history of the London Magazine.

61. But as Taylor continued in the post of editor, the magazine began to deteriorate. Although a friend to Keats and an admirer of his poetry, Taylor was not a good editor. He could not retain Hazlitt as a contributor; nothing that DeQuincey could offer was the equal of his Confessions. The London Magazine continued until 1829, but signs of decline were apparent as early as 1824. Taylor and Hessey sold the magazine in 1825.

62. Bauer discusses the London Magazine's treatment of the major Romantic Poets, pp. 180-203.

63. Review of Bacchus and Ariadne, II (July 1820), 45.

64. Graham, Periodicals, p. 238.

65. Ibid., p. 239.

66. "Blackwood's Magazine," London Magazine, II (November 1820), 511.

67. "The Mohock Magazine," London Magazine, II (December 1820), 682.

68. Blackwood's Magazine, II (January 1818), 417. An amusing addendum to this affair appears in the Edinburgh Advertiser of October 27, 1818, p. 270. A correspondence is published between Wilson and Lockhart, both of whom wrote under the signature "Z.," and the anonymous author of a pamphlet entitled Hypocrisy Unveiled and Calumny Detected in a Review of Blackwood's Magazine. Wilson's letter to the author declares,
    "As it is no part of a manly disposition to use insulting epithets to an unknown enemy who may perhaps have resolved to remain unknown, I shall not at present bestow any upon you. Long as you remain concealed you are a nonentity...."
    "It is possible, however, that you will come forward from your concealment, when you feel you cannot continue in it without consciousness of cowardice. I therefore request your name and address, that I may send a friend to you, to de-

liver my opinion of your character and to settle
time and place for a meeting, at which I may
exact satisfaction from you for the public insults
you have offered to me. "

Lockhart's letter also demands to know the
identity of the anonymous author.   The reply to
both men by the author of Hypocrisy Unveiled
makes the obvious parallel.   "If you be not the
secret traducer of ... Mr. Hazlitt and Mr.
Coleridge ... if you be not the writer of one or
the other of the letters addressed in the name of
Z to Mr. Leigh Hunt--and if you did not ... submit to be publicly stigmatized by him as a coward
and a scoundrel--then you have nothing to say to
me, for I speak only of the writer or writers who
have committed these enormities. "

This exchange of letters was also published in
the Examiner for November 1, 1818, p. 697.

69.   "The truth is, we from the beginning saw marks of
feeling and power in Mr. Keats' verses, which
made us think it very likely, he might become a
real poet of England, provided he could be persuaded to give up all tricks of Cockneyism, and
forswear for ever the potations of Mr. Leigh
Hunt..." (VIII [September 1820], 686).

70.   Geoffrey Carnall, "The Monthly Magazine," RES, n.s.
IV (1954), 162.

71.   John Middleton Murry, Studies in Keats (London, 1930),
pp. 6-11.   Following the assumption of Roberta
D. Cornelius ("Two Early Reviews of Keats's First
Volume," PMLA, XL [1925], 201), Murry named
Haydon as the author of a review of Poems in the
Champion of March 9, 1817, a review which
Mathew resented.   MacGillivray (p. 63) and Hyder
E. Rollins (Letters of Keats, I, 123), however,
identify the reviewer as Reynolds, whom Keats
thanks (presumably for the review) in a letter of
the same day.   Their judgment is confirmed by
Leonidas M. Jones in Selected Poetry and Prose
of John Hamilton Reynolds (Cambridge, Mass.,
1966), p. 451, n. 160.   Also, a letter-writer in
the Anti-Gallican Monitor (June 8, 1817, p. 5085)
indicates that Reynolds is the author of this review.   (See Chapter II, n. 44.)

72. Graham, Periodicals, p. 313.

73. Ibid., p. 315.

74. The Literary Chronicle and General Miscellany of Science, Arts, History, etc. (not to be confused with the Literary Chronicle and Weekly Review) was identical with the Literary Journal, except for a variation in the dating of issues. (William S. Ward, Index and Finding List of Serials Published in the British Isles, 1789-1832 [Lexington, Kentucky, 1953], p. 88.

75. The letters and the attribution are noted here for the first time. The case for Wilson's authorship is made in the headnote to Chapter II, item 7.

76. Eris was the goddess of discord. The reference relates to the charge that Keats's dress was grotesque. Although Keats did affect the uniform of a radical poet at about this time, the charge is exaggerated.

77. Attribution is given, among others, by MacGillivray, p. 65.

78. Attribution is given, among others, by MacGillivray, p. 66.

79. "When Perry died in 1821, the property which he had bought in 1780 for 1500 I. was sold for 42,000 I., and his profits during the last year amounted to 12,000 I." (H.R. Fox Bourne, English Newspapers [London, 1887], I, 363.)

80. Bourne (II, 87) lists Black's first name as Thomas, but the DNB and White (Hearth, p. 390) call him John Black. It is clear, however, that all three sources are referring to the same man.

81. His independent judgment attested to his intellectual honesty, but his views shocked the Whigs and offended the Radicals. As a result, the influence of the Morning Chronicle began to decline after 1821 (Bourne, II, 14-15, 87).

82. Both men were to make concurrent claims to the editor-

ship (Bourne, I, 368n.). The John Taylor referred to here was not Keats's publisher; he was
a friend of Godwin. (Kenneth N. Cameron, ed.
Shelley and His Circle [Cambridge, Mass., 1961],
II, 649.)

83. Richard Woodhouse was literary and legal advisor to
    Keats's publishers, Taylor and Hessey.

84. The review and the attribution are noted here for the
    first time. See Chapter IV, item 3.

85. Bourne, I, 360.

86. This attribution is given, among others, by E. V.
    Lucas in The Works of Charles and Mary Lamb
    (London, 1905), I, 203.

87. Marsh and White, pp. 51-54; Dorothy Hewlett, A Life
    of John Keats (New York, 1949), pp. 332-340;
    MacGillivray, pp. xxvii-xxviii; Robert Gittings,
    John Keats (Boston, 1968), pp. 401-402; Hayden,
    pp. 190-204.

88. [No reference]

89. In 1783 there was "on an average only one newspaper
    daily for every 300 inhabitants." By 1829 the
    newspaper reading audience had multiplied ten-
    fold. The yearly return of newspaper stamps in-
    dicates that the total number of newspapers sold
    in Great Britain in 1821, exclusive of Ireland,
    was almost twenty-five million. (A. Aspinall,
    "The Circulation of Newspapers in the Early
    Nineteenth Century," RES, XXII [1946], 29-30.)

90. Gittings, p. 132.

91. A favorable review of the Lamia volume in Baldwin's
    London Magazine mentions Keats's "frequent ob-
    scurity and confusion of language" (II [September
    1820], 321). Speaking of Keats's use of Greek
    mythology, Jeffrey expresses "doubts of the fit-
    ness of such personages to maintain interest with
    the modern public...." (Edinburgh Review, XXXIV
    [August 1820], 207.) Basil Willey's Seventeenth
    Century Background (London, 1934) helps explain

Jeffrey's critical dismay with Keats's mythological
subject matter.   The triumph of the mechanical
philosophy of Locke made it impossible to seriously employ mythological machinery in the poetry
of the eighteenth century; it continued to appear
only as a decoration (Willey, pp. 296-297).   Although Jeffrey recognized that the story of Endymion was only the framework upon which Keats
constructed his poem, he still occasionally confused Endymion's mythological framework with the
substance of Keats's poetry.   Those with less in-
sight than Jeffrey compounded the error.   Accordingly, Hyperion was also criticized for its mythological devices.   To many of his contemporaries,
it seemed that Keats was attempting to resurrect
a dead mythology which all standards of neoclassic
taste and decorum had dismissed a century before.
That the poet was attempting to "fabricate a genuine new mythology of his own (not necessarily re-
jecting all old material in so doing)" (Willey, p.
297), occurred to very few.

92.   Letters of William and Dorothy Wordsworth; the Middle
       Years, ed. Ernest de Selincourt [Oxford, 1937],
       I, 130.

93.   Keats Circle, I. 133-137.

94.   Taylor reconstructs the conversation.   Blackwood an-
       nounces his intention of speaking favorably of Keats,
       and Taylor replies, "After what has been said of
       his Talents I should think it very inconsistent.
       [Blackwood:] Certainly they found Fault with his
       former Poems, but that was because they thought
       they deserved it.   [Taylor:] But why did they
       attack him personally? [Blackwood:] They did
       not do so. [Taylor:] No? did not they speak of him
       in·ridicule as Johnny Keats, describe his Appear-
       ance while addressing a Sonnet [to] Ailsa Crag ...
       what can you say to that coldblooded Passage
       where they say they will take Care he shall never
       get 50 I. again for a Vol. of his poems--what
       had he done to cause such Attacks as these?
       [Blackwood:] Oh it was all a Joke, the writer
       meant nothing more than to be witty.   He certainly
       thought there was much affectation in his Poetry,
       and he expressed his Opinion only--It was done in

the fair Spirit of Criticism. [Taylor:] It was
done In the Spirit of the Devil, Mr. Blackwood
..." (Keats Circle, I, 134-135).

95. References in the Retrospective Review (II [August
       1820], 204) and the Honeycomb (August 12, 1820,
       p. 67) were favorable.   Those in the Dublin Maga-
       zine (I [March 1820], 228), New Bon Ton Magazine
       (V [September 1820], 282-284), and Déjeuné (Octo-
       ber 27, 1820, p. 45) were unfavorable.   Other
       references to Keats occur in this year, but they
       were in serials which also carried reviews of the
       poet.

96. "Death of Mr. John Keats," signed "L." (Baldwin's
       London Magazine, III [April 1821], 426-427); "Son-
       net, On the Death of the Poet J. Keats," possibly
       by John Taylor (Baldwin's London Magazine, III
       [May 1821], 526); "Sonnet, On the Death of John
       Keats, the Poet" (Kaleidoscope, n. s. I [August 29,
       1820], 69); "On Reading Lamia, and other Poems,
       by John Keats," signed "G. V. D." (Gossip [May 19,
       1821], p. 96).   The conjecture that Taylor may
       have been the author of the poem in the London
       Magazine was made by Edmund Blunden, Keats's
       Publisher: A Memoir of John Taylor (London,
       1936), p. 125.

97. The Complete Poetical Works of Percy Bysshe Shelley,
       ed. Thomas Hutchinson (Oxford, 1934), p. 425.

98. Speaking to Blackwood, John Taylor stated that the
       Quarterly was the first to attack Keats.   "I beg
       your pardon says B. we were the first" (Keats
       Circle, I, 135).

99. Complete Poetical Works of Shelley, p. 426.

100. Letters of Keats, II, 321.   The Lamia volume did not
        sell well, but Keats's initial impression was not
        inaccurate.   Dorothy Hewlett (A Life of John Keats,
        p. 206) tells us that one hundred and sixty copies
        were subscribed for at publication; then the trial
        of Queen Caroline, against whom George IV
        brought charges for "divorce and degredation,"
        drew attention away from the bookselling trade.
        Less than 500 copies of the volume were sold by
        March 1822.

101. Letters of Percy B. Shelley, ed. Frederick L. Jones
      (Oxford, 1964), II, 284. Robert Finch's often
      quoted letter on the death of Keats was not com-
      municated to Shelley by his friend, John Gisborne,
      until after Adonais was completed (Shelley to Gis-
      borne, June 16, 1821 in Letters of Shelley, II, 299-
      300). Finch's letter simply served as an addi-
      tional, if mistaken, verification. Complete details
      concerning Finch are given by Elizabeth Nitchie,
      The Reverend Colonel Finch (New York, 1940).

102. " 'Tis strange the mind, that very fiery particle, /
      Should let itself be snuff'd out by an article. "

103. White, Hearth, p. 27. Kenneth N. Cameron argues
      that Shelley had Southey in mind as the "base and
      unprincipled calumniator" mentioned in his Preface
      to Adonais. "That Shelley thus identified himself
      with Keats and the attacks on Keats with Southey's
      attacks on himself seems to be indicated..."
      ("Shelley vs. Southey: New Light on an Old Quar-
      rel, " PMLA, LVII [1942], 505). "Shelley ...
      linked the persecution of Keats by the Quarterly
      and (he seemed determined to believe) by Southey,
      with his own similar persecution" (p. 512).

104. William Hazlitt, A Reply to Z, ed. Charles Whibley
      (London, 1923), p. 38.

105. Review of the Round Table, XVII (April 1817), 154-
      159; review of Characters of Shakespear's Plays,
      XVIII (January 1818), 458-466; review of Lectures
      on the English Poets, XIX (July 1818), 424-434;
      review of Political Essays, XXII (November 1820),
      158-163; review of Table Talk, XXVI (October 1821),
      103-108.

106. "On Living to One's-Self, " Table Talk, I, 229-230.

107. Ibid. , p. 229.

108. Baker, p. 250. Another motive for Hazlitt's praise,
      which Baker does not mention, relates to his pre-
      conceived theory concerning the nature of fame.
      As reported by George Patmore in essentially
      favorable notices of Hazlitt's Lectures on English
      Poetry, "One would suppose he had a personal

quarrel with all living writers, good, bad, or indifferent. In fact, he seems to know little about
them, and to care less.... In his eyes, death,
like charity, 'covereth a multitude of sins.' In
short, if you want his praise, you must die for it"
(Blackwood's, III [April 1818], 75). These remarks are based on Patmore's report of Hazlitt's
eighth lecture "On the Living Poets." "Fame is
not the recompense of the living, but of the dead.
The temple of fame stands upon the grave.... He
who has ears truly touched to the music of fame,
is in a manner deaf to the voice of popularity....
He waits patiently and calmly for the award of
posterity, without endeavouring to forestall his
immortality, or mortgage it for a newspaper puff"
(p. 72). Hazlitt's stress upon death and lack of
popularity as keys to fame are repeated themes
in his later evaluations of Keats.

109. Severn neither believed in the myth nor accepted this
      assumption. In "The Vicissitudes of Keats's Fame,"
      Atlantic Monthly, XI (1863), he negates the im-
      portance of Blackwood's. "Certainly the 'Black-
      wood' attack was one of the least of his miseries,
      for he never even mentioned it to me" (p. 405).

110. Elsie Smith (An Estimate of William Wordsworth By
      his Contemporaries [Oxford, 1932], p. 225) sets
      the date for the rise of Wordsworth's popularity
      as shortly after the Excursion (1814), but in "The
      Establishment of Wordsworth's Reputation," T. M.
      Taysor argues for 1827.

Chapter II

KEATS'S RECEPTION THROUGH 1817

(The first two items in this chapter appeared
almost a year before the publication of Poems
[March 1817]. The remaining reviews and letters
relate to the reception of Keats's first volume.
Mathew's review in the European Magazine, like
his poem in that same journal, was not of essential
critical importance. The favorable review in the
Monthly Magazine and an exchange of comments in
the Champion were too short to be of major significance. The important reviews were by Reynolds in the Champion, Hunt in the Examiner,
and by the commentators in the Eclectic Review and the Edinburgh Magazine. Two of these
were entirely favorable. The review in the Edinburgh Magazine was mixed but not essentially un-
sympathetic. The Eclectic, however, was the only
quarterly review to notice Keats, and its estimate
was unfavorable. Moreover, Hunt's praise in the
Examiner [both before and after the publication of
Poems] caused some adverse effects. Wilson's
condemnation of Keats in the Anti-Gallican Monitor,
for instance, was a reply to Hunt's praise of his
friend in the "Young Poets." The major damage,
of course, was to be done by Tory critics in
Blackwood's and the Quarterly Review. However,
this is to anticipate the Tory reaction of 1818.
Although he did not gain wide critical attention,
Keats was generally well-received through 1817,
primarily as a result of the kindness and per-
ceptiveness of Hunt and Reynolds.)

1. George Felton Mathew's "To A Poetical Friend" in the
    European Magazine.

        (This poem, the earliest known public reference

to Keats, appeared in the European Magazine for
October 1816 [LXX, 365]. It is signed "G. F. M."
[clearly Mathew's initials] and was first discovered
by Roberta Cornelius in her PMLA article, "Two
Early Reviews of Keats's First Volume" [XL (1925),
193-211], where it was reprinted along with reviews
of Poems by Reynolds [Champion, March 9, 1817]
and Mathew [European Magazine, May 1817]. That
Keats is being addressed in the poem under discussion is clear from Mathews' footnote, which
alludes to his friend's medical character. Keats
completed his studies at Guy's Hospital in London
in July 1816 and continued to work occasionally at
the hospital as a wound-dresser through March
1817. As for the European Magazine, to which
Mathew contributed several poems in addition to
this one, details can be found in the introductory
chapter.)

O Thou who delightest in fanciful song,
    And tellest strange tales of the elf and the fay;
Of giants tyrannic, whose talismans strong
    Have power to charm gentle damsels astray;

Of courteous knights-errant, and high-mettled steeds:--
    Of forests enchanted, and marvellous streams:--
Of bridges, and castles, and desperate deeds:
    And all the bright fictions of fanciful dreams:--

Of captures, and rescues, and wonderful loves;
    Of blisses abounding in dark leafy bowers;--
Of murmuring music in shadowy groves,
    And beauty reclined on her pillow of flowers:--[1]

O where did thine infancy open its eyes?
    And who was the nurse that attended thy spring?--
For surè thou'rt exotic to these frigid skies,
    So splendid the song that thou lovest to sing.

Perhaps thou hast traversed the glorious East;
    And like the warm breath of its sun, and its gales,
That wander 'mid gardens of flowers to feast,
    Are tinctured with every rich sweet that prevails?

O no!--for a Shakespeare--a Milton are ours!
    And who e'er sung sweeter, or stronger than they?
As thine is, I ween was the spring of their powers;
    Like theirs, is the cast of thine earlier lay.

It is not the climate, or scenery round,
   It was not the nurse that attended thy youth;
That gave thee those blisses which richly abound.
   In magical numbers to charm, and to soothe. [2]

O no!--tis the Queen of those regions of air--
   The gay fields of Fancy--thy spirit has blest;
She cherish'd thy childhood with fostering care,
   And nurtur'd her boy with the milk of her breast.

She tended thee ere thou couldst wander alone,
   And cheer'd thy wild walks amidst terror and dread;--
She sung thee to sleep with a song of her own,
   And laid thy young limbs on her flowery bed.

She gave thee those pinions with which thou delightest
   Sublime o'er her boundless dominions to rove;
The tongue too she gave thee with which thou invitest
   Each ear to thy stories of wonder and love.

And when evening shall free thee from Nature's decays, [3]
   And release thee from Study's severest control,
Oh warm thee in Fancy's enlivening rays,
   And wash the dark spots of disease from thy soul.

And let not the spirit of Poesy sleep;
   Of Fairies and Genii continue to tell--
Nor suffer the innocent deer's timid leap
   To fright the wild bee from her flowery bell. [4]

                                      G. F. M.

2.   From Leigh Hunt's "Young Poets" in the <u>Examiner</u>

     (Hunt's unsigned article on the "Young Poets"
appeared in the <u>Examiner</u> of December 1, 1816,
pp. 761-762. It has been noted, identified, and
reprinted in several standard sources, which need
not be listed here. Hunt's article praises Shelley
and Reynolds, as well as Keats. In May of the
same year, Keats's "To Solitude" had appeared
in the <u>Examiner</u>, but without comment. The excerpts relating to Keats that follow linked the
young poet's name with Hunt's in the minds of
many Tory critics.)

In sitting down to this subject, we happen to be re-
stricted by time to a much shorter notice than we could wish:
but we mean to take it up again shortly. [5]   Many of our
readers however have perhaps observed for themselves, that
there has been a new school of poetry rising of late, which
promises to extinguish the French one that has prevailed
among us since the time of Charles the 2d. [6]   It began with
something excessive, like most revolutions, but this gradually
wore away; and an evident aspiration after real nature and
original fancy remained, which called to the mind the finer
times of the English Muse.   In fact it is wrong to call it a
new school, and still more so to represent it as one of
innovation, it's [sic] only object being to restore the same
love of Nature, and of thinking instead of mere talking, which
formerly rendered us real poets, and not merely versifying
wits, and bead-rollers of couplets.

We were delighted to see the departure of the old
school acknowledged in the number of the Edinburgh Review
just published, --a candour the more generous and spirited,
inasmuch as that work has hitherto been the greatest sur-
viving ornament of the same school in prose and criticism,
as it is now destined, we trust, to be still the leader in the
new.

We also felt the same delight at the third canto of
Lord Byron's Child Harolde [sic], in which, to our conceptions at least, he has fairly renounced a certain leaven
of the French style, and taken his place where we always
said he would be found, --among the poets who have a real
feeling for numbers, and who go directly to Nature for
inspiration. . . .

The object of the present article is merely to notice
three young writers, who appear to us to promise a considerable addition of strength to the new school. . . .

*   *   *

The last of these young aspirants whom we have met
with, and who promise to help the new school to revive
Nature and

"To put a spirit of youth in every thing, "--[7]

is, we believe, the youngest of them all, and just of age.
His name is John Keats.   He has not yet published any

thing except in a newspaper; but a set of his manuscripts
was handed us the other day, and fairly surprised us with
the truth of their ambition, and ardent grappling with Nature.
In the following Sonnet there is one incorrect rhyme, which
might be easily altered, but which shall serve as a peace-
offering to the rhyming critics. 8   The rest of the composition, with the exception of a little vagueness in calling the
regions of poetry "the realms of gold, " we do not hesitate
to pronounce excellent, especially in the last six lines.   The
word swims is complete; and the whole conclusion is equally
powerful and quiet:

> ["On First Looking Into Chapman's Homer, "
> dated October 1816, appears here in print for the
> first time.]

We have spoken with less scruple of these poetical
promises, because we really are not in the habit of lavishing praises and announcements, and because we have no fear
of any pettier vanity on the part of the young men, who
promise to understand human nature so well.

3.   John Hamilton Reynolds' review
     of Poems in the Champion

> (This unsigned review appeared in the Champion
> of March 9, 1817, p. 78, only a few days after
> Keats's first volume was published.   As with her
> Mathew discoveries, it was noted and reprinted by
> Miss Cornelius in her PMLA article of 1925.
> Cornelius attributes the review to Haydon, but the
> author is Reynolds.
> In the review Reynolds quotes at length from "I
> Stood Tiptoe Upon a Little Hill" and "Sleep and
> Poetry, " the longest and most ambitious poems in
> Keats's volume.   Extracts are also given from
> Keats's Epistles to Mathew and to Clarke, and from
> some of Keats's sonnets.   Reynolds says nothing,
> however, about "On First Looking Into Chapman's
> Homer. "   Possibly he felt Hunt's previous com-
> ments in the Examiner were sufficient.)

Here is a little volume filled throughout with very
graceful and genuine poetry.   The author is a very young
man, and one, as we augur from the present work, that is

likely to make a great addition to those who would overthrow
that artificial taste which French criticism has long planted
among us.   At a time when nothing is talked of but the
power and passion of Lord Byron, and the playful and elegant fancy of Moore, and the correctness of Rogers, and the
sublimity and pathos of Campbell (these terms we should
conceive are kept ready composed in the Edinburgh Review-
shop) a young man starts suddenly before us, with a genius
that is likely to eclipse them all.   He comes fresh from
nature, --and the originals of his images are to be found in
her keeping.   Young writers are in general in their early
productions imitators of their favourite poet; like young
birds that in their first songs, mock the notes of those
warblers, they hear the most, and love the best: but this
youthful poet appears to have tuned his voice in solitudes, --
to have sung from the pure inspiration of nature.   In the
simple meadows he has proven that he can

> "See shapes of light, aerial lymning
> And catch soft floating from a faint heard hymning."
> ["Sleep and Poetry," ll. 33-34.]

We find in his poetry the glorious effect of summer
days and leafy spots on rich feelings, which are in themselves a summer.   He relies directly and wholly on nature.
He marries poesy to genuine simplicity.   He makes her
artless, --yet abstains carefully from giving her an uncomely
homeliness:--that is, he shows one can be familiar with
nature, yet perfectly strange to the habits of common life.
Mr. Keats is fated, or "we have no judgment in an honest
face;"[9] to look at natural objects with his mind, as Shakespeare and Chaucer did, --and not merely with his eye as
nearly all modern poets do;--to cloth his poetry with a grand
intellectual light, --and to lay his name in the lap of immortality.   Our readers will think that we are speaking too
highly of this young poet--but luckily we have the power of
making good the ground on which we prophesy so hardily.
We shall extract largely from his volume:--It will be seen
how familiar he is with all that is green, light, and beautiful in nature;--and with what an originality his mind dwells
on all great or graceful objects.   His imagination is very
powerful, --and one thing we have observed with pleasure,
that it never attempts to soar on undue occasions.   The
imagination, like the eagle on the rock, should keep its eye
constantly on the sun, --and should never be started heaven-
ward, unless something magnificent marred its solitude.
Again, though Mr. Keats [sic] poetry is remarkably abstracted,

it is never out of reach of the mind; there are one or two
established writers of this day who think that mystery is the
soul of poetry--that artlessness is a vice--and that nothing
can be graceful that is not metaphysical;--and even young
writers have sunk into this error, and endeavoured to puzzle
the world with a confused sensibility.   We must however
hasten to the consideration of the little volume before us,
and not fill up your columns with observations, which extracts will render unnecessary.

The first poem in the book seems to have originated
in a ramble in some romantic spot, "with boughs pavillioned."[10]
The poet describes a delightful time, and a little world of
trees--and refreshing streams, --and hedges of filberts and
wild briar, and clumps of woodlime

> "--taking the [soft] wind
> Upon their summer thrones."
>   [" I Stood Tiptoe Upon A Little Hill, "
>   ll. 136-137.]

and flowers opening in the early sunlight.   He connects the
love of poetry with these natural luxuries.

> "For what has made the sage or poet write,
> But the fair paradise of Nature's light?"
>   [ll. 125-126.]

This leads him to speak of some of our olden tales; and
here we must extract the passages describing those of Psyche,
and Narcissus.   The first is exquisitely written.

> "So felt he, who first told, how Psyche went
> On the smooth wind to realms of wonderment;
> What Psyche felt, and Love, when their full lips
> First touch'd; what amorous and fondling nips
> They gave each other's cheeks; with all their sighs,
> And how they kist each others [sic] tremulous eyes;
> The silver lamp--the ravishment--the wonder--
> The darkness--loneliness--the fearful thunder;
> Their woes gone by, and both to heaven upflown,
> To bow for gratitude before Jove's throne."
>   [ll. 141-150.]

The following passage is not less beautiful,

[Quotes ll. 163-180.]

This poem concludes with a brief but beautiful recital of the tale of Endymion--to which indeed the whole poems seem to lean.   The address to the Moon is extremely fine.

[Quotes ll. 113-124.]

'The Specimen of an induction to a poem,' is exceedingly spirited,--as is the fragment of a Tale of Romance immediately following it; but we cannot stay to notice them particularly.   These four lines from the latter piece are very sweet.

> "The side-long view of swelling leafiness,
> Which the glad setting sun in gold doth dress;
> Whence ever and anon the jay outsprings,
> And scales upon the beauty of its wings."
> ["Calidore," ll. 34-37.]

The three poems following, addressed to Ladies, and the one to Hope are very inferior to their companions;-- but Mr. Keats informs us they were written at an earlier period than the rest. 11   The imitation of Spenser is rich. The opening stanza is a fair specimen.

[The excerpt follows.]

The two Epistles to his friends, and one to his brother are written with great ease and power.   We shall extract two passages, both equally beautiful.

[Quotes "Epistle to George Felton Mathew," ll. 31-52.]

The next passage is from the opening of the poet's letter to a friend.

[Keats's extended metaphor, in which he likens himself in the act of composing verse to a swan, is quoted from the first twenty lines of his "Epistle to Charles Cowden Clarke."]

Except in a little confusion of metaphor towards the end, the above passage is exquisitely imagined and executed.

A few Sonnets follow these epistles, and, with the exception of Milton's and Wordsworth's, we think them the most powerful ones in the whole range of English poetry.

We extract the first in the collection, with the assurance
that the rest are equally great.

[Quotes the sonnet "To My Brother George."]

We have been highly pleased with that Sonnet which
speaks--

> "Of fair hair'd Milton's eloquent distress,
>   And all his love for gentle Lycid drown'd;--
> Of lovely Laura in her light green dress,
>   And faithful Petrarch gloriously crown'd."
>   ["Keen, fitful gusts are whisp'ring
>   here and there," ll. 10-14.]

But the last poem in the volume, to which we are now
come, is the most powerful and the most perfect. It is entitled "Sleep and Poetry." The poet past a wakeful night at
a brother poet's house, [12] and has in this piece embodied the
thoughts which passed over his mind. He gives his opinion
of the Elizabethan age, --of the Pope's school, --and of the
poetry of the present day. We scarcely know what to select,
--we are so confused with beauties. In speaking of poetry,
we find the following splendid passage:--

[Quotes ll. 71-84.]

The following passage relating to the same, is even
greater. It is the very magic of imagination.

[Quotes ll. 125-137.]

We have not room to extract the passages on Pope
and his followers, who,

> "----With a puling force
> Sway'd them about upon a rocking horse,
> And thought it Pegasus."[13]
>   [ll. 185-187.]

Nor can we give those on the modern poets. We shall conclude our extracts with the following perfect and beautiful
lines on the busts and pictures which hung around the room
in which he was resting.

[Quotes ll. 381-395.]

We conclude with earnestly recommending the work

to all our readers.   It is not without defects, which may be
easily mentioned, and as easily rectified.   The author, from
his natural freedom of versification, at times passes to an
absolute faultiness of measure:--This he should avoid.   He
should also abstain from the use of compound epithets as
much as possible.   He has a few of the faults which youth
must have;--he is apt occasionally to make his descriptions
over-wrought, --But on the whole we never saw a book which
had so little reason to plead youth as its excuse.   The best
poets of the day might not blush to own it.

        We have two Sonnets presented to us, which were
written by Mr. Keats, and which are not printed in the
present volume.   We have great pleasure in giving them to
the public, --as well on account of their own power and
beauty, as of the grandeur of the subjects; on which we have
ourselves so often made observations.

            ["To Haydon" and "On Seeing the Elgin Marbles"
            follow.]

4.   A short review of Poems
     in the Monthly Magazine

            (This short, favorable notice appeared in the
            Monthly Magazine for March 1817 [XLIII, 248].
            It has been noted and reprinted by George L.
            Marsh and Newman I. White, "Keats and the
            Periodicals of His Time," MP, XXXII [August
            1934], 38.   A dissenting, liberal publication, the
            Monthly Magazine remained friendly to Keats
            throughout his career.)

        A small volume of poems, by Mr. Keats, has ap-
peared; and it well deserves the notice it has attracted, by
the sweetness and beauty of the compositions.   For the
model of his style, the author has had recourse to the age
of Elizabeth; and, if he has not wholly avoided the quaintness that characterises the writings of that period, it must
be allowed by every candid reader that the fertile fancy and
beautiful diction of our old poets, is not unfrequently rivaled
by Mr. Keats.   There is in his poems a rapturous glow and
intoxication of the fancy--an air of careless and profuse magnificence in his diction--a revelry of the imagination and
tenderness of feeling, that forcibly impress themselves on
the reader.

5.   Mathew's review of Poems
      in the European Magazine

> (Mathew's review, which appeared in the Euro-
> pean Magazine for May 1817 [LXXI, 434-437], was
> noted and reprinted for the first time in Cornelius'
> 1925 PMLA article.   There is a significant falling
> off in enthusiasm here from Mathew's poetic ef-
> fusion of 1816.   As Keats became friendly with
> Hunt and Reynolds, he saw little of Mathew; and
> the latter's resentment is clearly in evidence in
> this review.   Hunt is damned for his harmful in-
> fluence upon Keats, and Reynolds' dismissal of
> Keats's poems to Mathew's cousins is also resented.
> To make matters worse, Keats himself disavowed
> these and other early poems associated with Mathew.
> After the dedication to Hunt in Keats's 1817 vol-
> ume, the following disclaimer is inserted: "The
> Short Pieces in the middle of the Book as well as
> some of the Sonnets, were written at an earlier
> period than the rest of the Poems."   Piqued by
> these slights, Mathew's praise is grudging.   Keats's
> versification, he tells us, suffers from "slovenly
> independence"; and "savours too much ... of the
> foppery and affectation of Leigh Hunt!"   If Chap-
> man's Homer is a "fair specimen" of a sonnet, it
> is nevertheless, "absurd in its application"; and
> broken metaphor is to be found in this poem as
> well as in "Sleep and Poetry."   Condemnation such
> as this served as a balm to Mathew's hurt pride.)

There are few writers more frequent or more presumptuous in their intrusions on the public than, we know
not what to call them, versifiers, rhymists, metre-ballad
mongers, what you will but poets.   The productions of some
among them rise, like the smoke of an obscure cottage, clog
the air with an obtrusive vapour, and then fade away into
oblivion and nothingness.[14]   The composition of others
equally ephemeral, but possessing, perhaps a few eccentric
features of originality, come upon us with a flash and an
explosion, rising into the air like a rocket, pouring forth
its short-lived splendour and then falling, like Lucifer,
never to rise again.

The attention of the public, indeed, has been so frequently arrested and abused by these exhalations of ignorance,
perverted genius, and presumption, that "poems" has become

a dull feature upon a title page, and it would be well for the
more worthy candidates for regard and honour, particularly
at this physiognomical, or, rather craniological period, could
the spirit of an author be reflected there with more expressive fidelity. A quotation from, and a wood-engraving of
Spencer [sic], therefore, on the title page of Mr. Keats's
volume is very judiciously and appropriately introduced as
the poetical beauties of the volume we are about to review,
remind us much of that elegant and romantic writer.

For the grand, elaborate, and abstracted music of
nature our author has a fine ear, and now and then catches
a few notes from the passages of that never-ending harmony
which God made to retain in exaltation and purity the spirits
of our first parents. In "places of Nestling-green for poets
made,"[15] we have this gentle address to Cynthia:

"O maker of sweet poets! dear delight
Of this fair world, and all its gentle livers;
Spangler of clouds, halo of crystal rivers,
Mingler with leaves, and dew, and tumbling streams,
Closer of lovely eyes to lovely dreams,
Lover of loneliness and wandering,
Of upcast eyes and tender pondering!
Thee, must I praise, above all other glories
That smilest us on to tell delightful stories."
    ["I Stood Tiptoe Upon A Little Hill," ll. 116-124.]

And also in his last poem, concerning sleep, the
following interrogations and apostrophes are very pleasing:

"What is more gentle than a wind in summer?
What is more soothing than the pretty hummer
That stays one moment in an open flower,
And buzzes cheerily from bower to bower?
What is more tranquil than a musk rose, blowing
In a green island, far from all men's knowing?
More healthful than the leafings of dales?
More secret than a nest of nightingales?
More serene than Cordelia's countenance?
More full of visions than a high romance?
What but thee, sleep!"
                    ["Sleep and Poetry," ll. 1-11.]

The volume before us indeed is full of imaginations
and descriptions equally delicate and elegant with these; but,
although we have looked into it with pleasure, and strongly

recommend it to the perusal of all lovers of real poetry,
we cannot, as another critic has injudiciously attempted, [16]
roll the name of Byron, Moore, Campbell and Rogers, into
the milky way of literature, because Keats is pouring forth
his splendors in the Orient.   We do not imagine that the
fame of one poet, depends upon the fall of another, or that
our morning and our evening stars necessarily eclipse the
constellations of the meridian.

Too much praise is more injurious than censure, and
forms that magnifying lens, through which, the faults and
deformities of its object are augmented and enlarged; while
true merit looks more lovely beaming through the clouds of
prejudice and envy, because it adds to admiration and esteem
the association of superior feelings.

We cannot then advance for our author equal claim to
public notice for maturity of thought, propriety of feeling, or
felicity of style.   But while we blame the slovenly inde-
pendance of his versification, we must allow that thought,
sentiment, and feeling, particularly in the active use and
poetical display of them, belong more to the maturity of
summer fruits than to the infancy of vernal blossoms; to
that knowledge of the human mind and heart which is acquired
only by observation and experience, than to the early age, or
fervid imagination of our promising author.   But if the gay
colours and the sweet fragrance of bursting blossoms be the
promise of future treasures, then may we prophecy
boldly of the future eminence of our young poet, for we have
no where found them so early or so beautifully displayed as
in the pages of the volume before us.

The youthful architect may be discovered in the petty
arguments of his principal pieces.   These poetic structures
may be compared to no gorgeous places, no solemn temples;
and in his enmity to the French school, and to the Augustan
age of England, he seems to have a principle, that plan
and arrangement are prejudical to natural poetry.

The principal conception of his first poem is the same
as that of a contemporary author, Mr. Wordsworth, and pre-
sumes that the most ancient poets, who are the inventors of
the Heathen Mythology, imagined those fables chiefly by the
personification of many appearances in nature; just as the
astronomers of Egypt gave name and figure to many of our
constellations, and as the late Dr. Darwin[17] ingeniously
illustrated the science of Botany in a poem called "the Loves
of the Plants."

After having painted a few "places of nestling green,
for poets made" thus Mr. Keats:

[Quotes Keats's reference to Narcissus in "I Stood
Upon A Little Hill, " ll. 163-180.]

In the fragment of a Tale of Romance, young Calidore is amusing himself in a little boat in the park, till,
hearing the trumpet of the warder, which announces the
arrival of his friends at the castle, he hastens home to
meet them: in after times we presume he is to become the
hero of some marvellous achievements, devoting himself,
like Quixotte, to the service of the ladies, redressing wrongs,
dispelling the machinations of evil genii, encountering dragons,
traversing regions aerial, terestrial [sic], and infernal,
setting a price upon the heads of all giants, and forwarding
them, trunkless, like "a cargo of famed cestrian cheese, "
as a dutiful tribute to the unrivalled beauty of his fair Dul-
cenea del Toboso.   This fragment is as pretty and as innocent as childishness can make it, save that it savours
too much--as indeed do almost all these poems--of the
foppery and affectation of Leigh Hunt!

We shall pass over to the last of some minor pieces
printed in the middle of the book, of superior versification,
indeed, but of which, therefore, he seems to be partly
ashamed, from a declaration that they were written earlier
than the rest.   These lines are spirited and powerful:

"Ah! who can e'er forget so fair a being?
    Who can forget her half retiring sweets?
    God she is like a milk-white lamb that bleats
For man's protection.   Surely the All-seeing,
Who joys to see us with his gifts agreeing,
    Will never give him pinions, who intreats
    Such innocence to ruin; who vilely cheats
A dove-like bosom.   *   *   *   !"
    ["Woman! When I Behold Thee Flippant, Vain, "
    ll. 29-36.]

There are some good sonnets; that on first looking
into Chapman's Homer, although absurd in its application, is
a fair specimen:

[The poem is quoted here.]

"Till I heard Chapman speak out loud and bold" how-

ever is a bad line--not only as it breaks the metaphor--but
as it blows out the whole sonnet into an unseemly hyperbole.
Consistent with this sonnet[18] is a passage in his "Sleep and
Poetry."

> [Quotes Keats's attack on the neoclassical school
> and on Boileau, ll. 181-206.]

These lines are indeed satirical and poignant, but
levelled at the author of Eloise, and of Windsor Forest; of
the Essays and the Satires,[19] they will form no sun, no
centre of a system; but like the moon exploded from the
South Sea, the mere satellite will revolve only around the
head of its own author, and reflect upon him an unchanging
face of ridicule and rebuke.   Like Balaam's ass before the
angel, offensive only to the power that goads it on.[20]

We might transcribe the whole volume were we to
point out every instance of the luxuriance of his imagination,
and the puerility of his sentiments.   With these distinguishing features, it cannot be but many passages will appear
abstracted and obscure.   Feeble and false thoughts are
easily lost sight of in the redundance of poetical decoration.

To conclude, if the principal is worth encountering,
or the passage worth quoting, he says:

> "Let there nothing be
> More boist'rous than a lover's bended knee;
> Nought more ungentle than the placid look
> Of one who leans upon a closed book;
> Nought more untranquil than the grassy slopes
> Between two hills. --All hail delightful hopes!
> As she was wont, the imagination
> Into most lovely labyrinths will be gone,
> And they shall be accounted Poet Kings
> Who simply tell the most hearteasing things.
> O may these joys be ripe before I die."
>   ["Sleep and Poetry," ll. 259-269.]

Though he well adds:

> "Will not some say that I presumptuously
> Have spoken? that from hastening disgrace
> 'Twere better far to hide my foolish face?"
>   [ll.   270-272.]

Let not Mr. Keats imagine that the sole end of poesy
is attained by those

> "Who strive[21] with the bright golden wing
> Of genius, to flap away each sting
> Thrown by the pitiless world."
> ["Epistle to George Felton Mathew," ll. 63-65.]

But remember that there is a sublimer height to which
the spirit of the muse may soar; and that her arm is able to
uphold the adamantine shield of virtue, and guard the soul
from those insinuating sentiments, so fatally inculcated by
many of the most popular writers of the day, equally repugnant both to reason and religion, which, if they touch us with
their poisoned points, will contaminate our purity, innoculate
us with degeneracy and corruption, and overthrow among us
the dominion of domestic peace and public liberty. [22]

Religion and the love of virtue are not inconsistent
with the character of a poet: they should shine like the
moon upon his thoughts, direct the course of his enquiries,
and illuminate his reflections upon mankind. We consider
that the specimens here presented to our readers, will
establish our opinion of Mr. Keats's poetical imagination,
but the mere luxuries of imagination, more especially in
the possession of the proud egotist of diseased feelings and
perverted principles, may become the ruin of a people--
inculcate the falsest and most dangerous ideas of the condition of humanity--and refine us into the degeneracy of
butterflies that perish in the deceitful glories of a destructive
taper. These observations might be considered impertinent,
were they applied to one who had discovered any incapacity
for loftier flights--to one who could not appreciate the
energies of Milton or of Shakspeare--to one who could not
soar to the heights of poesy, --and ultimately hope to bind
his brows with the glorious sunbeams of immortality.

G. F. M.

6.   Hunt's review of Poems in the Examiner

(This review appeared in the Examiner of June
1, 1817, p. 345; July 6, 1817, pp. 428-429; and
July 13, 1817, pp. 443-444. It has been frequently
noted and has appeared in a wide number of re-

prints, which need not be mentioned here.   Hunt's
perceptive and well-written estimate of Keats ac-
curately indicates the strengths and weaknesses of
the poet's first volume.   In his opening paragraph,
Hunt speaks of his original association with Keats,
and his frank admission of friendship with the young
poet was to confirm the suspicions of Tory reviewers [whose suspicions were already aroused by
Hunt's article on the "Young Poets"] that Keats was
tainted with what they assumed were the radical
principles of the editor of the Examiner.)

[June 1, 1817]

      This is the production of a young writer, whom we
had the pleasure of announcing to the public a short time
since, and several of whose Sonnets have appeared meanwhile in the Examiner with the signature of J. K. 23   From
these and stronger evidences in the book itself, the readers
will conclude that the author and his critic are personal
friends; and they are so, --made however, in the first instance, by nothing but his poetry, and at no greater distance
of time than the announcement above-mentioned.   We had
published one of his Sonnets in our paper, without knowing
more of him than any other anonymous correspondent; but
at the period in question, a friend24 brought us one morning
some copies of verses, which he said were from the pen of
a youth.   We had not been led, generally speaking, by a
good deal of experience in these matters, to expect pleasure
from introductions of the kind, so much as pain; but we had
not read more than a dozen lines, when we recognized "a
young poet indeed."

      It is no longer a new observation, that poetry has of late
years undergone a very great change, or rather, to speak properly, poetry has undergone no change, but something which was
not poetry has made way for the return of something which is.
The school which existed till lately since the restoration of
Charles the 2d, was rather a school of wit and ethics in verse,
than any thing else; nor was the verse, with the exception of
Dryden's, of the best order.   The authors, it is true, are to be
held in great honour.   Great wit there certainly was, excellent
satire, excellent sense, pithy sayings; and Pope distilled as
much real poetry as could be got from the drawing-room world
in which the art then lived, --from the flowers and luxuries of
artificial life, --into that exquisite little toilet-bottle of essence,
the Rape of the Lock.   But there was little imagination, of a

higher order, no intense feeling of nature, no sentiment, no
real music or variety.   Even the writers who gave evidences
meanwhile of a truer poetical faculty, Gray, Thomson,
Akenside, and Collins himself, were content with a great
deal of second-hand workmanship, and with false styles made
up of other languages and a certain kind of inverted cant.
It has been thought that Cowper was the first poet who re-
opened the true way to nature and a natural style; but we
hold this to be a mistake, arising merely from certain nega-
tions on the part of that amiable but by no means powerful
writer.   Cowper's style is for the most part as inverted and
artificial as that of the others; and we look upon him to have
been by nature not so great a poet as Pope: but Pope, from
certain infirmities on his part, was thrown into the society
of the world, and thus had to get what he could out of an
artificial sphere:--Cowper, from other and more distressing
infirmities, (which by the way the wretched superstition that
undertook to heal, only burnt in upon him) was confined to a
still smaller though more natural sphere, and in truth did not
much with it, though quite as much perhaps as was to be
expected from an organization too sore almost to come in
contact with any thing.

It was the Lake Poets in our opinion (however grudg-
ingly we say it, on some accounts) [25] that were the first to
revive a true taste for nature; and like most Revolutionists,
especially of the cast which they have since turned out to
be, [26] they went to an extreme, calculated rather at first
to make the readers of poetry disgusted with originality and
adhere with contempt and resentment to their magazine common-places.   This had a bad effect also in the way of reaction; and none of those writers have ever since been able
to free themselves from certain stubborn affectations, which
having been ignorantly confounded by others with the better
part of them, have been retained by their self-love with a
still less pardonable want of wisdom.   The greater part indeed of the poetry of Mr. Southey, a weak man in all respects, is really made up of little else.   Mr. Coleridge
still trifles with his poetical as he has done with his metaphysical talent.   Mr. Lamb, in our opinion, has a more real
tact of humanity, a modester, Shakspearean wisdom, than
any of them; and had he written more, might have delivered
the school victoriously from all its' [sic] defects.   But it is
Mr. Wordsworth who has advanced it the most, and who in
spite of some morbidities as well as mistaken theories in
other respects, has opened upon us a fund of thinking and
imagination, that ranks him as the successor of the true and

abundant poets of the older time.   Poetry, like Plenty,
should be represented with a cornucopia, but it should be a
real one; not swelled out and insidiously optimized at the
top, like Mr. Southey's stale strawberry baskets, but fine
and full to the depth, like a heap from the vintage.   Yet
from the time of Milton till lately, scarcely a tree had been
planted that could be called a poet's own.   People got shoots
from France, that ended in nothing but a little barren wood,
from which they made flutes for young gentlemen and fan-
sticks for ladies.   The rich and enchanted ground of real
poetry, fertile with all that English succulance [sic] could
produce, bright with all that Italian sunshine could lend, and
haunted with exquisite humanities, had become invisible to
mortal eyes like the garden of Eden:--

"And from that time those Graces were not found. "27

[July 6, 1817]

These Graces, however, are re-appearing; and one
of the greatest evidences is the little volume before us; for
the work is not one of mere imitation, or a compilation of
ingenious and promising things that merely announce better,
and that after all might only help to keep up a bad system;
but here is a young poet giving himself up to his own impressions, and revelling in real poetry for its' own sake.
He has had his advantages, because others have cleared the
way into those happy bowers;28 but it shews the strength
of his natural tendency, that he has not been turned aside
by the lingering enticements of a former system, and by the
self-love which interests others in enforcing them.   We do
not, of course, mean to say, that Mr. Keats has as much
talent as he will have ten years hence, or that there are no
imitations in his book, or that he does not make mistakes
common to inexperience;--the reverse is inevitable at his
time of life.   In proportion to our ideas, or impressions of
the images of things, must be our acquaintance with the
things themselves.   But our author has all the sensitiveness
of temperament requisite to receive these impressions; and
wherever he has turned hitherto, he has evidently felt them
deeply.

The very faults indeed of Mr. Keats arise from a
passion for beauties, and a young impatience to vindicate
them; and as we have mentioned these, we shall refer to
them at once.   They may be comprised in two;--first, a

tendency to notice every thing too indiscriminately and without an eye to natural proportion and effect; and second, a
sense of the proper variety of versification without a due consideration of its principles.

The former error is visible in several parts of the
book, but chiefly though mixed with great beauties in the
Epistles, and more between pages 28 and 47, [29] where are
collected the author's earliest pieces, some of which, we
think, might have been omitted, especially the string of
magistrate-interrogatories about a shell and a copy of verses.
See also (p. 61) a comparison of wine poured out in heaven
to the appearance of a falling star, and (p. 62) the sight of
far-seen fountains in the same region to "silver streaks
across a dolphin's fin. "[30] It was by thus giving way to
every idea that came across him, that Marino, a man of
real poetical fancy, but no judgment, corrupted the poetry
of Italy; a catastrophe which however we by no means anticipate from our author, who with regard to this point is
much more deficient in age than in good taste.   We shall
presently have to notice passages of a reverse-nature, and
these are by far the most numerous.   But we warn him
against a fault, which is the more tempting to a young writer
of genius, inasmuch as it involves something so opposite to
the contented common-place.   It depends upon circumstances,
whether we are to consider ourselves near enough, as it
were, to the subject we are describing to grow microscopical
upon it.   A person basking in a landscape for instance, and
a person riding through it, are in two very different situations for the exercise of their eye-sight; and even where the
license is most allowable, care must be taken not to give
to small things and great, to nice detail and to general
feeling, the same proportion of effect.   Errors of this kind
in poetry answer to a want of perspective in painting, and
of a due distribution of light and shade.   To give an excessive instance in the former art, there was Denner, who
copied faces to a nicety amounting to a horrible want of it,
like Brobdignagian [sic] visages encountered by Gulliver;
and, who, according to the facetious Peter Pindar,

Made a bird's beak appear at twenty mile. [31]

And the same kind of specimen is afforded in poetry by
Darwin, a writer now almost forgotten and deservedly, but
who did good in his time by making unconscious caricatures
of all the poetical faults in vogue, and flattering himself
that the sum total went to the account of his original genius.

Darwin would describe a dragon-fly and a lion in the same
terms of proportion.   You did not know which he would have
scrambled from the sooner.   His pictures were like the two-
penny sheets which the little boys buy, and in which you see
J Jackdaw and K King, both of the same dimensions.

Mr. Keats's other fault, the one in his versification,
arises from a similar cause, --that of contradicting over-
zealously the fault on the opposite side.   It is this which
provokes him now and then into mere roughness and dis-
cords for their own sake, not for that of variety and contrasted harmony.   We can manage, by substituting a greater
feeling for a smaller, a line like the following:--

I shall roll on the grass with two-fold ease;--
["Epistle to Charles Cowden Clarke," l. 79.]

but by no contrivance of any sort can we prevent this from
jumping out of the heroic measure into mere rhythmicality, --

How many bards gild the lapses of time!
[Sonnet IV, l. 1.]

We come now however to the beauties; and the reader
will easily perceive that they not only outnumber the faults
a hundred fold, but that they are of a nature decidedly opposed to what is false and inharmonious.   Their characteristics indeed are a fine ear, a fancy and imagination at will,
and an intense feeling of external beauty in it's most natural
and least expressible simplicity.

We shall give some specimens of the least beauty
first, and conclude with a noble extract or two that will
shew the second, as well as the powers of our young poet
in general.   The harmony of his verses will appear throughout.

The first poem consists of a piece of luxury in a
rural spot, ending with an allusion to the story of Endymion
and to the origin of other lovely tales of mythology, on the
ground suggested by Mr. Wordsworth in a beautiful passage
of his Excursion.   Here, and in the other largest poem,
which closes the book, Mr. Keats is seen to his best advantage, and displays all that fertile power of association
and imagery which constitutes the abstract poetical faculty
as distinguished from every other.   He wants age for a
greater knowledge of humanity, but evidences of this also

bud from here and there. --To come however to our specimens:--

        The first page of the book presents us with a fancy,
founded, as all beautiful fancies are, on a strong sense of
what really exists or occurs.   He is speaking of

                A gentle Air in Solitude. *

                        There crept
            A little noiseless noise among the leaves,
            Born of the very sign that silence heaves.
            ["I Stood Tiptoe Upon A Little Hill," [ll. 10-12.]

                    Young Trees.

                        There too should be
            The frequent chequer of a youngling tree,
            That with a score of light green brethren shoots
            From the quaint mossiness of aged roots:
            Round which is heard a spring-head of clear waters.
                                        [ll. 37-41.]

Any body who has seen a throng of young beeches, furnish-
ing those natural clumpy seats at the root, must recognize
the truth and grace of this description.   The remainder of
this part of the poem, especially from--

            Open afresh your round of starry folds,
            Ye ardent marigolds!--
                                        [ll. 47-48.]

down to the bottom of page 5, affords an exquisite proof of
close observation of nature as well as the most luxuriant
fancy.

                    The Moon.

                        Lifting her silver rim
            Above a cloud, and with a gradual swim
            Coming into the blue with all her light.
                                        [ll. 113-115.]

_____
*This and all other introductory headings are by Hunt.

A starry Sky.

                    The dark silent blue
With all it's diamonds trembling through and through.
        ["Epistle to My Brother George," ll. 57-58.]

Sound of a Pipe.

And some are hearing eagerly the wild
Thrilling liquidity of dewy piping.
                ["Sleep and Poetry," ll. 370-371.]

    The Specimen of an Induction to a Poem, and the frag-
ment of the Poem itself entitled Calidore, contain some very
natural touches on the human side of things; as when speaking of a lady who is anxiously looking out on the top of a
tower for her defender, he describes her as one

        Who cannot feel for cold her tender feet;
            ["Specimen of an Induction to a Poem," l. 14.]

and when Calidore has fallen into a fit of amorous abstraction, he says that

        --The kind voice of good Sir Clerimond
        Came to his ear, as something from beyond
        His present being.
                        ["Calidore," ll. 99-101.]

                                [July 13, 1817]

    The Epistles, the Sonnets, and indeed the whole of
the book, contain strong evidences of warm and social feelings, but particularly the Epistle to Charles Cowden Clarke,
and the Sonnet to his own Brothers, in which the "faint
cracklings" of the coal-fire are said to be

        Like whispers of the household gods that keep
        A gentle empire o'er fraternal souls.
                    ["To My Brothers," ll. 3-4.]

The Epistle to Mr. Clarke is very amiable as well as
poetical, and equally honourable to both parties, --to the
young writer who can be so grateful towards his teacher,
and to the teacher who had the sense to perceive his genius,
and the qualities to call forth his affection. It consists

chiefly of recollections of what his friend had pointed out to
him in poetry and in general taste; and the lover of Spenser
will readily judge of his preceptor's qualifications, even
from a single triplet, in which he is described, with a deep
feeling of simplicity, as one

> Who had beheld Belphoebe in a brook,
> And lovely Una in a leafy nook,
> And Archimago leaning o'er his book.
>   [ll. 35-37.]

The Epistle thus concludes:--

Picture of Companionship
                [Hunt quotes 1. 109, 11. 115-130.]

And we can only add, without any disrespect to the graver
warmth of our young poet, that if Ought attempted it, [32]
Ought would find he had stout work to do with more than one
person.

The following passage in one of the Sonnets passes,
with great happiness, from the mention of physical associa-
tions to mental: and concludes with a feeling which must
have struck many a contemplative mind, that has found the
sea-shore like a border, as it were, of existence. He is
speaking of

The Ocean

> The Ocean with it's vastness, it's blue green,
> It's ships, it's rocks, it's caves, --it's hopes,
>   it's fears, --
> It's voice mysterious, which whoso hears
> Must think on what will be, and what has been.
>   ["To My Brother George," ll. 5-8.]

We have read somewhere the remark of a traveller, who
said that when he was walking alone at night-time on the sea-
shore, he felt conscious of the earth, not as the common
every day sphere it seems, but as one of the planets, rolling
round with him in the mightiness of space. The same feeling is common to imaginations that are not in need of similar local excitements.

The best poem is certainly the last and longest, entitled Sleep and Poetry. It originated in sleeping in a room

adorned with busts and pictures, [33] and is a striking specimen of the restlessness of the young poetical appetite, obtaining its food by the very desire of it, and glancing for fit
subjects of creation "from earth to heaven." Nor do we
like it the less for an impatient, and as it may be thought
by some, irreverend [sic] assault upon the late French
school of criticism and monotony, which has held poetry
chained long enough to render it somewhat indignant when it
has got free.

The following ardent passage is highly imaginative:--

An Aspiration after Poetry
[Hunt quotes ll. 47-48, ll. 55-84.]

Mr. Keats takes an opportunity, though with very different feelings towards the school than he has exhibited towards the one above-mentioned, to object to the morbidity
that taints the productions of the Lake Poets. [34] They might
answer perhaps, generally, that they chuse to grapple with
what is unavoidable, rather than pretend to be blind to it;
but the more smiling Muse may reply, that half of the evils
alluded to are produced by brooding over them; and that it
is much better to strike at as many causes of the rest as
possible, than to pretend to be satisfied with them in the
midst of the most evident dissatisfaction.

Happy Poetry Preferred.
[Hunt quotes ll. 230-247.]

We conclude with the beginning of the paragraph which follows this passage, and which contains an idea of as lovely
and powerful a nature in embodying an abstraction, as we
ever remember to have seen put into words:--

Yet I rejoice: a myrtle fairer than
E'er grew in Paphos, from the bitter weeds
Lift's it's sweet head into the air, and feeds
A silent space with ever sprouting green.
[ll. 248-251.]

Upon the whole, Mr. Keats's book cannot be better
described than in a couplet written by Milton when he too
was young, and in which he evidently alludes to himself.
It is a little luxuriant heap of

Such sights as youthful poets dream
On summer eves by haunted stream. [35]

7. From two letters by Wilson in
    the Anti-Gallican Monitor

> (These two letters appeared in the Anti-Gallican
> Monitor on June 8, 1817, p. 5085, and July 16,
> 1817, p. 6019, under the heading "Original Criti-
> cisms." The author, who uses the signature "Ob-
> servator," directs his comments to the poetry of
> Hunt, Shelley, Keats, and Reynolds. The last
> three named are the same authors whom Hunt
> praised in his article, "Young Poets," and Obser-
> vator's letters were conceived as a reply to Hunt.
> The letters under discussion attack the poetry
> of Hunt and Keats, and the first letter links Keats
> with the republican principles of Milton. At such
> points these letters seem strikingly similar to the
> political attacks on Hunt and Keats that began to
> appear in Blackwood's in the fall of 1817, and for
> good reason, because Observator was, in fact,
> John Wilson (Christopher North).
> The personal references of the letter writer
> identify him as Wilson. He tells us that he is a
> poet. By 1817, Wilson had published a substantial
> amount of verse, including The Isle of Palms (1812),
> The Magic Mirror (1812), and The City of Plague
> (1816). Furthermore, we can gather from one of
> his allusions that Observator was a friend of
> Thomas Campbell. Again, Wilson fits the descrip-
> tion. He was a former classmate and a close
> friend of Campbell, whom he met in 1797 while
> both were attending Glasgow University.[36] Author-
> ship of these letters also is established by com-
> paring them with Wilson's contributions to Black-
> wood's, and this has been done by me in "Keats's
> Reception in Newspapers of His Day," article to be
> published in Keats-Shelley Journal, 1973.
> With one exception, these letters are repro-
> duced in their entirety. Although there are some
> passages which are not directly relevant to Keats,
> the opportunity is taken to make Wilson's com-
> ments on Hunt and Shelley available to the reader.)

To the EDITOR of the ANTI-GALLICAN MONITOR

SIR, --As your page is always open to those whom,
from having more time than yourself are better enabled to
notice occurrences, which, though of a general nature, are
not liable to your observation, I take the liberty of addressing
you under the title of "Observator."

You will perceive, by the heading of my letter
["Original Criticisms"], that I have taken to myself the
name of Critic:--Such is the case, though not in the common acceptation of the word.   I intend to find fault, but
unlike other great men, of critical, as well as other dignity,
I propose to offer prospect of amendment.

I beg pardon for troubling you with this preliminary
matter, but I have introduced it lest my title should frighten
you.   To be somewhat more brief:--I am one of those, who,
from a certain smattering of rhime, generally at variance in
my own head, and a continual communication with this misfortune, in that of others, has dubbed himself a Poet.   In
my researches some little time since, I was tempted to
read an article in the "Examiner," a Sunday Newspaper,
touching on this very subject;[37] and naturally anxious to
look on any thing so near home, I attacked it with great
glee.

The style of Poetry that went abroad in the time of
Chaucer, is, fortunately, nearly abolished--and it is time,
Mr. Editor; it was a style that then attracted, principally
for its novelty, but even more through the depravity of taste
in those days.   I venture to assert that, with a conviction
of Chaucer's genius, and even with good master Godwin's
life of that poet, before me,[38] his was the conception, not
the execution of Poetry.   Devoted to nature, he lived only
in her fields and bowers; and thus infatuated, felt the
Poet's ardour: but the more domestic beauties of the Poet's
mind play'd false with him.   He had little purity, and no
refinement of language; some judgment, but no taste; and
harmony fled from his in wonderment.   This is individual
opinion; but it is, as such conviction.   The school of poetry,
that is adduced in the article I have quoted, is an attempt,
in part, to revive the "days of good Queen Bess."   There
are sundry Genii yclep'd--Leigh Hunt, John Keats, John
Reynolds, Percy Shelley, and I believe I may add a few
&c.'s &c.'s &c.'s at the head of this desperate gang--Mr.
Hunt, the high Priest of Opollo, nemcon, in the Chair.

This gentlemen, as present Editor of the "Examiner,"
late writer in the "News," the "Reflector," and maker of
sundry "Round Tables,"[39] has obtained, and very deservedly
so, a reputation in the metropolis.   He is, in this style of
composition, a fine writer; (I do not allude, in any shape,
to his principles), and equally as good a critic: but not
withstanding his opinion, that prose and verse are the same

thing,[40] and his late attempt to establish this doctrine, he
will find many disagree with him. I do not think Mr. Hunt
a Poet--(at least his Sonnets to the puddles on Hampstead
heath, are no more like poetry, than if he had splashed
himself in them:) yet I know some one who think [sic] him
the first one living. He is a man of talent--great ingenuity
--much wit; and wonderful contrivance: but genius never
troubled him, whatever he may have done to genius. Poetry,
with the exception of a few great men, (our first, generally
allowed, living Poets), in these days, consists in a certain
jingling of words, sundry affectations, and much quaintness;
brought into public notice, by interest with Editors and Reviewers; or, with the assistance of a long purse. A celebrated writer lately observed to me, that, on his first publication, in 1799,[41] he was looked upon as a good--nay, a
great Poet: and that in 1814, he heard himself spoken of
with a pretended ignorance of his ever having written before;
very odd this!--If it is to the Editors of Papers and Pam-
phlets, we owe our reputation; and if these said Editors
should happen, as some are called, to be Poets, what is to
become of the fatherless bard in these times? There be
Leigh Hunt, Editor and Poet. He writes a poem on the
story of Rimini, which the booksellers can't think good
enough to buy; but which Wm. Hazlitt, critic-general to the
"Examiner," (Mr. Hunt's paper), introduces into the pages
of the "Edinburgh Review," (for which Wm. Hazlitt is also
Surveyor), as a fine work indeed;[42] yet Mr. Southey, in
the "Quarterly Review," thinks otherwise of it:[43] (vide these
respective publications). I was of opinion, forsooth, that
Mr. Southey would think so. Then the said Hunt, in his
"Examiner," his own little judgment-seat, yokes Messrs,
Keats, Reynolds, and Shelley, as "young Poets;" and then
the fore-named Reynolds, in the "Champion," brings forward John Keats.[44] This is really droll. Still there is a
mystery attached to it. Hunt, the patron of these gentlemen,
is in the dark. He has turned School master, before he knew
his lesson as school boy: for, with the exception of Keats,
the two others named are very superior writers, as Poets
to the aforesaid Hunt. I hesitate not to assert, that, with
the exception of its principles, the "Spirit of Solitude"
[Alastor], by Mr. Shelley, is among the best of modern
poems. Mr. Reynolds, in an earlier production of "Safie,"
was not fortunate, for it was bad: but his Ode to Napoleon,
for reflection, and his Eden of Imagination, and Naiad for
fancy, are far superior to Mr. Hunt's Rimini; or, Descent
of Liberty. Keats is an original, but of the Eristotratus
species.[45] I hear, while quoting him, that his dress

is made by a great grand-child of Milton, after that Poet's
mode; and that the white crape in his button-hole, a token
of grief for the loss of his liberty, is on the ground of
Milton's political principles. --Poor youth! The suspenders
of the Habeas Corpus Act, (his loss of liberty), would do
well to suspend him in Bedlam. His poems, just published,
are the echo of Mr. Hunt's: his [Hunt's] style in every
respect--faulty or not. This is a sad affair, be assured
Mr. Editor. Genius and originality, Sir, are different attributes; and though the former should possess the latter,
to be perfect, the reverse is by no means apparent. In
this case, it is quite to the contrary: for it amounts to
mere folly--nay, most positive ridicule; and far from en-
hancing the value of his poetry, it will aid its annihilation.

    I am sorry for having trespassed thus long on you;
but as I have more to say on the present subject, I will,
with your good leave, defer till next week, when I shall resume it, illustrated by quotations from my authors; being,
in the internim [sic],

               Your obliged and obedient Servant,

London, June 4   OBSERVATOR

To the EDITOR of the ANTI-GALLICAN MONITOR.

    SIR--I left you in my last criticism very abruptly.
I resume my attempt to anatomize the diseases I then com-
plained of. I began with introducing CHAUCER to you, and
then somewhat suddenly, ran down to the days of SPENCER.
I was induced so to do from necessity. CHAUCER and
GOWER are considered the first of English Poets--their
style was somewhat similar; but, as rather singular, it
nearly died with them; nor was it viewed in any alarming
shape till the days of SPENCER. Though CHAUCER was
deemed a great wit, and very extravagant in its application--
and though deep in study and research, a great scholar al-
together--still with all these attributes I shall not retract
my opinion on his Poetry. SPENCER, the next school, was
a better Poet. --His genius was wonderful really; his expression grand; his fancy delicious; and his descriptive beauti-
ful--still he wanted harmony: and though esteemed so highly
at that period, his fame is less appreciated now. Be it so,
or not, it is very rash for men, particularly of the class I
mentioned in my last, to attempt its revival. He who would

do so, should be esteemed a great Poet before he essayed;
and then we might pardon his eccentricity: but to begin a
doubtful career, such as this is, in such a way as this too,
is folly or madness--perhaps both: example shall speak.
Mr. Hunt's first publication as a boy, is his best work--
his "Palace of Pleasure" (after Spencer), is almost an exception to my foregoing observation: indeed, the whole of
the work is good--but the translation of the celebrated
anacreontic beginning

"The tippling earth drinks up the dew"[46]

is fine. Then the "Feast of the Poets" is another very good
thing--but his "Descent of Liberty" is not worth naming; and
though passages of "The story of Rimini" are good, the
whole is indifferent. 'Tis as ungain and unmetrical as
Chaucer, with none of his sterling strokes in it. The
opening fourteen lines are very good: but then the account
of the horses with bits in their mouths, and their tails
hanging behind, their sundry decorations, with the description of riders and walkers, including the general outline of
the procession, is hardly worth reading, certainly not writing
on. The quaintness of phrase and jingling of words is horrid, and the attempt to call the whole poetry, is tremendous.
The most curious scene in the book is, where Mr. Paulo
goes to visit the lady in her bower, for the purpose of reading to her. He is of course full of sighs and flutters, some
grunts and a few fears; and thus caparison'd, proceeds: he
begs leave to enter, and he with the most perfect butter-
shop politeness, brings an "Oh, yes, certainly," into rhyme.
Now this is beyond precedent: but enough,--Mr. Hunt has
evidently made a mistake, and will, I feel convinced, write
no more poetry. His preface and general style is vain and
egotistical, and his dedication is presumptive and ridiculous.
When he writes in his own style, he is clever indeed. I
should say more about him: but unfortunately, his poetry is
more generally known than what I am about to subjoin. Now
Mr. Keats, who has lately been publishing, is the worst of
the whole fry. His dedication is almost as bad as that of
another youth who patronized Mr. Hunt's school.--(I think I
saw a sonnet of his lately in the Anti-Gallican)[47] and is as
perfectly incomprehensible. The opening poem--description
of fields, flowers, fish, and water, is a shameful imposi-
tion on the ear and understanding: particularly so, where
we find these lines:--

"A little noiseless noise."
    ["I Stood Tiptoe Upon A Little Hill," l. 11.]

"Ye ardent marigolds."
                                        [l. 48.]

"--sweet peas, on tip-toe for a flight."
                                        [l. 57.]

                    --"blades of grass
"Slowly across the chequer'd shadows pass,
"Why, you might [read] two sonnets, ere they reach
"To where the hurrying freshness, aye preach
"A natural sermon o'er their pebbly beds."
                                        [ll. 67-71.]

"The soul is lost in pleasant smotherings!"
                                        [l. 132.]

"Stepping, like Homer, at the trumpet's call"
                                        [l. 217.]

                    --"a field of drooping oats,
"Through which the poppies shew their scarlet coats:
"So pert and useless, that they bring to mind
"The scarlet coats that pester human kind"48
        ["Epistle to My Brother George, ll. 127-130.]

"More serene than Cordelia's countenance."
                    ["Sleep and Poetry," l. 9.]

"And other spirits there are standing apart."
                    ["Great spirits" sonnet, l. 9.]

Some of these for sense, and others for harmony are shocking; added to which there is a vile manufactory of words--a
"cloud-let,"--"banneral,"--"Ken," are inexcusable. The
whole is very bad indeed. The "Sonnet to Solitude" pleases
me most--but the line of

        "Born of the very sign that silence heaves,"
                    ["I Stood Tiptoe," l. 12.]

is really beautiful, the rest is leather and prunello....

            *   *   *

"Alastor, or the Spirit of Solitude, " by Mr. Shelley, is a
fine work.   I shall say no more, but give you a trifling
proof: these lines--

> [Quotes from Alastor ll.   29-34, 65-66, 137-139,
> 153-154, 224-227, 314-315, 350-351, 631-632,
> 717-720.]

There are a hundred passages I could produce equally
beautiful, but have no limits.   I enter not on Mr. Shelley's
work, excepting as to the Poetry, and there I dwell with
much delight.   I veil in obscurity his principles. 49   I say no
more, Mr. Editor, judge for yourself.   I must take another
opportunity of pointing out the means of amending--50 but
hope in the mean time the Gentlemen I have alluded to, excepting Mr. Shelley, will give themselves some assistance.

Your Obedient Servant

June 12, 1817   OBSERVER

8.   An exchange on Keats in the Champion

(The first comment appeared in the form of a
letter under the heading "Original Poetry" in the
Champion of August 3, 1817, p. 245.   The rejoinder of August 17, 1817, p. 261, under the
same heading, was probably by Reynolds. [John
M. Turnbull, "Keats, Reynolds, and the Champion, "
London Mercury, XIX (1929), 393.] The exchange
was first noted and reprinted by Turnbull [pp. 391-
393], who speculated that Keats himself might
have written the August 3 letter and used the signature "Pierre. " If so, Turnbull concludes, the
exchange was a hoax [p. 394].   However, Turnbull does not identify the author of the two poems
listed in note 51 below.   They certainly were not
by Keats.)

[August 3, 1817]

TO THE EDITOR OF THE CHAMPION
Sir,

If you can make room for the lines below, I shall

feel obliged. [51]   Perhaps the last stanzas may plead better
than I can for an introduction. [52]   I have seen some lines in
your paper, occasionally signed J. H. R. which have pleased
me much.   I think that the writer (whoever he is) can
furnish something much better than your favorite Mr. Keats,
whom my perverseness of taste, forbids me to admire.   I
cannot understand this circumstance altogether, as in every
other instance I have felt the beauty of your selections in
poetry.   Pray indulge us with some more.   Miltons [sic]
minor poems--Carew--Drayton--Suckling, &c. &c. will
furnish you with an opportunity, and your readers with a
treat.

                              Your constant reader and admirer,

                                            Pierre

                                    [August 17, 1817]

        The following Sonnet is from the pen of Mr. Keats.
It is quite sufficient, we think, to justify all the praises we
have given him--and to prove to our correspondent Pierre,
his superiority over any poetical writer in the Champion. --
J. H. R. would be the first to acknowledge this himself.

        [Keats's sonnet "On the Sea" follows.]

9.   A review of Poems in the Eclectic Review[53]

                (This review appeared in September 1817 [s. 2.
        VIII, 267-275].   Although noted before, it is re-
        produced here for the first time.   Keats's volume
        is used as a point of departure for the reviewer's
        extended discussion of poetry and the lack of thought
        and moral purpose in modern poetic compositions.
        If Keats's first production is clearly lacking in sub-
        ject matter, it is equally clear that the reviewer's
        distaste for Poems stems from his distaste for
        poetry in general.   This same distaste is evident
        in the reviewer's evaluation of Wordsworth and
        Scott.   Of Wordsworth, we are told, his thoughts
        "are not worth being expressed at all."   Two
        sentences toward the end of this review make it
        clear that the author considers poetry to be no

> more than a minor, and somewhat shameful, avo-
> cation: "When a man has established his character
> in any useful sphere of exertion, the fame of the
> poet may be safely sought as a finish to his reputa-
> tion.   When he has shewn he can do something
> else besides writing poetry, then, and not till then,
> may he safely trust the public with his secret.")

There is perhaps no description of publication that
comes before us, in which there is for the most part discovered less of what is emphatically denominated thought,
than in a volume of miscellaneous poems.   We do not speak
of works which obviously bear the traits of incapacity in the
Author.   Productions of this kind abound in more than one
department of literature; yet in some of these which rank at
the very lowest degree of mediocrity, there is occasionally
displayed a struggling effort of mind to do its best, which
gives an interest and a character to what possesses no
claims to originality of genius, or to intrinsic value.   But
poetry is that one class of written compositions, in which the
business of expression seems often so completely to en-
gross the Author's attention, as to suspend altogether that
exercise of rational faculties which we term thinking; as if
in the same limited sense as that in which we speak of the
arts of music and painting, poetry might also be termed an
art; and in that case indeed the easiest of arts, as requiring
less previous training of faculty, and no happy peculiarity
either in the conformation of the organs, or in the acquired
delicacy of the perceptions.   So accustomed however are we
to find poetry thus characterized, as consisting in the
mysteries of versification and expression, so learnedly
treated of in all the "Arts "of Poetry" [sic] extant, from
Horace down to Mr. Bysshe, [54] that it is not surprising
that the generality of those who sit down to write verses,
should aim at no higher intellectual exertion, than the
melodious arrangement of 'the cross readings of memory.'[55]
Poetry is an art, and it is an elegant art: and so is the
writing of prose, properly speaking, an art likewise; and
they are no otherwise distinguishable from each other, than
as being different styles of composition suited to different
modes of thought.   Poetry is the more ornate, but not,
perhaps, in its simpler forms, the more artificial style of
the two: the purpose, however, to which it is directed, requires a more minute elaboration of expression, than prose.
But what should we think of a person's professedly sitting
down to write prose, or to read prose composition, without
reference to any subject, or to the quality of the thoughts,

without any definite object but the amusement afforded by
the euphonous [sic] collection of sentences? As a school
exercise, the employment, no doubt, would be beneficial;
but were the writer to proceed still further, and publish
his prose, nor for any important or interesting sentiment
conveyed in his work, but as presenting polished specimens
of the beautiful art of prose-writing, it would certainly be
placed to the account of mental aberration.

On what ground, then, does the notion rest, that
poetry is a something so sublime, or that so inherent a
charm resides in words and syllables arranged in the form
of verse, that the value of the composition is in any degree
independent of the meaning which links together the sentences? We admit that rhythm and cadence, and rhymed
couplets, have a pleasurable effect upon the ear, and more
than this, that words have in themselves a power of awaken-
ing traits of association, when the ideas which they convey
are very indistinct, and do not constitute or account for the
whole impression. It may be added, that the perception of
skill or successful art, is also attended with pleasurable
emotions; and this circumstance forms, in addition to what
we have already mentioned, a powerful ingredient in the
whole combination of effect produced by genuine poetry: but
that the mere art of setting words to the music of measure,
should come to be regarded as the chief business of poetry,
and the ultimate object of the writer, is so whimsical a
prejudice, that after a brief exposition of the fact, it may
be worth while to inquire a little into its cause.

As to the fact, it would be travelling too far out of
the record, to make this notice of a small volume of poems,
a pretence for instituting an examination of all the popular
poets of the day. Suffice it to refer to the distinct schools
into which they and their imitators, as incurable mannerists,
are divided, as some evidence that mode of expression has
come to form too much the distinguishing characteristic of
modern poetry. Upon an impartial estimate of the intellectual quality of some of those poems which rank the
highest in the public favour, it will be found to be really of
a very humble description. As works of genius, they may
deservedly rank high, because there is as much scope for
genius in the achievements of art as in the energies of
thought; but as productions of mind, in which respect their
real value must after all be estimated, they lay the reader
under small obligations. Wordsworth is by far the deepest
thinker of our modern poets, yet he has been sometimes

misled by a false theory, to adopt a puerile style of composition; and it is remarkable, that the palpable failure should
be charged on his diction, which is attributable rather to the
character of the thoughts themselves; they were not adapted
to any form of poetical expression, inasmuch as they are
not worth being expressed at all.   Scott, of all our leading
poets, though the most exquisite artist, occupies the lowest
rank in respect to the intellectual quality of his productions.
Scarcely an observation or a sentiment escapes him, in the
whole compass of his poetry, that even the beauty of expression can render striking or worth being treasured up by the
reader for after reference.   The only passages recurred to
with interest, or cited with effect, are those admirable
specimens of scenic painting in which he succeeds beyond
almost every poet, in making one see and hear whatever he
describes.   But when we descend from such writers as con-
fessedly occupy the first rank, to the ὁι πολλοι [hoi
polloi] of their imitators, respectable as many of them are,
and far above mediocrity considered as artists, the characters of sterling thought, of intellect in action, becomes
very faint and rare.   It is evident that, in their estimation,
to write poetry is an achievement which costs no laborious
exercise of faculty; is an innocent recreation rather, to
which the consideration of any moral purpose would be altogether foreign.

    Now, on turning from the polished versification of the
elegant artists of the present day, to the rugged numbers of
our early poets, the most obvious feature in the refreshing
contrast is, the life and the vividness of thought diffused
over their poetry.   We term this originality, and ascribe
the effect either to their pre-eminent genius, or to the early
age in which they flourished, which forced upon them the
toil of invention.   But originality forms by no means a test
of intellectual pre-eminence; and we have proof sufficient,
that originality does not necessarily depend on priority of
time.   Provided the person be capable of the requisite
effort of abstraction, nothing more is necessary in order to
his attaining a certain degree of originality, than that his
thoughts should bear the stamp of individuality, which is
impressed by self-reflective study.   In the earlier stages of
the arts, we behold mind acting from itself, through the
medium of outward forms, consulting its own purpose as the
rule of its working, and referring to nature as its only
model.   But when the same arts have reached the period of
more refined cultivation, they cease to be considered as
means through which to convey to other minds the energies of

thought and feeling: the productions of art become themselves the ultimate objects of imitation, and the mind is
acted upon by them instead of acting through them from itself.   Mind cannot be imitated; art can be: and when imi-
tative skill has brought an art the nearest to perfection, it is
then that its cultivation is the least allied to mind: its
original purpose, as a mode of expression, becomes wholly
lost in the artificial object, --the display of skill.

We consider poetry as being in the present day in
this very predicament; as being reduced by the increased
facilities of imitation, to an elegant art, and as having
suffered a forcible divorce from thought.   Some of our
young poets have been making violent efforts to attain
originality, and in order to accomplish this, they have been
seeking with some success for new models of imitation in
the earlier poets, presenting to us as the result, something
of the quaintness, as well as the freedom and boldness of
expression characteristic of those writers, in the form and
with the effect of novelties.   But after all, this specious
sort of originality lies wholly in the turn of expression; it
is only the last effort of the cleverness of skill to turn
eccentric, when the perfection of correctness is no longer
new.   We know of no path to legitimate originality, but one,
and that is, by restoring poetry to its true dignity as a
vehicle for noble thoughts and generous feelings, instead of
rendering meaning the mere accident of verse.   Let the
comparative insignificance of art be duly appreciated, and
let the purpose and the meaning be considered as giving the
expression all its value; and then, so long as men think and
feel for themselves, we shall have poets truly and simply
original.

We have no hesitation in pronouncing the Author of
these Poems, to be capable of writing good poetry, for he has
the requisite fancy and skill which constitute the talent.   We
cannot however, accept this volume as any thing more than
an immature promise of possible excellence.   There is, indeed, little in it that is positively good, as to the quality of
either the thoughts of the expressions.   Unless Mr. Keats
has designedly kept back the best part of his mind, we must
take the narrow range of ideas and feelings in these Poems, as
an indication of his not having yet entered on the business
of intellectual acquirement, or attained the full development
of his moral faculties.   To this account we are disposed to
place the deficiencies in point of sentiment sometimes border-
ing upon childishness, and the nebulous character of the

meaning in many passages which occur in the present volume.
Mr. Keats dedicates his volume to Mr. Leigh Hunt, in a
sonnet which, as possibly originating in the warmth of gratitude, may be pardoned its extravagance; and he has obviously been seduced by the same partiality, to take him as
his model in the subsequent poem, to which is affixed a
motto from the "Story of Rimini. "56   To Mr. Hunt's poetical
genius we have repeatedly borne testimony, but the affectation which vitiates his style must needs be aggravated to a
ridiculous excess in the copyist.   Mr. Hunt is sometimes a
successful imitator of the manner of our elder poets, but
this imitation will not do at second hand, for ceasing then to
remind us of those originals, it becomes simply unpleasing.

Our first specimen of Mr. Keats's powers, shall be
taken from the opening of the poem alluded to.

[Quotes "I Stood Tiptoe Upon A Little Hill, " ll.
1-60.]

There is certainly considerable taste and sprightli-
ness in some parts of this description, and the whole poem
has a sort of summer's day glow diffused over it, but it
shuts up in mist and obscurity.

After a 'specimen of an induction to a poem,' we
have next a fragment, entitled Calidore, which, in the same
indistinct and dreamy style, describes the romantic adventure of a Sir Somebody, who is introduced 'paddling o'er
a lake,' edged with easy slopes and 'swelling leafiness,'
and who comes to a castle gloomy and grand, with halls and
corridor, where he finds 'sweet-lipped ladies,' and so forth;
and all this is told with an air of mystery that holds out
continually to the reader the promise of something interesting
just about to be told, when, on turning the leaf, the Will o'
the Wisp vanishes, and leaves him in darkness.   However
ingenious such a trick of skill may be, when the writer is
too indolent, or feels incompetent to pursue his story, the
production cannot claim to be read a second time; and it
may therefore be questioned, without captiousness, whether
it was worth printing for the sake of a few good lines which
ambitiously aspired to overleap the portfolio.

The 'epistles' are much in the same style, all about
poetry, and seem to be the first efflorescence of the un-
pruned fancy, which must pass away before any thing like
genuine excellence can be produced.   The sonnets are per-

haps the best things in the volume.   We subjoin one addressed 'To my brother 'George.'

[The sonnet is quoted here.]

The 'strange assay' entitled Sleep and Poetry, if its
forming the closing poem indicates that it is to be taken as
the result of the Author's latest efforts, would seem to shew
that he is indeed far gone, beyond the reach of the efficacy
either of praise or censure, in affectation and absurdity.
We must indulge the reader with a specimen.

[Quotes ll. 270-293.   The last lines of the quotation speak of the end and aim of poetry.]

We must be allowed, however, to express a doubt
whether its nature has been as clearly perceived by the
Author, or he surely would never have been able to impose
even upon himself as poetry the precious nonsense which he
has here decked out in rhyme.   Mr. Keats speaks of

'The silence when some rhymes are coming out,
And when they're come, the very pleasant rout;'
[ll. 321-322.]

and to the dangerous fascination of this employment we
must attribute this half-awake rhapsody.   Our Author is a
very facetious rhymer.   We have Wallace and solace, tenderness and slenderness, burrs and sepulchres, favours and
behaviours, livers and rivers;--and again,

'Where we may soft humanity put on,
And sit and rhyme, and think on Chatterton.'
["Epistle to George Felton Mathew," ll. 55-56.]

Mr. Keats has satirized certain pseudo poets, who,

'With a puling infant's force,
Sway'd about upon a rocking horse,
And thought it Pegasus.'
["Sleep and Poetry," ll. 185-187.]

Satire is a two-edged weapon: the lines brought irresistibly to our imagination the Author of these poems in
the very attitude he describes.   Seriously, however, we
regret that a young man of vivid imagination and fine talents,
should have fallen into so bad hands, as to have been flat-

tered into the resolution to publish verses, of which a few
years hence he will be glad to escape from the remembrance.
The lash of a critic is the thing the least to be dreaded, as
the penalty of premature publication. To have committed
one's self in the character of a versifier, is often a for-
midable obstacle to be surmounted in after-life, when other
aims require that we should obtain credit for different, and
what a vulgar prejudice deems opposite qualifications.   No
species of authorship is attended by equal inconvenience in
this respect.   When a man has established his character in
any useful sphere of exertion, the fame of the poet may be
safely sought as a finish to his reputation.   When he has
shewn that he can do something else besides writing poetry,
then, and not till then, may he safely trust the public with
his secret.   But the sound of a violin from a barrister's
chamber, is not a more fatal augury than the poet's lyre
strummed by a youth whose odes are as yet all addressed
to Hope and Fortune.

But perhaps the chief danger respects the individual
character, a danger which equally attends the alternative of
success or failure.   Should a young man of fine genius, but
of half-furnished mind, succeed in conciliating applause by
his first productions, it is a fearful chance that his energies
are not dwarfed by the intoxication of vanity, or that he
does not give himself up to the indolent day-dream of some
splendid achievement never to be realized.   Poetical fame,
when conceded to early productions, is, if deserved, seldom
the fruit of that patient self-cultivation and pains-taking, which
in every department of worthy exertion are the only means
of excellence; and it is by the natural consequence of this
easy acquisition of gratification, that it induces a distaste
for mental labour.   Should, however, this fatal success be
denied, the tetchy aspirant after fame is sometimes driven
to seek compensation to his mortified vanity, in the plaudits of
some worthless coterie, whose friendship consists in mutual
flattery, or in community in crime, or, it may be, to vent
his rancour in the satire of envy, or in the malignity of
patriotism.

Exceptions, brilliant exceptions, are to be found in
the annals of literature, and these make the critic's task
one of peculiar delicacy.   The case has occurred, when a
phlegmatic Reviewer, in a fit of morning spleen, or of
after-dinner dulness, has had it in his power to dash to the
ground, by his pen, the innocent hopes of a youth struggling
for honourable distinction amid all the disadvantages of

poverty, or to break the bruised reed of a tender and
melancholy spirit; but such an opportunity of doing mischief
must of necessity be happily rare. Instances have also
been, in which the performances of maturer life have fully
redeemed the splendid pledge afforded by the young Author,
in his first crude and unequal efforts, with which he has had
to thank the stern critic that he did not rest self-satisfied.
Upon the latter kind of exceptions, we would wish to fix Mr.
Keats's attention, feeling perfectly confident, as we do, that
the patronage of the friend he is content to please, [57] places
him wholly out of the danger of adding to the number of
those who are lost to the public for want of the smile of
praise.

    Mr. Keats has, however, a claim to leave upon our
readers the full impression of his poetry; and we shall therefore give insertion to another of his sonnets, which we have
selected as simple and pleasing.

[Quotes "Happy is England!"]

10.   A review of Poems in the Edinburgh
      Magazine and Literary Miscellany

          (This mixed review appeared in the Edinburgh
      Magazine for October 1817 [n. s. I, 254-257]. It
      has been noted before, but it is reproduced here
      for the first time. The identity of the reviewer
      is not known, but despite his advice that Keats
      abandon the affectations, conceits, and prosodic
      weaknesses of Hunt's style [faults which were
      clearly present in Poems], the tone of his review
      is essentially sympathetic. For further details
      about the Edinburgh Magazine, see the introductory
      chapter.)

    Of the author of this small volume we know nothing
more than that he is said to be a very young man, and a
particular friend of the Messrs Hunt, the editors of the
Examiner, and of Mr. Hazlitt. [58] His youth accounts well
enough for some injudicious luxuriances and other faults in
his poems; and his intimacy with two of the wittiest writers
of their day, sufficiently vouches both for his intellect and
his taste. Going altogether out of the road of high raised
passion and romantic enterprise, into which many ordinary

versifiers have been drawn after the example of the famous
poets of our time, he has attached himself to a model more
pure than some of these, we imagine; and, at the same time,
as poetical as the best of them.   "Sage, serious" Spencer,
the most melodious and mildly fanciful of our old English
poets, is Mr. Keats's favourite.   He takes his motto from
him, 59--puts his head on his title-page, --and writes one of
his most luxurious descriptions of nature in his measure. 60
We find, indeed, Spencerianisms scattered through all his
other verses, of whatsoever measure or character.   But,
though these things sufficiently point out where Mr. K. has
caught his inspiration, they by no means determine the general character of his manner, which partakes a great deal
of that picturesqueness of fancy and licentious brilliancy of
epithet which distinguishes the early Italian novelists and
amorous poets.   For instance, those who know the careless,
sketchy, capricious, and yet archly-thought manner of Pulci
and Ariosto will understand what we mean from the following specimens, better than from any laboured or specific
assertion of ours.

> [Quotes "I Stood Tiptoe Upon A Little Hill," ll.
> 61-68, 87-106 and the "Epistle to My Brother
> George," ll. 110-142. In the lines cited from
> the second poem, Keats speaks of his poetic am-
> bitions.]

This is so easy, and so like the ardent fancies of
an aspiring and poetical spirit, that we have a real pleasure
in quoting, for the benefit of our readers, another fragment of one of Mr. Keats's epistles:

> [Quotes the opening fourteen lines of Keats's swan
> simile in the "Epistle to Charles Cowden Clarke."]

All this is just, and brilliant too, --though rather ambitious to be kept up for any length of time in a proper and
fitting strain.   What follows appears to us the very pink of
the smart and flowing conversational style.   It is truly such
elegant badinage as should pass between scholars and gentlemen who can feel as well as judge.

[ll. 109-132.]

These specimens will be enough to shew that Mr. K.
has ventured on ground very dangerous for a young poet;--
calculated, we think, to fatigue his ingenuity, and try his

resources of fancy, without producing any permanent effect
adequate to the expenditure of either. He seems to have
formed his poetical predilections in exactly the same direction as Mr. Hunt; and to write, from personal choice,
as well as emulation, at all times, in that strain which can
be most recommended to the favour of the general readers
of poetry, only by the critical ingenuity and peculiar refinements of Mr. Hazlitt. That style is vivacious, smart,
witty, changeful, sparkling, and learned--full of bright points
and flashy expressions that strike and even seem to please
by a sudden boldness of novelty,--rather abounding in
familiarities of conception and oddnesses of manner which
shew ingenuity, even though they be perverse, or common,
or contemptuous. The writers themselves seem to be persons of considerable taste, and of comfortable pretensions,
who really appear as much alive to the socialities and sensual enjoyments of life; as to the contemplative beauties of
nature. In addition to their familiarity, though,--they appear
to be too full of conceits and sparkling points, ever to excite
any thing more than a cold approbation at the long-run--and
too fond, even in their favourite descriptions of nature, of
a reference to the factitious resemblances of society, ever
to touch the heart. Their verse is straggling and uneven,
without the lengthened flow of blank verse, or the pointed
connection of couplets. They aim laudably enough at force
and freshness, but are not so careful of the inlets of vul-
garity, nor so self-denying to the temptations of indolence,
as to make their force a merit. In their admiration of
some of our elder writers, they have forgot the fate of
Withers and Ben Jonson, and May: And, without forgetting
that Petrarch and Cowley are hardly read, though it be decent to profess admiration of them,--they seem not to bear
in mind the appaling doom which awaits the faults of man-
nerism or the ambition of a sickly refinement. To justify
the conclusions of their poetical philosophy, they are brave
enough to sacrifice the sympathetic enthusiasm of their art,
and that common fame which recurs to the mind with the
ready freshness of remembered verse,--to a system of which
the fruits come, at last, to make us exclaim with Lycidas,

"<u>Numeros</u> memini, si verba tenerem."[61]

   If Mr. Keats does not forwith cast off the unclean-
nesses of this school, he will never make his way to the
truest strain of poetry in which, taking him by himself, it
appears he might succeed. We are not afraid to say before
the good among our readers, that we think this true strain

dwells on features of manly singleness of heart, or feminine
simplicity and constancy of affection, --mixed up with feelings
of rational devotion, and impressions of independence spread
over pictures of domestic happiness and social kindness, --
more than on the fiery and resolute, the proud and repulsive
aspects of misnamed humanity.   It is something which bears,
in fact, the direct impress of natural passion, --which depends for its effect on the shadowings of unsophisticated
emotion   and takes no merit from the refinements of a
metaphysical wit, or the giddy wanderings of an untamed
imagination, --but is content with the glory of stimulating,
rather than of oppressing, the sluggishness of ordinary conceptions.

It would be cold and contemptible not to hope well of
one who has expressed his love of nature so touchingly as
Mr. K. has done in the following sonnets:

["To Solitude" and "To one who has been long in
city pent" follow.]

Another sonnet, addressed to Mr. Haydon the painter,
appears to us very felicitous. The thought, indeed, of the
first eight lines is altogether admirable; and the whole has
a veritable air of Milton about it which has not been given,
in the same extent, to any other poet except Wordsworth.

[Quotes Keats's second sonnet addressed to Haydon, beginning "High-mindedness, a jealousy for
good,".]

We are sorry that we can quote no more of these
sweet verses which have in them so deep a tone of moral
energy, and such a zest of the pathos of genius.   We are
loth to part with this poet of promise, and are vexed that
critical justice requires us to mention some passages of
considerable affectation, and marks of offensive haste, which
he has permitted to go forth into his volume. "Leafy
luxury," "jaunty streams," "lawny slope," "the moon-beamy
air," "a sun-beamy tale"; these, if not namby-pamby, are,
at least, the "holiday and lady terms" of those poor affected creatures who write verses "in spite of nature and
their stars."62--

"A little noiseless noise among the leaves,
Born of the very sigh that silence heaves."
["I Stood Tiptoe, ll. 48-49.]

This is worthy only of the Rosa Matildas whom the strong-
handed Gifford put down. 63

> "To possess but a span of the hour of leisure. "
> ["To Some Ladies, " l. 27.]

> "No sooner had I stepped into these pleasures. "
> ["Epistle to Charles Cowden Clarke, " 1. 97.]

These are two of the most unpoetical of Mr. K.'s lines, --
but they are not single.   We cannot part, however, on bad
terms with the author of such a glorious and Virgilian conception as this:

> "The moon lifting her silver rim
> Above a cloud, and with a gradual swim
> Coming into the blue with all her light. "
> ["I Stood Tiptoe, " ll. 113-115.]

A striking natural vicissitude has hardly been expressed
better by Virgil himself, --though the severe simpleness of
his age, and the compact structure of its language, do so
much for him in every instance:

> "Ipse Pater, mediâ nimborum in nocte, coruscâ
> Fulmina molitur dextra. "64

Notes

1.   "To A Poetical Friend" was written in November 1815,
        months before Keats composed such romantic
        poems as "Specimen of an Induction" and "Cali-
        dore. "   These three stanzas do not refer to the
        preceding poems.   Mathew is simply alluding to
        the romantic tales that he and Keats read together
        during the early period of their friendship.   (See
        Claude L. Finney, The Evolution of Keats's Poetry,
        I [Cambridge, Mass., 1936], 70.)

2.   John Middleton Murry (Studies in Keats [London, 1920],
        pp. 2-3) tells us that Mathew copied this stanza
        from Keats's poem, "On Receiving a Curious Shell
        and a Copy of Verses from the Same Ladies. "
        The pertinent stanzas from Keats's poem read,
           "Ah! courteous Sir Knight, with large joy thou
               art crowned;

> Full many the glories that brighten thy youth!
> I will tell thee my blisses, which richly abound
> In magical powers to bless, and to soothe."
> *   *   *
>
> "Adieu, valiant Eric! with joy thou art crown'd;
> Full many the glories that brighten thy youth,
> I too have my blisses, which richly abound
> In magical powers, to bless and to soothe."

The meter of Keats's poem was also copied by Mathew.

3. "Alluding to his medical character." (Mathew's note.)

4. In this stanza Mathew is alluding to Keats's Solitude sonnet. According to Robert Gittings (John Keats [Boston, 1968], p. 55), Mathew is criticizing his friend for abandoning the romantic style of earlier poems and following the homely nature imagery of Wordsworth in "To Solitude."

5. This article was not continued, but the Examiner printed numerous reviews and notices of Shelley, Reynolds, and Keats over the next six years. The Examiner's review of Reynolds' Wordsworth lampoon, Peter Bell, a Lyrical Ballad, was written by Keats himself (April 25, 1819, p. 270).

6. The neoclassic canons of the Augustans were associated with the French School.

7. Shakespeare's Sonnet XCVIII, 1. 3. For "To put" read "Hath put."

8. Hunt is referring to the false rhyme "Demesne" and "mean" in 11. 6-7 of "Chapman's Homer." This error was corrected in a later version of the sonnet which was published in Keats's 1817 volume.

9. Othello, III, iii, 1. 50. For "we" read "I."

10. A paraphrase of " 'Mongst boughs pavillion'd" in "To Solitude," 1. 7.

11. The poems addressed to ladies are "To Some Ladies," "On Receiving a Curious Shell, and a Copy of Verses from the Same Ladies," and "To---." The

ladies in the titles of the first two poems were
cousins of George Felton Mathew (Murry, p. 3),
and Mathew resented Reynolds' dismissal of these
poems as "very inferior" (Murry, p. 10). When
Mathew later reviewed Poems in the European
Magazine, his attitude towards Keats's volume was
influenced, in part, by his angry reaction against
Reynolds' review. (See the headnote to Mathew's
review and note 16.)

12.   Hunt's cottage in Hampstead Heath.

13.   These lines, misquoted by Reynolds, should read:
                    "... with a puling infant's force
      They sway'd about upon a rocking-horse
      And thought it Pegasus."
      Byron, among others, was offended at this attack
      on the Augustans. His anger also might have been
      motivated by Keats's allusions to him in 11. 235-
      240 of "Sleep and Poetry."

14.   Mathew's last image is taken from the opening of
      Endymion, where Keats remarks that "A thing of
      beauty ... will never / Pass into nothingness."
      (I. 11. 1-3.) Keats was at work on the Endymion
      theme as early as December 1816; and Mathew,
      although no longer a close friend, may have seen
      these lines in a rough draft.

15.   From Leigh Hunt's The Story of Rimini, 1. 432.
      Keats uses this line for the motto of "I Stood
      Tiptoe Upon A Little Hill."

16.   Mathew is referring to Reynolds' review of March 9
      in the Champion. In his opening paragraph, it
      will be recalled, Reynolds claimed that Keats's
      poetry would soon eclipse the poems of Byron,
      Moore, Campbell, and Rogers. Mathew makes his
      rejoinder in this paragraph.

17.   Erasmus Darwin (1731-1802), the English physiologist
      and poet.

18.   That is, also containing broken metaphor.

19.   In his attack, Keats does not mention Pope by name.

20. Balaam was a prophet hired to curse the Israelites. After beating his donkey three times, he was rebuked by the animal (Numbers 22-24). Pope also used Sir Balaam as a tag name in his "Epistle to Lord Bathurst" (ll. 339-402), and Mathew's preceding defense of Pope may have brought the story of Balaam to mind.

21. For "strive" read "strove."

22. Byron is certainly one of the popular writers Mathew has in mind here. After his separation from Lady Byron and his departure from England in 1816, the legend of Byron's "immorality" grew.

23. Hunt's announcement to the public was in the "Young Poets." The sonnets of Keats which appeared in the Examiner prior to this review were "To Solitude" (May 5, 1816, p. 282), "On First Looking into Chapman's Homer" (December 1, 1816, p. 762), "To Kosciusko" (February 16, 1817, p. 107), "After dark vapours" (February 23, 1817, p. 124), "To Haydon" and "On Seeing the Elgin Marbles" (March 9, 1817, p. 155), and on "The Floure and the Lefe" (March 16, 1817, p. 173).

24. Charles Cowden Clarke.

25. Hunt's praise was grudging because of his dislike of the political conservatism of the Lake Poets: Southey, Coleridge, and Wordsworth.

26. In terms of the political conversion of Southey, Coleridge, and Wordsworth from revolutionists to conservatives, Hunt's comment here, although literary in nature, also contains an accusation of political apostasy against the Lake Poets.

27. Unidentified.

28. Hunt is alluding to himself and to Wordsworth. He may also have Shelley in mind.

29. The poems found on these pages are the two album verses to Mathew's cousins, "To---," and Keats's "Imitation of Spenser."

30. And, when upheld, the wine from each bright jar
     Pours with the lustre of a falling star.
               ("Epistle to My Brother George," ll. 41-42.)
               *   *   *
     All that's reveal'd from the far seat of blisses,
     Is, the clear fountains' interchanging kisses,
     As gracefully descending, light and thin.
     Like silver streaks across a dolphin's fin.
                                              (ll. 47-50.)

31. Peter Pindar was the pseudonym of John Wolcot (1738-
          1819). The line is from Wolcot's "Lyric Odes to
          the Royal Academicians for MDCCLXXXIII," Ode
          VIII, l. 52, and should read "Makes a bird's beak
          appear at twenty mile."

32. An allusion to l. 130 of Keats's "Epistle to Clarke":
          "It cannot be that ought will work him [Clarke]
          harm."

33. The room was the library of Hunt's cottage in Hamp-
          stead.

34. Although Keats does criticize the Lake Poets, Hunt
          fails to mention that ll. 235-240 of "Sleep and
          Poetry" are also a specific attack on the grandiose
          nature of Byron's poetry:
                              "... We've had
               Strange thunders from the potency of song;
               Mingled indeed with what is sweet and strong,
               From majesty: but in clear truth the themes
               Are ugly clubs, the Poets' Polyphemes
               Disturbing the grand sea."

35. "L'Allegro," ll. 121-122.

36. Elsie Swann in Christopher North (London: Oliver
          and Boyd, 1934), p. 11, refers to this meeting:
          "Thomas Campbell, the future poet of The Pleas-
          ures of Hope and Gertrude of Wyoming, joined the
          logic class at Glasgow College, while Wilson was
          also a member, and Wilson constituted himself the
          champion of the little black-eyed 'smalley' boy who
          ran about firing off paper pellets and vocal epi-
          grams against the bigger lads."

37. Hunt's article on the "Young Poets," December 1, 1816.

38. William Godwin, The Life of Chaucer, 2 vols. (London, 1803).

39. "I do not mean by this," Wilson remarks in a footnote, "to give Hunt credit for being a good Cabinetmaker in general." Carpenters make both cabinets and round tables, but this pun on the title of a collection of essays by Hunt and Hazlitt is political in nature. Should Hunt, a man with liberal, independent ideas, have formed a governmental cabinet, his appointees would have opposed Wilson's Tory interests.

40. This idea was first proposed by Wordsworth in his Preface to the second edition of Lyrical Ballads: "a large portion of the language of every good poem can in no respect differ from prose." His remark led to critical controversy, and Wordsworth was attacked by, among others, Jeffrey in the Edinburgh. In English Bards and Scotch Reviewers, Byron refers to Wordsworth as "that mild apostate of poetic rule" who "both by precept and example, shows/That prose is verse, and verse is merely prose." Wilson was probably reminded of the preceding controversy by Hunt's statement in his Preface to The Story of Rimini (London, 1816) that he will "endeavour to recur to a freer spirit of versification" by "having a free and idiomatic cast of language ... the proper language of poetry is in fact nothing different from that of real life, and depends for its dignity upon the strength and sentiment of what it speaks." (pp. xv-xvi).

41. Thomas Campbell's The Pleasures of Hope.

42. Rimini was reviewed in the Edinburgh of June 1816 (XXVI, 476-491). Walter Houghton in The Wellesley Index to Victorian Periodicals, I Toronto, 1966), 455, states that the article was probably Hazlitt's, but "so very heavily revised by Jeffrey as to have seemed his own work.

43. A review of Hunt's Rimini appeared in the Quarterly for January 1816 (XIV, 473-481), but Walter Graham (Tory Criticism in the Quarterly Review [New York, 1921], p. 47) identifies the author as Croker rather than Southey.

44. At the time of the present letter, the only reference to
     Keats in the Champion was Reynolds' review of
     Poems on March 9, 1817. It is significant that
     Wilson knew the reviewer to be Reynolds, for until
     1949, this article was assigned to Haydon.   The
     attribution to Reynolds was first made by MacGil-
     livray in Bibliography, p. 63, and confirmed by
     Rollins in Letters, I, 123, and Leonidas M. Jones
     in Selected Poetry and Prose of John Hamilton
     Reynolds (Cambridge, Mass., 1966), p. 451 n.
     160.   Perhaps Wilson learned of Reynolds' identity
     from the author himself.   In later years, Reynolds
     was certainly familiar with the Blackwood's group;
     Jones in "Reynolds and Keats," K-SJ, VII (1958),
     50, tells us that in 1818 Reynolds unsuccessfully
     attempted to forestall further attacks of Black-
     wood's on Keats by introducing the poet to Lock-
     hart's friend, John Christie.

45. See Chapter One, n. 76.

46. Anacreon, Ode XII, l. 1 in Hunt's Juvenilia (London,
     1801), p. 47.

47. Although no definite identification of this youth is pos-
     sible, he obviously was not one of the writers under
     discussion in Wilson's letters.   The name of
     Cornelius Webb (c. 1790-c. 1848), a young poetas-
     ter who attached himself to Hunt's circle, might
     be offered in conjecture.   In the Anti-Gallican
     for March 16, 1817, over the signature "C.," is
     an unidentified translation of Petrarch's Sonnets
     CCV and CXXXI.   Outside of the initial of his
     first name, no further connection between Webb
     and "C." can be established.

48. "This, I suppose, is meant for a political pun." (Ob-
     servator's note.)

49. Shelley's principles are veiled in obscurity because of
     his radical and anti-religious views.

50. No further criticisms by Observator appear in the
     Anti-Gallican Monitor. By October 1817, letters
     to the editor were no longer necessary; Wilson had
     found his own vehicle in Blackwood's.

51. Two poems by "Pierre," "On Liberty" and "Aurea
     Libertas," follow the letters.

52. That is, "Aurea Libertas."

53. Bate (John Keats [New York, 1966], p. 223) identifies
     the reviewer as Josiah Conder, the editor of the
     Eclectic Review, but he gives no evidence for his
     attribution.

54. Edward Bysshe was a late seventeenth and early eighteenth
     century literary hack whose dates are uncertain.
     His best known work, The Art of English Poetry,
     appeared in 1702.

55. Unidentified.

56. See p. 63 and n. 15 of this chapter.

57. The friend is Hunt.

58. Keats was an admirer of Hazlitt but not a close friend.

59. The title-page of the 1817 volume bore the following
     motto:
     　　　"What more felicity can fall to creature
     　　　Than to enjoy delight with liberty?
     　　　　　　　Fate of the Butterfly--Spenser."

60. The reference is to the Keats poem entitled "Imita-
     tion of Spenser."

61. "The measure I remember, could I but keep the words,"
     Eclogues, IX, l. 45, transl., H. R. Clough, Virgil
     (New York, 1920), I, 69.

62. Samuel Butler's Hudibras, Part I, Canto I, ll. 647-
     648.

63. Makers of inferior, sentimentalized poems. More
     specifically, a reference to Hanna Cowley (1743-
     1809), a playwright who, under the pseudonym
     "Anna Matilda," contributed sentimentalized verse
     to the World. Gifford ridicules her verse in the
     Baviad (1791) and the Maeviad (1795).

64.   "The Father, enthroned in midnight clouds, hurls
           from a flashing/Right hand his lightning," Georgics,
           I, ll. 328-329, trans. C. Day Lewis (New York,
           1947), p. 13.

Chapter III

THE RECEPTION OF ENDYMION
AND OTHER NOTICES THROUGH 1820

(Endymion was published toward the end of
April 1818. The first reviews and notices of the
poem were generally favorable. However, a review in the Champion of June 7, 1818 nervously
sensed the possibility of an ensuing Tory attack.
The attack came, first by Blackwood's Edinburgh
Magazine in its August number [published on
September 1] and then by the Quarterly Review and
the British Critic toward the end of September.
Lokhart's article in Blackwood's was far more
scurrilous than Croker's review in the Quarterly.
"In fairness to Croker," Walter Graham has
argued, "it must be admitted that he exposed a
few of the worst effects of Hunt's baleful influence
on the young poet's style. The review was short
and much less damaging than is generally believed."
[Tory Criticism in the Quarterly Review (New York,
1921), p. 21.] Despite this, the Quarterly was
singled out for attack by Keats's defenders in the
Morning Chronicle, Alfred, West of England Journal and General Advertiser, Sun, and Chester
Guardian. The reason was simple. By affixing
Blackwood's label of Cockney to Keats, and by
criticizing the poet in other ways, the influential
Quarterly seemed to confirm the slanders of the
less prestigious monthly magazine. These reviews,
in conjunction with the censure of the British
Critic, resulted in a serious, but temporary, set-
back to Keats's reputation. At the same time,
however, it should be remembered that the Provincial and London newspaper press clearly recognized Keats's worth and future potential.
1819 was a year of composition for Keats.
Outside of occasional poems which appeared in
serials and other sources, he did not publish.
However, some substantive allusions to him did

occur in the Literary Journal and General Miscellany of Science, Arts, History, Politics, etc.
and in Blackwood's. These allusions were unfavorable, and they all continued to link Keats
with Hunt in the same way that the attacks of 1818
had done. Keats's general reputation did not im-
prove in 1819.

The reception of Endymion continued through
1820, but the tenor of critical commentary was significantly different from the Tory attacks of 1818.
A highly favorable review of the poem appeared in
April 1820 in one of the first numbers of Baldwin's
London Magazine. Four months later the influential Edinburgh Review praised Endymion. During
the same month, the Edinburgh Magazine and Literary Miscellany [formerly the Scot's Magazine]
praised Keats's second volume. In each of these
instances, the reviewer clearly disassociated himself from the attacks of 1818. In point of fact,
these two reviews considered Endymion in retro-
spect. The achievement of the Lamia volume
could not be ignored, and Endymion was now seen
as a precursor of future "clouds of glory."
Jeffrey's praise in the Edinburgh and the continued championship of Keats by the press were
indicators of this change in critical climate.
Keats's reputation had reached its nadir in 1818
and 1819; it was to move steadily upward in 1820.)

1.   A review of Endymion in the Literary Journal

(This favorable review appeared on May 7, 1818,
pp. 114-115 and May 24, 1818, p. 121. Although
noted in several sources, it is reproduced here
for the first time. With only minimal critical
commentary, the author, whose identity is not
known, contents himself with a plot summary of
Keats's poem.)

[May 7, 1818]

In this poetizing age we are led to look with an eye
of suspicion on every work savouring of rhyme; especially
if (as in this case) its author is but little known in the
literary world. It was with this feeling that we took up

the present volume, and we regret to add, that it remained
undiminished for the first thirty lines; when, like the Great
Chamberlain in the exquisite poem of Lalla Rookh, we began
to elevate our critical eye-brows, and exclaim, "And this
is poetry!"[1] A few seconds, however, taught us, that this
severity of criticism, like that of Fadladeen's, was premature; and the admiration we felt at the beautiful simplicity of
the following lines, amply compensated for any previous defects in the versification:--

[Quotes from Endymion, I. ll. 34-62.]

The plot of the poem, to which the preceding passage
is an introduction, is founded on the most beautiful portion
of the Greek mythology. Endymion, Prince of Caria, reposing on Mount Latmos, is discovered by Diana, who
causes a deep sleep to fall upon him: his dream, as related to his sister Peona, who seeks to discover the cause
of his melancholy, evidently bespeaks its author to possess
a vivid imagination and refined mind, though the verse is
frequently irregular, and sometimes unmetrical:--

[Quotes I. ll. 578-671.]

The following lines bear a strong analogy to a beautiful passage in the "Arabian Tales," in which Prince Ahmed
is led, in search of an arrow, to the residence of the fairy
Banou:--

[Quotes I. ll. 929-971, lines which summarize
Endymion's melancholy wanderings.]

After having been led by a Naiad, in search of the
"fair unknown," to a most beautiful cavern, he invokes the
assistance of Venus, who directs him onward, and he is
shortly wafted by an eagle from the regions of "middle air"
to a delightful garden: his description of this spot, and
subsequent meeting with Diana, is written with a warmth
of feeling, and a tenderness of expression, we seldom find
exceeded even in some of our most popular poets:--

[Quotes II. ll. 670-773, 806-853.]

[May 24, 1818]

After awaking from the slumber into which he had

fallen on the departure of Diana, Endymion commences a
pilgrimage through the "vasty deep:" in the course of his
wanderings he meets with a solitary man, who afterwards
relates his adventures, which consist chiefly of his transformation from youth to age, by Circe, as the consequence
of having freely indulged in her enchanting luxuries.   In
this state of premature debility he is doomed to remain,
until released by the appearance of a young stranger.   The
meeting with Endymion convinces the old man that his hour
of freedom is at hand.   The anxious desire of liberty, and
almost maddening anticipation of its possession, expressed
by Glaucus, after having been spell bound for a thousand
years, is described with considerable spirit.   Indeed the
whole passage will strongly remind the reader of the rapturous exclamations of Ariel, when promised his freedom by
Propsero.

> "Thou art the man!   Now shall I lay my head
> In peace upon my watery pillow: now
> Sleep will come smoothly to my weary brow.
> O Jove!   I shall be young again; be young!
> O, shell-borne Neptune, I am pierc'd and stung
> With new-born life!   What shall I do?   Where go,
> When I have cast this serpent-skin of woe?--
> I'll swim to the syrens, and one moment listen
> Their melodies, and see their long hair glisten;
> Anon upon that giant's arm I'll be,
> That writhes about the roots of Sicily:
> To northern seas I'll in a twinkling sail,
> And mount upon the snortings of a whale
> To some black cloud; thence down I'll madly sweep
> On forked lightning, to the deepest deep,
> Where through some sucking pool I will be hurl'd
> With rapture to the other side of the world!
> O, I am full of gladness! sisters three,
> I bow full hearted to your old decree!
> Yes, every god be thank'd, and power benign,
> For I no more shall wither, droop, and pine.
> Thou art the man!"
>
> [III. ll.   234-255.]

The fourth book opens with the following invocations
to the muse of Britain:--

[Quotes ll.   1-29.]

The following passage, descriptive of the aërial passage of Endymion, accompanied by Diana, contains some

beautiful lines:--

[Quotes IV. ll. 484-512.]

The measure of this poem, which is nearly allied to
that of Chaucer, frequently reminds us of Mr. Hunt's "Rimini,"
though many of the faults so justly attributed to that author,
have been avoided in the present work.   Indeed, with the exception of two passages, we are induced to give our most
unqualified approbation of this poem: and, first,

> --"The sleeping kine,
> Couch'd in thy brightness, dream of fields divine."
>   [III. ll. 57-58.]

This may be a very happy thought, and extremely
poetical; but in our finite judgment, the giving to the brute
creation one of the greatest and most glorious attributes of
a rational being, is not only very ridiculous, but excessively
impious.   And from the following passage we dissent most
decidedly, as we feel persuaded, that genius, like that possessed by Mr. K., may with safety venture in the highest
walk of poetry:--

> --"O 'tis a very sin
> For one so weak to venture his poor verse
> In such a place as this.   O do not curse.
> High Muses! let him hurry to the ending."
>   [III. ll. 937-940.]

2.   Two letters on Endymion by Benjamin Bailey
       in the Oxford University and City Herald

> (These letters in praise of Endymion appeared
> on May 20 and June 6, 1818 over the signature
> "N.Y."   They were first reprinted by H.B. and
> M.B. Forman in the Hampstead Edition of Keats's
> Poetical Works and Other Writings [New York,
> 1938-1939], II, 237-243.   The author, whose
> identity was known long before the reprints in the
> Formans, was Keats's friend, Benjamin Bailey,
> whom Keats thanks in a letter of June 10, 1818.
> Bailey, a student at Oxford, had shared his lodgings
> with Keats in September 1817 while the poet was
> at work on the third book of Endymion.)

[May 20, 1818]

To the EDITOR of the OXFORD HERALD

Sir,

Let me recommend to the perusal of your readers
the poem of "Endymion," which is the most original production I ever read.   Some account of its author may not be
uninteresting.

John Keats, the author of "Endymion," is a very
young man, about 22 years of age.   About a year ago he
published a small volume of Poems, in which was the
richest promise I ever saw of an etherial imagination maintained by vast intellectual power.   One passage from the
largest poem in the volume may give the reader some idea
of the conscious capability of real genius:--

> "What, though I am not wealthy in the dower
> Of spanning wisdom; though I do not know
> The shifting of the mighty winds that blow
> Hither and thither all the changing thoughts
> Of man: though no great minist'ring[2] sorts
> Out the dark mysteries of human souls
> To clear conceiving: yet there ever rolls
> A vast idea before me, and I glean
> Therefrom my liberty; thence too I've seen
> The end and aim of poesy. "
>   Sleep and Poetry [ll. 284-293.]

This is no common language.   It is the under-breath
of a "master-spirit."   It is the deep yearning of genius after
the beauty and the fair.   It is, as it were, the brooding of
an earthquake.   It is "the first virgin passion of a soul com-
muning with the glorious universe. "[3]

I could say much more, but must desist for the
present.   I beg, however, to add, that I am impelled by no
unworthy motive in recommending "Endymion" to the public.
I am confident of its extraordinary merit, and cannot com-
promise my firm opinion out of respect to the mere "forms,
modes, and shows," of the world.   I call upon the age to
countenance and encourage this rising genius, and not to let
him pine away in neglect, lest his memory to after ages
speak trumpet-tongued the disgrace of this.   I love my
country, and admire our literature.   Our poets are our glory.

I am no bookseller's tool; I am no pandar to poetical vanity;
but I would not for worlds witness the insensibility of Old
England to her own glory, in the neglect of the vernal genius
of her sons.

I am, Sir, your obedient Servant,

N. Y.

[June 6, 1818]

To the EDITOR of the OXFORD HERALD

Sir,

In my last I gave a very hasty sketch of John Keats,
the author of "Endymion." I took the liberty of recommending that poem in very strong and confident terms to the
public. Far from retracting anything I there advanced, I
shall be rather induced to add to it. I referred to his first
volume as a book of great promise, wherein might be observed the seeds of genius, swelling, as it were, like the
seeds, in the bosom of the earth at spring time, to rise
into "the paths of upper air,"[4] and "dwell not unvisited of
heaven's fair light."[5] "Endymion" is but the second child
of great promise. It will shew that, in so short a space,
the author has "plumed his feathers, and let grow his wings."[6]
We may see in it the germs of immortality. What Milton,
with the modest, yet confident tone of deathless mind, said
in a letter to his friend Deodati [sic], when very young, I
can imagine this young poet to have felt, though he may not
have given it utterance:

"Multa solicitè quaeris etiam, quid cogitem. Audi,
Theodote, verum in aurem, ut ne rubeam, et sinito paulis-
per apud te grandia loquar; quid cogitam? Ita me bonus
Deus, immortalitatem."[7]--You may perhaps think, Sir, I
am culpable in making this allusion. I am not going to
compare him with Milton as a full-grown man whose
"stature reached the sky,"[8] but with Milton as a young
enthusiast panting for fame;--not with Milton, when in his
blindness and old age, he speaks of fame as "that last in-
firmity of noble minds,"[9]--but with him who said, "Fame
is the spur that the clear spirit doth raise," as in his
"Comus,"[10] which he wrote at 23. Let it be remembered
too, that our great epic poet had many advantages of learn-

ing and leisure from his youth upwards; but if, without
these advantages, this young poet" with his soft pipe and
smooth-dittied song, "11 can come at all within the sphere
of that "mighty orb of song, the divine Milton;"12 if likewise his genius be found in any respect kindred to our
national Glory, Shakespeare, (and I think it is so, more
than with Milton);--let not his countrymen withhold from
him their suffrages, nor refuse to bind the laurel round his
brows.

    Suffer me, Sir, to detain you a short while longer
before I proceed to the poem of "Endymion" itself. --Before
he wrote the poems which comprise his first volume, he had
not written above 200 lines of poetry.   He was unconscious
of his power; it had slumbered in him like "a stream in-
audible by day-light. "13   To apply a beautiful image of his
own, --

> " 'Twas Might half-slumbering on his own right
>   arm. "
>
> ["Sleep and Poetry, " l. 237.]

He next undertook "Endymion, " a poem of 4000 lines.   It
was a daring undertaking.   Enterprize is the offspring of
Genius.   He has accomplished it. --I shall now proceed to
speak of it more exclusively, and make such extracts as
your limits will allow me; but were I to stop at every
striking beauty, I must transcribe the whole poem.   The
flowers of spring do not "broider the ground with richer
inlay"14 than exquisite passages of poetry float--

> "With many a winding bout
> "Of linked sweetness long drawn out"15

through this poem.   For--

> "Here be all the pleasures
> "That Fancy can beget on youthful thoughts,
> "When the fresh blood grows lively; and returns
> "Brisk as the April buds in primrose season. "16

Every one knows the beautiful story of "Endymion, " of
which Keats says, --

> "The very music of the name has gone
> "Into my being, and each pleasant scene

"Is growing fresh before me as the green
"Of our own vallies."
[Endymion, II. ll. 36-39.]

But it is very wonderful how so long a poem could
be constructed upon so simple a fable.   Nothing but very
original genius could have done it.   I can but give your
readers a faint idea of his management of the story--The
Poem is in four books.   Endymion is a "Shepherd King."
In the first book there is a feast to Pan, and an exquisitely
fine Pastoral Hymn, to which I must refer the reader, it
being too long for quotation. [17]   Endymion has a sister,
Peona, who is his confidante, and to whom he describes his
first two scenes with Diana.   In the second book Endymion
wanders underneath the earth--

"Through winding passages where sameness breeds
"Vexing conceptions of some hidden[18] change."
[ll.   235-236.]

In this book he gives a beautiful turn to the Story of
Adonis.   In the third book he wanders through the sea:

"The visions of the earth are gone and fled,
"He saw the giant sea above his head."
[ll.   1022-1023.]

In the fourth book he is again upon the earth--

"And forest green
"Cooler than all the wonders he had seen."
[ll.   1029-1030.]

He meets with and becomes enamoured of a beautiful
Indian.   This gives the poet an opportunity, of which he
takes a noble advantage, of describing a procession of
Bacchus.   I shall extract this, to give the reader some idea
of the lyrical beauty of his description:--

[Quotes IV. ll. 182-267.]

I fear your limits will not suffer me to make any
other extract.   The catastrophe of the Poem is this young
Indian's being changed into Diana.   It is worthy of remark,
as a singular, and I am sure, an unconscious coincidence
on the part of the author of "Endymion," that the conclusion
bears great resemblance to the close of "Paradise Regained."

After the angels, having "brought him on his way with joy,"
have left our Saviour,--

"He unobserved,
"Home to his mother's house private returned."[19]

When Diana assumes her own form and person, she
and Endymion take their leave of his sister, and "vanish
far away"--

"Peona went
"Home through the gloomy wood in wonderment."
[IV. ll. 1002-1003.]

I must be suffered, Sir, to make a few remarks before I conclude. I am aware of the suspicious and invidious
task of thus publicly bestowing such high encomiums upon
the productions of any one. It is the vice of this age that
literature is a trade. Trade is employed upon the lower
interests of the world. A book, therefore, is valued according to the standard of Sir Hudibras, for "as much as it
will bring."[20]

All I wish to be understood is, that no such petty
and paltry motives have induced me to come forward as I
have. I do not disguise that I am acquainted with the
author; but I was first acquainted with his poetry, and hence
sought the knowledge of himself. I have found that personal
acquaintance answerable to my expectations of what a poet
should be in character. He has the most of that character
I ever knew or shall know.--I mean not to affirm that his
poetry is faultless. Far from it. But his faults are those
of an ardent genius, not sufficiently curbed. His youth has
not yet "tempered his tresses in Aquarius' beam."[21] Let
not the cold unfeeling world freeze up his enthusiasm by
neglect.--Poetry is no trivial toy, however "this world's
true worldling"[22] may sneer at it. The finest book in the
world teems with the sublimest poetry. Nature nourishes it
at her bosom, and cherishes it in her heart. It "goes to
bed with the sun, and rises with him."[23] It is the breath
of spring, and "comes before the swallow dares, and takes
the winds of March with beauty." It is "sweeter than the
lids of Juno's eyes, or Cytherea's breath."[24] All this is
felt by this young poet; and I envy not that man his heartless
indifference, though he should think it philosophy, who cannot feel this influence of nature. Poetry is but the language
of nature. Poetasters swarm "thick" as the motes that

people the sunbeam."25   Poets, in the true meaning of the
title, are very rare.   If ever fair morning gave smiling
promise of a lovely day, I repeat it, that the poems already
published by the author of "Endymion" are the germs of
future greatness.

> "Some there be, that by due steps aspire
> "To lay their just hands on that golden key,
> "That hopes the palace of eternity. "26

I am, Sir,

Your obedient Servant,

N. Y.

3.   A review of Endymion in the Champion

(This favorable review appeared on June 7, 1818,
pp. 362-364.   It has been noted in several sources,
but it is reproduced here in its entirety for the
first time.   The author cannot be definitely identified; but John Scott, who was then editor of the
Champion, is a likely candidate.   The reviewer
speaks of the tyranny of judgment in the influential
quarterlies, a theme that Scott was to frequently
re-echo in articles which he later wrote as editor
of Baldwin's London Magazine.   The author's appeal
for fair criticism went unheeded, and if Scott had
framed this appeal, it might account for the level
of his consistent hostility toward Blackwood's and
the Quarterly in 1820.
The article itself is judicious, well-reasoned,
and written on a high enough level to also suggest
that Scott was the author.   The reviewer's estimate of Endymion is sympathetic, but he foresees
the possibility of a future attack on Keats's poem.
Some may tack "the introduction of the first book
[the Preface], to the fag end of the last" and
"swear the whole is an unintelligible jumble...."
This was actually done by the British Critic in
September 1818.   The author's fear that not all
future reviewers would treat Keats's poem fairly,
proved, all to unfortunately, correct in terms of
Blackwood's and the Quarterly as well.)

Although this poem has very lately appeared, the
short delay between its publication and our notice, was in-
tentional.   We are sincerely anxious for its ultimate success: we were willing that the age should do honour to itself by its reception of it; and cared little for having been
the first to notice it.   We were fearful, that if we ventured
to decide on it, and could induce the few to take its consideration into their own hands, our great critical authorities
would choose, as usual, to maintain an obstinate silence,
or to speak slightingly, perhaps contemptuously, to keep up
the etiquette; for they have a spice of Cicero, and "never
follow any thing that other men begin. " Neither have we
altered our opinion, but having seen more than one public
notice of the work, do not choose longer to delay it.   That
the consequences will be pretty nearly as we predict we have
little doubt.   If the reviews play the sure game and say
nothing, to nothing can we object; but if they really notice
it, let us have something like a fair and liberal criticism--
something that can be subjected to examination itself.   Let
them refer to principles: let them shew us the philosophic
construction of poetry, and point out its errors by instance
and application.   To this we shall not object: but this we
must think they owe to Mr. Keats himself, and all those who
have written and spoken highly of his talent.   If however,
they follow their old course, and having tacked the introduction of the first book, to the fag end of the last, swear the
whole is an unintelligible jumble, we will at least exert ourselves to stop their chuckling and self congratulation.

We cannot, however, disguise from ourselves that the
conduct that may be pursued by these reviews will have its
influence, and a great influence, on public opinion: but,
excepting as to the effect that opinion may have on the poet
himself, we care not two straws for it.   Public opinion is
not a comprehensive or comprehending thing: it is neither
a wit nor a wise man: a poet nor a philosopher: it is the
veriest "king of shadows:" it is nothing but the hollow echoing of some momentary oracle: and if we estimate the work
of the reviews themselves, we have it, for they are the
things now in authority: they are your only substantials:
they give currency to our poets: and what chance has an
original genius that differs from all our poets, when nearly
all our poets write for one or other of them.   These men
have it in their own hands, to meet our praise and censure,
for half the population.   We only hope they do not flatter
themselves on the general assent: if they really mistake
their popularity for immortality, they trick out an ideot in

motely, and having stuck a Bartholomew trumpet[27] in his
hand, persuade themselves it is fame. But we do fear even
public opinion from our knowledge of human nature. No man
ever lived but he had a consciousness of his own power, and
if he chose to make a fair estimate was perhaps a better
judge than any other of his own ability. If then with this
consciousness he find nothing in unison with his own feeling,
no fair and liberal estimate made of his own worth, no con-
cessions made, no deference paid to him by the opinion that
for the time passes current, he is driven by necessity upon
his self-love for satisfaction, his indignation lashes his
pride, he is unsupported by others w[h]ere he has an undoubted assurance of being right, and he maintains those
errors that have been justly objected against him, because
they have been urged too far, and refuses to concede any
thing because too much has been demanded. This, however,
is a speculation, and we trust, it will remain so.

It is ever hazardous to predict the fate of a great
original work; and of Endymion, all we dare to venture in
this way is an opinion, that an inferior poem is likely to
excite a more general interest. The secret of the success
of our modern poets, is their universal presence in their
poems--they give to every thing the colouring of their own
feeling; and what a man has felt intensely--the impressions
of actual existence--he is likely to describe powerfully:
what he has felt we can easily sympathize with. But Mr.
Keats goes out of himself into a world of abstractions:--
his passions, feelings are all as much imaginative as his
situations. Neither is it the mere outward signs of passions
that are given: there seems ever present some being that
was equally conscious of its internal and most secret imaginings. There is another objection to its ever becoming
popular that it is, as the Venus and Adonis of Shakespeare,
a representation and not a description of passion. Both
these poems, would, we think, be more generally admired
had the poets been only veiled instead of concealed from us.
Mr. Keats conceives the scene before him, and represents
it as it appears. This is the excellence of dramatic poetry;
but to feel its truth and power in any other, we must
abandon our ordinary feeling and common consciousness, and
identify ourselves with the scene. Few people can do this.
In representation, which is the ultimate purpose of dramatic
poetry, we should feel something of sympathy though we
could merely observe the scene, or the gesticulation, and
no sound could reach us; but to make an ordinary reader
sensible of the excellence of a poem, he must be told what

the poet felt; and he is affected by him and not by the scene.
Our modern poets are the shewmen of their own pictures,
and point out its beauties.

      Mr. Keats' very excellence, we fear, will tell against
him.   Each scene bears so actually the immediate impress
of truth and nature, that it may be said to be local and
peculiar, and to require some extrinsic feeling for its full
enjoyment:--perhaps we are not clear in what we say.
Every man, then, according to his own particular habit of
mind, not only gives a correspondent colouring to all that
surrounds him, but seeks to surround himself with corresponding objects, in which he has more than other people's
enjoyment.   In every thing then that art or nature may
present to man, though gratifying to all, each man's gratification and sympathy will be regulated by the disposition
and bent of his mind.   Look at Milton's Sonnets.   With what
a deep and bitter feeling would a persecuted religious enthusiast select and dwell "On the late Massacre in Preniout
[Piemont]. " Has a social man no particular enjoyment in
those to Laurence [Lawrence] and Skynner? or a patriot in
those to Fairfax, Cromwell, and Vane?   What is common
to humanity we are all readily sensible of, and all men
proportioned to their intelligence, will receive pleasure on
reading that on his birth day:28--it wants nothing exclusive
either in persons or age:--but would not a young and fearful
lover find a thousand beauties in his address to the nightingale that must for ever escape the majority.   In further
illustration, we would adduce the first meeting of Endymion
and Cynthia in the poem before us; which, though wonderfully
told, we do not think most likely to be generally liked. 29
It is so true to imagination, that passion absorbs every
thing.   Now, as we have observed, to transfer the mind to
the situation of another, to feel as he feels, requires an
enthusiasm, and an abstraction, beyond the power or the
habit of most people.   It is in this way eloquence differs
from poetry, and the same speech on delivery affects people,
than, on an after reading would appear tame and unimpas-
sioned.   We have certain sympathies with the person addressing us, and what he feels, we feel in an inferior degree; but
he is afterwards to describe to us his passion; to make us
feel by telling us what he felt: and this is to be done by
calculating on the effect on others feelings, and not by
abandoning ourselves to our own.   If Mr. Keats can do this,
he has not done it. 30   When he writes of passion, it seems
to have possessed him.   This, however, is what Shakespeare
did, and if Endymion bears any general resemblance to any

other poem in the language, it is to Venus and Adonis on this very account. In the necessarily abrupt breaking off of this scene of intense passion, however, we think he has exceeded even his ordinary power. It is scarcely possible to conceive any thing more poetically imaginative; and though it may be brought in rather abruptly, we cannot refuse ourselves the pleasure of immediately extracting it.

[Quotes II. ll. 827-854.]

The objection we have here stated is equally applicable to the proper and full appreciation of many other beautiful scenes in the poem: but having acknowledged this, we shall extract the hymn to Pan, that our readers may be satisfied there are others to which universal assent must be given as among the finest specimens of classic poetry in our language.

[Quotes I. ll. 232-262, 279-306.]

We shall trespass a little beyond the hymn itself, and must then postpone our further observations.

[Quotes I. ll. 307-319. The last line reads "But in old marbles ever beautiful."]

This last line is as fine as that in Shakespeare's Sonnets,

And beauty making beautiful old rhyme:[31]

and there are not a dozen finer in Shakespeare's poems.

(To be continued.)[32]

4.   John Gibson Lockhart's "Cockney School of Poetry. No. IV." in Blackwood's Edinburgh Magazine

(Over the signature "Z." in Blackwood's Edinburgh Magazine for October 1817 (II, 38-41), Lockhart and Wilson initiated the first of a series of articles "On the Cockney School of Poetry."[33] Hunt, who was labeled founder of the school, was the primary victim; but Keats's name was also mentioned. The focus shifted directly to Keats in the fourth number of the Cockney School [IV (August 1818), 519-524].

Although Wilson may have had some slight hand
in this article, all major authorities agree that it
is primarily the work of Lockhart. The attack,
by far the most scathing contemporary criticism
of Keats to ever appear, was inspired by Tory
malice. The article is as much a review of
Poems as it is of Endymion, and this fit well into
Lockhart's purposes. Keats's first volume was in-
herently weaker than Endymion, and the fault-
finding critic was able to build part of his case
against Keats by exposing these weaknesses. In
the main, however, Lockhart simply relies on
personal invective. Repeatedly, Keats's name is
linked with Hunt's.)

                  --OF KEATS
THE MUSES' SON OF PROMISE, AND WHAT FEATS
HE YET MAY DO, &c.
                  Cornelius Webb. 34

Of all the manias of this mad age, the most incurable, as
well as the most common, seems to be no other than the
Metromanie. 35 The just celebrity of Robert Burns and
Miss Baillie36 has had the melancholy effect of turning the
heads of we know not how many farm-servants and unmar-
ried ladies; our very footmen compose tragedies, and there
is scarcely a superannuated governess in the island that does
not leave a roll of lyrics behind her in band-box. To witness the disease of any human understanding, however
feeble, is distressing; but the spectacle of an able mind reduced to a state of insanity is of course ten times more
afflicting. It is with such sorrow as this that we have contemplated the case of Mr. John Keats. This young man
appears to have received from nature talents of an excellent,
perhaps even of a superior order--talents which, devoted to
the purposes of any useful profession, must have rendered
him a respectable, if not an eminent citizen. His friends,
we understand, destined him to the career of medicine, and
he was bound apprentice some years ago to a worth apothecary in town. 37 But all has been undone by a sudden attack
of the malady to which we have alluded. Whether Mr. John
had been sent home with a diuretic or composing draught to
some patient far gone in the poetical mania, we have not
heard. This much is certain, that he has caught the infec-
tion, and that thoroughly. For some time we were in hopes,
that he might get off with a violent fit or two; but of late the

symptoms are terrible.   The phrenzy of the "Poems" was
bad enough in its way; but it did not alarm us half so seriously as the calm, settled, imperturbable drivelling idiocy
of " Endymion. " We hope, however, that in so young a person, and with a constitution originally so good, even now the
disease is not utterly incurable.   Time, firm treatment, and
rational restraint, do much for many apparently hopeless
invalids; and if Mr. Keats should happen, at some interval
of reason, to cast his eye upon our pages, he may perhaps
be convinced of the existence of his malady, which, in such
cases, is often all that is necessary to put the patient in a
fair way of being cured.

The readers of the Examiner newspaper were informed, some time ago, by a solemn paragraph, in Mr.
Hunt's best style, of the appearance of two new stars of
glorious magnitude and splendour in the poetical horizon of
the land of Cockaigne. 38   One of these turned out, by and
by, to be no other than Mr. John Keats.   This precocious
adulation confirmed the wavering apprentice in his desire to
quit the gallipots, and at the same time excited in his too
susceptible mind a fatal admiration for the character and
talents of the most worthless and affected of all the versifiers of our time.   One of his first productions was the
following sonnet, "written on the day when Mr. Leigh Hunt
left prison. " It will be recollected, that the cause of Hunt's
confinement was a series of libels against his sovereign,
and that its fruit was the odious and incestuous "Story of
Rimini. "

> "What though, for shewing truth to flattered state,
> Kind Hunt was shut in prison, yet has he,
> In his immortal spirit been as free
> As the sky-searching lark, and as elate.
> Minion of grandeur! think you he did wait?
> Think you he nought but prison walls did see,
> Till, so unwilling, thou unturn'dst the key?
> Ah, no! far happier, nobler was his fate!
> In Spenser's halls! he strayed, and bowers fair,
> Culling enchanted flowers; and he flew
> With daring Milton! through the fields of air;
> To regions of his own his genius true
> Took happy flights.   Who shall his fame impair
> When thou art dead, and all thy wretched crew?39

The absurdity of the thought in this sonnet is, however, if
possible, surpassed in another, "addressed to Haydon" the

painter, that clever, but most affected artist, who as little
resembles Raphael in genius as he does in person, notwithstanding the foppery of having his hair curled over his
shoulders in the old Italian fashion.   In this exquisite piece
it will be observed, that Mr. Keats classes together Wordsworth, Hunt, and Haydon, as the three greatest spirits of
the age, and that he alludes to himself, and some others of
the rising brood of Cockneys, as likely to attain hereafter
an equally honourable elevation. [40] Wordsworth and Hunt! what
a juxta-position! The purest, the loftiest, and, we do not
fear to say it, the most classical of living English poets,
joined together in the same compliment with the meanest,
the filthiest, and the most vulgar of Cockney poetasters.
No wonder that he who could be guilty of this should class
Haydon with Raphael, and himself with Spencer.

> "Great spirits now on earth are sojourning;
>   He of the cloud, the cataract, the lake,
>   Who on Helvellyn's summit, wide awake,
> Catches his freshness from Archangel's wing:
> He of the rose, the violet, the spring.
>   The social smile, the chain for Freedom's sake:
>   And lo!--whose stedfastness would never take
> A meaner sound than Raphael's whispering.
> And other spirits there are standing apart
>   Upon the forehead of the age to come;
> These, these will give the world another heart,
>   And other pulses. Hear ye not the hum
> Of mighty workings?-----
>   Listen awhile ye nations, and be dumb. [41]

The nations are to listen and be dumb! and why, good
Johnny Keats? because Leigh Hunt is editor of the Examiner,
and Haydon has painted the judgment of Solomon, and you and
Cornelius Webb, and a few more city sparks, are pleased to
look upon yourselves as so many Shakespeares and Miltons!
The world has really some reason to look to its foundations!
Here is a tempestas in matulâ[42] with a vengeance.   At the
period when these sonnets were published, Mr. Keats had
no hesitation in saying, that he looked on himself as "not
yet a glorious denizen of the wide heaven of poetry,"[43] but
he had many fine soothing visions of coming greatness, and
many rare plans of study to prepare him for it.   The following we think is very pretty raving.

[Quotes "Sleep and Poetry," ll. 89-121.]

Having cooled a little from this "fine passion," our youthful poet passes very naturally into a long strain of foaming abuse against a certain class of English Poets, whom, with Pope at their head, it is much the fashion with the ignorant unsettled pretenders of the present time to undervalue. Begging these gentlemens' pardon, although Pope was not a poet of the same high order with some who are now living, yet, to deny his genius, is just about as absurd as to dispute that of Wordsworth, or to believe in that of Hunt. Above all things, it is most pitiably ridiculous to hear men, of whom their country will always have reason to be proud, reviled by uneducated and flimsy striplings, who are not capable of understanding either their merits, or those of any other men of power--fanciful dreaming tea-drinkers, who, without logic enough to analyse a single idea, or imagination enough to form one original image, or learning enough to distinguish between the written language of Englishmen and the spoken jargon of Cockney's, presume to talk with contempt of some of the most exquisite spirits the world ever produced, merely because they did not happen to exert their faculties in laborious affected descriptions of flowers seen in window-pots or cascades heard at Vauxhall; in short, because they chose to be wits, philosophers, patriots, and poets, rather than to found the Cockney school of versification, morality, and politics, a century before its time. After blaspheming himself into a fury against Boileau, &c. Mr. Keats comforts himself and his readers with a view of the present more promising aspect of affairs: above all, with the ripened glories of the poet of Rimini. [44] Addressing the manes of the departed chiefs of English poetry, he informs them, in the following clear and touching manner, of the existence of "him of the Rose," [45] &c.

> "From a thick brake,
> Nested and quiet in a valley mild,
> Bubbles a pipe; fine sounds are floating wild
> About the earth. Happy are ye and glad."
> ["Sleep and Poetry," ll. 216-219.]

From this he diverges into a view of "things in general." We smile when we think to ourselves how little most readers will understand of what follows.

[Quotes "Sleep and Poetry," ll. 248-276.]

From some verses addressed to various amiable individuals of the other sex, [46] it appears, notwithstanding all

this gossamer-work, that Johnny's affections are not entirely
confined to objects purely etherial.   Take, by way of specimen, the following prurient and vulgar lines, evidently meant
for some young lady east of Temple-bar. [47]

> "Add too, the sweetness
> Of thy honied voice; the neatness
> Of thine ankle lightly turn'd:
> With those beauties, scarce discern'd,
> Kept with such sweet privacy,
> That they seldom meet the eye
> Of the little loves that fly
> Round about with eager pry.
> Saving when, with freshening lave,
> Thou dipp'st them in the taintless wave;
> Like twin water lilies, born
> In the coolness of the morn.
> O, if thou hadst breathed then,
> Now the Muses had been ten.
> Couldst thou wish for lineage higher
> Than twin sister of Thalia?
> At last for ever, evermore,
> Will I call the Graces four."
> ["To --," ll. 23-40.]

Who will dispute that our poet, to use his own phrase (and
rhyme),

> "Can mingle music fit for the soft ear
> Of Lady Cythera."
> [Endymion, III. ll. 974-975.]

So much for the opening bud; now for the expanded flower.
It is time to pass from the juvenile "Poems," to the mature
and elaborate " Endymion, a Poetic Romance."   The old
story of the moon falling in love with a shepherd, so prettily
told by a Roman Classic, [48] and so exquisitely enlarged and
adorned by one of the most elegant of German poets, [49] has
been seized upon by Mr. John Keats, to be done with as
might seem good unto the sickly fancy of one who never
read a single line either of Ovid or of Wieland. [50]   If the
quantity, not the quality, of the verses dedicated to the story
is to be taken into account, there can be no doubt that Mr.
John Keats may now claim Endymion entirely to himself.
To say the truth, we do not suppose either the Latin or the
German poet would be very anxious to dispute about the
property of the hero of the "Poetic Romance."   Mr. Keats

has thoroughly appropriated the character, if not the name.
His Endymion is not a Greek shepherd, loved by a Grecian
goddess; he is merely a young Cockney rhymester, dreaming a phantastic dream at the full of the moon.   Costume,
were it worth while to notice such a trifle, is violated in
every page of this goodly octavo.   From his prototype Hunt,
John Keats has acquired a sort of vague idea, that the Greeks
were a most tasteful people, and that no mythology can be
so finely adapted for the purposes of poetry as theirs.   It is
amusing to see what a hand the two Cockneys make of this
mythology; the one confesses that he never read the Greek
Tragedians, [51] and the other knows Homer only from Chapman; and both of them write about Apollo, Pan, Nymphs,
Muses, and Mysteries, as might be expected from persons
of their education.   We shall not, however, enlarge at
present upon this subject, as we mean to dedicate an entire
paper to the classical attainments and attempts of the Cockney poets.   As for Mr Keats' "Endymion," it has just as
much to do with Greece as it has with "old Tartary the
fierce;"[52] no man, whose mind has ever been imbued with
the smallest knowledge or feeling of classical poetry or
classical history, could have stooped to profane and vulgarise
every association in the manner which has been adopted by
this "son of promise."   Before giving any extracts, we
must inform our readers, that this romance is meant to
be written in English heroic rhyme.   To those who have
read any of Hunt's poems, this hint might indeed by needless.
Mr Keats has adopted the loose, nerveless versification, and
Cockney rhymes of the poet of Rimini; but in fairness to
that gentleman, we must add, that the defects of the system
are tenfold more conspicuous in his disciple's work than in
his own.   Mr Hunt is a small poet, but he is a clever man.
Mr Keats is still a smaller poet, and he is only a boy of
pretty abilities, which he has done every thing in his power
to spoil.

  The poem sets out with the following exposition of the
reasons which induced Mr Keats to compose it.

   [Quotes Endymion, I. ll. 1-35.]

After introducing his hero to us in a procession, and preparing us, by a few mystical lines, for believing that his
destiny has in it some strange peculiarity, Mr Keats represents the beloved of the Moon as being conveyed by his
sister Peona into an island in a river.   This young lady
has been alarmed by the appearance of the brother, and

questioned him thus:

> [Quotes I. ll. 505-515.]

Endymion replies in a long speech, wherein he describes his
first meeting with the Moon.   We cannot make room for the
whole of it, but shall take a few pages here and there.

> [Quotes I. ll. 554-567, 598-616, 633-645.]

Not content with the authentic love of the Moon, Keats makes
his hero captivate another supernatural lady, of whom no
notice occurs in any of his predecessors.

> [Quotes II. ll. 98-130.]

But we find that we really have no patience for going over
four books filled with such amorous scenes as these, with
subterraneous journeys equally amusing, and submarine pro-
cessions equally beautiful; but we must not omit the most
interesting scene of the whole piece.

> [Quotes II. ll. 707-741, mediocre lines which
> make it clear that the sentence above is ironic.]

After all this, however, the "modesty," as Mr Keats expresses it, of the Lady Diana prevented here from owning
in Olympus her passion for Endymion.   Venus, as the most
knowing in such matters, is the first to discover the change
that has taken place in the temperament of the goddess.   "An
idle tale,"[53] says the laughter-loving dame,

> "A humid eye, and steps luxurious,
> When these are new and strange, are ominous."
> [III. ll. 910-911.]

The inamorata, to vary the intrigue, carries on a romantic
intercourse with Endymion, under the disguise of an Indian
damsel.   At last, however, her scruples, for some reason
or other, are all overcome, and the Queen of Heaven owns
her attachment

> "She gave her fair hands to him, and behold,
> Before three swiftest kisses he had told,
> They vanish far away!--Peona went
> Home through the gloomy wood in wonderment."
> [IV. ll. 1000-1003.]

And so, like many other romances, terminates the "Poetic Romance" of Johnny Keats, in a patched-up wedding.

We had almost forgot to mention that Keats belongs to the Cockney School of Politics, as well as the Cockney School of Poetry. [54]

It is fit that he who holds Rimini to be the first poem, should believe the Examiner to be the first politician of the day. We admire consistency, even in folly. Hear how their bantling has already learned to lisp sedition.

> [Quotes III. ll. 1-22, lines which the British Critic was to describe the next month as a "jacobinical apostrophe."]

And now, good-morrow to "the Muses' son of Promise;" as for "the feats he yet may do," as we do not pretend to say, like himself, "Muse of my native land am I inspired,"[55] we shall adhere to the safe old rule of pauca verba. We venture to make one small prophecy, that his bookseller will not a second time venture £50 upon any thing he can write. It is a better and a wiser thing to be a starved apothecary than a starved poet; so back to the shop Mr John, back to "plasters, pills, and ointment boxes,"[56] &c. But, for Heaven's sake, young Sangrado,[57] be a little more sparing of extenuatives and soporifics in your practice than you have been in your poetry.   Z.

5. John Wilson Croker's review of Endymion
    in the Quarterly Review

> (This attack on Keats's second volume is ac-
> knowledged by all major authorities to have been
> written by Croker for the April 1818 issue of the
> Quarterly Review [XIX, 204-208], an issue that
> was not published until September of that year. [58]
> The Edinburgh, the only literary review to rival
> the Quarterly in size and influence, remained
> silent about Keats's poem until 1820; and its si-
> lence was incorrectly construed by many, Keats
> included, as an acquiescence to the unfavorable
> judgment of the Quarterly. Developments in 1820
> proved Croker's condemnation less significant than
> it appeared to be at the time; but with the publica-

tion of this review in 1818, Keats's reputation sank
to its lowest ebb.

In Blackwood's, Lockhart had sarcastically alluded to the Preface of Endymion, just as the reviewer in the Champion had predicted.   Croker
also employed this tactic in the Quarterly.   Keats's
friends, Reynolds in particular, had advised him
to revise his original Preface; they feared, and
quite correctly so, that Keats's frank admission of
Endymion's flaws would be turned against him by
hostile reviewers.   Keats took their advice and revised his Preface, but the following published version did not sufficiently guard against the same
danger:

"Knowing within myself the manner in which this
Poem has been produced, it is not without a feeling of regret that I make it public.

"What manner I mean, will be quite clear to
the reader, who must soon perceive great inexperience, immaturity, and every error denoting a
feverish attempt, rather than a deed accomplished.
The two first books, and indeed the two last, I
feel sensible are not of such completion to war-
rant their passing the press; nor should they if I
thought a year's castigation would do them any
good;--it will not: the foundations are too sandy.
It is just that this youngster should die away: a
sad thought for me, if I had not some hope that
while it is dwindling I may be plotting, and fitting
myself for verses fit to live. 59

"This may be speaking too presumptuously, and
may deserve a punishment: but no feeling man will
be forward to inflict it: he will leave me alone,
with the conviction that there is not a fiercer hell
than failure in a great object.   This is not written
with the least atom of purpose to forestall criticisms of course, but from the desire I have to
conciliate men who are competent to look, and who
do look with a zealous eye, to the honour of
English literature.

"The imagination of a boy is healthy, and the
mature imagination of a man is healthy; but there
is a space of life between, in which the soul is in
a ferment, the character undecided, the way of life
uncertain, the ambition thick-sighted: thence proceeds mawkishness, and all the thousand bitters
which those men I speak of must necessarily taste

in going over the following pages.
   "I hope I have not in too late a day touched the
beautiful mythology of Greece, and dulled its brightness: for I wish to try once more, before I bid
it farewel [sic]. ")

Reviewers have been sometimes accused of not reading the
works they affected to criticise.   On the present occasion
we shall anticipate the author's complaint, and honestly confess that we have not read his work.   Not that we have been
wanting in our duty--far from it--indeed, we have made
efforts almost as superhuman as the story itself appears to
be, to get through it; but with the fullest stretch of our perseverance, we are forced to confess that we have not been
able to struggle beyond the first of the four books of which
this Poetic Romance consists.   We should extremely lament
this want of energy, or whatever it may be, on our parts,
were it not for one consolation--namely, that we are no
better acquainted with the meaning of the book through which
we have so painfully toiled, than we are with that of the
three which we have not looked into.

   It is not that Mr. Keats, (if that be his real name,
for we almost doubt that any man in his senses would put
his real name to such a rhapsody,) it is not, we say, that
the author has not powers of language, rays of fancy, and
gleams of genius--he has all these; but he is unhappily a
disciple of the new school of what has been somewhere called
Cockney poetry; which may be defined to consist of the most
incongruous ideas in the most uncouth language.

   Of this school, Mr. Leigh Hunt, as we observed in
a former Number, 60 aspires to be the hierophant. 61   Our
readers will recollect the pleasant recipes for harmonious
and sublime poetry which he gave us in his preface to
'Rimini, ' and the still more facetious instances of his harmony and sublimity in the verses themselves; and they will
recollect above all the contempt of Pope, Johnson, and such
like poetasters and pseudo-critics, which so forcibly contrasted itself with Mr. Leigh Hunt's self-complacent approbation of

            --'all the things itself had wrote
         Of special merit though of little note. '62

   This author is a copyist of Mr. Hunt; but he is more

unintelligible, almost as rugged, twice as diffuse, and ten
times more tiresome and absurd than his prototype, who,
though he impudently presumed to seat himself in the chair
of criticism, and to measure his own poetry by his own
standard, yet generally had a meaning. But Mr. Keats has
advanced no dogmas which he was bound to support by examples; his nonsense therefore is quite gratuitous; he writes
it for its own sake, and, being bitten by Mr. Leigh Hunt's
insane criticism, more than rivals the insanity of his poetry.

Mr. Keats's preface hints that his poem was produced
under peculiar circumstances.

> 'Knowing within myself (he says) the manner
> in which this Poem has been produced, it is not
> without a feeling of regret that I make it public. --
> What manner I mean, will be quite clear to the
> reader, who must soon perceive great inexperience,
> immaturity, and every error denoting a feverish
> attempt, rather than a deed accomplished.'--
> Preface, p. vii.

We humbly beg his pardon, but this does not appear
to us to be quite so clear--we really do not know what he
means--but the next passage is more intelligible

> 'The two first books, and indeed the two last,
> I feel sensible are not of such completion as to
> warrant their passing the press.'63--Preface,
> p. vii.

Thus 'the two first books' are, even in his own judgment, unfit to appear, and 'the two last' are, it seems, in
the same condition--and as two and two make four, and as
that is the whole number of books, we have a clear and,
we believe, a very just estimate of the entire work.

Mr. Keats, however, deprecates criticism on this
'immature and feverish work' in terms which are themselves sufficiently feverish; and we confess that we should
have abstained from inflicting upon him any of the tortures
of the 'fierce hell' of criticism, which terrify his imagination, if he had not begged to be spared in order that he
might write more; if we had not observed in him a certain
degree of talent which deserves to be put in the right way,
or which, at least, ought to be warned of the wrong; and if,
finally, he had not told us that he is of an age and temper

which imperiously require mental discipline.

Of the story we have been able to make out but little;
it seems to be mythological, and probably relates to the
loves of Diana and Endymion; but of this, as the scope of
the work has altogether escaped us, we cannot speak with
any degree of certainty; and must therefore content ourselves with giving some instances of its diction and versification:--and here again we are perplexed and puzzled.-- At
first it appeared to us, that Mr. Keats had been amusing
himself and wearying his readers with an immeasurable game
at bouts-rimés;[64] but, if we recollect rightly, it is an in-
dispensable condition at this play, that the rhymes when
filled up shall have a meaning; and our author, as we have
already hinted, has no meaning. He seems to us to write
a line at random, and then he follows not the thought excited
by this line, but that suggested by the rhyme with which it
concludes. There is hardly a complete couplet inclosing a
complete idea in the whole book. He wanders from one subject to another, from the association, not of ideas but of
sounds, and the work is composed of hemistichs which, it
is quite evident, have forced themselves upon the author by
the mere force of the catchwords on which they turn.

We shall select, not as the most striking instance,
but as that least liable to suspicion, a passage from the
opening of the poem.

> --'Such the sun, the moon,
> Trees old and young, sprouting a shady boon
> For simple sheep; and such are daffodils
> With the green world they live in; and clear rills
> That for themselves a cooling covert make
> 'Gainst the hot season; the mid forest brake,
> Rich with a sprinkling of fair musk-rose blooms:
> And such too is the grandeur of the dooms
> We have imagined for the mighty dead; &c. &c.'--
> pp. 3, 4.

[I. ll. 13-21.]

Here it is clear that the word, and not the idea,
moon produces the simple sheep and their shady boon, and
that 'the dooms of the mighty dead' would never have in-
truded themselves but for the 'fair musk-rose blooms.'

Again.

'For 'twas the morn: Apollo's upward fire
Made every eastern cloud a silvery pyre
Of brightness so unsullied, that therein
A melancholy spirit well might win
Oblivion, and melt out his essence fine
Into the winds: rain-scented eglantine
Gave temperate sweets to that well-wooing sun;
The lark was lost in him; cold springs had run
To warm their chilliest bubbles in the grass;
Man's voice was on the mountains; and the mass
Of nature's lives and wonders puls'd tenfold,
To feel this sun-rise and its glories old. '--p. 8.
[I. ll. 95-106.]

Here Apollo's fire produces a pyre, a silvery pyre
of clouds, wherein a spirit might win oblivion and melt his
fine, and scented eglantine gives sweets to the sun, and cold
springs had run into the grass, and then the pulse of the
mass pulsed tenfold to feel the glories old of the new-born
day, &c.

One example more.

'Be still the unimaginable lodge
For solitary thinkings; such as dodge
Conception to the very bourne of heaven,
Then leave the naked brain: be still the leaven,
That spreading in this dull and clodded earth
Gives it a touch etheral--a new birth. '--p. 17.
[I. ll. 293-298.]

Lodge, dodge--heaven, leaven--earth, birth; such, in six
words, is the sum and substance of six lines.

We come next to the author's taste in versification.
He cannot indeed write a sentence, but perhaps he may be
able to spin a line.   Let us see.   The following are specimens of his prosodical notions of our English heroic metre.

'Dear as the temple's self, so does the moon,
The passion poesy, glories infinite. '--p. 4.
[I. ll. 28-29.]

'So plenteously all weed-hidden roots. '--p. 6.
[I. l. 65.]

'Of some strange history, potent to send. '--p. 18.
[I. l. 324.]

'Before the deep intoxication.'--p. 27.
                    [I. 1. 502.]

'Her scarf into a fluttering pavilion.'--p. 33.
                    [I. 1. 628.]

'The stubborn canvass for my voyage prepared--.'--
p. 39.
                              [I. 1. 772.]

' "Endymion! the cave is secreter
Than the isle of Delos. Echo hence shall stir
No sighs but sigh-warm kisses, or light noise
Of thy combing hand, the while it travelling cloys
And trembles through my labyrinthine hair."'--p. 48
                              [I. ll. 965-969.]

By this time our readers must be pretty well satisfied as to the meaning of his sentences and the structure of
his lines; we now present them with some of the new words
with which, in imitation of Mr. Leigh Hunt, he adorns our
language.

We are told that 'turtles passion their voices' (p.
15); that 'an arbour was nested,' (p. 23); and a lady's locks
'gordian'd up,' (p. 32); and to supply the place of the nouns
thus verbalized Mr. Keats, with great fecundity, spawns
new ones; such as 'men-slugs and human serpentry,' (p.
410) the 'honey-feel of bliss,' (p. 45); 'wives prepare need-
ments,' (p. 13)--and so forth.

Then he has formed new verbs by the process of
cutting off their natural tails, the adverbs, and affixing
them to their foreheads; thus, 'the wine out-sparkled,' (p.
10); the 'multitude up-followed,' (p. 11); and 'night up-took,'
(p. 29). 'The wind up-blows,' (p. 32); and the 'hours are
down-sunken,' (p. 36).

But if he sinks some adverbs in the verbs he com-
pensates the language with adverbs and adjectives which he
separates from the parent stock. Thus, a lady 'whispers
pantingly and close,' makes 'hushing signs,' and steers her
skiff into a 'ripply cove,' (p. 23); a shower falls 'refresh-
fully,' (45); and a vulture has a 'spreaded tail,' (p. 44).

But enough of Mr. Leigh Hunt and his simple neo-
phyte. --If any one should be bold enough to purchase this
'Poetic Romance,' and so much more patient, than ourselves,

as to get beyond the first book, and so much more fortunate
as to find a meaning, we entreat him to make us acquainted
with his success; we shall then return to the task which we
now abandon in despair, and endeavour to make all due
amends to Mr. Keats and to our readers.

6.   A review of Endymion in the British Critic

            (According to Walter J. Bate [John Keats (Cam-
       bridge, Mass., 1963), p. 366], the June 1818
       issue of the British Critic did not appear until
       some time in September. 65   The Critic was a
       guardian of morality and the Established Church,
       and its disapproval of Keats can be traced to his
       friendship with the freethinking Hunt.   Keats's
       poetry is linked with Hunt's at the outset of the
       review.   Moreover, the Critic also assumed that
       there were political links between the two friends:
       the opening lines of Book III of Endymion, we are
       told, contain "a jacobinical apostrophe to 'crowns,
       turbans, and tiptop nothings.'"   In general, the
       reviewer attempts to reduce Keats's poem to
       absurdity by a series of quotations which are some-
       times inaccurate and always out of context.   The
       identity of the author is not known, but his review
       is characterized throughout by a contemptuous,
       condescending humor.   The article itself has fre-
       quently been noted by students of the period, but it
       is reproduced here in its entirety for the first
       time.)

This is the most delicious poem, of its kind, which has
fallen within our notice, and if Mr. Leigh Hunt had never
written, we believe we might have pronounced it to be sui
generis without fear of contradiction.   That gentleman, however, has talked so much about "daisies and daffodils,
clover and sweet peas, blossomings and lushiness, "66 that
we fear Mr. Keats must be content to share but half the
laurel, provided always, and we can most consciously assert
it, that the disciple be recognized as not one whit inferior
to his mighty master.   All the world knows that the moon
fell in love with Endymion, just as Aurora intrigued with
Cephalus, till, as the author of the Pursuits of Literature tells
us, she jilted him for Mr. Steevens; 67 but it remained for
a muse of modern days to acquaint us with the whole pro-

gress of this demi-celestial amour. "A thing of beauty (as
Mr. Keats says, or sings, we know not which, in the first
line of his poem,) is a joy for ever!" And, "as the year
grows lush in juicy stalks," "many and many a verse he
hopes to write." Endymion is a very handsome young man,
"but there were some who feelingly could scan a lurking
trouble in his nether lip."--" [sic] then they would[68] sigh
and think of yellow leaves and owlets cry and (what else in
the name of wonder does the reader expect?) of logs pil'd
solemnly, [69] (B. I. 1. 180.) One day after the priest of
Patmos had sung a song to Pan, whom he represents, rather
indecorously, we must acknowledge, as a god "who loves[70]
to see the Hamadryads dress;" and also, one "for whose
soul-soothing quiet, turtles passion their voices cooingly
among myrtles," with many other things about "broad
leaved fig-trees, freckled butterflies, solitary thinkings,
shorn peers, and dodging conceptions;" a shout arises among
the multitude, just as "when Ionian shoals of dolphins bob
their noses through the brine," (1. 310). In consequence
of this noise, and "Niobe's caressing tongue," which "lay
a lost thing upon her paly lip" (1. 340). Endymion goes to
sleep among some "pouting zephyr-sighs," where, while
his sister sits "guarding his forehead with her round elbow,"
he lies "aye, e'en as dead still as a marble man, frozen
in that old tale Arabian," (1. 405.) after sleeping his
"magic sleep, O comfortable bird!" for a "triple hour," he
"opens his eyelids with a healthier brain." Peona "shuts
her pure sorrow drops with loud exclaim," and he explains
to her what has made him who used to be able to "frown a
lion into growling," lose his "toil-breeding fire;" it seems
that one evening when the sun had done driving "his snorting
four," "there blossom'd suddenly a magic bed of sacred
ditamy," (Qu. dimity?)[71] and he looked up to the "lidless-
eyed train of planets," where he saw "a completed form of
all completeness," "with gordian'd locks and pearl round
ears," and kissed all these till he fell into a "stupid sleep"
from which he was roused by "a gentle creep," (N. B. Mr.
Tiffin[72] is the ablest bug-destroyer of our days), to look
at some "upturn'd gills of dying fish." This very intelligible
communication to his sister relieves him a good deal, but
he is not quite easy till "amid his pains he seem'd to taste
a drop of manna dew," (1. 767.) and he continues to tell her
of his wish to "wipe away all slime left by men-slugs and
human serpentry," and winds up with a passage by far too
pathetic not to be given at length:

--"But who, of men, can tell
That flowers would bloom, or that green fruit would swell
To melting pulp, that fish would have bright mail,
That earth its dower of river, wood, and vale,
The meadows runnels, runnels pebble-stones,
The seed its harvest, or the lute its tones,
Tones ravishment, or ravishment its sweet,
If human souls did never kiss and greet?" P. 42
[I. ll. 835-842.]

"Honey-feels," "honey whispers," which come "re-
freshfully," "obscure and hot hells," "secreter caves,"
"sigh-warm kisses and combing hands which travelling cloy
and tremble through labyrinthine hair," (l. 970) conclude
book the first.

Book the second opens, for the sake of contrast, with
"stiff-holden shields, far-piercing spears, keen blades,
struggling, and blood, and shrieks," and proceeds, without
ceremony, to use very foul language to one "History," who
is represented, like an old country attorney, as a "swart
planet in the universe of deeds." After this Endymion sets
out in search of the moon, and meets with a good-natured
young woman, whose calling may be easily guessed by the
present she offers to make him, of "all her clear-eyed
fish, golden or rainbow-sided, or purplish, vermilion-tail'd,
or finn'd with silv'ry gauze," but he stands on "the pebble
head of doubt," and runs "into the fearful deep to hide his
head from the clear moon (not very wise when he is in
pursuit of her), the trees, and coming madness;" from this
he passes into "a vast antre," where he "seeth" (and this
rhymes to "beneath,)" many things, "which misery most
drowningly doth sing," there he wishes to "noint" his eyes
(l. 325.) which, perhaps, he would do if the poet could
restrain the following burst of inspiration from himself.

"O did he ever live, that lonely man,
Who lov'd--and music slew not? 'Tis the pest
Of love, that fairest joys give most unrest;
That things of delicate and tenderest worth
Are swallow'd all, and made a seared dearth,
By one consuming flame: it doth immerse
And suffocate true blessings in a curse." P. 70.
[II. ll. 364-370.]

This music introduces Adonis between two cupids "a
slumbering," with "a faint damask mouth tenderly unclos'd

to slumbery pout. " And we are told of his coyness to Venus,
"when her lips and eyes were clos'd in sullen moisture, and
quick sighs came vex'd and pettish through her nostrils
small, " (l. 470.) then cupid stands up while "a soverign
quell is in his waving hands, " and "new-born Adon" springs
to life again: the scene very soon shifts, and Endymion
finds "a hurried change" "working within him into something
dreary, vex'd like a morning eagle lost and weary, " (l. 635.)
till Cybele comforts him; she is described as drawn by four
lions, whose "toothed maws" (we presume these lions are
ruminating animals, of a new species, who masticate in the
stomach,)[73] are solemn "their" surly eyes "brow hidden, "
their "heavy paws uplifted drowsily, " and their "nervy tails
cowering their tawny brushes. " When she has done speaking, " 'bove his head flew a delight half-graspable"--but we
must pause here--for Mr. Keats is not contented with a
half initiation into the school he has chosen. And he can
strike from un-meaning absurdity into the gross slang of
voluptuousness with as much skill as the worthy prototype
whom he has selected. We will assure him, however, that
not all the flimsy veil of words in which he would involve
immoral images, can atone for their impurity; and we will
not disgust our readers by retailing to them the artifices of
vicious refinement, by which, under the semblance of
"slippery blisses, twinkling eyes, soft completion of faces,
and smooth excess of hands, " he would palm upon the un-
suspicious and the innocent imaginations better adapted to
the stews.[74]

> "How he does love me; his poor temples beat,
> To the very tune of love! how sweet, sweet, sweet. "
>   B. II. l. 66. [75]

To recur to the story: Endymion next goes into a
"cool wonder" where "whales arbour close to brood and
sulk;" and there he has an interview with Arethusa in the
shape of "a misty spray. "

The third book begins in character, with a jacobinical
apostrophe to "crowns, turbans, and tiptop nothings"; we
wonder how mitres escaped from their usual place. Then
we have "thunder-tents, abysm-births, gentlier-mightiest,
and eterne Apollo"; and are told that the moon makes "old
boughs feel palpitations, and lisp out a holier din, " that she
is "a relief to the poor patient oyster, " and teaches "far-
spooming ocean" how to bow. Moreover, that when Mr.
Keats was a very young man, she (the moon) was all the

following things to him

> "--Thou wast the deep glen;
> Thou wast the mountain-top--the sage's pen--
> The poet's harp--the voice of friends--the sun[76]
> Thou wast the river--thou wast glory won;
> Thou wast the clarion's blast--thou wast my steed--
> My goblet full of wine--my topmost deed:--
> Thou wast the charm of women, lovely moon!" P. 113.
> [III. ll. 163-169.]

Now all this reads very like a rebus, but we have
not yet found any solution to it.   After his last adventure
Endymion meets with a very strange old man, who is right
glad to see him, because, as he says,

> "To northern seas I'll in a twinkle sail,
> And mount upon the snortings of a whale." P. 117
> [III. ll. 245-246.]

This elderly stranger is an acute physiognomist,
and informs him that he knows

> "He cannot feel a drouth,
> By the melancholy corners of his mouth." P. 124.
> [III. ll. 395-396.]

He warbles to him "for very joy mellifluous sorrow,"
gives him a history of some "nectarous camel-droughts"
which he had drank, and concludes with an account of some
"sights too fearful for the feel of fear," which, as far as
we can understand, were nothing more than

> "A tooth, a tusk, and venom-bag, and sting,
> Laughing and wailing, grovelling, serpenting."[77] P. 129.
> [III. ll. 501-502.]

Against "whose eyes (i. e. the eyes of the tooth, task,
venom-bag, and sting) Circe whisked a sooty oil."

> "Until their grieved bodies 'gan to bloat
> And puff from the tail's end to stifled throat." P. 130.
> [III. ll. 525-526.]

And then,

> "The whole herd, as by a whirlwind writhen,
> Went through the dismal air like one hugh Python

Antagonizing Boreas. " P. 130.
[III. ll. 529-531.]

Soon after this there is "a mighty consumation";
"death falls a weeping in his charnel house, " and

"When each their old love found, a murmuring rose,
Like what was never heard in all the throes
Of wind and waters: 'tis past human wit
To tell; 'tis dizziness to think of it. "   P. 144
[III. ll. 824-827.]

"Large Hercules" and "large Neptune" joins the
assembly; Cupid, "empire-sure, " "flutters and laughs";
"Eolus skulks to his cavern 'mid the gruff complaint of all
his rebel tempests, " and the third book comes to an end.

In the beginning of the last book we are informed of
a new discovery in natural history, namely, that there is
"no authentic dew but in the eye of love. " Somebody sings
a very pitiful song to sorrow; and somebody else gets upon
horseback with Endymion, to "win an immortality ere a
lean bat could plump his wintry skin. " While he was on
horseback with this lady, the poet tells us, "so fond, so
beauteous was his bed-fellow, he could not help but kiss her. "
We suspect that some confusion must have arisen here between a pillion and a pillow. When "vespers begin to throe, "
the hero "drops hawkwise to the earth, " where he listens to
another song about some "tender bibbers of rain and dew, "
and raves about his saddle-bed-fellow, who he calls his
"Indian bliss, and river-lily bud, " and asks her for "one
gentle squeeze warm as a dove's nest among summer trees";
but finding himself "enlarged to his hunger, and caught in
trammels of perverse deliciousness, he could bear no more,
and so bent his soul fiercely like a spiritual bow, and
twang'd it inwardly, " till he was able to "trip lightly on in
sort of deathful glee. " In the conclusion "Cynthia bright
Peona kiss'd, and bless'd with fair good night"; Endymion
falls into a swoon, and "Peona went home through the
gloomy wood in wonderment"; a feeling which we are by no
means surprized that she should entertain after all that had
happened.

We do most solemnly assure our readers that this
poem, containing 4074 lines, is printed on very nice hot-
pressed paper, and sold for nine shillings, by a very respectable London bookseller. Moreover, that the author has

put his name in the title page, and told us, that though he
is something between man and boy, he means by and by to
be "plotting and fitting himself for verses fit to live."[78]
We think it necessary to add that it is all written in rhyme,
and, for the most part, (when there are syllables enough)
in the heroic couplet.

7.   Two letters on Endymion in the Morning Chronicle

         (On October 3 and October 8, 1818, two letters
     attacking Croker's review in the Quarterly appeared
     in this newspaper.   H. B. and M. B. Forman reprint
     them in their Hampstead Edition of Keats [II, 268-
     270].   The letter signed "J. S." was probably
     written, as Sidney Colvin claimed, by John Scott
     [John Keats (London, 1917), p. 167 n.].[79] J. S.
     states that he was first led to Keats's poem by the
     unfavorable review of the Quarterly, but this may
     simply be a pretense. (See note 80 below.)   The
     Champion had reviewed Endymion in June; and Scott,
     either as author of this review or editor of this
     newspaper, probably read Keats's poem at this
     time.   The identity of the author of the second
     letter, who signed himself "R. B.," is not known.
         Keats comments on his two defenders in a letter
     of October 8, 1818 to his publisher, James Hessey.
     "You are very good in sending me the letters from
     the Chronicle....   I cannot but feel indebted to
     these Gentlemen who have taken my part--As for
     the rest, I begin to get acquainted with my own
     strength and weakness. --Praise or blame have but
     a momentary effect on the man whose love of beauty
     in the abstract makes him a severer critic on his
     own Works.   My own domestic criticism has given
     me pain without comparison beyond what Blackwood
     or the Quarterly could possibly inflict....   J. S. is
     perfectly right in regard to the slip-shod Endymion."
     [Letters, I, 373-374.])

                                        [October 3, 1818]

         To the EDITOR of the MORNING CHRONICLE

SIR,

Although I am aware that literary squabbles are of
too uninteresting and interminable a nature for your Journal,
yet there are occasions when acts of malice and gross injustice towards an author may be properly brought before
the public through such a medium. --Allow me, then, without
further preface, to refer you to an article in the last Number of The Quarterly Review, professing to be a Critique on
"The Poems of John Keats." Of John Keats I know nothing;
from his Preface I collect that he is very young--no doubt
a heinous sin; and I have been informed that he has incurred
the additional guilt of an acquaintance with Mr. Leigh Hunt.
That this latter Gentleman and the Editor of The Quarterly
Review have long been at war, must be known to every one
in the least acquainted with the literary gossip of the day.
Mr. L. Hunt, it appears, has thought highly of the poetical
talents of Mr. Keats; hence Mr. K. is doomed to feel the
merciless tomahawk of the Reviewers, termed Quarterly, I
presume from the modus operandi. From a perusal of the
criticism, I was led to the work itself. [80] I would, Sir,
that your limits would permit a few extracts from this poem.
I dare appeal to the taste and judgment of your readers,
that beauties of the highest order may be found in almost
every page--that there are also many, very many passages
indicating haste and carelessness, I will not deny; I will go
further, and assert that a real friend of the author would
have disuaded him from an immediate publication.

Had the genius of Lord Byron sunk under the dis-
couraging sneers of an Edinburgh Review the nineteenth
century would scarcely yet have been termed the Augustan
æra of poetry. Let Mr. Keats too persevere--he has talents
of common stamp;[81] this is the hastily written tribute of a
stranger, who ventures to predict that Mr. K. is capable of
producing a poem that shall challenge the admiration of
every reader of true taste and feeling; nay if he will give up
his acquaintance with Mr. Leigh Hunt, and apostatise in his
friendships, his principles and his politics (if he have any),
he may even command the approbation of the Quarterly Review.

I have not heard to whom public opinion has assigned
this exquisite morceau of critical acumen. If the Translator
of Juvenal[82] be its author, I would refer him to the manly
and pathetic narrative prefixed to that translation, to the
touching history of genius oppressed by and struggling with

innumerable difficulties, yet finally triumphing under <u>patron-
age and encouragement.</u>   If the Biographer of Kirke White[83]
have done Mr. Keats this cruel wrong, let him remember
his own just and feeling expostulation with the Monthly Reviewer, who <u>"sat down to blast the hopes of a boy, who had
confessed to him all his hopes and all his difficulties.</u>"[84]
If the 'Admiralty Scribe'[85] (for he too is a Reviewer) be
the critic, let him compare the "Battle of Talavera" with
"Endymion."

I am, Sir,

Your obedient servant,

J. S.

[October 8, 1818]

To the EDITOR of the MORNING CHRONICLE

SIR,

The spirited and feeling remonstrance of your Correspondent J. S. against the cruelty and injustice of the Quarterly Review, has most ably anticipated the few remarks
which I had intended to address to you on the subject.   But
your well known liberality in giving admission to every thing
calculated to do justice to oppressed and injured merit, induces me to trespass further on your valuable columns, by
a few extracts from Mr. Keat's [sic] Poem.   As the Reviewer professes to have read only the first book, I have
confined my quotations to that part of the Poem; and I leave
your readers to judge whether the Critic who could pass
over such beauties as these lines contain, and condemn the
whole Poem as "consisting of the most incongruous ideas
in the most uncouth language," is very implicitly to be relied on.

I am, Sir, your obedient servant,

Temple, Oct. 3, 1818   R. B.

> [After the signature the following excerts from
> Book I of <u>Endymion</u> are quoted: ll. 163-184, 231-
> 305, 453-463, 721-738, 797-831.]

8.   J. H. Reynolds' "The Quarterly Review--Mr. Keats"
      in the Alfred, West of England Journal and General
      Advertiser[86]

> (This defense, reprinted by the Formans in the
> Hampstead edition of Keats [II, 260-267] and later
> by Leonidas F. Jones [Selected Prose of John
> Hamilton Reynolds (Cambridge, Mass., 1966), pp.
> 225-230] originally appeared in the Alfred on
> October 6, 1818. Reynolds' authorship is ac-
> knowledged by Keats in a journal letter of October
> 14-31, 1818 to his brother and sister-in-law,
> George and Georgiana. Like Keats's defenders in
> the Morning Chronicle, Reynolds ignores the attack
> of Blackwood's, choosing instead to direct his com-
> ments to Croker's article in the Quarterly Review.
> As J. S. did in the Chronicle, Reynolds also makes
> it perfectly clear that the Quarterly's attack on
> Keats was politically inspired.)

We have met with a singular instance, in the last
number of the Quarterly Review, of that unfeeling arrogance,
and cold ignorance, which so strongly marked the minds and
hearts of Government sycophants and Government writers.
The Poem of a young man of genius, which evinces more
natural power than any other work of this day, is abused
and cried down, in terms which would disgrace any other
pens than those used in the defence of an Oliver or a
Castles. [87] We have read the Poetic Romance of Endymion
(the book in question) with no little delight; and could hardly
believe that it was written by so young a man as the preface
infers. [88] Mr. Keats, the author of it, is a genius of the
highest order; and no one but a Lottery Commissioner and
Government Pensioner, (both of which, Mr. William Gifford,
the Editor of the Quarterly Review, is) [89] could, with a
false and remorseless pen, have striven to frustrate hopes
and aims, so youthful and so high as this young Poet nurses.
The Monthly Reviewers, it will be remembered, endeavoured
some few years back, to crush the rising heart of Kirk [sic]
White; and indeed they in part generated that melancholy
which ultimately destroyed him;[90] but the world saw the
cruelty, and with one voice, hailed the genius which
malignity would have repressed, and lifted it to fame.   Reviewers are creatures that "stab men in the dark:"[91] --young
and enthusiastic spirits are their dearest prey.   Our readers
will not easily forget the brutality with which the Quarterly
Reviewers, in a late number of their ministerial book, com-

mented on the work of an intelligent and patriotic woman, [92]
whose ardour and independence happened to be high enough to
make them her enemies. The language used by these
Government critics, was lower than man would dare to utter
to female ears; but Party knows no distinctions, --no pro-
prieties, --and a woman is the best of prey for its malignity,
because it [sic] is the gentlest and the most undefended.
We certainly think that Criticism might vent its petty passions on other subjects; that it might chuse its objects from
the vain, the dangerous, and the powerful, and not from the
young and the unprotected.

> "It should strike hearts of age and care,
> And spare the youthful and the fair."[93]

The cause of the unmerciful condemnation which has
been passed on Mr. Keats, is pretty apparent to all who
have watched the intrigues of literature, and the wily and unsparing contrivances of political parties. This young and
powerful writer was noticed some little time back, in the
Examiner;[94] and pointed out, by its Editor, as one who was
likely to revive the early vigour of English poetry. Such a
prediction was a fine, but dangerous compliment, to Mr.
Keats: it exposed him instantly to the malice of the Quarterly Review. Certain it is, that hundreds of fashionable
and flippant readers, will henceforth set down this young
Poet as a pitiable and nonsensical writer, merely on the
assertions of some single heartless critic, who has just
energy enough to despise what is good, because it would
militate against his pleasantry, if he were to praise it.

The genius of Mr. Keats is peculiarly classical; and,
with the exception of a few faults, which are the natural
followers of youth, his imagination and his language have a
spirit and an intensity which we should in vain look for in
half the popular poets of the day. Lord Byron is a splendid
and noble egotist. --He visits classical shores; roams over
romantic lands, and wanders through magnificent forests;
courses the dark and restless waves of the sea, and rocks
his spirit on the midnight lakes; but no spot is conveyed to
our minds, that is not peopled by the gloomy and ghastly
feelings of one proud and solitary man. It is as if he and
the world were the only two things which the air clothed. --
His lines are majestic vanities;--his poetry always is marked
with a haughty selfishness;--he writes loftily, because he is
the spirit of an ancient family;--he is liked by most of his
readers, because he is a Lord. If a common man were to

dare to be as moody, as contemptuous, and as misanthropical,
the world would laugh at him.   There must be a coronet
marked on all his little pieces of poetical insolence, or the
world would not countenance them.   Mr. Keats has none of
this egotism--this daring selfishness, which is a stain on the
robe of poesy--His feelings are full, earnest, and original,
as those of the olden writers were and are; they are made
for all time, not for the drawing-room and the moment.
Mr. Keats always speaks of, and describes nature, with an
awe and a humility, but with a deep and almost breathless
affection. --He knows that Nature is better and older than he
is, and he does not put himself on an equality with her.
You do not see him, when you see her.   The moon, and the
mountainous foliage of the woods, and the azure sky, and the
ruined and magic temple; the rock, the desart, and the sea;
the leaf of the forest, and the embossed foam of the most
living ocean, are the spirits of his poetry; but he does not
bring them in his own hand, or obtrude his person before
you, when you are looking at them.   Poetry is a thing of
generalities--a wanderer amid persons and things--not a
pauser over one thing, or with one person.   The mind of Mr.
Keats, like the minds of our older poets, goes round the
universe in its speculations and its dreams.   It does not set
itself a task.   The manners of the world, the fictions and
wonders of other worlds, are its subjects; not the pleasures
of hope, or the pleasures of memory. 95   The true poet con-
fines his imagination to no one thing--his soul is an invisible ode to the passions. 96   --He does not make a home for
his mind in one land--its productions are an universal story,
not an eastern tale. 97   The fancies of Moore are exquisitely
beautiful, as fancies, but they are always of one colour;--
his feelings are pathetic, but they are "still harping on my
daughter."98   The true pathetic is to be found in the reflections on things, not in the moods and miseries of one
person.   There is not one poet of the present day, that enjoys any popularity that will live; each writes for his booksellers and the ladies of fashion, and not for the voice of
centuries.   Time is a lover of old books, and he suffers
few new ones to become old.   Posterity is a difficult mark
to hit; and few minds can send the arrow full home.   Wordsworth might have safely cleared the rapids in the stream of
time, but he lost himself by looking at his own image in
the waters.   Coleridge stands bewildered in the cross-road
of fame;--his genius will commit suicide, and be buried in
it.   Southey is Poet Laureate, "so there is no heed to be
taken of him."99   Campbell has relied on two stools, "The
Pleasures of Hope," and "Gertrude of Wyoming," but he

will come to the ground, after the fashion of the old proverb. The journey of fame is an endless one; and does Mr. Rogers think that pumps and silk stockings (which his genius wears) will last him the whole way?   Poetry is the coyest creature that ever was wooed by man: she has something of the coquette in her; for she flirts with many, and seldom loves one.

Mr. Keats has certainly not perfected any thing yet; but he has the power, we think, within him, and it is in consequence of such an opinion that we have written these few hasty observations.   If he should ever see this, he will not regret to find that all the country is not made up of Quarterly Reviewers.   All that we wish is, that our Readers would read the Poem, as we have done, before they assent to its condemnation--they will find passages of singular feeling, force, and pathos.   We have the brightest hopes of this young Poet.   We are obscure men, it is true, and not gifted with the perilous power of mind, and truth of judgment, which are possessed by Mr. Croker, Mr. Canning, Mr. Bar- row, or Mr. Gifford, (all "honourable men," and writers in the Quarterly Review).   We live far from the world of let- ters, --out of the pale of fashionable criticism, --aloof from the atmosphere of a Court; but we are surrounded by a beautiful country, and love Poetry, which we read out of doors, as well as in.   We think we see glimpses of a high mind in this young man, and surely the feeling is better that urges us to nourish its strength, than that which prompts the Quarterly Review to crush it in its youth, and for ever. If, however, the mind of Mr. Keats be of the quality we think it to be of, it will not be cast down by this wanton and empty attack.   Malice is a thing of the scorpion--It drives the sting into its own heart.   The very passages which the Quarterly Review quotes as ridiculous, have in them the beauty that sent us to the Poem itself. [100]   We shall close these observations with a few extracts from the romance itself:--If our Readers do not see the spirit and beauty in them to justify our remarks, we confess ourselves bad judges, and never more worthy to be trusted.

The following address to Sleep, is full of repose and feeling:--

"O magic sleep! Oh comfortable bird,
That broodest o'er the troubled sea of the mind,
Till it is hush'd and smooth! O unconfined
Restraint! Imprisoned Liberty! Great key

To golden palaces, strange minstrelsy,
Fountains grotesque, new trees, bespangled caves,
Echoing grottoes, full of tumbling waves,
And moonlight!"

[I. 11. 453-460.]

This is beautiful--but here is something finer,

"--That men, who might have tower'd in the van
Of all the congregated world, to fan
And winnow from the coming step of time,
All chaff of custom, wipe away all slime
Left by men slugs and human serpentry,
Have been content to let occasion die,
Whilst they did sleep in Love's Elysium.
And truly I would rather be struck dumb,
Than speak again this ardent listlessness:
For I have ever thought that it might bless
The world with benefits unknowingly;
As does the nightingale up-perched high,
And cloister'd among cool and bunched leaves,
She sings but to her love, nor e'er conceives
How tiptoe night holds back her dark grey hood."

[I. 11. 817-831.]

The turn of this is truly Shakesperian [sic], which
Mr. Keats will feel to be the highest compliment we can
pay him, if we know any thing of his mind.   We cannot refrain from giving the following short passage, which appears
to us scarcely to be surpassed in the whole range of English
Poetry.   It has all the naked and solitary vigour of old
sculpture, with all the energy and life of old poetry:--

"--At this, with madden'd stare,
And lifted hands, and trembling lips he stood,
Like old Deucalion mounted o'er the flood,
Or blind Orion hungry for the morn."

[II. 11. 195-198.]

Again, we give some exquisitely classical lines, clear
and reposing as a Grecian sky--soft and lovely as the waves
of Ilyssus.

"--Here is wine,
Alive with sparkles. --Never, I aver,
Since Ariadne was a vintager,
So cool a purple; taste these juicy pears,

Sent me by sad Vertumnus, when his fears
Were high upon Pomona: here is cream,
Deepening to sickness from a snowy gleam;
Sweeter than that nurse Amalthea skimm'd
For the boy Jupiter. "

[II. ll. 441-449.]

This is the very fruit of poetry. --A melting repast
for the imagination.   We can only give one more extract--
our limits are reached.   Mr. Keats is speaking of the story
of Endymion itself.   Nothing can be more imaginative than
what follows:

"--Ye who have yearn'd
With too much passion, will here stay and pity,
For the mere sake of truth; as 'tis a ditty
Not of these days, but long ago 'twas told
By a cavern'd wind unto a forest old;
And then the forest told it in a dream
To a sleeping lake, whose cool and level gleam
A Poet caught as he was journeying
To Phoebus' shrine; and in it he did fling
His weary limbs, bathing an hour's space,
And after, straight in that inspired place
He sang the story up into the air,
Giving it universal freedom. "

[II. ll. 827-839.]

We have no more room for extracts.   Does the author
of such poetry as this deserve to be made the sport of so
servile a dolt as a Quarterly Reviewer?--No.   Two things
have struck us on the perusal of this singular poem.   The
first is, that Mr. Keats excels, in what Milton excelled--
the power of putting a spirit of life and novelty into the
Heathen Mythology.   The second is, that in the structure of
his verse, and the sinewy quality of his thoughts, Mr. Keats
greatly resembles old Chapman, the nervous translator of
Homer.   His mind has "thews and limbs like to its an-
cestors. "[101] Mr. Gifford, who knows something of the old
dramatists, [102] ought to have paused before he sanctioned
the abuse of a spirit kindred with them.   If he could not
feel, he ought to know better.

9.   A short review of Endymion in the Sun

(The following brief but favorable commentary

appeared on October 21, 1818 under the heading
"LITERARY REVIEW." The author is not known,
but it is significant that the review appeared in a
Tory newspaper. The reviewer quotes from and
contradicts Croker's article in the <u>Quarterly</u>. Obviously, there was a feeling among some fair-
minded Tories that the attack on Keats was un-
justified.

   The <u>Sun</u> continued to favor Keats through 1820,
and the reason for it may have been that Richard
Woodhouse, a friend of Keats and literary and legal
advisor to Keats's publishers, has access to the
newspaper. Woodhouse is the author of a review
of Keats's <u>Lamia</u> volume that appeared in the <u>Sun</u>
on July 10, 1820. [See Chapter Four, item 3.])

We present our Readers with a few more extracts
from this Work, 103 evidently the production of a young man
of considerable genius, and we think of much promise. The
Poem has certainly many faults, and betrays throughout more
carelessness than is quite pardonable in a young author
making his first appearance before an enlightened, and even
a fastidious public. But this carelessness seems to proceed
from a bold consciousness of superior powers; and in almost
every page are to be found passages of the highest poetical
merit, and marks of the most elegant fancy. We regret that
he should have given any occasion for the severe remarks
which have recently been made on him; but h e has shewn that
he possesses not only "powers of language, rays of fancy,
and gleams of genius,"104 but a strength of mind and an
ardour of pursuit which will enable him, we trust, to achieve
something truly great, and "fit to live."105

We have merely selected a few passages from various
parts of the Poem, without attempting a regular criticism,
or a sketch of the plan of the work, which would exceed our
present limits.

   [Quotes from Endymion, I. ll. 169-184, 466-474,
   672-678; II. ll. 393-419; III. ll. 52-66, 318-321,
   338-341; IV. ll. 119-124; II. ll. 639-649. These
   excerpts, which fill almost a complete column,
   constitute the bulk of the review.]

10. The <u>Examiner</u> reprints a defense of Keats
     from the <u>Chester Guardian</u>

(The following reprint from an unavailable copy
of the Chester Guardian appeared in the Examiner
for November 1, 1818, p. 696. Although long
known to exist, it is presented here for the first
time.)

Mr. Keats's Endymion--We are happy to add the following valuable testimony to the various ones that have come
forward on this occasion and shewn their contempt of the
would-be authorities whom the public are so rapidly leaving
behind them:[106] --"It must be evident to all who are acquainted with the extent of the province of poetry, that there
is a mountainous part of it where the atmosphere is too rare
for common breathing; in other words, that a very high
degree of poetical inspiration exists which cannot be made
popular.   Such we fear is the case with Mr. Keats's Endymion, which calls for a knowledge of the more erudite or
second sense of classical mythology.   Thus, in the Hymn
to Pan, we are called to a glance not only of the more
pastoral Diety, but to that typification of general nature, the
great and mystic Pan, who, as an universal intelligence,
formed one of the fine indistinct dreams of antiquity.   Where
this sort of apprehension has been acquired, the lines will
be doubly relished; but even by the less informed, making
a little allowance for the Arcadian cast of the scenery, the
beauty and felicity of the rural imagery and painting will
be duly appreciated.   Mr. Keats has evidently borrowed his
taste from the school of which Milton is the head, and those
who are thoroughly acquainted with Lycidas, Comus, and the
Faithful Shepherdess, [107] will feel the Masters in the Disciple.   We observe all this in the face of a contemptible
piece of flippancy in the Quarterly Review, intended to put
down the young aspirant, because forsooth, his politics and
friendships are not agreeable to the managers of that liberal
vehicle.   Injustice of this kind, too, may be ventured; first,
because he is young, and hope, at such a season, may, with
some temperaments, be depressed almost to annihilation;
secondly, his subject cannot be felt generally, consequently
the mob who wait for these quarterly oracles to tell them
what to admire, may the more easily be wrought upon.
How well principled and magnanimous all this!   One thing,
however, is comfortable, it is almost too late in the day
for such sort of oppression to succeed, and in the present
instance it has happily failed. "--The Chester Guardian.

11.   Three sonnets to Keats in Hunt's Foliage

> (Although Foliage was published in March 1818,
> Hunt's poems to Keats are included at this point
> for purposes of continuity with items 12 and 13.
> The poems to Keats appeared on pp. cxxv-cxxvii of
> Hunt's volume. Hunt's sonnet "To John Keats"
> was reprinted in the Alfred for October 13, 1818.)

TO JOHN KEATS

'Tis well you think me truly one of those,
Whose sense discerns the loveliness of things;
For surely as I feel the bird that sings
Behind the leaves, or dawn as it up grows,
Or the rich bee rejoicing as he goes,
Or the glad issue of emerging springs,
Or overhead the glide of a dove's wings,
Or turf, or trees, or, midst of all, repose.
And surely as I feel things lovelier still,
The human look, and the harmonious form
Containing woman, and the smile in ill,
And such a heart as Charles's,[108] wise and warm, --
As surely as all this, I see, ev'n now,
Young Keats, a flowering laurel on your brow.[109]

ON RECEIVING A CROWN OF IVY FROM THE SAME

A crown of ivy! I submit my head
To the young hand that gives it, --young, 'tis true,
But with a right, for 'tis a poet's too.
How pleasant the leaves feel! and how they spread
With their broad angles, like a nodding shed
Over both eyes! and how complete and new,
As on my hand I lean, to feel them strew
My sense with freshness, --Fancy's rustling bed!
Tress-tossing girls, with smell of flowers and grapes
Come dancing by, and downward piping cheeks,
And up-thrown cymbals, and Silenus old
Lumpishly borne, and many trampling shapes, --
And lastly, with his bright eyes on her bent,
Bacchus, --whose bride has of his hand fast hold.

ON THE SAME

It is a lofty feeling, yet a kind,
Thus to be topped with leaves;--to have a sense
Of honour-shaded thought, --an influence
As from great Nature's fingers, and be twined
With her old, sacred, verdurous ivy-bind,
As though she hallowed with that sylvan fence
A head that bows to her benevolence,
Midst pomp of fancied trumpets in the wind.
'Tis what's within us crowned.   And kind and great
Are all the conquering wishes it inspires, --
Love of things lasting, love of the tall woods,
Love of love's self, and ardour for a state
Of natural good befitting such desires,
Towns without gain, and haunted solitudes.

12.   A burlesque of Hunt by "Beppo"
        in the Literary Journal

> (The following lampoon, noted before but re-
> produced here for the first time, appeared in the
> Literary Journal on March 20, 1819, p. 192.   In
> May 1818 this same weekly had reviewed Endymion
> favorably; now, less than one year later, it printed
> a parody which ridiculed the poetry of Hunt and
> Keats.   Clearly, the effects of the Tory attack of
> 1818 were still in evidence.
> The identity of Beppo is not known, but he de-
> rived his pseudonym from Byron's satire of the
> same name, which was published in 1818.   The
> motto at the head of Beppo's poem is a burlesque
> of the opening lines of Hunt's sonnet "To John
> Keats. ")

PLEASANT WALKS;

A COCKNEY PASTORAL,

In the manner of Leigh Hunt, Esq.

" 'Tis well I see the beautiful of things"--Myself

'Tis well I see the beautiful of things,
Else, K--, there thousands are who wouldn't see

Scarce any thing, in this most stupid age,
Worth calling poetry.
Aye, and it's well, too, I do not engage
To any niceties of measure in my rhyme,
Because, such beautiful thoughts as I,
At times, let fly,
Would, were they confin'd,
Before and behind
By your silky Pope-like tethers, [110] be,
Like over-fondled children--ill and rickety.

You know, K. I sometimes use your little lines
That drop,
In this short manner, like a rotten prop
From under a bunch of streaky woodbines,
Letting the whole beautiful superstructure
Of my flowers poetical,
Whate'er I cull,
Fall smack adown upon the muddy ground,
Scattering, all o'er every where around,
Their perfumes into air!
Wonder ye?--poo! now none of your scurvy jokes--
I cannot bear to do like other folks.
What! waste my time in measurings and rules?[111]
Let Byron, Scott, and Campbell--precious fools!
Be, to such things, mere mercenary tools.
'Tis well for them to trim old-madish wings,
But I can see--"the beautiful of things."

Listen, (if Nature's loveliness ought bind ye)
Whom kindred wanderings have brought behind me,
And I will map ye out some pleasant walks,
O'er furrowy lands, and green grass banks,
Where Nature hath dropt her wild, unpolish'd showers,
And bought up heaps of wild unpolish'd flowers,
And unfurl'd,
The glorious forest world.
How nice it is to stray all among brooks,
In dark green nooks,
That, hid in their drowsy windings, snore,
In their stuff'd up, rushy, weedy beds,
Dreamingly: how sweet to see
The glib eel, nibbling hastily
The newly-caught worm, held by her neck fast,
Making his summer breakfast:
Or hear the hoarse frog,
In the reedy bog,
Singing the poor worm's elegy.

How sweet to stroll up chequer'd lanes and highways,
(Provided they are bye-ways)
To feel the soft come-o'er-ye-breeze, that dreads,
As 'twere, to touch your hatty heads,
Lest it should ruffle your curly locks,
And fling your beavers
Into the unaccomodating, saucy rivers;--
A sweet breeze, that won't set you in the stocks
Of coughy colds, and still-limb'd catarrhs,
And such-like stay-at-home wars,
As we, in playing life's poor game at loo,
Are subject to!

And, O! to ramble all about some heath--
A lovely one--(and not
One like Hampstead's up-and-down pathy spot) 112
To take, as 'twere a pill, a breath
Of nutmeg-smelling air, cutting, like knife,
From off our lungs the city's filthy soot,
And smoke to boot;
So as to bless,
And raise to liveliness,
With freshening draughts, the nauseous-cup of life;
Especially where the sun-toasted gypsies,
Hang out, all over the branched trees,
Their sunny draperies
Because, in our ramblings, we
Like good company.
Like you this plumage of my muse's wings?
Ah! I can see the "beautiful of things."
Do you not like where a dark wood covers,
With her leafy hood all things, and hovers
Above some up-hill and down-dale track,
(The sun in your face, and the wind in your back,)
To go, and see the industrious pig root up
The buried acorn, where the oaks shoot up,
Making itself "green head-dresses," 113
And "leafy wildernesses,"
Lovely dryad!--and the "young-eyed" lambs
That walk by their dams,
With their milk-white dresses, 114
And their light prettinesses,
And feet that go skipity-skip!
And the sage cow,
That munches the drooping newly-clad bough,
Hanging its fresh'ning leaves o'er her head
And her back's glossy red;

O! these are objects for Castalian springs!
But I, you know, can see "the beautiful of things!"
Stop!--there's something of the gypsies, O dear,
I forgot to mention: I'll do it here.
Like not ye to sit with them and chat,
And all that,
(Beneath the over-hanging bunchy leaves,)
With that enlighten'd, independent few!
I love it, K--, and so, I think, do you;
For theirs, look ye,
Whom kindred fancies have brought after me,
Is, like the quiv'ring blown-off leaves
On which they tread, real unpoluted liberty,
That never grieves!
And love ye not to walk where flings
Some old wind-mill her muttering flys about?
Or like ye, where some white-wash'd farms peep out,
To hear the clapping of the old hens' wings,
Where the quick wind, round the hay-stack sings
A delicious tune,
In the month of June,
When the sun pops out,
And spreads, all about
The cornfields' yellow dress,
His yellower loveliness?
And, O! to hear the rural ding-a-dings,
Where the sweet little old village church up springs
Its dumpy spire, becrown'd
With tall trees, and ivy-bound!--
Don't, don't I paint the--"the beautiful of things?"

                                                    Beppo

13.   Blackwood's "Cockney School of Poetry.   No. VI."

        (This article, which appeared in October 1819
     [VI, 70-76], is a review of Foliage. It was written
     by either or both Lockhart and Wilson, who signed
     themselves "Z." The excerpt relating to Keats that
     follows is from pp. 75-76. Although noted before, it
     is reproduced here for the first time.)

     [The reviewer speaks of Hunt's love of himself.]   Then
follows a sonnet to John Keats,

'Tis well you think me truly one of those
Whose sense discerns the loveliness of things, &c.

And then again comes another sonnet on "receiving a crown of ivy from the same."

[The octave of Hunt's sonnet is quoted.]

This sonnet presents to us a very laughable picture, which, spite of Mr. Hunt's decease, [115] we hope there can be no great harm in enjoying. Mr. John Keats was, we believe, at this time, a young apothecary, and if, instead of crowning poor Mr. Hunt with ivy, he had clapped a blister upon his head, he would have acted in a way much more suitable to his profession. Such an opportunity probably never occurred again. Well--behold the Cockney--strutting about the room, for we hope there was no "out of doors"[116] exposure, with his ivy-crown, dressing gown, yellow breeches, and red slippers--followed, in all his movements by young Esculapius, [117] and ever and anon coquetting with himself in the magic mirror. No doubt, he rung the bell for the ladies, and the children, and the servants, and probably sent out his favorite "washer-woman."[118] When he dressed for dinner, did the ivy wreath still continue to deck his regal temples? Did he sip tea in it? Play a rubber of whist? And finally, did he go to bed in it--and, if so, did he shroud its glories in a night-cap, or did he lay his head on the pillow like Bacchus by the side of Ariadne? All these little interesting circumstantialities are, no doubt, mentioned in his autobiography.

But one sonnet--two sonnets to John Keats, do not suffice--and we have a third "on the same."

[Quotes the first nine lines of Hunt's sonnet beginning "It is a lofty feeling...."]

There is a pair of blockheads for you! John Keats has no more right to dress up Leigh Hunt in this absurd fashion, than he had to tar and feather him--and we do not doubt, that if Leigh Hunt had ever had the misfortune to have been tarred and feathered, he would have written a sonnet on his plumification, and described himself as a Bird of Paradise.

[The reviewer then speaks of the "idolatry" of Reynolds and "of a certain [unnamed and unidentified] Doctor" towards Hunt.]

See what it is to be a favourite of Apollo! Apothecaries and physicians flock in upon you from every side. -- And well might it be said of-- --, M. D. , in reference to Keats and Reynolds,

> "The force of nature could not farther go--
> To make one Fool, she joined the other two."119

Z.

14.   John Wilson in Blackwood's alludes to Keats in
       a review of Hunt's Literary Pocketbook for 1820
       published in December 1819)

> (In his Literary Pocketbook, a combination of
> annual calendar and literary almanac, Hunt prints
> for the first time Keats's sonnets "The Human
> Seasons" and "To Ailsa Rock." Blackwood's re-
> viewed Hunt's publication in December 1819 [VI,
> 235-247]. During the course of the unsigned re-
> view, the author reveals that he is Christopher
> North [the pseudonym of John Wilson]. The ex-
> cerpts relating to Keats that follow are from pp.
> 219-220; they have been reprinted only in part by
> MacGillivray, pp. 67-68.)

Two sonnets, with the signature I., we opine to be
the property of the "Muse's Son of Promise,"--two feats
of Johnny Keates." We cannot be mistaken of them. Whatever be the name of the supposed father--Tims or Tom-
kins[120] --Johnny Keates gignated these sonnets. To each
of them we may say,

> "Sleep image of thy Father, sleep my Boy!"[121]

As we are anxious to bring this young writer into
notice, we quote his sonnets.

> ["The Human Seasons" and "To Ailsa Rock" follow.]

The first of these compositions is very well--a common and hackneyed thought is illustrated in a novel and also
natural manner--and we thank Mr. Keates for his sonnet.
But who but himself could form a collocation of words to
produce such portentuous folly as in the second? Mister
John Keates standing on the sea-shore at Dunbar, without
a neckcloth, according to the custom of Cockaigne, and
cross-questioning the Craig of Ailsa!

> "Thou answerest not for thou art dead asleep!"
> [l. 9 of Keats's sonnet.]

This reminds us of an exclamation in an ode lately
submitted to our perusal by an ingenious and modest young
man, in which, about half way down, he exclaims, as if
prophetically, "READER AWAKE!" There is much smart-
ness in the idea of "two dead eternities."[122] An eternity

especially, past with whales, is enough to make the stoutest
reader blubber.   Do not let John Keates think we dislike
him.   He is a young man of some poetry; but at present he
has no more than about a dozen admirers, --Mr Leigh Hunt
whom he feeds on the oil-cakes of flattery till he becomes
flatulent of praise, --Mr Benjamin Haydon, who used to laugh
at him till that famous sonnet--123 three engrossing clerks--
and six or seven medical students, who chaunt portions of
Endymion as they walk the hospitals, because the author was
once an apothecary.   We alone like him and laugh at him.
He is at present a very amiable, silly, lisping, and prag-
matical young gentleman--but we hope to cure him of all
that--and should have much pleasure in introducing him to
our readers in a year or two speaking the language of this
country, counting his fingers correctly, and condescending
to a neckcloth.

*   *   *

It would greatly amuse us, to meet in company together Johnny Keates and Percy Bysshe Shelley, --and as
they are both friends of Mr Leigh Hunt, we do not despair
of witnessing the conjunction of these planets on Hampstead
Hill, when we visit London in spring.   A bird of praise and
a Friezeland fowl would not look more absurdly, on the
same perch.   Hear with what a deep voice of inspiration
Shelley speaks. 124

[Quotes Shelley's poem, "Marianne's Dream, "
which appeared in Hunt's Literary Pocketbook.]...

15.   A review of Endymion in Baldwin's London Magazine

(This favorable, sympathetic review "From A
Correspondent" appeared in Baldwin's for April
1820 [II, 380-389].   It is assigned by Haydon
[The Romantic Reviewers, p. 283] to P. G. Patmore, but without confirming evidence.   The
article, reproduced here for the first time, is an
important turning point in Keats's reputation.   It
ushered in a widespread reaction against the Tory
attacks of 1818, a reaction which was to continue
throughout 1820 and 1821.)

(From A Correspondent)

That the periodical criticism of the present day, <u>as</u>
criticism enjoys but a slender portion of public respect, --
except among mere book-buyers and blue-stockings;--cannot
be denied. It would be unjust not to confess that it has its
uses. But, in return, it has its reward. The public, and
public critics, mutually serve and despise each other; and
if both, for the most part, know that this is the case, the
latter are too politic to complain of injustice, and the
former too indolent to resent it. Each party is content to
accept the evil with the good. But a feeling much stronger
than that of contempt has attached itself to this part of the
public press, in consequence of certain attempts of modern
criticism to blight and wither the maturity of genius; or--
still worse--to change its youthful enthusiasm into despair,
and thus tempt it to commit suicide; or--worst of all--to
creep to its cradle, and strangle it in the first bloom and
beauty of its childhood. To feel that all this has been attempted, and most of it effected, by modern criticism, we
need only pronounce to ourselves the names of Chatterton
and Kirke White among the dead, of Montgomery, [125] and
Keats, and Wordsworth among the living;--not to mention
Byron, Shelley, Hunt, &c. It is only necessary to refer,
in particular, to the first four of these names; for the
others, with an equal share of poetic "ambition," have less
of "the illness does attend it;"[126] --less of its over-refine-
ment and morbid sensibility.

The miraculous boy, Chatterton, might have been
alive, glorying in, and glorifying himself, his country, and
his age at this day, if he had not encountered a shallow-
thoughted and cold-blooded critic:[127] for though he was one
of the true "children of the sun"[128] of poetry, his more
than human power was linked to more than human weakness.
Poor Kirke White, too! different as they were in almost
every thing--the one a star, the other a flower--yet both
received their light and beauty from the same sun, and both
participated in the same fate. To think that the paltry drudge
of a bookseller[129] should be permitted to trample in the dirt
of a review such as amaranthine flower as this--worthy as
it was, to have bloomed in the very Eden of Poetry!--And
what had the brilliant, and witty, and successful creator of a
new era in criticism to do with the plaintive and tender
Montgomery?[130]--If he was too busy or too happy to discover any music in sighs, or any beauties in tears, at least
he might have been too philosophical, or too good-natured, to

laugh at them.   Suppose the poet did indulge a little too
much in the "luxury of grief,"[131]--if it was weakness, at
least it was not hypocrisy; and there was small chance of
it infecting either the critic or his readers--so that he
exhibited little either of skill or courage in going out of his
way to pick a quarrel with it.   The poet, with all his fine
powers, has scarcely yet recovered from the effects of the
visitation; and the critic, with all his cleverness, never
will.

It would lead us too far from our present purpose, --
and indeed does not belong to it, --to do more than refer to
the exploits of the same work against the early attempts of
the two writers who at present share the poetic throne of
the day.[132]   Whatever else they might want, these attacks
had at least boldness; and they could do little mischief, for
the objects of them were armed at all points against the
assault.   It is not to these latter, but to such as those on
Kirke White and Montgomery, and a late one on the work
which we are about to notice,[133] that the periodical criticism
of the day owes that resentment and indignation which is at
present felt against it, by the few whose praise (in matters
of literature) is not censure.   To make criticism subser-
vient to pecuniary or ambitious views is poor and paltry
enough; but there is some natural motive, and therefore
some excuse, for this: but to make it a means of de-
pressing true genius, and defrauding it of its dearest re-
ward--its fair fame--is unnaturally, because it is gratui-
tously, wicked.   It is a wickedness, however, that might
safely be left to work out its own punishment, but that its
anonymous offspring too frequently do their mischievous
bidding for a time, and thus answer the end of their birth.

In thinking of these things we are tempted to express
an opinion which perhaps it would be more prudent to keep
to ourselves, --viz. that poetical criticism is, for the most
part, a very superfluous and impertinent business; and is to
be tolerated at all only when it is written in an unfeigned
spirit of admiration and humility.   We must therefore do
ourselves the justice to disclaim, for once, any intention
of writing a regular critique in the present instance.   Criticism, like every thing else, is very well in its place; but,
like every thing else, it does not always know where that
is.   Certainly a poet, properly so called, is beyond its
jurisdiction;--for good and bad, when applied to poetry, are
words without a meaning.   One might as well talk of good
or bad virtue.   That which is poetry must be good.   It may

differ in kind and in degree, and therefore it may differ in
value; but if it be poetry, it is a thing about which criticism
has no concern, any more than it has with other of the
highest productions of Fine Art.   The sublimities of Michael
Angelo are beyond the reach of its ken--the divine forms of
Raphael were not made to be meddled with by its unhallowed
fingers--the ineffable expressions of Corregio must not be
sullied by its earthy breath.   These things were given to the
world for something better than to be written and talked
about; and they have done their bidding hitherto, and will do
it till they cease to exist.   They have opened a perpetual
spring of lofty thoughts and pure meditations; they have
blended themselves with the very existence, and become a
living principle in the hearts of mankind;--and they are,
now, no more fit to be touched and tampered with than the
stars of heaven--for like them

<u>Levan di terra al ciclo nostr' intelletto.</u> [134]

We will not shrink from applying these observations, pro-
spectively, to the young poet whose work we are about to
notice.   Endymion, if it be not, technically speaking, a
poem, is poetry itself.   As a promise, we know nothing
like it, except some things of Chatterton.   Of the few
others that occur to us at the moment, the most remarkable are Pope's Pastorals, and his Essay on Criticism;--
but these are proofs of an extraordinary precocity, not of
genius, but of taste, as the word was understood in his day;
and of a remarkably early acquaintance with all the existing
common-places of poetry and criticism.   It is true that
Southey's Joan of Arc, and Campbell's Pleasures of Hope,
were both produced before their authors were one-and-
twenty.   But Joan of Arc, though a fine poem, is diffuse,
not from being rich, but from being diluted; and the Pleasures of Hope is a delightful work--but then it is a work--
and one cannot help wishing it had been written at thirty
instead of twenty.

Endymion is totally unlike all these, and all other
poems.   As we said before, it is not a poem at all.   It
is an ecstatic dream of poetry--a flush--a fever--a burning
light--an involuntary out-pouring of the spirit of poetry--
that will not be controuled.   Its movements are the starts
and boundings of the young horse before it has felt the bitt--
the first flights of the young bird, feeling and exulting in
the powers with which it is gifted, but not yet acquainted
with their use or their extent.   It is the wanderings of the

butterfly in the first hour of its birth; not as yet knowing
one flower from another, but only that all are flowers.   Its
similitudes come crowding upon us from all delightful things.
It is the May-day of poetry--the flush of blossoms and weeds
that start up at the first voice of spring.   It is the sky-
lark's hymn to the day-break, involuntarily gushing forth as
he mounts upward to look for the fountain of the light which
has awakened him.   It is as if the muses had steeped their
child in the waters of Castaly, [135] and we beheld him
emerging from them, with his eyes sparkling and his limbs
quivering with the delicious intoxication, and the precious
drops scattered from him into the air at every motion,
glittering in the sunshine, and casting the colours of the
rainbow on all things around.

Almost entirely unknown as this poem is to general
readers, [136] it will perhaps be better to reserve what we
have further to say of its characteristics, till we have
given some specimens of it.   We should premise this, however, by saying that our examples will probably exhibit almost as many faults as beauties.   But the reader will have
anticipated this from the nature of the opinion we have already given--at least if we have succeeded in expressing
what we intended to express.   In fact, there is scarcely a
passage of any length in the whole work, which does not
exhibit the most glaring faults--faults that in many instances
amount almost to the ludicrous: yet positive and palpable
as they are, it may be said of them generally, that they
are as much collateral evidences of poetical power, as the
beauties themselves are direct ones.   If the poet had had
time, or patience, or we will even say taste, to have
weeded out these faults as they sprang up, he could not
have possessed the power to create the beauties to which
they are joined.   If he had waited to make the first half
dozen pages of his work faultless, the fever--the ferment
of mind in which the whole was composed would have sub-
sided for ever.   Or if he had attempted to pick out those
faults afterwards, the beauties must inevitably have gone
with them--for they are inextricably linked together.

The title of Endymion will indicate the subject of it.
It is, in one word, the story of the mutual loves of Endymion and the Moon, --including the trials and adventures
which the youthful shepherd was destined to pass through,
in order to prepare and fit him for the immortality to which
he at last succeeds.

It is not part of our plan to follow the poet and his
hero--for they go hand in hand together--through their adventures; for, as a tale, this work is nothing.   There is
no connecting interest to bind one part of it to another.   Almost any two parts of it might be transposed, without disadvantage to either, or to the whole.   We repeat, it is not
a poem, but a dream of poetry; and while many of its
separate parts possess that vivid distinctness which frequently belongs to the separate parts of a dream, the impression it leaves as a whole is equally indistinct and confused. --The poet begins by noticing the delightful associa-
tions we are accustomed to attach to beautiful thoughts and
objects, and continues,

> --therefore 'tis that I
> Will trace the story of Endymion.
> The very music of his[137] name has gone
> Into my being.
>   [I. ll. 34-37.]

Then, after dallying a little with the host of beautiful images which are conjured up by that name, he exclaims

> And now at once, adventuresome, I send
> My herald thought into a wilderness.
>   [I. ll. 58-59.]

These two lines are very characteristic.   It is the
bold boy plunging for the first time into the stream, without
knowing or caring whither it may carry him.   The story,
such as it is, commences with the description of a procession and festival, in honour of the god Pan.   The following
are parts of this description.

[Quotes I. ll. 107-121, 135-152.]

After this comes Endymion, the "Shepherd Prince."

[Quotes I. ll. 175-181.]

The following are parts of a hymn to Pan, sung by
a chorus of shepherds.   We direct the reader's attention to
the imagery as well as the rythm of these extracts in
particular.   They are, likewise, almost entirely free from
the writer's characteristic faults.

[Quotes I. ll. 232-246, 279-292.]

After this hymn the sports begin, and--

> --They danc'd to weariness
> And then in quiet circles did they press
> The hillock turf, and caught the latter end
> Of some strange history, potent to send
> A young mind from its bodily tenement.
> [I. ll. 321-325.]

The love-stricken Endymion cannot partake in the sports, but is led by his sister Peona, to her own favourite bower, where,

[Quotes I. ll. 442-452, lines which describe Peona serenely watching over the sleeping Endymion.]

Nothing can be more exquisitely beautiful than this-- nothing more lulling-sweet than the melody of it.--And let us here, once for all, direct the readers' attention to the rythm of the various extracts we lay before them; and add that, upon the whole, it combines more freedom, sweetness, and variety than are to be found in that of any other long poem written in the same measure, without any exception whatever. In the course of more than four thousand lines it never cloys by sameness, and never flags. To judge of the comparative extent of this praise, turn at random to Pope's Homer, or even Dryden's Virgil, and read two or three pages. Sweetness and variety of music in the versi-fiction of a young writer, are among the most authentic evidences of poetical power. These qualities are peculiarly conspicuous in Shakespeare's early poems of Lucrece, and Venus and Adonis. It should be mentioned, however, that in the work before us, these qualities seem to result from-- what shall we say?--a fine natural ear?--from any thing, however, rather than system--for the verse frequently runs riot, and loses itself in air. It is the music of the happy wild-bird in the woods--not of the poor caged piping-bull-finch.

The following description of the impressions Endy-mion receives from various external objects,--on awaking from an Elysian dream of love, and finding that it was but a dream,--is finely passionate and natural:

[Quotes I. ll. 682-705.]

Peona succeeds in rousing her brother from the list-
less trance into which he has fallen, and he again feels the
true dignity of his being, and its mysterious bridal with the
external forms and influences of Nature.   The following
strikes us as being exceedingly fine, notwithstanding some
obvious faults in the diction. --It is the very faith, the religion, of imaginative passion.

[Quotes I. ll. 783-797.]

They who do not find poetry in this, may be assured
that they will look for it in vain elsewhere. --At the end of
the first book, Endymion confides the secret of his mysterious passion, and all the circumstances attending it, to his
sister Peona; and at the beginning of the second book we
find him wandering about, without end or aim,

> Through wilderness, and woods of mossed oaks;
> Counting his woe-worn minutes, by the strokes
> Of the lone wood-cutter;
>
> [II. ll. 49-51.]

till at length he meets with a winged messenger, who seems
commissioned from heaven to direct his steps; and who leads
him

> Through buried paths, where sleepy twilight dreams
> The summer time away. One track unseams
> A wooded cleft, and, far away, the blue
> Of ocean fades upon him; then, anew,
> He sinks adown a solitary glen,
> Where there was never sound of mortal men,
> Saving, perhaps, some snow-light cadences
> Melting to silence, when upon the breeze
> Some holy bark let forth an anthem sweet,
> To cheer itself to Delphi.
>
> [II. ll. 73-82.]

"Snow-light cadences, " &c. may be a little fantastical, perhaps; but it is very delicate and poetical, nevertheless.   The passage in italics [supplied by the reviewer]
is also very still and lonely. --The following delightful little
picture of cool quietude is placed in contrast to the restless fever of Endymion's thoughts, when his winged con-
ductor leaves him:--

[Quotes II. ll. 131-137.]

After this he yields up his whole soul to the dominion
of passion and imagination, and they at last burst forth with
an extatic address to his unearthly mistress, the moon--
though he does not yet know her as such.   The latter part
of this address follows: and amidst numerous faults, both
of thought and diction, the reader will not fail to detect
much beauty.   In the picture which follows the close of this
address there is great power, and even sublimity.

[Quotes II. ll. 179-198.]

At this moment a caverned voice is heard, bidding
the young lover descend into the hollows of the earth; and
adding

> --He ne'er is crown'd
> With immortality who fears to follow
> Where airy voices lead.
> [II. ll. 211-213.]

From this time Endymion quits the surface of the
earth, and passes through a multitude of strange adventures
in "the sparry hollows of the world," [II. l. 204] and in the
other mysterious regions of the air, the sea, and the sky--
meeting, in the course of his journeyings, with Glaucus and
Sylla, Alpheus and Arethusa, Adonis, &c. part of whose
stories are related.   Till at length, having fulfilled the
measure of his destinies, we find him once more on the
earth, and near his own home; where, after an interview
with his sister Peona, his immortal mistress appears to
him under her proper form, and they ascend the sky together.

It will be seen that here is a rich fund of materials,
fitted for almost every variety and degree of poetical power
to work upon.   And if the young builder before us has not
erected from them a regular fabric, which will bear to be
examined by a professional surveyor, with his square and
rule and plumb-line, --he has at least raised a glittering
and fantastic temple, where we may wander about, and de-
lightedly lose ourselves while gazing on the exquisite pictures which every here and there hang on its sun-bright
walls--the statues and flower-vases which ornament its
painted niches--the delicious prospects opening upon us from
its arabesque windows--and the sweet airs and romantic
music which come about when we mount upon its pleasant
battlements.   And it cannot be denied that the fabric is at

least as well adapted to the airy and fanciful beings who
dwell in it, as a regular Epic Palace--with its grand geo-
metrical staircases, its long dreary galleries, its lofty
state apartments, and its numerous sleeping-rooms--is to
its kings and heroes.

The whole of the foregoing extracts are taken from
the first and the beginning of the second book. We had
marked numerous others through the rest of the work; but
the little space that we have left for quotations must be
given to a few of the fancies, images, and detached thoughts
and similes--the pictures, statues, flowers, &c. --which
form the mere ornaments of the building, and are scattered
here and there, almost at random.

The little cabinet gems which follow may take their
place in any collection. The first might have been cut out
of a picture by Salvator:139

> Echoing grottos full of tumbling waves
> And moonlight.   p. 25.
>   [I. ll. 459-460.]

The next we can fancy to have formed a part of one
of Claude's140 delicious skies. It is Venus ascending from
the earth.

>   --At these words up flew
> The impatient doves, up rose the floating car,
> Up went the hum celestial. High afar
> The Latmian saw them 'minish into nought.
>   [II. ll. 579-582.]

The third reminds us of a sublime picture of the
Deluge, by Poussin. It is a lover who loses his mistress,
he knows not how, and afterwards, while swimming, finds
her dead body floating in the sea.

> Upon a dead thing's face my hand I laid;
> I look'd--'twas Scylla--
>   --Cold, O cold indeed
> Were her fair limbs, and like a common weed
> The sea-swell took her hair.
>   [III. ll. 618-619, 623-625.]

The fourth picture has all the voluptuous beauty of
Titian:

Do not those curls of glossy jet surpass
For tenderness the arms so idly lain
Amongst them?   Feelest not a kindred pain,
Too see such lovely eyes in swimming search
After some warm delight, <u>that seems to perch</u>
<u>Dovelike in the dim cell lying beyond</u>
<u>Their upper lids</u>?

> [IV. ll. 60-66.]

The following are a few of the wild flowers of Fancy
that are scatter'd up and down.

> [Quotes I. ll. 920-923.]

A brook running between mossy stones

> [Described in I. ll. 938-941.   Then, under the
> title "LOVER'S TALK," II. ll. 737-738 are
> quoted.]

The following are a few of the detached thoughts
which float about like clouds, taking their form and colour
from the position and the medium through which they are
seen.

> [With titles supplied by the reviewer, a series of
> quotes follow: "SUPPOSED EMPLOYMENTS OF
> DISEMBODIED SPIRITS," I. ll. 362-365, 368-369;
> "A POET," I. ll. 723-725; "THE END OF UN-
> REQUITED LOVE," I. ll. 735-736; "LOVE," II.
> ll. 536, 538-540, 542-544; "REMEMBRANCE OF
> PAST YEARS," III. ll. 327-332.]

The following similes are as new as they are
beautiful:

> > --his eyelids
> Widened a little, as when Zephyr bids
> A little breeze to creep between the fans
> of careless/butterflies.
>
> > [I. ll. 762-765.]

> --As delicious wine doth, sparkling, dive
> In nectar'd clouds and curls through water fair,
> So from the arbour roof down swell'd an air
> Odorous and enlivening.
>
> > [II. ll. 511-514.]

> --like taper-flame
> Left sudden by a dallying breath of air,
> He rose in silence.
> > [III. ll. 116-118.]

One more cluster of beautiful thoughts, fancies, and images meeting together, and one example of a totally different style of composition,--and we have done with quotations. The first is part of an address to the Moon, by the poet in his own character:

> [Quotes III. ll. 42, 44-71.]

If there be such a thing as inspiration, breathed forth by the forms and influences of the external world, and echoed back again from the inner shrine of the poet's breast --this is it. The image of the wren, is, in its kind, not to be surpassed in the whole circle of poetry. [141] We remember nothing equal to it, except Burns's morning picture, which is an exact companion to it, and probably suggested it.

> Just when the lark,
> 'Twixt light and dark,
> Awakens, by the daisy's side. [142]

Our last extract shall be part of a song, supposed to be sung by an Indian maid, who has wandered far away from her own native streams:

> [Quotes IV. ll. 146-163, 182-187, 279-290.]

This is, to be sure

> --Silly sooth,
> And dallies with the innocence of grief; [143]

but it is very touching and pathetic, nevertheless. Perhaps we like it the better from its reminding us (we do not very well know why) of two little elegies that are especial favourites with us,--one by Chatterton, beginning "O sing unto my roundelay;"--and the other by Kirke White, "Edwy, Edwy, ope thine eye!" It was perhaps suggested by Fletcher's divine song to Melancholy, in the Passionate Madman. [144]

We cannot refrain from asking, Is it credible

that the foregoing extracts are taken, almost at random,
from a work in which a writer in the most popular--we will
say deservedly the most popular--critical journal of the day,
has been unable to discover any thing worthy to redeem it
from mere contempt? Those who have the most respect for
the Quarterly Review will feel most pain at seeing its pages
disgraced by such an article as that to which we allude.
Almost anywhere else it would have been harmless, and unworthy of particular notice; but there it cannot fail to gain
a certain degree of credit from the company which it keeps.
It would be foolish to doubt or to deny the extensive effect
which such an article is likely to produce, appearing as it
does in a work which is read by tens of thousands, nine-
tenth of whom are not able to judge for themselves, and half
of the other tenth will not take the trouble of doing so. Its
chief mischief, however, is likely to take effect on the poet
himself, whose work is the subject of it. Next to the necessity of pouring forth that which is within him, the strongest
active principle in the mind of a young poet is the love of
fame. Not fame weighed and meted out by scales of strict
justice. Not fame, properly so called. But mere fame--
mere praise and distinction. He loves it for itself alone.
During a certain period, this love exists almost in the form
of an instinct in a poet's nature; and seems to be given him
for the purpose of urging or leading him on to that "hereafter" which is to follow. If it is not the food and support
of his poetical life, it is at least the stimulus without which
that life would be too apt to flag and faulter in its appointed
course. Woe to the lovers of poetry, when poets are content merely to deserve fame! Let that pest of the literary
republic, the mere versifier, be derided and put down as
a common nuisance. But let us, even for our own sakes,
beware of withholding from youthful poets the fame which
they covet;--let us beware of heaping ridicule even upon
their faults; lest, in revenge, they learn to keep to themselves the gift which was bestowed on them for the benefit
of their fellow-beings, and be satisfied with finding in poetry
"its own reward." But we willingly return to our more
immediate subject. We at first intended to have accompanied
the foregoing extracts by a few of a contrary description,
shewing the peculiar faults and deficiencies of the work before us. But as, in the present instance, we disclaim any
intention of writing a regular criticism, we feel that this
would be superfluous. It is not our object to give a distinct
idea of the work as a whole; and we repeat, it is not a fit
one to be judged of by rules and axioms. We only wish to
call the public notice to the great and remarkable powers

which it indicates, --at the same time giving encouragement--
as far as our sincere suffrage is of any value--to the poet
himself; and bespeaking, --not favour, --but attention, --to
any thing that he may produce hereafter. It is, therefore,
surely sufficient--for it is saying a great deal--to confess
that Endymion is as full of faults as of beauties. And it is
the less needful to point out those faults, as they are exactly of such a description that any one who has relish for
the amusement may readily discover them for himself.
They will not hide themselves from his search. He need
only open a page at random, and they will look him boldly,
but not impudently, in the face--for their parent is, as yet,
too inexperienced himself to know how to teach them better.

        The same reasons which make it unnecessary to point
out the peculiar faults of this work, make it difficult, if
not impossible, to state its peculiar beauties as a whole, in
any other than general terms. And, even so, we may ex-
haust all the common-places of criticism in talking about
the writer's active and fertile imagination, his rich and
lively fancy, his strong and acute sensibility, and so forth, --
without advancing one step towards characterising the work
which all these together have produced: because, though the
writer possesses all these qualities in an eminent degree,
his poetical character has not yet taken up any tangible or
determinate ground. So that, though we know of no poetical
work which differs from all others more than Endymion
does, yet its distinguishing feature is perhaps nothing more
than that exuberant spirit of youth, --that transport of imagination, fancy, and sensibility--which gushes forth from every
part, in a glittering shower of words, and a confused and
shadowy pomp of thoughts and images, creating and hurrying
each other along like waves of the sea. And there is no
egotism in all this, and no affectation. The poet offers
himself a willing sacrifice to the power which he serves:
not fretting under, but exulting and glorying in his bondage.
He plunges into the ocean of Poetry before he has learned
to stem and grapple with the waves; but they "bound beneath
him as a steed that knows its rider;"[145] and will not let him
sink. Still, however, while they bear him along triumphantly,
it is, evidently, at their will and pleasure, not at his. He
"rides on the whirlwind" safely; but he cannot yet "direct the
storm."[146]

        We have spoken of this work as being richer in
promise than any other that we are acquainted with, except
those of Chatterton. It by no means follows that we con-

fidently anticipate the fulfillment of that promise to its utmost extent.   We are not without our fears that it may be
like the flush of April blossoms which our fine soil almost
always sends forth, but which our cloudy and uncertain skies
as often prevent from arriving at maturity.   Notwithstanding
the many living poets that we possess, the times in which we
live are essentially unpoetical; and powerful and resolute indeed must that spirit be, which, even in its youth, can
escape their influence.   When the transports of enthusiasm
are gone by, it can hardly dare hope to do so.   It must
submit to let "the years being on the inevitable yoke."[147]
This has been one strong inducement for us to notice the
young writer before us; and we cannot conclude these
slight and desultory remarks without entreating him not to
be cast down or turned aside from the course which nature
has marked out for him.   He is and must be a poet--and
he may be a great one.   But let him never be tempted to
disregard this first evidence of that power which at present
rules over him--much less affect to do so: and least of
all let him wish or attempt to make it any thing but what
it is.   Nothing can ever tame and polish this wild and way-
ward firstling, and make it fit to be introduced to "mixed
company"; but let him not therefore be ashamed to cherish
and claim it for his own.   He may live to see himself surrounded by a flourishing family, endowed with all sorts of
polite accomplishments, and able not only to make their own
way in the world, but to further his fortunes too.   But this
--first-born of his hopes--the child of his youth--whatever
he may say or think to the contrary--must ever be the
favourite. He may admire those which are to come, and
pride himself upon them; but he will never love them as he
has loved this; he will never again watch over the infancy
and growth of another with such full and unmixed delight:
for this was born while his muse was his mistress, and he
her rapturous lover.   He will marry her by and bye--or
perhaps he has already--and then he may chance to love her
better than ever; but he will cease to be her lover.

16.   Francis Jeffrey reviews Endymion
        in the Edinburgh Review

            (This generally favorable review appeared in
        the Edinburgh for August 1820 [XXXIV, 202-213]
        and was acknowledged as his by Jeffrey when he
        reprinted it in Vol. III of his Contributions to the

Edinburgh Review (1844). In the past forty years,
Jeffrey's important review has been widely reprinted in a number of anthologies and other texts.
For a more detailed discussion of Jeffrey and the
Edinburgh, see the introductory chapter.
    The Edinburgh's circulation and prestige in 1820
was not significantly less than the Quarterly's; and
praise by Jeffrey, notwithstanding some qualifications concerning Keats's extravagant fancy and his
use of mythology, served as an effective, if late,
rejoinder to the attacks on Endymion of two years
before. As the editor of a Whig journal, Jeffrey
most assuredly had a political motive for opposing
the Tory attacks of 1818, and it must also be
granted that his claim of not having seen Keats's
second volume "till very lately" was highly unlikely. The editor of the Edinburgh had simply
waited until the climate of opinion began to turn in
Keats's favor. Jeffrey, speaking for the Whig
establishment, gave the sanction of the Edinburgh
to the general critical impression that Blackwood's,
the Quarterly, and the British Critic had overex-
tended themselves in their earlier attacks on the
poet.
    The review was occasioned by the publication
of the Lamia volume, but Jeffrey's treatment of
Keats's last effort is perfunctory. In essence,
Jeffrey was reviewing Endymion.)

We had never happened to see either of these volumes till
very lately--and have been exceedingly struck with the genius
they display, and the spirit of poetry which breathes through
all their extravagance. That imitation of our older writers,
and especially of our older dramatists, to which we cannot
help flattering ourselves that we have somewhat contributed
has brought on, as it were, a second spring in our poetry;--
and few of its blossoms are either more profuse of sweetness or richer in promise, than this which is now before
us. Mr. Keats, we understand, is still a very young
man;[148] and his whole works, indeed, bear evidence enough
of the fact. They are full of extravagance and irregularity,
rash attempts at originality, interminable wanderings, and
excessive obscurity. They manifestly require, therefore,
all the indulgence that can be claimed for a first attempt:
--but we think it no less plain that they deserve it; for they
are flushed all over with the rich lights of fancy, and so
coloured and bestrewn with the flowers of poetry, that even

while perplexed and bewildered in their labyrinths, it is impossible to resist the intoxication of their sweetness, or to
shut our hearts to the enchantments they so lavishly present.
The models on which he has formed himself, in the Endymion, the earliest and by much the most considerable of
his poems, are obviously the Faithful Shepherdess of Fletcher,
and the Sad Shepherd of Ben Jonson;[149] --the exquisite
metres and inspired diction of which he has copied with
great boldness and fidelity--and, like his great originals,
has also contrived to impart to the whole piece that true
rural and poetical air which breathes only in them and in
Theocritus--which is at once homely and majestic, luxurious
and rude, and sets before us the genuine sights and sounds
and smells of the country, with all the magic and grace of
Elysium.   His subject has the disadvantage of being mythological; and in this respect, as well as on account of the
raised and rapturous tone it consequently assumes, his
poetry may be better compared perhaps to the Comus and
the Arcades of Milton, of which, also, there are many
traces of imitation.   The great distinction, however, between him and these divine authors, is, that imagination in
them is subordinate to reason and judgment, while, with him,
it is paramount and supreme--that their ornaments and
images are employed to embellish and recommend just
sentiments, engaging incidents, and natural characters, while
his are poured out without measure or restraint, and with
no apparent design but to unburden the breast of the author,
and give vent to the overflowing vein of his fancy.   The thin
and scanty tissue of his story is merely the light frame
work on which his florid wreaths are suspended; and while
his imaginations go rambling and entangling themselves
everywhere, like wild honeysuckles, all idea of sober reason, and plan, and consistency, is utterly forgotten, and
are [sic] 'strangled in their waste fertility.'[150]   A great
part of the work indeed, is written in the strangest and
most fantastical manner that can be imagined.   It seems as
if the author had ventured everything that occurred to him
in the shape of a glittering image or striking expression--
taken the first word that presented itself to make a rhyme,
and then made that word the germ of a new cluster of images
--a hint for a new excursion of the fancy--and so wandered
on, equally forgetful whence he came, and heedless whither
he was going, till he had covered his pages with an interminable arabesque of connected and incongruous figures,
that multiplied as they extended, and were only harmonized
by the brightness of their tints, and the graces of their
forms.   In this rash and headlong career he has of course

many lapses and failures.   There is no work, accordingly,
from which a malicious critic could cull more matter for
ridicule, or select more obscure, unnatural, or absurd
passages.   But we do not take that to be our office;--and
just beg leave, on the contrary, to say, that any one who,
on this account, would represent the whole poem as despicable, must either have no notion of poetry, or no regard
to truth.

        It is, in truth, at least as full of genius as of ab-
surdity; and he who does not find a great deal in it to admire and to give delight, cannot in his heart see much beauty
in the two exquisite dramas to which we have alluded, 151
or find any great pleasure in some of the finest creations of
Milton and Shakespeare.   There are very many such persons, we verily believe, even among the reading and judicious part of the community--correct scholars we have no
doubt many of them, and, it may be, very classical
composers in prose and in verse--but utterly ignorant of the
true genius of English poetry, and incapable of estimating
its appropriate and most exquisite beauties.   With that spirit
we have no hesitation in saying that Mr K. is deeply im-
bued--and of those beauties he has presented us with many
striking examples.   We are very much inclined indeed to
add, that we do not know any book which we would sooner
employ as a test to ascertain whether any one had in him
a native relish for poetry, and a genuine sensibility to its
intrinsic charm.   The greater and more distinguished poets
of our country have so much else in them to gratify other
tastes and propensities, that they are pretty sure to captivate and amuse those to whom their poetry is but an
hindrance and obstruction, as well as those to whom it constitutes their chief attraction.   The interest of the stories
they tell--the vivacity of the characters they delineate--the
weight and force of the maxims and sentiments in which
they abound--the very pathos and wit and humor they display, which may all and each of them exist apart from their
poetry and independent of it, are quite sufficient to account
for their popularity, without referring much to that still
higher gift, by which they subdue to their enchantments those
whose souls are attuned to the finer impulses of poetry.   It
is only where those other recommendations are wanting, or
exist in a weaker degree, that the true force of the attraction exercised by the pure poetry with which they are so often
combined, can be fairly appreciated--where, without much
incident or many characters, and with little wit, wisdom, or
arrangement, a number of bright pictures are presented to

the imagination, and a fine feeling expressed of those
mysterious relations by which visible external things are
assimilated with inward thoughts and emotions, and become
the images and exponents of all passions and affections.
To an unpoetical reader such passages always appear mere
raving and absurdity--and to this censure a very great part
of the volume before us will certainly be exposed, with this
class of readers.   Even in the judgment of a fitter audience,
however, it must, we fear, be admitted, that, besides the
riot and extravagance of his fancy, the scope and substance
of Mr K. 's poetry is rather too dreary and abstracted to
excite the strongest interest, or to sustain the attention
through a work of any great compass or extent.   He deals
too much with shadowy and incomprehensible beings, and is
too constantly rapt in an extramundane Elysium, to command
a lasting interest with ordinary mortals--and must employ
the agency of more varied and coarser emotions, if he
wishes to take rank with the seducing poets of this or of
former generations.   There is something very curious too,
we think, in the way in which he, and Mr Barry Cornwall
also, have dealt with the Pagan mythology, of which they
have made so much use in their poetry.   Instead of presenting its imaginary persons under the trite and vulgar
traits that belong to them in the ordinary systems, little
more is borrowed from these than the general conception of
their conditions and relations; and an original character and
distinct individuality is bestowed upon them, which has all
the merit of invention, and all the grace and attraction of
the fictions on which it is engrafted.   The antients, though
they probably did not stand in any great awe of their deities,
have yet abstained very much from any minute or dramatic
representation of their feelings and affections.   In Hesiod
and Homer, they are coarsely delineated by some of their
actions and adventures, and introduced to us merely as the
agents in those particular transactions; while in the Hymns,
from those ascribed to Orpheus and Homer, down to those
of Callimachus, we have little but pompous epithets and invocations, with a flattering commemoration of their most
famous exploits--and are never allowed to enter into their
bosoms, or follow out the train of their feelings, with the
presumption of our human sympathy.   Except the love-song
of the Cyclops to his Sea Nymph in Theocritus[152]--the
Lamentation of Venus for Adonis in Moschus[153] --and the
more recent Legend of Apuleius, [154] we scarcely recollect
a passage in all the writings of antiquity in which the passions of an immortal are fairly disclosed to the scrutiny
and observation of men.   The author before us, however,

and some of his contemporaries, have dealt differently with
the subject;--and, sheltering the violence of the fiction under
the ancient traditionary fable, have created and imagined an
entire new set of characters, and brought closely and
minutely before us the loves and sorrows and perplexities
of beings, with whose names and supernatural attributes we
had long been familiar, without any sense or feeling of their
personal character.   We have more than doubts of the fit-
ness of such personages to maintain a permanent interest
with the modern public;--but the way in which they are here
managed, certainly gives them the best chance that now remains for them; and, at all events, it cannot be denied that
the effect is striking and graceful.   But we must now proceed to our extracts.

        The first of the volumes before us is occupied with
the loves of Endymion and Diana--which it would not be very
easy, and which we do not at all intend to analyze in detail.
In the beginning of the poem, however, the Shepherd Prince
is represented as having had strange visions and delirious
interviews with an unknown and celestial beauty; soon after
which, he is called on to preside at a festival in honour
of Pan; and his appearance in the procession is thus
described.

              [Quotes I. ll. 169-181.]

        There is then a choral hymn addressed to the sylvan
deity, which appears to us to be full of beauty; and reminds
us, in many places, of the finest strains of Sicilian or
English poetry.   A part of it is as follows.

              [Quotes I. ll. 232-241, 247-287.]

        The enamoured youth sinks into insensibility in the
midst of the solemnity, and is borne apart and revived by
the care of his sister; and, opening his heavy eyes in her
arms, says---

              [Quotes I. ll. 466-472, 476-497.]

        He then tells her all the story of his love and mad-
ness; and is afterwards led away by butterflies to the haunts
of Naiads, and by them sent down into enchanted caverns,
where he sees Venus and Adonis, and great flights of Cupids,
and wanders over diamond terraces among beautiful fountains
and temples and statues, and all sorts of fine and strange

things.   All this is very fantastical: But there are splendid
pieces of description, and a sort of wild richness on the
whole.   We cull a few little morsels.   This is the picture
of the sleeping Adonis.

[Quotes II. ll.   393-394,   403-414,   418-427.]

There is another and more classical sketch of Cybele.

[Quotes II. ll.   639-649.]

In the midst of all these spectacles, he has, we do
not very well know how, a ravishing interview with his unknown goddess; and, when she melts away from him, he
finds himself in a vast grotto, where he overhears the
courtship of Alpheus and Arethusa, and, as they elope together, discovers that the grotto has disappeared, and that
he is at the bottom of the sea, under the transparent arches
of its naked waters.   The following is abundantly extravagant;
but comes of no ignoble lineage, nor shames its high descent.

[III. ll.   119-136.]

There he finds antient Glaucus enchanted by Circe--
hears his wild story--and goes with him to the deliverance
and restoration of thousands of drowned lovers, whose bodies
were piled and stowed away in a large submarine place.
When this feat is happily performed, he finds himself again
on dry ground, with woods and waters around him; and cannot help falling desperately in love with a beautiful damsel
whom he finds there pining for some such consolations, and
who tells a long story of her having come from India in the
train of Bacchus, and having strayed away from him into
that forest:--so they vow eternal fidelity, and are wafted up
to heaven on flying horses, on which they sleep and dream
among the stars;--and then the lady melts away, and he is
again alone upon the earth; but soon rejoins his Indian love,
and agrees to give up his goddess, and live only for her:
But she refuses, and says she is resolved to devote herself
to the service of Diana; and when she goes to dedicate herself, she turns out to be the goddess in a new shape, and
exalts her lover with her to a blest immortality.

We have left ourselves room to say but little of the
second volume, which is of a more miscellaneous character.
Lamia is a Greek antique. story, in the measure and taste of
Endymion.   Isabella is a paraphrase of the same tale of

Boccacio, which Mr Cornwall has also imitated under the
title of 'a Sicilian Story.' It would be worth while to compare the two imitations; but we have no longer time for such
a task.   Mr K. has followed his original more closely, and
has given a deep pathos to several of his stanzas.   The
widowed bride's discovery of the murdered body is very
strikingly given.

[Quotes st. XLVII; XLVIII, ll. 1-7; LI-LII.]

The following lines from an ode to a Nightingale,
are equally distinguished for harmony and feeling.

[Quotes ll. 15-28, 63-70.]

We must close our extracts with the following lively
lines to Fancy.

[Quotes ll. 9-24, 39-66.]

There is a fragment of a projected Epic, entitled
'Hyperion,' on the expulsion of Saturn and the Titanian
deities by Jupiter and his younger adherents, of which we
cannot advise the completion: For, though there are passages of some force and grandeur, it is sufficiently obvious,
from the specimen before us, that the subject is too far removed from all the sources of human interest, to be successfully treated by any modern author.   Mr Keats has
unquestionably a very beautiful imagination, and a great
familiarity with the finest diction of English poetry; but
he must learn not to misuse or misapply these advantages;
and neither to waste the good gifts of nature and study on
intractable themes, nor to luxuriate too recklessly on such
as are more suitable.

17.   A review of Endymion in the Edinburgh
      Magazine and Literary Miscellany

(Like Jeffrey's preceding piece, this review
was occasioned by the publication of Keats's Lamia
volume.   It appeared in the Edinburgh Magazine
for August 1820 [n.s. VII, 107-110] and deals almost exclusively with Endymion: it was continued
in October 1820 when the Lamia volume was reviewed [see Chapter IV, item 8].

The Edinburgh Magazine had reviewed Poems unfavorably in October 1817; here it offers a sympathetic appraisal of Keats and continues to do so in
its October 1820 issue as well.   The poet was now
receiving praise from those who had condemned him
three years before.
          The article itself is not distinguished.   Despite
a disclaimer to the contrary, much of the commentary that follows is plot summary.   The review has been noted before, but it is reprinted
here for the first time.   The author is not known.)

REMARKS ON KEATS'S POEMS[155]

Mr Keats is a poet of high and undoubted powers.
He has evident peculiarities, which some of the London
critics, who are averse to his style, have seized upon and
produced as fair specimens of his writings; and this has
operated, of course, to his disadvantage with the public, who
have scarcely had an opportunity of judging what his powers
really are.   Some of his friends, indeed, have put in a word
or two of praise, but it has been nearly unqualified; and this,
when viewed at the same time with the criticism produced
in an opposite spirit, has tended very much to confirm the
objections made to his poetry.

Mr Keats has produced three volumes of verse: the
first is very inferior in power to the others, but containing
very delightful passages, and some sonnets of great beauty.
The second volume consists of the old mythological story of
Endymion, and over which is scattered a multitude of thoughts
and images, conceived and produced in the highest spirit of
poetry.   Perhaps the "Endymion," though it contains more
positive faults than the last book, ("Lamia,") is more completely in Mr Keats's own style; and we think that it contains, at least, as many beauties.   It is more careless,
perhaps, but there is a greater freshness about it than
about the last book, which (in "Hyperion" at least) reminds
us occasionally of other writers, but which we must not be
understood to speak of otherwise than in terms of the sin-
cerest admiration.

The poem of Endymion contains about 4000 lines,
and the story of the hero is not, perhaps, very interesting
in itself; indeed, it is scarcely possible to endure, with a
lively interest, a tale so slight and shadowy as that of the

Loves of Diana and the Shepherd of Latmos.   While this is
stated, however, great praise must be ceded to the author,
who, by force of poetry alone, can claim and compel the
attention of the reader, for any length of time, to so bare
(although graceful) a subject.

    Mr Keats commences his poem with an evident de-
light.   Shapes and stories of beauty, he tells us, are joys
for ever.   They

> Haunt us till they become a cheering light
> Unto our souls.
> > [II. ll. 30-31.]

Therefore, he says, and how beautifully does he say it--

> Therefore, 'tis with full happiness that I
> Will trace the story of Endymion,
> The very music of whose name has gone
> Into my being.   p. 5
> > [Slightly misquoted from I. ll. 34-37.]

    We do not profess to give a summary of the contents
of this volume.   Our intention is merely to give a few extracts, and to let our readers judge for themselves.   It
will save a wonderful deal of insisting on our parts; and
after all, poetry is a matter of feeling rather than argument.

    The first book opens with a procession in honour of
Pan, in which the Latmian Prince Endymion appears.   Part
of this, and the hymn subsequent to it, are told in words
that would shed lustre upon any age of poetry.   After dam-
sels, who carry baskets of April flowers, come on

> A crowd of shepherds, with as sunburnt looks
> As may be read of in Arcadian books,
> Such as sate listening round Apollo's pipe,
> When the great deity, for earth too ripe,
> Let his divinity, o'erflowing, die
> In music thro' the vales of Thessaly
> > p. 10.
> > [I. ll. 139-144.]

Of Endymion it is said, --

> A smile was on his countenance; he seemed
> To common lookers on, like one who dreamed
> Of idleness, in groves Elysian; p. 11.
> [I. 11. 175-177.]

and yet he had a "lurking trouble" [I. 1. 179] in his nether
lip, which, to a keener observer, would have betrayed his
incipient passion. The procession stops at last, and ranges
itself in a circle, in the midst of which a venerable priest
rises, and invites the "Men of Latmos" [I. 1. 196] to address
their vows to the great god Pan. They obey; and the following hymn is sung. It is worthy of any of the gods.

> [Quotes I. 11. 232-246, 263-319 of the "Hymn to
> Pan."]

We hope that our readers begin to feel that there
are some (not ordinary) beauties in the volumes of Mr
Keats. He is, perhaps, the poet, above all others, that
we should refer to, in case we are challenged to produce
single lines of extraordinary merit. He is very unequal in
his earlier volumes certainly, (and what poet is not?) but
there are beauties which might redeem ten times the amount
of any defects that they may contain.

Speaking of Zephyr, before sunrise, he says, he

> Fondles the flower amid the sobbing rain.
> [I. 1. 331.]

This seems to us very charming, and it is quite in the
spirit of that mythology which has invested the west wind and
the flowers with such delicate personifications. 156 Again,
speaking of Peona, the sister of Endymion, who sits by him
while he sleeps, he says,

> --as a willow keeps
> A patient watch over the stream that creeps
> Windingly by it, so the quiet maid
> Held her in peace: so that a whispering blade
> Of grass, p. 24
> [I. 11. 446-450.]

or any other trivial thing, might be heard.

We have given the title of Mr Keats's second volume
of poetry, and it was our intention to notice it, but this we

must defer doing at present, and we have only space enough
to give a few more single lines, or ideas from Endymion,
but these our readers will, we doubt not, appreciate.   It is
sufficient to say, that the flowers which we select are by
no means rare.   Look at the effect of a single word, --

> --Sometimes
> A scent of violets, and blossing limes,
> Loiter'd around us, p. 34
> [I. ll. 666-668.]

    The following lines were quoted against the author,
in a London Review. [157]   They are irregular, perhaps, but
still very beautiful, we think.

> Endymion! the cave is secreter
> Than the isle of Delos.   Echo hence shall stir
> No sighs, but sigh warm kisses, or light noise
> Of thy combing hand, the while it travelling cloys
> And trembles thro' my labyrinthine hair.
>   p. 48
>   [I. ll. 965-969.]

Endymion wanders for many days

> Thro' wilderness and woods of mossed oaks,
> Counting his woe-worn minutes, by the strokes
> Of the lone wood-cutter.   p. 55.
>   [II. ll. 49-51.]

A butterfly is sent to guide him: he follows it

> Thro' the green evening quiet in the sun,
> O'er many a heath, and many a woodland dun,
> Thro' buried paths, where sleepy twilight dreams
> The summer time away.   p. 56, 57.
>   [II. ll. 71-74.]

    If this be not poetry, we do not know what is; but
we must, perforce, leave Endymion, begging our readers
to refer to it without more ado, both for their sakes and
our own.

(To be continued.)

Notes

1. From the prose introduction which precedes "The Fire-
   Worshippers" section of Moore's poem.

2. Bailey omits the word "reason," which follows at this
   point in Keats's poem.

3. Wordsworth's Excursion, I. ll. 285-286.

4. Wordsworth's Laodamia, l. 22.

5. Paradise Lost II. l. 398.

6. This may simply be an aphorism rather than a literary
   allusion. There is another instance later in
   Bailey's letter when he uses quotation marks to
   indicate an obvious aphorism.

7. Letter of September 23, 1637 to Charles Diodati in
   Milton's Epistolae Familiares. For "quid cogitam?"
   in the second sentence of Bailey's quote read "quid
   cogitem quaeris?" The translation that follows is
   by David Masson from The Works of John Milton,
   ed. Frank A. Patterson et. al. (New York, 1931-
   1940), XII, 27. "You make many anxious in-
   quiries, even as to what I am at present thinking
   of. Hearken, Theodotus, but let it be in your
   private ear, lest I blush; and allow me for a little
   to use big language with you. You ask what I
   am thinking of. So may the good Diety help me,
   of immortality!"

8. Paradise Lost, IV. l. 988.

9. Lycidas, l. 71. For "minds" read "mind." Bailey,
   who probably attributed this line to Paradise Lost,
   is incorrect. Milton was only thirty when he published Lycidas in 1638; he did not become totally
   blind until 1652.

10. Again, Bailey is in error. His quote is from Lycidas,
    l. 70.

11. Comus, l. 86.

12. The Excursion, I. ll. 249-250.

13. A paraphrase of Wordsworth's <u>White Doe of Rylstone,</u>
    l. 965.

14. A paraphrase of <u>Paradise Lost</u>, IV. l. 272.

15. "L'Allegro," ll. 139-140.

16. <u>Comus</u>, ll. 668-671.

17. See ll. 232-306 of Keats's poem.

18. For "hidden" read "sudden."

19. <u>Paradise Regained</u>, IV. ll. 638-639.

20. A paraphrase from Samuel Butler's <u>Hudibras</u>, Part II,
    Canto I, l. 466.

21. Unidentified.

22. Unidentified. This quote may be general, or it may
    apply specifically to Byron. The fourth canto of
    <u>Childe Harold</u> was published less than six months
    before Bailey's letter, and Byron's worldly tone
    was hardly likely to impress Keats's somewhat
    priggish friend.

23. Unidentified.

24. This quote and the one that precedes it are from <u>The
    Winter's Tale</u>, IV. iv. ll. 119-121.

25. A paraphrase of "Il Penseroso," ll. 7-8.

26. <u>Comus</u>, ll. 12-14. "Hopes" in l. 14 is a misprint
    for "opes."

27. Meant in the sense of a bauble. In this case, a cheap
    trumpet or noisemaker sold on St. Bartholomew's
    day (August 24) at the fair in West Smithfield.
    The <u>OED</u> tells us that the proper noun was applied
    in both a favorable and unfavorable sense to dif-
    ferent articles sold at the fair: Bartholomew-
    pig, Bartholomew-ware, etc.

28. This is hopelessly confused and, like the misspellings
    of Piemont and Lawrence above, it was probably

the fault of the printer who, in this case, omitted
a clause.   These blunders suggest that the review
was published in some haste.

29.   The British Critic was to object to this passage in its
review of September 1820.

30.   If, in Endymion, Keats did not always keep his audience
in mind, he soon became aware of the need to do
so.   In a letter of October 27, 1818 to Richard
Woodhouse, he speaks of the poet's need to suppress
his own identity, substituting in its place the identity of his creation.   "A Poet is the most unpoetical of any thing in existence; because he has
no Identity--he is continually ... filling some
other Body...." (Letters of John Keats, ed.
Hyder E. Rollins [Cambridge, Mass., 1958], I,
387.)

31.   Sonnet CVI, l. 3.

32.   It is clear that the author intended to continue his review, but there is no evidence that he did so.
J. R. MacGillivray states (Keats: A Bibliography
and Reference Guide [Toronto, 1949], p. 65) that
it was "completed in the next day's issue of the
paper," but the Monday issue of the Champion,
published for the provinces, merely reprinted the
same review.   The original conclusion of Marsh
and White ("Keats and the Periodicals of His Time,"
MP, XXXII [August 1934], 41) is correct: "It is
announced that this review is to be continued, or
concluded, but nothing further appeared in The
Champion. "

33.   One specialized meaning of the term "Cockney," the
OED tells us, is to signify "One born in the city
of London....   Always more or less contemptuous
... and particularly used to connote the characteristics in which the born Londoner is supposed
to be inferior to other Englishmen. "   The poetry of
Hunt and Keats, both of whom were Londoners,
was considered meretricious and vulgar by Blackwood's, an Edinburgh publication.

34.   Webb is identified in the previous chapter.   At
the head of each of the first two articles on

the Cockney School, the following extract from
Webb's poem appeared:
> Our talk shall be (a theme we never tire on)
> Of Chaucer, Spenser, Shakespeare, Milton, Byron,
> (Our England's Dante)--Wordsworth--Hunt and
>   Keats,
> The Muses' son of promise; and of what feats
> He yet may do.

35. The reviewer chooses the French form, "metromanie,"
     instead of the English equivalent, "metromania."

36. Joanna Baillie (1762-1851), the Scottish dramatist and
     poet.

37. In an attempt to forestall the expected attack of
     Blackwood's, Keats's friends, Bailey and Reynolds,
     unwittingly supplied Lockhart with information con-
     cerning the poet's medical background that was
     turned to ridicule.

38. Hunt's article on the Young Poets (December 1, 1816)
     praised both Shelley and Reynolds, as well as
     Keats. Lockhart should have more accurately
     spoken of the appearance of "three new stars" on
     the poetical horizon.

39. Lockhart gibes at Keats's references to Hunt, Spenser,
     and Milton by means of italics and exclamation
     marks.

40. [No reference]

41. Italics are by Lockhart.

42. Tempest in a teapot.

43. An allusion to "Sleep and Poetry," ll. 48-49.

44. Hunt was the author of The Story of Rimini (1816).

45. Shakespeare. The allusion to the rose is to Romeo
     and Juliet, II. i. ll. 43-44.

46. Lockhart is referring to the two album verses written
     to the cousins of George Felton Mathew, "To Some
     Ladies" and "On Receiving a Curious Shell ...

from the Same Ladies," as well as to the poem
"To --."

47. Cheapside, where fishmongers and peddlers hawked
    their wares, is east of Temple-bar. Thus, the
    lady addressed in the poem is, according to Lock-
    hart, a prostitute; and Keats is singing her praise.

48. Ovid's Metamorphoses.

49. Christoph M. Wieland (1733-1813). Among Wieland's
    minor pieces is "Endymion" (1771).

50. Keats knew neither Latin nor German, but he did read
    Sandys' 1626 translation of The Metamorphoses and
    William Sothbey's 1798 translation of Wieland's
    Oberon. He read Oberon "with George Felton
    Mathew in 1815 ... and thought very highly of it."
    (Werner W. Beyer, Keats and the Daemon King
    [New York, 1947], p. 322.) It was this work
    rather than Wieland's "Endymion," Beyer tells us,
    which had an influence on Keats's poem.

51. Hunt makes this admission on p. xvii of his Introduc-
    tion to The Story of Rimini.

52. Endymion, IV. l. 242.

53. For "tale" read "tongue," III. l. 909.

54. Here Lockhart states the major motive for his hostile
    review; he considers Keats a radical of the same
    ilk as Hunt. Although Lockhart attempted to be
    offhand about the charge, the cause of the ad
    hominem attack upon Keats was the poet's "Cock-
    ney Politics."

55. An allusion to the opening lines of Book IV of Endy-
    mion.

56. Unidentified.

57. A medical quack in Alain René LeSage's picaresque
    novel, L'Historie de Gil Blas de Santillane (1715-
    1735).

58. J. R. MacGillivray (p. 65) lists this review according
    to the Quarterly's April 1818 date of issue.

59. Keats's phrase, "verses fit to live," may possibly be
    an echo of Milton's letter to Diodati in which the
    aspiring poet tells his friend of his desire for
    literary immortality.
    Bailey quotes from Milton's letter in the Oxford
    Herald of June 6, 1818, and it is more than likely
    that he discussed this same letter with Keats the
    year before when the latter visited him at Oxford.

60. Quarterly, XIV (January 1816), 473-481.

61. The chief priest of the Eleusinian mysteries. By ex-
    tension, any high priest.

62. Probably a quotation from Hunt, but not from The
    Story of Rimini. The exact source remains uni-
    dentified.

63. A comparison with the complete Preface shows that
    Keats's sentence does not end at this point.
    Croker deliberately omits the qualifying clause
    that follows.

64. Bouts-rimés are defined by Edmund Gosse in the 11th
    edition of the Encyclopaedia Brittanica as "lit-
    erally (from the French) 'rhymed ends,' the name
    given in all literatures to a kind of verse ...
    which ... Addison in the Spectator ... described
    as 'lists of words that rhyme to one another,
    drawn up by another hand, and given to a poet,
    who was to make a poem to the rhymes in the
    same order that they were placed upon the list
    ....' The invention of bouts-rimés is attributed
    to a minor French poet of the 17th century, Dulot,
    of whom little else is remembered" (IV, p. 356 b).
    It became the fashion among French writers of the
    seventeenth and eighteenth centuries and was in-
    dulged in later by William and Dante Rossetti in
    the nineteenth century.

65. MacGillivray (p. 65), using the Critic's date of issue,
    lists this review after the June 1818 article in
    the Champion.

66. These references are culled from the opening three
    stanzas of Endymion. Clusters of similar para-
    phrases from Keats's poem comprise the major

part of the review.   Accordingly, it is impractical
to include line references in most instances.   As
a general guide, the reader may use the paren-
thetical references of the reviewer.   They are in
error, but never by more than a line or two, unless otherwise noted.   The reviewer also refers
to the page numbers of Keats's 1818 volume.   In
these instances, references to line numbers within
brackets are by me.

67.   Thomas James Mathias (1754-1835) was the author of
        The Pursuits of Literature (1794-1797), a tedious
        series of satiric dialogues, modeled on Pope,
        which denounced all traces of revolutionary think-
        ing.   George Steevens (1736-1800), collaborator
        with Dr. Johnson in the work of editing the plays
        of Shakespeare, as well as the detector of Chat-
        terton's forgeries, was one of Mathias' satiric
        butts in the poem.

68.   Should read "would they."

69.   The quotation should be closed at this point.

70.   Should read "lov'st."

71.   The word Keats had in mind was "dittany."

72.   Unidentified.

73.   Keats is not incorrect; the noun "maw" can be used
        to mean the mouth of a voracious animal.

74.   The reviewer is referring to Endymion's union with
        Cynthia in a dream (II. ll. 717-853).   The
        author's moral outrage is in keeping with the
        pious façade of the British Critic.   Hunt's Story
        of the Rimini had been attacked for its immorality
        in several publications; and Keats, the friend of
        Hunt, was now being scored for the same im-
        morality.

75.   This reference should read II. ll. 764-765.

76.   "A very odd thing for the moon to be."   (Reviewer's
        note.)

77.   These lines should read, "Laughing, and wailing,
        grovelling, serpenting, /Showing tooth, tusk, and
        venom bag, and sting!"

78.   A quote from Keats's Preface to Endymion. (The
        Preface is reprinted in the headnote to item five
        of this chapter.)

79.   An allusion to this letter is found in the October 11,
        1818 issue of the Examiner, p. 648.   "A manly
        and judicious letter, signed J.S. appeared in the
        Morning Chronicle the other day, respecting the
        article in the Quarterly Review on the Endymion
        of the young poet Mr. Keats.   It is one of several
        public animadversions, which that half-witted, half-
        hearted Review has called indignantly forth on the
        occasion.   'This is the hastily-written tribute,'
        says the writer, 'of a stranger who ventures to
        predict that Mr. K. is capable of producing a
        poem that shall challenge the admiration of every
        reader of true taste and feeling; nay, if he will
        give up his acquaintance with Mr. Leigh Hunt, and
        apostatise in his friendships, his principles, and
        his politics (if he have any), he may even com-
        mand the approbation of the Quarterly Review.'--
        We really believe so; but Mr. Keats is of a
        spirit which can afford to dispense with such
        approbation, and stand by his friend."

80.   If this is so, then it is unlikely Scott is the author of
        this letter.   However, it is also possible that
        Scott, if he is the author, is simply employing a
        stratagem here to indicate that the attack of the
        Quarterly will result in attracting more, rather
        than less, readers to Keats's poem.   Such pre-
        tenses were not uncommon at the time.   (See n.
        88 below for a comparable instance of deception
        by Reynolds.)

81.   Obviously, an error by "J.S." or by the typesetter.
        For "common" read "uncommon" or "no common."

82.   Gifford wrote a translation of Juvenal (1803).

83.   Southey compiled The Remains of Henry Kirke White
        ... with an Account of his Life in two volumes
        (1807).   White (1785-1806) was a young poet of

unexceptional merit, whose Clifton Grove (1803)
was reviewed courteously but unfavorably in the
Monthly Review for February 1804.   Southey
championed his cause and insisted that the young
man had been maligned by a hostile reviewer.
Because of his early death, White, like Chatterton before him and Keats after him, became the
sumbol of youthful genius hounded to death by
critical abuse.

84.   A quote from Southey's biography of White (I, 18).
       Italics are by "J. S."

85.   John Wilson Croker was Secretary to the Admiralty
       (1810-1830) and, among other works, wrote The
       Battles of Talavera (1809).   In his list of possi-
       bilities, "J. S." finally includes the actual re-
       viewer.

86.   Reynolds' article was reprinted in the Examiner for
       October 11, 1818, pp. 648-649.

87.   "Government spies," Leonidas F. Jones tells us, "who
       were the subject of heated Parlimentary debates
       in 1817" (Selected Prose, p. 401).

88.   Reynolds was only one year older than Keats, but
       here he adopts the persona of a middle-aged,
       general reader (far removed "from the world of
       letters," he later tells us) who marvels at the
       ability of the youthful author of Endymion.

90.   From these sinecures Gifford earned annually £100
       and £1000 respectively.

90.   See note 83 above.

91.   A cut at the evils of critical anonymity.

92.   Lady Morgan, Sydney Owenson (1776-1859), an Irish
       woman of letters who had sympathized with the
       French revolutionists and had also gained the sup-
       port of some Whig leaders, was continually at-
       tacked by the Quarterly.   One of the most vicious
       of such attacks occurred in a review of her book,
       France (1817), in the Quarterly for April 1817
       (XVII, 260-286).

93.   Unidentified.

94.   Hunt's "Young Poets," December 1, 1816.

95.   As mentioned in the text below, Thomas Campbell
      was the author of The Pleasures of Hope (1799).
      Samuel Rogers was the author of The Pleasures of
      Memory (1792).

96.   Probably an allusion to William Collins' "The Pas-
      sions: An Ode for Music" (1746).

97.   Eastern tales were frequent enough in this period to
      make this reference general; but in terms of the
      specifics of this paragraph, Reynolds probably had
      Byron's series of Oriental Tales and Moore's Lalla
      Rookh in mind.

98.   Polonius' aside in Hamlet, II. ii. ll. 187-188.
      Moore's early poems, The Poetical Works of
      Thomas Little, Esq. (1802) in particular, are
      filled with amatory, erotic verses.

99.   Between the time of Dryden and Wordsworth, a period
      of more than 150 years, the laureatship was not
      held by a poet of major importance. Southey, who
      preceded Wordsworth, was no exception.

100. A further expansion of Reynolds' persona; it echoes
      the statement of "J. S." in the Morning Chronicle of
      October 3.

101. An allusion to Julius Caesar, I. iii. l. 481.

102. Gifford had edited the plays of Massinger (1805) and
      Jonson (1816).

103. On October 5, 1818 "The Triumph of Bacchus" was
      quoted from Endymion, IV. ll. 182-272.

104. The quotation is from Croker's review in the
      Quarterly.

105. Keats uses this phrase in his Preface to Endymion.

106. The Examiner did not review Endymion, perhaps be-
      cause Hunt originally hoped, fruitlessly as events

developed, to forestall the inevitable Tory assault
that would result from his praise of Keats.   Instead, he came to Keats's aid by reprinting
articles such as this one.   It will be remembered
that Hunt had already reprinted part of the letter
of "J. S. " in the Morning Chronicle and the entire
Reynolds article from the Alfred.

107.   The title of Fletcher's pastoral, tragicomic play.

108.   "Charles C. C. [Cowden Clarke], a mutual friend. "
       (Hunt's note.)

109.   The episode of the crowns of laurel and ivy exchanged
       by Hunt and Keats before or on March 1, 1817 is
       told by Walter J. Bate in John Keats (New York,
       1966), pp. 137-140.   The two friends wrote son-
       nets on the occasion.   (Hunt's sonnets appeared
       in Foliage and are reprinted below this poem;
       Keats's sonnet, beginning "Minutes are flying
       swiftly, " was never published by him and did not
       appear in print until 1914.)   Visitors then arrived.
       Hunt suggested that he and Keats take off their
       crowns, but Keats insisted on wearing his.
       Later he was to feel acute embarrassment over
       the incident.

110.   Hunt speaks of the limitations of Pope and his pres-
       ent-day followers (Byron and Moore excluded) in
       his Preface to Foliage (pp. xiii-xiv).   Keats had
       also attacked the Augustans in "Sleep and Poetry, "
       ll. 181-206.

111.   In his Preface to Foliage, Hunt states "that Pope and
       the French school of versification ... have mis-
       taken mere smoothness for harmony..." (pp. xiii-
       xiv).   "With the endeavour to recur to a freer
       spirit of versification, " Hunt continues, "I have
       joined one of still greater importance, --that of
       having a free and idiomatic cast of language" (p.
       xv).   Beppo's line is an exaggeration of these
       statements.

112.   Hunt owned a cottage near Hampstead Heath that
       Keats frequently visited.

113.   An allusion to the laurel and ivy crowns that Hunt

and Keats exchanged.   Another allusion occurs in
the last lines of the poem.

114.   A parody of the line "God! she is like a milk-white
lamb that bleats" from Keats's poem beginning
"Woman! when I behold thee flippant, vain. "

115.   Earlier in the review "Z. " claimed that Hunt "died,
as might have been prophesied, within a few hours
saunter of the spot where he was born, and without having been once beyond the well-fenced meadows of his microcosm" (p. 74).

116.   It is not clear why this adjective is placed in quotation marks.

117.   Aesculapius, the son of Apollo, was both the Greek
and Roman god of medicine and of healing.   The
reference, of course, is to Keats.

118.   Hunt wrote an essay "On Washerwomen" in the Examiner of September 15, 1816.   It was later reprinted over the initials "L. H. " in the second volume of Hazlitt's Round Table (1817).

119.   This quote is an improvisation on Dryden's "Epigram
on Milton, " which follows:
"Three poets, in three distant ages born,
Greece, Italy, and England did adorn.
The first in loftiness of thought surpass'd,
The next in majesty, in both the last:
The force of Nature could no farther go;
To make a third, she join'd the former two. "

120.   These names do not seem to have any special significance, other than the suggestion of derogatory
pseudonyms for Keats.

121.   Wilson is probably paraphrasing rather than quoting
directly.   As a result, it is difficult to identify
the exact source of the quote.   The general idea
may have come from Dryden.   In Mac Flecknoe,
Shadwell receives the mantle of dullness from
Richard Flecknoe "With double portion of his
father's art. "

122.   This allusion and the one to whales that follows are

from 11. 10-12 of "To Ailsa Rock":
"Thy life is but two dead eternities--
The last in the air, the former in the deep;
First, with the whales, last with eagle-skies...."

123. Keats's "Great spirits" sonnet, addressed to Haydon.

124. Although Blackwood's disliked Shelley's liberal principles, it frequently praised his poetry. Wilson,
in particular, had "a firm conviction of Shelley's
great genius...." (Newman I. White, The Unextinguished Hearth [Durham, 1938], p. 23.)

125. James Montgomery (1771-1854), poet, editor, and pro-
prietor of the Sheffield Iris, a newspaper.

126. Slightly misquoted from Macbeth, I. v. 1. 19.

127. George Steevens, as mentioned in note 67 above.

128. Unidentified.

129. Ralph Griffiths, owner and editor of the Monthly
Review. In February 1804 an unfavorable review of White's Clifton Grove appeared in the
Monthly. Southey vehemently attacked this review in his Remains and Life of White (see n.
83).

130. Francis Jeffrey wrote a caustic review of Montgomery's The Wanderer of Switzerland, and other
Poems in the Edinburgh for January 1807 (IX,
347-354).

131. The phrase is taken from the title of Montgomery's
poem, "The Joy of Grief," which is found in The
Wanderer of Switzerland (1806).

132. The two writers are Byron and Wordsworth. Byron's
Hours of Idleness was reviewed unfavorably in the
Edinburgh for January 1808 (XI, 285-289). Wordsworth was attacked several times in the Edinburgh,
the most infamous instance being Jeffrey's review
of The Excursion on November 1814 (XXIV, 1-30).

133. This reference, as it will later be established, is to

Croker's review of Endymion in the Quarterly,
XIX (April 1818), 204-208.

134. "Exalt our earthly minds to paradise," Petrarch,
      Sonnet X, 1. 9 from The Sonnets of Petrarch,
      trans. Joseph Auslander (New York, 1931), p. 10.
      The Italian is quoted "Levan di terra al ciel
      nostr' intellecto" in this dual language text.

135. A variant of Castalia.

136. A questionable assertion. In a survey limited to
      newspapers for the year 1818, reviews defenses
      and/or excerpts from Endymion appeared in the
      Yellow Dwarf (May 9), Oxford Herald (June 6),
      Champion (June 7), Morning Chronicle (October
      3, 8), Sun (October 5, 21), Alfred (October 6),
      and Examiner (October 12, November 1). Of
      these newspapers, the Morning Chronicle and the
      Sun had large, mass circulations.

137. For "his" read "the."

138. [No reference]

139. Salvator Rosa

140. Claude Lorrain

141. The image, which is applied to Diana, appears in III.
      ll. 63-66:

                              "the nested wren
          Has thy fair face within its tranquil ken,
          And from beneath a sheltering ivy leaf
          Takes glimpses of thee...."

142. Slightly misquoted from Burns's "Song Composed in
      Spring."

143. Slightly misquoted from Twelfth Night, II. iv. ll. 42-
      43.

144. Fletcher's The Mad Lover.

145. Slightly misquoted from Byron's Childe Harold, III. ll.
      11-12.

146.   Addison's The Campaign, l. 292.   Pope repeats this
        line in his Dunciad, III. l. 264.

147.   Slightly misquoted from Wordsworth's "Immortality
        Ode, " l. 125.

148.   As Leonidas M. Jones tells us ("Reynolds and Keats,"
        K-SJ, VII [1958], 52), Reynolds, in an effort to
        influence the editor of the Edinburgh in favor of
        Keats, wrote to Jeffrey on July 13, 1820.   Al-
        though Keats was almost twenty-five at the time,
        Reynolds informs Jeffrey that the poet is only
        twenty-two deliberately exaggerating "Keats's
        youth in order to make his accomplishment seem
        more remarkable..." (p. 53).   The letter under
        discussion was published in the London Times,
        October 30, 1928, p. 19, and is worth quoting at
        length.   Reynolds informs Jeffrey that "Mr. Keats
        is young--22 I should think.   He was educated for
        a Surgeon, but he has been foolish enough to aban-
        don his profession and trust to his books and a
        very trifling income left by his Father.   [It was
        his grandfather who left Keats an income.]   He is
        an orphan.   His health is now in the worst state,
        for as his medical man [Dr. George Darling] tells
        me he is in a decided consumption, of which
        malady his mother and Brother died.   He is ad-
        vised--nay ordered--to go to Italy; but in such a
        state it is a hopeless doom.   Owing to Leigh
        Hunt's patronage, Keats' name and fate have been
        joined with him in the Quarterly and Blackwoods
        magazine.   By his friends he is very much be-
        loved; and I know of no one who with such talents
        is so unaffected and sincere, or who with [such]
        rich personal abuse, as he has suffered, could
        be so cheerful and so firm.   His politics are
        strongly against the Quarterly Review.   I do not,
        my dear sir, at all ask you to review his book,
        unless you are disposed to do it, from reading it,
        as it were a book put into your hands by a
        Stranger. "   By calling his friend foolish in leav-
        ing his profession, Reynolds "made it clear to
        Jeffrey that Keats needed a friendly review"
        (Jones, p. 53).

149.   Both Fletcher's and Jonson's plays were seventeenth
        century pastoral dramas.   Endymion, of course,

is a pastoral poem.

150. Comus, 1. 729.

151. An allusion to the editor of the Quarterly. Gifford
      had edited the plays of Jonson in 1816.

152. The love song of Polyphemus (the Cyclops) for
      Galatea (the sea-nymph) is found in Theocritus'
      Bucolics, XI.

153. The lamentation of Venus for Adonis was by Bion
      rather than Moschus. Keats retells the story of
      Venus and Adonis in Endymion, I. ll. 457-579.

154. The legend to which Jeffrey refers is the story of
      Cupid and Psyche from Apuleius' Metamorphoses,
      or The Golden Ass. The parallel with Endymion
      and Cynthia is clear: in both instances the love
      of an immortal (Cupid, Cynthia) for a mortal
      (Psyche, Endymion) results in the deification of
      the latter.

155. Endymion and the Lamia volume are identified in the
      reviewer's footnote.

156. The author may be thinking of Shelley's "Ode to the
      West Wind," which was published with Prometheus
      Unbound in August 1820, the same month as this
      review of Keats. However, no attribution to
      Shelley can be made on this basis. It is clear
      from Shelley's comments and letters that he pre-
      ferred Hyperion to Endymion; he never would have
      claimed "greater freshness" for Endymion, as this
      reviewer does.

157. Quarterly Review, XIX (April 1818), 207.

Chapter IV

THE LAMIA VOLUME AND THE REVIEWS OF 1820

(Lamia, Isabella, The Eve of St. Agnes, and other Poems was published on either June 30 or July 1, 1820. By October, Keats's third volume had occasioned fourteen reviews in a wide variety of serials. Most of these items were favorable. The Lamia volume was praised by Richard Woodhouse in the Sun, Charles Lamb in the New Times, Leigh Hunt in the Indicator, John Scott in Baldwin's London Magazine, and by the Edinburgh Magazine and Literary Miscellany. There were still four other less important, but equally favorable, reviews and one favorable notice. In addition to the Sun and the New Times, Keats was praised by a third Tory newspaper, the St. James's Chronicle. Of those reviews which were mixed or unfavorable, only the Guardian's was completely without praise. To be sure, not everything that was written about the Lamia volume was perceptive [contemporary estimates of a literary masterpiece rarely are], but Keats's harshest critics were forced to assume a defensive posture. No better indication of this change in critical climate can be found than in the grudging admission of the British Critic that its previous censure of Endymion was too severe. With the exception of the Guardian and the Eclectic Review, the feeling was prevalent that the poet had been dealt with unfairly in 1818, and that the same injustice should not occur again in 1820.

It should be emphasized that a majority of the items in this chapter are reproduced for the first time. Accordingly, a significant body of material pertinent to Keats and the Lamia volume is now available to specialists in the period.)

1.   A review of the <u>Lamia</u> volume in the <u>Monthly Review</u>

> (This mixed but not unfriendly article appeared
> in the <u>Monthly Review, or Literary Journal,</u> XCII
> [July 1820], 305-310. [For further details con-
> cerning this magazine, see the introductory chap-
> ter, pp. 19-20.] The author is not known, but
> his neoclassical biases are clear from his "pre-
> conceived notions of the <u>manner</u> in which a poet
> ought to write," his admission that Keats's orig-
> inality shocks "our ideas of poetical decorum,"
> and his dislike of the poet's use of Greek and
> Roman mythology.   Nevertheless, these objections
> are expressed with a degree of tolerance.   <u>Endy-</u>
> <u>mion</u>, it is mentioned, did not receive "a fair
> <u>trial</u> before the public"; <u>Hyperion,</u> we are told, is
> a poem of great power.   Nothing is said about
> <u>Lamia</u> or <u>The Eve of St. Agnes</u>, however, and
> there is an imperceptive reference to the "Ode on
> a Grecian Urn."   If the author is not a discrim-
> inating critic, neither does he show any hostile
> intent.   Although noted before, the review is re-
> produced here for the first time.)

        This little volume must and ought to attract attention,
for it displays the ore of true poetic genius, though mingled
with a large portion of dross.   Mr. Keats is a very bold
author, bold perhaps because (as we learn) he has yet but
little more than touched the "years of discretion"; and he
has carried his peculiarities both of thought and manner to
an extreme which, at the first view, will to many persons
be very displeasing.   Yet, whatever may be his faults, he
is no <u>Della Crusca</u> poet;[1] for, though he is frequently involved in ambiguity, and dressed in the affectation of quaint
phrases, we are yet sure of finding in all that he writes the
proof of deep thought and energetic reflection.   Poetry is
now become so antient an art, and antiquity has furnished
such a store-house of expression and feeling, that we daily
meet with new worshippers of the Muse who are content to
repeat for the thousandth time her prescriptive language.
If any would deviate from the beaten track, and from those
great landmarks which have so long been the guides of the
world in all matters of taste and literary excellence, he will
find that it requires no timid foot to strike into new paths,
and must deem himself fortunate if he be not lost amid the
intricacies of a region with which he is unacquainted.   Yet,
even should this be partially the case, the wild and beauti-

ful scenery, which such an excursion is frequently the
means of developing, is a fair remuneration for the in-
equalities and obstructions which he may chance to experience on his ramble. We must add that only by attempts
like these can we discover the path of true excellence;
and that, in checking such efforts by illiberal and ill-timed
discouragement, we shut out the prospect of all improvement. Innovations of every kind, more especially in matters
of taste, are at first beheld with dislike and jealousy; it is
only by time and usage that we can appreciate their claims
to adoption.

        Very few persons, probably, will admire Mr. Keats
on a short acquaintance; and the light and the frivolous never
will. If we would enjoy his poetry, we must think over it;
and on this very account, which is perhaps the surest proof
of its merit, we are afraid that it will be slighted. Unfortunately, Mr. Keats may blame himself for much of this
neglect; since he might have conceded something to established taste, or (if he will) established prejudice, without
derogating from his own originality of thought and spirit.
On the contrary, he seems to have written directly in
despite of our preconceived notions of the manner in which
a poet ought to write; and he is continually shocking our
ideas of poetical decorum, at the very time when we are
acknowleging the hand of genius. In thus boldly
running counter to old opinions, however, we cannot conceive that Mr. Keats merits either contempt or ridicule;
the weapons which are too frequently employed when liberal
discussion and argument would be unsuccessful. At all
events, let him not be pre-judged without a candid examination of his claims. --A former work by this very young poet,
(Endymion,) which escaped our notice, cannot certainly be
said to have had a fair trial before the public; and now that an
opportunity is afforded for correcting that injustice, we trust
that the candour of all readers will take advantage of it.

        For ourselves, we think that Mr. Keats is very
faulty. He is often laboriously obscure; and he sometimes
indulges in such strange intricacies of thought, and peculiarities of expression, that we find considerable difficulty
in discovering his meaning. Most unluckily for him, he is
a disciple in a school in which these peculiarities are virtues:[2] but the praises of this small coterie will hardly
compensate for the disapproval of the rest of the literary
world. Holding, as we do, a high opinion of his talents,
especially considering his youth[3] and few advantages, we

regret to see him sowing the seeds of disappointment where
the fruit should be honour and distinction.   If his writings
were the dull common-places of an every-day versifier, we
should pass them by with indifference or contempt: but, as
they exhibit great force and feeling, we have only to regret
that such powers are misdirected.

The wild and high imaginations of antient mythology,
the mysterious being and awful histories of the deities of
Greece and Rome, form subjects which Mr. Keats evidently
conceives to be suited to his own powers: but, though
boldly and skilfully sketched, his delineations of the im-
mortals give a faint idea of the nature which the poets of
Greece attributed to them.   The only modern writer, by
whom this spirit has been completely preserved, is Lord
Byron, in his poem of "Prometheus."[4]   In this mould, too,
the character of Milton's Satan is cast.

The fragment of Hyperion, the last poem in the
volume before us, we consider as decidedly the best of Mr.
Keats's productions; and the power of both heart and hand
which it displays is very great.   We think, too, that it has
less conceit than other parts of the volume.   It is the
fable of the antient gods dethroned by the younger.

[Quotes I. 11. 1-14, 22-36.]

The appearance of Saturn among the Titans is splen-
didly told:

[Quotes II. 11. 105-128.]

The description of Hyperion also is really fine:

[Quotes II. 11. 371-391.]

The story of Isabella, or the Pot of Basil, from Boccaccio, is the worst part of the volume; and Mr. Barry
Cornwall's versification of this fable in his Sicilian Story[5]
is in some respects superior to Mr. Keats's attempt.   The
latter gentleman seems inclined, in this poem, to shew us
at once the extent of his simplicity and his affectation; witness the following tirade against the mercantile pride of
the brothers of Isabella:

[Quotes St. XVI, a rather overdone stanza, beginning "Why were they proud?"]

    Mr. Keats displays no great nicety in his selection
of images.   According to the tenets of that school of poetry
to which he belongs, he thinks that any thing or object in
nature is a fit material on which the poet may work; forgetting that poetry has a nature of its own, and that it is
the destruction of its essence to level its high being with
the triteness of every-day life.   Can there be a more
pointed concetto than this address to the Piping Shepherds
on a Grecian Urn?

            'Heard melodies are sweet, but those unheard
                 Are sweeter; therefore, yet soft pipes, play on;
            Not to the sensual ear, but, more endear'd,
                 Pipe to the spirit ditties of no tone:'
                                             [ll. 11-14.]

but it should be irksome to point out all the instances of
this kind which are to be found in Mr. K.'s compositions.

    Still, we repeat, this writer is very rich both in
imagination and fancy; and even a superabundance of the
latter faculty is displayed in his lines 'On Autumn,' which
bring the reality of nature more before our eyes than almost any description that we remember.

    [Quotes "To Autumn."]

    If we did not fear that, young as is Mr. K., his
peculiarities are fixed beyond all the power of criticism
to remove, we would exhort him to become somewhat less
strikingly original,--to be less fond of the folly of too new
or too old phrases,--and to believe that poetry does not
consist in either the one or the other.   We could then venture to promise him a double portion of the readers, and
a reputation which, if he persist in his errors, he will
never obtain.   Be this as it may, his writings present us
with so many fine and striking ideas, or passages, that we
shall always read his poems with much pleasure.

2.   A short review of the Lamia volume
        in the St. James's Chronicle

            (This brief commentary, favorable in intent,
        appeared in the St. James's Chronicle for July 1-4,
        1820.   The review itself is routine, and the au-

thor's contention that Keats's "peculiarity of expression" ruins the shorter poems in his 1820
volume--poems on which a large part of his pres-
ent-day reputation now stands--is obviously absurd; nevertheless, it is clear from the carefully
qualified tone of the following two paragraphs that
the Tories were retreating from their previous
position.)

THE POT OF BASIL

(From Mr. Keats's new Volume of Poems,
published this day.)

   The poetry of Mr. Keats is marked with an affected
peculiarity of expression which prevails, perhaps, too generally among his tuneful brethren of the present day.   This
characteristic is, indeed, soon lost sight of amid the lively
painting and exquisite tenderness with which his larger poems
abound; but it is fatal to his shorter pieces, and renders it
almost impossible to present any detached specimen even of
his best poems without creating an impression as unfavour-
able, as it is unjust.   The eminent injury which an author
distinguished by any singularity of style, is open to, from a
partial acquaintance, can be well appreciated by recollecting
the shock which Mr. Wordsworth's reputation has suffered
from the disingenuous selections made from his most
beautiful poems by the Edinburgh Review: but the Reviewers
might have spared their malignant industry.   To exhibit Mr.
Wordsworth in a ridiculous point of view, it was enough to
show him in parts; as the Scythian savage, we are told, was
convulsed with laughter at the bold tones and violent gesticulation of Pericles, because he was unable to comprehend
the heat of sentiment and full tide of feeling which gave a
peculiar propriety to both.   These considerations have
hitherto prevented us from offering any specimens of Mr.
Keats's poetry; and are now our motive for offering an extract rather longer than those to which our readers are accustomed.

   Isabel, the heroine, is instructed by a vision that
her lover Lorenzo has been murdered by her brothers,
and buried in a particular part of the forest:--

   [Quotes from Isabella, sts. XLIII-LXIII.]

3. Richard Woodhouse's review of
    the Lamia volume in the Sun

>   (This favorable review, which concentrates al-
>   most entirely upon Hyperion, appeared in the Sun
>   for July 10, 1820. Although it was first noted by
>   Dorothy Hewlett in her 1937 biography of Keats,
>   without any indication of the author, and again
>   mentioned, in somewhat greater detail, in her
>   second edition of A Life of John Keats [New York,
>   1949], p. 326, it seems to have escaped the at-
>   tention of J.R. MacGillivray, who does not list it
>   in Keats: A Bibliography and Reference Guide.
>   The review was written by Woodhouse, the
>   literary and legal advisor to Keats's pub-
>   lishers.
>
>   In his annotated copy of Endymion, Woodhouse
>   observes of Hyperion: "The poem if completed
>   would have treated of the dethronement of Hyperion,
>   the former God of the Sun, by Apollo, -- and inci-
>   dentally of those of Oceanus by Neptune, of Saturn
>   by Jupiter, etc. and of the war of the Giants for
>   Saturn's re-establishment...." (The Poems of
>   Keats, ed. Horace E. Scudder [Cambridge, Mass.,
>   1899], p. 198.) The phrasing of this note runs
>   parallel to the fourth paragraph of the review under
>   discussion: "The Poem it appears was intended to
>   contain the History of the Dethronement of Hyperion
>   from the Empire of the Sun, and the assumption of
>   his place by Apollo; an event said in the old Myth-
>   ology to have immediately succeeded the overthrow
>   of Saturn and his Titan brethren by Jupiter, Nep-
>   tune, and Pluto." Moreover, the high order of
>   praise for Keats and the passing references to the
>   "promise" of Poems and to Endymion not only sug-
>   gest that the review was written by someone with-
>   in Keats's circle, but are entirely consistent with
>   the esteem which Woodhouse expressed for the poet
>   in letters and notes. Additional evidence of Wood-
>   house's authorship, and the reason he chose not to
>   reveal it to Keats, is given in note 7 below. As
>   for the Sun, details about this newspaper are
>   given in the introductory chapter.)

[FROM A CORRESPONDENT.]

There are few things more delightful than the perusal of a new Volume of beautiful Poetry. Gray's "eternal
new Romances"6 are not to be compared with it. This delight we have just experienced in a very eminent degree,
and as we have reason to believe very few of our Readers
can have seen the Volume which has contributed to our enjoyment, we shall endeavour to impart to them some portion of our pleasure, in a short account of the Work before
us, which contains, besides the three Poems named in the
title [Lamia, Isabella, and The Eve of St. Agnes], several
smaller Pieces, and an unfinished Poem in blank verse, entitled HYPERION.

Mr. Keats is known to the Public as the Author of
a Volume of juvenile Poems of much promise, and of Endymion, a poetic Romance, founded on the classical story of
the loves of Endymion and Diana.

An Advertisement from the Publishers of the Volume
before us states, that the unfinished Poem of Hyperion,
which is now printed in its imperfect state, "was intended
to be of equal length with Endymion, but the reception given
to that Work discouraged the Author from proceeding."7 We
cannot but regret this circumstance for our own sake, as
well as from sympathy with the feelings of the Author, and
we shall be very much mistaken if our Readers, especially
such of them as shall be induced by our extracts to refer
to the Volume itself, do not join with us in the same
feeling. As our attention has been called to this fragment,
we shall proceed to give some account of it in the first
place, though it is last in order in the Volume.

The Poem it appears was intended to contain the
History of the Dethronement of Hyperion from the Empire
of the Sun, and the assumption of his place by APOLLO;
an event said in the old Mythology to have immediately succeeded the overthrow of SATURN and his TITAN bretheren
by JUPITER, NEPTUNE, and PLUTO. It opens as follows:

[Quotes I. ll. 1-51, 72-94.]

Saturn's speech ends with a determination to attempt
the recovery of his lost empire, and Thea conducts him to
a cavern, where the other fallen Titans are assembled.

We are then introduced to Hyperion, who alone--

                          --"still kept
          His sov'reignty, and rule, and majesty:"--
                          [I. ll. 164-165.]

and have the following beautiful description:--

          [Quotes I. ll. 203-213.]

for he had been perplexed with unpropitious omens, and
"horrors, portion'd to a giant's nerve"; [I. l. 175] and he
paces about his splendid halls, in restless anxiety for the
return of morning, when he might again begin his course
through the heavens. The blazing orb is prepared "six
dewy hours before the dawn in season due should blush, "
[I. ll. 264-265] and remains at the porch of heaven, waiting
for his command, but

          "He might not;--No, though a primeval God;
          The sacred seasons might not be disturb'd. "--
                          [I. ll. 292-293.]

          [Quotes I. ll. 299-304.]

          At length he determines to visit his fallen brethren,
and

          "--With a slow incline of his broad breast,
          Like to a diver in the pearly seas,
          Forward he stoop'd over the airy shore,
          And plung'd all noiseless into the deep night. "
                          [I. ll. 354-357.]

          The second book opens with a powerful description
of "that sad place where Cybele and the bruised Titans
mourn'd" [II. l. 4].

          [Quotes II. ll. 33-38.]

          Saturn and Thea arrive among the Titans, and a
council is held. The speeches of Oceanus Clymene and
Euceladus are exceedingly fine, and exhibit great discrimination of character with abundance of poetical beauty.
In the midst of their debate Hyperion approaches, and his
appearance is thus beautifully described;--

[Quotes II. ll. 367-378.]

The third Book introduces us to Apollo, in the Island
of Crete, before he was aware of his high destiny and immortal nature, and, after a beautiful description of the
young God, and his interview with Mnemosyne, it breaks suddenly off at the very interesting point where Apollo becomes
conscious of his Divinity, and is about to assume his true
character. We could scarcely have thought it possible, out
of such materials, to have produced a Poem of such interest,
and we again are compelled to express our regret that it
was not finished. It certainly, even in its present unfinished
state, is the greatest effort of Mr. Keats' genius, and
gives us reason to hope for something great from his pen.

Our limits prevent us from particularising the other
Poems which form the volume; they are very various in
their style, but all of great merit. The story of Isabella,
from Boccacio, is a specimen of beautiful simplicity and
affecting tenderness: the smaller Poems, especially the
Odes to a Nightingale, and on a Grecian Urn, deserve
high praise. We regret that we cannot insert them.

4.   Charles Lamb's review of the Lamia volume
      in the New Times.

(This favorable review appeared in the New
Times for July 19, 1820 and was then reprinted
in the Examiner for July 30, 1820, pp. 494-495.
It is acknowledged by all authorities to be the
work of Lamb and is included in E. V. Lucas'
edition of The Works of Charles and Mary Lamb
[London, 1905], I. 203, as well as in several
other sources. Lamb gained access to the New
Times through his friend, John Stoddart, who was
founder and editor of the newspaper. [See the
introductory chapter pp. 26-27 for further details
about the New Times.]
As noted by Lucas, Lamb was not a close
friend of Keats; they met only a few times, once
at Benjamin Haydon's "immortal dinner" in December 1817. "But he admired his work (he told
Crabb Robinson he considered it next to Wordsworth's), and he hated the treatment Keats received from certain critics" [I, 471]. In his re-

view, Lamb concentrates on the three principal
poems included in the title of Keats's 1820 volume.
He says nothing about either the great Odes or
Hyperion, but on July 21 the _New Times_ printed
extracts from these poems which Lucas suggests
were "presumably crowded out of the [July 19]
article..." [I, 470].)

[Quotes Sts. XXIV; XXV, ll. 1-8; XXVI-XXVII
from _The Eve of St. Agnes_.]

Such is the description which Mr. Keats has given
us, with a delicacy worthy of Christabel, of a high-born
damsel, in one of the apartments of an baronial castle, laying herself down devoutly to dream, on the charmed Eve
of St. Agnes; and like the radiance, which comes from those
old windows upon the limbs and garments of the damsel, is
the almost Chaucer-like painting, with which this poet illumes every subject he touches.   We have scarcely any thing
like it in modern description.   It brings us back to ancient
days, and

Beauty making-beautiful old rhymes. [8]

The finest thing in the volume is the paraphrase of
Boccacio's story of the Pot of Basil.   Two Florentines,
merchants, discovering that their sister Isabella has placed
her affections upon Lorenzo, a young factor in their employ, when they had hopes of procuring for her a noble
match, decoy Lorenzo, under pretence of a ride, into a
wood, where they suddenly stab and bury him.   The anticipation of the assassination is wonderfully conceived in one
epithet, in the narration of the ride--

So the two brothers, and their murder'd man,
   Rode past fair Florence, to where Arno's stream
Gurgles--
                                    [St. XXVII. ll. 1-3.]

Returning to their sister, they delude her with a story of
their having sent Lorenzo abroad to look after their mer-
chandises; but the spirit of her lover appears to Isabella
in a dream, and discovers how and where he was stabbed,
and the spot where they have buried him.   To ascertain
the truth of the vision, she sets out to the place, accompanied by her old nurse, ignorant as yet of her wild purpose.

Her arrival at it, and digging for the body, is described in
the following stanzas, than which there is nothing more
awfully simple in diction, more nakedly grand and moving
in sentiment, in Dante, in Chaucer, or in Spenser:--

[Quotes Sts. XLVI-XLVIII.]

        To pursue the story in prose. --They find the body,
and with their joint strengths sever from it the head, which
Isabella takes home, and wrapping it in a silken scarf, en-
tombs it in a garden-pot, covers it with mould, and over
it she plants sweet basil, which, watered with her tears,
thrives so that no other basil tufts in all Florence throve
like her basil. How her brothers, suspecting something
mysterious in the herb, which she watched day and night,
at length discover the head, and secretly convey the basil
from her; and how from the day that she loses her basil
she pines away, and at last dies, we must refer our readers
to the poem, or to the divine germ of it in Boccacio. It
is a great while ago since we read the original; and in this
affecting revival of it we do but

Weep again a long-forgotten woe. [9]

        More exuberantly rich in imagery and painting is the
story of the Lamia. It is of as gorgeous stuff as ever
romance was composed of. Her first appearance in ser-
pentine form--

        --a[10] beauteous wreath with melancholy eyes--
                                        [I. 1. 84.]

her dialogue with Hermes, the Star of Lethe [I. 1. 81] as
he is called by one of those prodigal phrases which Mr.
Keats abounds in, which are each a poem in a word, and
which in this instance lays open to us at once, like a picture, all the dim regions and their inhabitants, and the sudden coming of a celestial among them; the charming of her
into woman's shape again by the God; her marriage with the
beautiful Lycius; her magic palace, which those who knew
the street, and remembered it complete from childhood,
never remembered to have seen before; the few Persian
mutes, her attendants.

                --who that same year
        Were seen about the markets: none knew where
        They could inhabit;--
                                        [I. 11. 390-392.]

the high-wrought splendours of the nuptial bower, with the
fading of the whole pageantry, Lamia, and all, away, before
the glance of Apollonius, --are all that fairy land can do for
us. They are for younger impressibilities. To us an
ounce of feeling is worth a pound of fancy; and therefore we
recur again, with a warmer gratitude, to the story of Isabella and the pot of basil, and those never-cloying stanzas
which we have cited, and which we think should disarm criticism, if it be not in its nature cruel; if it would not deny
to honey its sweetness, nor to roses redness, nor light to
stars in Heaven; if it would not bay the moon out of the
skies, rather than acknowledge she is fair.

5.   A review of the Lamia volume in the
     Literary Chronicle and Weekly Review

             (This rather perfunctory review, unfavorable in
        the main, appeared in the Literary Chronicle for
        July 29, 1820, pp. 484-485. The author, whose
        identity can not be definitely established, quotes
        with approval the "Ode on a Grecian Urn" and
        "Bards of Passion and of Mirth, " but he makes
        only the most general comment about the title
        poems in the volume. [One suspects he may not
        have read them.] Keats is accused of affectation,
        unintelligible quaintness, and excessive word coin-
        age, faults which if they apply to Keats at all,
        should have been assigned to Poems. However,
        the reviewer perversely states that "Keats's
        former productions augured better things. "
        George Felton Mathew, who only approved of
        Keats's early, inferior poems, was capable of
        such insensitivity; but there is no evidence avail-
        able to document this conjecture. Although noted
        before, the review is reproduced here for the first
        time.)

It is customary in Paris and some other places, to present
their friends on New Year's Day with some expressive wishes
for their future happiness, wealth, or success, in such matters as may be deemed most agreeable. Following this example, we will, at Midsummer instead of Christmas, offer
Mr. Keats our wishes, and, whether they may be agreeable
or not, we assure him they are sincere. First, then, we
wish that he would renounce all acquaintance with our metro-

politan poets. 11   Secondly, that he would entirely abandon
their affected school, instead of being a principal supporter
of it; and, exiling himself for twelve months to North Wales
or the Highlands of Scotland, trust to nature's ever varying
scene and his own talents.   And, lastly, until he does all
this, we wish that he would never write any poem of more
than an hundred verses at the utmost.   Of the propriety of
this last piece of advice, we believe all who have read
his works will become sensible, and were any other argument wanting, the volume before us would furnish it.

We believe there is a sort of fashion observed by
authors or booksellers, to place the longest poems at the
commencement of a volume, although we are convinced it
is often an injudicious one; we would rather tempt the
reader by some short and delicate morceau than run the
hazard of exhausting his patience or exciting his disgust,
by putting the worst piece in the front ranks, because it is
largest.   Lamia and Isabella, and the Eve of St. Agnes
have some fine passages, but we can award them no higher
praise.   Among the minor poems, many of which possess
considerable merit, the following appears to be the best:--

[Quotes "Ode on a Grecian Urn. "]

There is a pretty idea, happily expressed, in the
following ode:--

[Quotes "Bards of Passion and of Mirth. "]

We confess this volume has disappointed us; from
Mr. Keats's former productions, we had augured better
things, and we are confident he can do better; let him
avoid all sickly affectation on one hand, and unintellible
quaintness on the other.   Let him avoid coining new
words, and give us the English language as it is taught and
written in the nineteenth century, and he will have made
considerable progress toward improvement.   These poems
contain many beautiful passages, but they are too thickly
strewed with the faults we have noticed, to entitle them
to more than a very qualified approval.

6.   Hunt's review of the Lamia volume in the Indicator

(This favorable review appeared in Hunt's

Indicator for August 2 and August 9, 1820, pp. 337-
344, 345-352. [For further details about this
weekly, see the introductory chapter, p. 23.] The
review has been noted in several sources and was
reprinted by Edmund Blunden in Leigh Hunt's
"Examiner Examined" [London, 1928], pp. 141-157,
and by H. B. and M. B. Forman in their Hampstead
Edition of Keats's Poetical Works and Other Writings [New York, 1938-1939], III, 290-306. The
writer's proprietary reference in the last paragraph
of this review to the Examiner and the Indicator
as "our own," and his earlier allusion to his
friendship with Keats, clearly indicates Hunt's
authorship. Despite more plot summary than is
necessary, Hunt's critical comments on the "Ode
to a Nightingale," Hyperion, and the title poems
in the 1820 volume are generally sensitive and intelligent. Like Lamb, Hunt was fully aware of
Keats's achievement. "Mr. Keats," he tells us,
"undoubtedly takes his seat with the oldest and best
of our living poets.")

[August 2, 1820]

In laying before our readers an account of another
new publication, it is fortunate that the nature of the work
again falls in with the character of our miscellany; part of
the object of which is to relate the stories of old times.
We shall therefore abridge into prose the stories which Mr.
Keats has told in poetry, only making up for it, as we go,
by cutting some of the richest passages out of his verse,
and fitting them in to our plainer narrative. They are such
as would leaven a much greater lump. Their drops are rich
and vital, the essence of a heap of fertile thoughts.

The first story, entitled Lamia, was suggested to
our author by a passage in Burton's Anatomy of Melancholy,
which he has extracted at the end of it. We shall extract
it here, at the beginning, that the readers may see how he
has enriched it. Burton's relation is itself an improvement
on the account in Philostratus. The old book-fighter with
melancholy thoughts is speaking of the seductions of phan-
tasmata.

"Philostratus, in his fourth book 'DeVita Apolloni,'
hath a memorable instance in this kind, which I may not

omit, of one Menippus Lycius, a young man twenty-five
years of age, that going betwixt Cenchreas and Corinth,
met such a phantasm in the habit of a fair gentlewoman,
which taking him by the hand, carried him home to her
house, in the suburbs of Corinth, and told him she was a
Phoenician by birth, anf if he would tarry with her, he
should hear her sing and play, and drink such wine as never
any drank, and no man should molest him; but she, being
fair and lovely, would live and die with him, that was fair
and lovely to behold. The young man, a philosopher,
otherwise staid and discreet, able to moderate his passions,
though not this of love, tarried with her awhile to his great
content, and at last married her, to whose wedding,
amongst other guests, came Apollonius; who, by some
probable conjectures, found her out to be a serpent, a
lamia; and that all her furniture was, like Tantalus' gold,
described by Homer, no substance but mere illusions.
When she saw herself descried, she wept, and desired
Apollonius to be silent, but he would not be moved, and
therefore she, plate, house, and all that was in it, vanished
in an instant: many thousands took notice of this fact, for
it was done in the midst of Greece."--Anat. of Mel. Part
3, Sect. 2.

According to our poet, Mercury had come down from
heaven, one day, in order to make love to a nymph, famous
for her beauty. He could not find her; and he was halting
among the woods uneasily, when he heard a lonely voice,
complaining. It was

> A mournful voice,
> Such as once heard, in gentle heart, destroys
> All pain but pity: thus the lone voice spake.
> "When from this wreathed tomb shall I awake!
> "When move in a sweet body fit for life,
> "And love, and pleasure, and the ruddy strife
> "Of hearts and lips! Ah, miserable me!"
>   [Lamia I. ll. 35-41.]

Mercury went looking about among the trees and grass,

> Until he found a palpitating snake,
> Bright, and cirque-couchant in a dusky brake.
>   [I. ll. 45-46.]

The admiration, pity, and horror, to be excited by humanity
in a brute shape, were never perhaps called upon by a

greater mixture of beauty and deformity than in the picture
of this creature.   Our pity and suspicions are begged by
the first word: the profuse and vital beauties with which
she is covered seem proportioned to her misery and natural
rights; and lest we should lose sight of them in this gor-
geousness, the "woman's mouth" [I. l. 60] fills us at once
with shuddering and compassion.

[Quotes I. ll. 47-63.]

The serpent tells Mercury that she knows upon what quest
he is bound, and asks him if he has succeeded.   The god,
with the usual eagerness of his species to have his will,
falls into the trap; and tells her that he will put her in
possession of any wish she may have at heart, provided she
can tell him where to find his nymph.   As eagerly, she
accepts his promise, making him ratify it by an oath, which
he first pronounces with an earnest lightness, and afterwards with a deeper solemnity.

[Quotes I. ll. 112-114.]

The creature tells him that it was she who had rendered
the nymph invisible, in order to preserve her from the im-
portunities of the ruder wood gods.   She adds, that she was
a woman herself, that she loves a youth of Corinth and
wishes to be a woman again, and that if he will let
her breathe upon his eyes, he shall see his invisible beauty.
The god sees, loves, and pervails.   The serpent undergoes
a fierce and convulsive change, and flies toward Corinth,

A full-born beauty, new and exquisite.
[I. l. 172.]

Lamia, whose liability to painful metamorphosis was re-
lieved by a supernatural imagination, had been attracted by
the beauty of Lycius, while pitching her mind among the
enjoyments of Corinth.   By the same process, she knew
that he was to pass along, that evening, on the road from
the sea-side to Corinth; and there accordingly she contrives
to have an interview, which ends in his being smitten with
love, and conducting her to her pretended home in that city.
She represents herself as a rich orphan, living 'but half-
retired,' [I. l. 312] and affects to wonder that he never
saw her before.   As they enter Corinth, they pass the
philosopher Apollonius, who is Lycius's tutor, and from
whom he instinctively conceals his face.   Lamia's hand

shudders in that of her lover; but she says she is only
wearied; and at the same moment, they stop at the entrance
of a magnificent house:--

[Quotes I. ll. 379-382.]

Here they lived for some time, undisturbed by the world,
in all the delight of a mutual passion. The house remained
invisible to all eyes, but those of Lycius. There were a
few Persian mutes, 'seen that year about the markets' [I.
ll. 390-391]; and nobody knew whence they came; but the
most inquisitive were baffled in endeavouring to track them
to some place of abode.

But all this while, a god was every night in the
house, taking offence. Every night

With a[12] terrific glare,
Love, jealous grown of so complete a pair,
Hovered and buzzed his wings with fearful roar
Above the lintel of their chamber door,
And down the passage cast a glow upon the floor.
[II. ll. 11-15.]

Lycius, to the great distress of his mistress, who saw in
his vanity a great danger, persuaded her to have a public
wedding-feast. She only begged him not to invite Apollonius;
and then, resolving to dress up her bridals with a sort of
despairing magnificence, equal to her apprehensions of
danger, she worked a fairy architecture in secret, served
only with the noise of wings and a restless sound of music--

A haunting music, sole perhaps and lone
Supportress of the faery-roof, made moan
Throughout, as fearful the whole charm might fade.
[II. ll. 122-124.]

This is the very quintessence of the romantic. The walls
of the long vaulted room were covered with palms and
plantain-trees imitated in cedar-wood, and meeting over
head in the middle of the ceiling; between the stems were
jasper pannels, from which 'there burst forth creeping
imagery of slighter trees'; [II. ll. 139-140] and before each
of these 'lucid pannels'

Fuming stood
A censer filled[13] with myrrh and spiced wood,

> Whose slender feet wide-swerved upon the soft
> Wool-woofed carpets: fifty wreaths of smoke
> From fifty censers their light voyage took
> To the high roof, still mimicked as they rose
> Along the mirrored walls by twin-clouds odorous.
> > [II. ll. 175-176, 178-182.]

Twelve tables stood in this room, set round with circular
couches, and on every table was a noble feast and the
statue of a god.

> [Quotes II. ll. 133-137, 142-145.]

The guests came. They wondered and talked; but
their gossiping would have ended well enough, when the wine
prevailed, had not Apollonius, an unbidden guest, come with
them. He sat right opposite the lovers, and

> --Fixed his eye, without a twinkle or stir
> Full on the alarmed beauty of the bride,
> Brow-beating her fair form, and troubling her
> > sweet pride.
> > > [II. ll. 246-248.]

Lycius felt her hand grow alternately hot and cold, and
wondered more and more both at her agitation and the conduct of his old tutor. He looked into her eyes, but they
looked nothing in return: he spoke to her, but she made
no answer: by degrees the music ceased, the flowers
faded away, the pleasure all darkened, and

> A deadly silence step by step increased,
> Until it seemed a horrid presence there,
> And not a man but felt the terror in his hair.
> > [II. ll. 266-268.]

The bridegroom at last shrieked out her name; but it was
only echoed to him by the room. Lamia sat fixed, her
face of a deadly white. He called in mixed agony and rage
to the philosopher to take off his eyes; but Apollonius, re-
fusing, asked him whether his old guide and instructor who
had preserved him from all harm to that day, ought to see
him made the prey of a serpent. A mortal faintness came
into the breath of Lamia at this word; she motioned him,
as well as she could, to be silent; but looking her sted-
fastly in the face, he repeated Serpent! and she vanished
with a horrible scream. Upon the same night, died Lycius,

and was swathed for the funeral in his wedding-garments.

Mr. Keats has departed as much from common-place
in the character and moral of this story, as he has in the
poetry of it.   He would see fair play to the serpent, and
makes the power of the philosopher an ill-natured and dis-
turbing thing.   Lamia though liable to be turned into painful shapes had a soul of humanity; and the poet does not see
why she should not have her pleasures accordingly, merely
because a philosopher saw that she was not a mathematical
truth.   This is fine and good.   It is vindicating the greater
philosophy of poetry.   At the same time, we wish that for
the purpose of his story he had not appeared to give into the
common-place of supposing that Apollonius's sophistry must
always prevail, and that modern experiment has done a
deadly thing to poetry by discovering the nature of the rainbow, the air, &c. 14: that is to say, that the knowledge of
natural history and physics, by shewing us the nature of
things, does away [with] the imaginations that once adorned
them.   This is a condescension to a learned vulgarism,
which so excellent a poet as Mr. Keats ought not to have
made.   The world will always have fine poetry, as long as
it has events, passions, affections, and a philosophy that
sees deeper than philosophy.   There will be a poetry of the
heart, as long as there are tears and smiles; there will
be a poetry of the imagination, as long as the first causes
of things remain a mystery.   A man who is not poet, may
think he is none, as soon as he finds out the physical cause
of the rainbow; but he need not alarm himself:--he was none
before.   The true poet will go deeper.   He will ask himself
what is the cause of that physical cause; whether truths to
the senses are after all to be taken as truths to the imagination; and whether there is not room and mystery enough in
the universe for the creation of infinite things, when the
poor matter-of-fact philosopher has come to the end of his
own vision.   It is remarkable that an age of poetry has
grown up with the progress of experiment; and that the very
poets, who seem to countenance these notions, accompany
them by some of their finest effusions.   Even if there were
nothing new to be created,--if philosophy, with its line and
rule, could even score the ground, and say to poetry 'Thou
shalt go no further,' she would look back to the old world,
and still find it inexhaustible.   The crops from its fertility
are endless.   But these alarms are altogether idle.   The
essence of poetical enjoyment does not consist in belief,
but in a voluntary power to imagine.

The next story, that of the Pot of Basil, is from
Boccaccio. After the narrative of that great writer, we
must make as short work of it as possible in prose. To
turn one of his stories into verse, is another thing. It is
like setting it to a more elaborate music. Mr. Keats is
so struck with admiration of his author, that even while
giving him this accompaniment, he breaks out into apology
to the great Italian, asking pardon for this

--Echo of him[15] in the north-wind sung.
[St. XX. l. 8.]

We might waive a repetition of the narrative altogether, as
the public have lately been familiarized with it in the Sicilian
Story of Mr. Barry Cornwall: but we cannot help calling to
mind that the hero and heroine were two young and happy
lovers, who kept their love a secret from her rich brothers;
that her brothers, getting knowledge of their intercourse,
lured him into a solitary place, and murdered him; that
Isabella, informed of it by a dreary vision of her lover,
found out where he was buried, and with the assistance of
her nurse, severed the head from the body that she might
cherish even that ghastly memorial of him as a relic never
to be parted with; that she buried the head in a pot of
earth, and planting basil over it, watered the leaves with
her continual tears till they grew into wonderful beauty and
luxuriance; that her brothers, prying into her fondness for
the Pot of Basil, which she carried with her from place to place,
contrived to steal it away; that she made such lamentations
for it, as induced them to wonder what could be its value,
upon which they dug into it, and discovered the head; that
the amazement of the discovery struck back upon their
hearts, so that after burying the head secretly, they left
their native place, and went to live in another city; and that
Isabella continued to cry and moan for her Pot of Basil,
which she had not the power to cease wishing for; till, under
the pressure of that weeping want, she died.

Our author can pass to the most striking imaginations
from the most delicate and airy fancy. He says of the
lovers in their happiness,

Parting they seemed to tread upon the air,
Twin roses by the zephyrs blown apart
Only to meet again more close, and share
The inward fragrance of each other's heart.
[St. X. ll. 1-4.]

These pictures of their intercourse terribly aggravate the
gloom of what follows.   Lorenzo, when lured away to be
killed, is taken unknowingly out of his joys, like a lamb out of
the pasture.   The following masterly anticipation of his end,
conveyed in a single word, has been justly admired:16--

> So the two brothers and their murder'd man
> Rode past fair Florence....
>   [St. XXVII. ll. 1-2. Hunt con-
>   tinues to quote ll. 2-3 and 7-8.]

When Mr. Keats errs in his poetry, it is from the ill
management of a good thing,--exuberance of ideas.   Once
or twice, he does so in a taste positively bad, like Marino17
or Cowley, as in a line in his Ode to Psyche

> At tender eye-dawn of aurorean love;
>   [l. 20.]

but it is once or twice only, in his present volume.   Nor
has he erred much in it in a nobler way.   What we allude
to is one or two passages in which he over-informs the
occasion or the speaker; as where the brothers, for instance,
whom he describes as a couple of mere 'money-bags,' are
gifted with the power of uttering the following exquisite
metaphor:--

> 'To day we purpose, ay, this hour we mount
>   To spur three leagues toward the Apennine:
> Come down, we pray thee, ere the hot sun count
>   His dewy rosary on the eglantine.'18
>   [St. XXIV. ll. 1-4.]

But to return to the core of the story.19   Observe the fervid misery of the following.

> [Quotes Sts. XLVI-XLVIII.]

It is curious to see how the simple pathos of Boccaccio, or (which is the same feeling) the simple intensity
of the heroine's feelings, suffices our author more and
more, as he gets to the end of his story.   And he has related it as happily, as if he had never written any poetry
but that of the heart.   The passage about the tone of her
voice,--the poor lost-witted coaxing,--the 'chuckle,' in
which she asks after her Pilgrim20 and her Basil,--is as
true and touching an instance of the effect of a happy

familiar word, as any in all poetry. The poet bids his
imagination depart,

> For Isabel, sweet Isabel, will die....
> [St. LXI. l. 6.   Hunt continues to quote from
> St. LXI. ll. 7-8 and Sts. LXII-LXIII.]

The Eve of St. Agnes, which is rather a picture than
a story, may be analysed in a few words. It is an account
of a young beauty, who going to bed on the eve in question
to dream of her lover, while her rich kinsmen, the opposers
of his love, are keeping holiday in the rest of the house,
finds herself waked by him in the night, and in the hurry of
the moment agrees to elope with him. The portrait of the
heroine, preparing to go to bed, is remarkable for its
union of extreme richness and good taste; not that those two
properties of description are naturally distinct; but that they
are too often separated by very good poets, and that the
passage affords a striking specimen of the sudden and strong
maturity of the author's genius. When he wrote Endymion
he could not have resisted doing too much. To the description before us, it would be a great injury either to add or
diminish. It falls at once gorgeously and delicately upon
us, like the colours of the painted glass. Nor is Madeline
hurt by all her encrusting jewelry and rustling silks. Her
gentle, unsophisticated heart is in the midst, and turns
them into so many ministrants to her loveliness.

> [Quotes Sts. XXIV-XXVII.]

Is not this perfectly beautiful?

> [Want of room compels us to break off here. We
> cannot leave the reader at a better place. The remainder
> of the criticism must occupy the beginning of our next
> number.]

[August 9, 1820]

As a specimen of the Poems, which are all lyrical,
we must indulge ourselves in quoting entire the Ode to a
Nightingale. There is that mixture in it of real melancholy
and imaginative relief, which poetry alone presents us in
her 'charmed cup,'[21] and which some over-rational critics
have undertaken to find wrong because it is not true. It
does not follow that what is not true to them, is not true
to others. If the relief is real, the mixture is good and

sufficing. A poet finds refreshment in his imaginary wine,
as other men do in their real; nor have we the least doubt,
that Milton found his grief for the loss of his friend King,
more solaced by the allegorical recollections of Lycidas,
(which were exercises of his mind, and recollections of a
friend who would have admired them) than if he could have
anticipated Dr. Johnson's objections, and mourned in nothing
but broadcloth and matter of fact. He yearned after the
poetical as well as social part of his friend's nature; and
had as much right to fancy it straying in the wilds and oceans
of romance, where it had strayed, as in the avenues of
Christ's College where his body had walked. In the same
spirit the imagination of Mr. Keats betakes itself, like the
wind, 'where it listeth, '22 and is as truly there, as if his feet
could follow it. The poem will be the more striking to the
reader, when he understands what we take a friend's liberty
in telling him, that the author's powerful mind has for some
time past been inhabiting a sickened and shaken body, and
that in the mean while it has had to contend with feelings that
make a fine nature ache for its species, even when it would dis-
dain to do so for itself;--we mean, critical malignity, --that unhappy envy, which would wreak its own tortures upon others,
especially upon those that really feel for it already. 23

[Quotes "Ode to a Nightingale"]

   The Hyperion is a fragment, --a gigantic one, like a
ruin in the desert, or the bones of the mastodon. It is
truly of a piece with its subject, which is the downfall of
the elder gods. It opens with Saturn, dethroned, sitting in
a deep and solitary valley, benumbed in spite of his huge
powers with the amazement of the change.

[Quotes I. ll. 1-41.]

   By degrees, the Titans meet in one spot, to con-
sult how they may regain their lost empire; but Clymene
the gentlest, and Oceanus the most reflective of those
earlier deities, tell them that it is irrevocable. A very
grand and deep-thoughted cause is assigned for this by the
latter. Intellect, he gives them to understand, was inevitably displacing a more brute power.

[Quotes II. ll. 182-190, 202-215.]

   The more imaginative parts of the poem are worthy
of this sublime moral. Hyperion, the God of the Sun, is

the last to give way; but horror begins to visit his old
beatitude with new and dread sensations. The living beauty
of his palace, whose portals open like a rose, the awful
phaenomena that announce a change in heaven, and his inability to bid the day break as he was accustomed, --all this
part, in short, which is the core and inner diamond of the
poem, we must enjoy with the reader.

[Quotes I. ll. 176-304.]

The other Titans, lying half lifeless in their valley
of despair, are happily compared to

> A dismal cirque
> Of Druid stones, upon a forlorn moor,
> When the chill rain begins at shut of eve,
> In dull November, and their chancel vault,
> The Heaven itself, is blinded throughout night.
> [II. ll. 34-38.]

The fragment ends with the deification of Apollo. It
strikes us that there is something too effeminate and human in the way in which Apollo receives the exaltation
which his wisdom is giving him. He weeps and wonders
somewhat too fondly; but his powers gather nobly on him
as he proceeds. He exclaims to Mnemosyne, the Goddess
of Memory,

> Knowledge enormous makes a God of me,
> Names, deeds, gray legends, dire events, rebellions,
> Majesties, sovran voices, agonies,
> Creations and destroying, all at once
> Pour into the wide hollows of my brain,
> And deify me, as if some blithe wine
> Or bright elixir peerless I had drunk,
> And so become immortal.
> [III. ll. 113-120.]

After this speech, he is seized with a glow of aspiration,
and an intensity of pain, proportioned to the causes that are
changing him; Mnemosyne upholds her arms, as one who
prophesied; and

> At length
> Apollo shrieked;--and lo! from all his limbs
> Celestial   *   *   *   *   *   *
> [III. ll. 134-136.]

Here the poem ceases, to the great impatience of the poetical
reader.

     If any living poet could finish this fragment, we be-
lieve it is the author himself.   But perhaps he feels that he
ought not.   A story which involves passion, almost of
necessity involves speech; and though we may well enough
describe beings greater than ourselves by comparison, unfortunately we cannot make them speak by comparison.   Mr.
Keats, when he first introduces Thea consoling Saturn, says
that she spoke

> Some mourning words, which in our feeble tongue
> Would come in these like accents; O how frail
> To that large utterance of the early Gods!
>   [I. 11. 49-51.]

This grand confession of want of grandeur is all that he
could do for them.   Milton could do no more.   Nay, he did
less, when according to Pope he made

> God the father turn a school divine. [24]

The moment the Gods speak, we forget that they did not
speak like ourselves.   The fact is, they feel like ourselves;
and the poet would have to make them feel otherwise, even
if he could make them speak otherwise, which he cannot,
unless he venture upon an obscurity which would destroy our
sympathy: and what is sympathy with a God, but turning
him into a man?   We allow, that superiority and inferiority
are, after all, human terms, and implying something not so
truly fine and noble as the levelling of a great sympathy
and love; but poems of the present nature, like Paradise
Lost, assume a different principle; and fortunately perhaps,
it is one which it is impossible to reconcile with the other.

     We have now to conclude the surprise of the reader,
who has seen what solid stuff these poems are made of,
with informing him of what the book has not mentioned, --
that they were almost all written four years ago, when the
author was but twenty. [25] Ay, indeed! cries a critic, rubbing
his hands delighted (if indeed even criticism can do so, any
longer). 'then that accounts for the lines you speak of
written in the taste of Marino. '--It does so; but, sage Sir,
after settling the merits of those one or two lines you speak
of, what accounts, pray, for a small matter which you
leave unnoticed, namely, all the rest?--The truth is, we

rather mention this circumstance as a matter of ordinary
curiosity, than anything else; for great faculties have great
privileges, and leap over time as well as other obstacles.
Time itself, and its continents, are things yet to be discovered.   There is no knowing even how much duration one
man may crowd into a few years, while others drag out
their slender lines.   There are circular roads full of hurry
and scenery, and straight roads full of listlessness and bar-
renness; and travellers may arrive by both, at the same
hour.   The Miltons, who begin intellectually old, and still
intellectual, end physically old, are indeed Methusalems;
and may such be our author, their son.

Mr. Keats's versification sometimes reminds us of
Milton in his bland verse, and sometimes of Chapman both
in his blank verse and rhyme; but his faculties, essentially
speaking, though partaking of the unearthly aspirations and
abstract yearnings of both these poets, are altogether his
own.   They are ambitions, but less directly so.   They are
more social, and in the finer sense of the word, sensual,
than either.   They are more coloured by the modern
philosophy of sympathy and natural justice.   Endymion,
with all its extraordinary powers, partook of the faults of
youth, though the best ones; but the reader of Hyperion and
these other stories would never guess that they were written
at twenty.   The author's versification is now perfected, the
exuberances of his imagination restrained, and a calm power,
the surest and loftiest of all power, takes place of the impatient workings of the younger god within him.   The character of his genius is that of energy and voluptuousness,
each able at will to take leave of the other, and possessing,
in their union, a high feeling of humanity not common to
the best authors who can less combine them.   Mr. Keats
undoubtedly takes his seat with the oldest and best of our
living poets.

We have carried our criticism to much greater
length than we intended; but in truth, whatever the critics
might think, it is a refreshment to us to get upon other
people's thoughts, even though the rogues be our contemporaries.   Oh! how little do those minds get out of themselves, and what fertile and heaven-breathing prospects do
they lose, who think that a man must be confined to the
mill-path of his own homestead, merely that he may avoid
seeing the abundance of his neighbours!   Above all, how
little do they know of us eternal, weekly, and semi-weekly
writers!   We do not mean to say that it is not very pleas-

ant to run upon a smooth road, seeing what we like, and
talking what we like; but we do say, that it is pleasanter
than all, when we are tired, to hear what we like, and to
be lulled with congenial thoughts and higher music, till we
are fresh to start again upon our journey.   What we would
not give to have a better Examiner and a better Indicator
than our own twice every week, uttering our own thoughts in
a finer manner, and altering the world faster and better
than we can alter it!   How we should like to read our present number, five times bettered; and have nothing to do, for
years and years, but to pace the green lanes, forget the tax-
gatherer, and vent ourselves now and then in a verse.

7.   A review of the Lamia volume in the Guardian

> (This unfavorable review, noted before but re-
> produced here for the first time, appeared in the
> Guardian of August 6, 1820. [For further details
> about this newspaper, see the introductory chapter,
> p. 24.] The author's identity is not known, but
> his aspish comments are reminiscent of the tone
> of Keats's Tory attackers of 1818.   In his first
> two paragraphs, the reviewer inveighs against re-
> cent critical praise of the Lamia volume.   His
> displeasure seems to be increased by the uneasy
> feeling that where once Keats's defenders were
> forced to justify their praise, the burden of proof
> for any adverse judgment has now become the re-
> sponsibility of Keats's detractors.)

We open this volume with an indescribable feeling of
reverence and curiosity.   We approach it as a gentleman
from the country takes his seat in the third row of the pit
at the Lyceum, to banquet upon the sweets of 'Woman's
Will--a Riddle,'[26] after being told in the play-bills that 'it
has received the decided approbation of the first critics
of the day.'   Mr. Keats has been praised by all 'men of
mark,'[27] from the Editor of the New Times[28] to the Editor
of the Examiner.[29]   Principles the most opposite unite in
lauding this 'Muses' Son of Promise:'[30] --He is 'a fresh
and true poet,' says one;[31] and 'No criticism can deny his
merits,' proclaims another, 'but such as would disprove
that moonlight is beautiful, or roses fragrant.'[32]   This is
oracular--and we bow to it.

What a blessing it is to be a poet now-a-days! Ten
years ago we rhyming aspirants used to give an entertain-
ment to our friends if the monopolizing dulness of the
Monthly Review or the British Critic afforded us half a page
of notice, with some parting formula of benediction; such as
Mr. --- is a young man of promising talents; and we hope
that when experience has matured his imagination, ' &c. &c.[33]
--But now the sun of criticism is ever shining upon us. We
have a perfect polar quarter of never-failing light. The long
day of brightness first beams in extracts in 'The Morning
Post, '[34] or eulogies in 'The New Times, '--(the Old is, very
properly, above such things.) This blaze is gradually diffused over the country by the Evening Suns.[35] The three
times a-week journals reflect the diurnal brightness; and
the flame at last lights the whole land through the potential
agency of the Sunday prints. But it does not yet die.
There is a new tribe of Illuminati sprung up under the
names of Indicators, and Honeycombs, and Talismans,
and Citizens, and Londoners, and Critics, and Mouse-
Traps,[36] and--look on the walls--all devoted to 'Literature
and the Arts. ' For a week or two there may be an eclipse
--but then come the Magazines--here is a new-born day.
The Ephemcon yet lives--and if, after six weeks, his wings
tire, and his buzzing is no longer heard--if darkness gather
round him, and the world fade from his sight--there is
a gleam of hope in the rising of the Quarterly or the Edinburgh, who may confer on him immortality, by not suffering
him to die a natural death. Thus we are 'nothing if not
critical;'[37] --thus we preserve 'flies in amber;'[38] --thus
we will not let a modest man, like Mr. Keats, commit the
sin of scribbling in secret;--thus--but to our vocation.

The first great merit of Mr. Keats' poetry consists
in the exercise which it affords to the thinking faculties.
It is not to be classed with the common-place performances
which tell us what every body has seen, in language which
every body can understand. It is deep and mystical--it has
all the stimulating properties of a Christian riddle--it is a
nosegay of enigmas. And then, what is most delightful, the
mysterious is so mixed up with the simple, that the mind is
not exhausted by its own conjectures--'est modus in
REBUS. '[39] He never begins 'riddle-me, riddle-me, ree, '
with a solemn face; but offers his problems with the utmost
gentility in the midst of the most agreeable and easy narrative. This is very well for a poet, but it will never do
for a critic. It is our province to digest and systematize;
and we also are determined to revive the much-neglected

practice of calling forth juvenile industry and invention, in
the manner of the primative magazines, or the last Ladies'
Diary. 40 We therefore hereby offer two splendid prizes
for the first and second best solutions of the following
Enigmas, viz:--a copy of 'Endymion' in yellow morocco;
and of the Volume before us, in double extra calf, or red
basil:41

> [Under the headings "RIDDLE I, II, III," the re-
> viewer quotes Sts. XVII, XXVII. 11. 1-2, and
> XLVII. 11. 1-6 of Isabella.]

But why are we, to use Mr. Keats' own words, to

> 'look
> Like puzzled urchin, on an aged crone,
> Who keepth close a wondrous riddle-book.'
> [The Eve of St. Agnes, St. XV. 11. 2-4.]

and not endeavour to make some guesses ourselves? Our
readers shall not have all the honours of discovery, and
all the rewards of perseverance. --Spirits of Scaliger and
Hayne, 42 assist us!

> 'A palpitating snake,
> Bright, and cirque-couchant,'
> [Lamia, I. 11. 45-46.]

means a snake curled up.

> 'The brilliance feminine' [Lamia, I. 1. 92] means a
brightness neither masculine nor neuter.

> 'I took compassion on her, bade her steep
> Her hair in weird syrops, that would keep
> Her loveliness invisible,'
> [Lamia, I. 11. 106-108.]

means that the lady should buy a bottle of 'Essence of
Tyre,'43 for changing red hair to black

> 'A swooning love
> [Lamia, I. 1. 219.]

is a love that falls into a swoon; beautiful, but uncommon.

'A pillowy cleft'
[Isabella, St. XLI. l. 5.]

is certainly an indention that the nose has made in a pillow.

'Divine liquids come with odorous ooze
Through the cold-serpent pipe,'
[Isabella, St. LII. ll. 3-4.]

are strong waters made in a portable still.

But there are some passages, which, with all our
pains, must remain, for us, in their own mystical beauty.
We cannot understand 'a milder-mooned body'; [Lamia, I.
l. 156]--or 'the ruddy strife of hearts and lips'; [Lamia, I.
ll. 40-41]--or how 'Love'

-buzz'd his wings, with fearful roar,
Above the lintel of their chamber-door,
And down the passage cast a glow upon the floor.'
[Lamia, II. ll. 13-15.]

But we do not offer any reward for their explanation.

However we may have dwelt upon the power which
Mr. Keats thus possesses of setting us to think, we cannot
pass over the equally happy influence with which he sways us
to laughter. We think that our language cannot furnish any
conceits half so agreeable, and airy, and provoking, as the
following:--

'In Cupid's college she had spent
Sweet days, a lovely graduate';
[Lamia, I. ll. 197-198.]

or,

'Love in a hut, with water and a crust,
Is--Love forgive us--cinders, ashes, dust';
[Lamia, II. ll. 1-2.]

or two lovers reposing

'with eyelids clos'd,
Saving a tithe which love still open kept,
That they might see each other while they almost
slept';
[Lamia, II. ll. 23-25.]

or,

> 'He answer'd, bending to her open eyes,
> Where he was mirror'd small, in Paradise';
>   [Lamia, II. ll. 46-47.]

or,

> 'My voice is not a bellows unto ire!'
>   [Hyperion, II. 1. 176.]

Our readers will by this time conclude that Mr. Keats is a very original poet. We perfectly accord with them. But he yet has his faults;--he sometimes descends to write naturally, and to the use of the common language of humanity[44] in the expression of pleasure or grief. We hope he may correct this fault ere the Cockney chair shall become vacant.

8.   A review of the Lamia volume in the
     Edinburgh Magazine and Literary Miscellany

> (This favorable review appeared in the Edinburgh Magazine for October 1820 [n. s. VII, 313-316]. As the heading and footnote announce, it is a continuation of the August 1820 review which had considered Endymion [see Chapter III, item 17].)

CONTINUATION OF REMARKS ON THE POETRY OF KEATS[45]

Lamia is the poem in which, in Mr Keats's second volume, the greatest fancy is displayed. It is more in the style of the Endymion, and we shall therefore forbear quoting from it, excepting only three lines, which, for the imagination contained in them, and the beauty with which they are executed, have seldom been equalled: the poet is speaking of a palace built by the magic power of Lamia.

> A haunting music, sole perhaps and lone
> Supportress of the faery-roof, made moan
> Throughout, as fearful the whole charm might fade.
>   p. 34.
>   [II. ll. 122-124.]

"Isabella, or the Pot of Basil," is a story from Boccaccio, and is the same as was given to the public sometime
ago by Mr Barry Cornwall, under the title of "A Sicilian
Story." We can safely recommend "Isabella" as eminently
beautiful. What can be sweeter than this? The days pass
sadly,

> Until sweet Isabella's untouched cheek
> Fell sick with the rose's just domain,
> Fell thin as a young mother's, who doth seek
> By every lull to cool her infant's pain.
>
> p. 51.
> [St. V. ll. 1-4.]

The progress of the love of Lorenzo and Isabella
is told in this delightful manner.

[Quotes Sts. II-III, IV. ll. 1-2.]

The brothers of Isabella discover that their sister
loves Lorenzo: they entice him to a forest, and murder
and bury him: his ghost appears to Isabella, who seeks
the body, and cutting off the head, buries it beneath a pot
of Basil, which she waters with her tears. There are some
terms in the poem which Mr Keats inflicts upon the brothers
of Isabella, which we think in bad taste. He calls them
"money-bags," "ledger-men," [St. XVIII. ll. 1, 6] &c.
which injures, in some respect, this delightful story. Mr
K. indeed, himself seems to have some doubts of this,
and in the following beautiful stanzas intreats the forgive-
ness of his master [Boccaccio]. They are enough, to say
the least, to wipe away the sin committed.

[Quotes Sts. XIX-XX.]

What a beautiful picture might not Stothard[46] make
from the following exquisite stanza?

[Quotes St. XXV.]

Isabella, as we have said, buries the head of the
lover in the pot of Basil, and weeps over it continually.

[Quotes St. LIII.]

The brothers, discovering at last the cause of her
grief, take the Basil-pot away: she having nothing then left

to console her, pines and dies.

[Quotes Sts. LXII-LXIII.]

The "Eve of St. Agnes" consists merely of one scene.
Porphyro, a young cavalier, is in love with, and beloved by
Madeline; he enters her chamber on the eve of St Agnes,
when she is dreaming of him under the supposed influence of
the Saint.   He persuades her to fly with him.   We have only
room for the following stanzas, which will speak for themselves sufficiently.

[Quotes Sts. XXIV-XXVIII.]

Amongst the minor poems we prefer the "Ode to the
Nightingale." Indeed, we are inclined to prefer it beyond
every other poem in the book; but let the reader judge.   The
third and seventh stanzas have a charm for us which we
should find it difficult to explain.   We have read this ode
over and over again, and every time with increased delight.

[Quotes Sts. II-VII.]

As our object is rather to let Mr Keats's verses be
seen in justification of themselves, than to insist upon their
positive beauty, we shall quote part of another of the minor
poems.   It is entitled "Robin Hood," whose days, the poet
says, "are gone away."

[Quotes ll. 33-62.]

The ode to "Fancy," and the ode to "Autumn," also
have great merit.   "Hyperion," we confess, we do not like
quite so well, on the whole, as some others; yet there is
an air of grandeur about it, and it opens in a striking manner.

> Deep in the shady sadness of a vale
> Far sunken from the healthy breath of morn,
> Far from the fiery noon, and eve's one star,
> Sat grey-hair'd Saturn, quiet as a stone,
> Still as the silence round about his lair;
> Forest on forest hung about his head
> Like cloud on cloud.   p. 145.
>   [I. ll. 1-7.]

One expression here reminds us of a line in the old

poem called the "Mirror for Magistrates, "

> By him lay heavie sleep, cosen of death,
> Flat on the ground, and still as any stone;[47]

and also of another line in Chaucer. [48]

The picture of Thea, in p. 147, is very beautiful, and
the effect of a word (it is where Saturn is deploring the loss
of his kingdom) is given with exceeding power and simplicity.
Saturn speaks,

> Where is another chaos? where? That word
> Found way unto Olympus.
>   [I. ll. 145-146.]

The description, too, of Hyperion, "a vast shade in
midst of his own brightness, " [II. ll. 372-373] is very fine;
though the preceding part of it,

> Golden his hair of short Numidian curl,
> Regal his shape majestic,
>   [II. ll. 371-372.]

is not like Mr Keats, but like Milton.

Upon the whole, we have felt great pleasure from
the perusal of Mr Keats's volumes, and we can safely com-
mend them to our readers, as--not faultless books indeed,
--but as containing, perhaps, as much absolute poetry as
the works of almost any contemporary writer.

9.   A review of the Lamia volume in
     Gold's London Magazine

> (This review, noted before but reproduced here
> for the first time, appeared in August 1820 [II,
> 160-173]. The exact date of Gold's August pub-
> lication cannot be determined, but it was after
> August 9th. (See n. 54 below for an explanation.)
> The author, whose identity is not know, seems to
> be at cross-purposes. Although he defends Keats
> against "the foul injustice" of the Quarterly Review,
> he loses no opportunity to expose the "idiot's
> praise" of Baldwin's London Magazine. [For a

discussion of Gold's Magazine and its rivalry with
Baldwin's, see the introductory chapter, p. 22.]
He mentions that Keats belongs to the Cockney
School, makes several ironic and slashing references to the poet's affectations and misuse of
Greek mythology, and suggests that many readers
will "fear to undertake the task of wading through"
Isabella, or the Pot of Basil; yet, at the end of
his review, the author expresses the hope that
Keats's "uncharitable enemies may learn to repent
them of their enmity, and set that value on his
labours which the perusal of our extracts [most of
which are either italicized to indicate Keats's absurdity, or followed with the reviewer's ironic
comments] may induce them to form." It is possible that the reviewer is not as muddle-headed
as he seems to be: an editor, without any concern for consistency, may have made a number of
unauthorized changes in the review before its publication.)

"Bonis nocet, quisquis pepercerit malis."--Publius Syrus. [49]

We do not think the poetical merits of Mr. Keats
have been duly estimated; and that apparently for the worst
of all reasons--because he is said to be a disciple of Leigh
Hunt's. Now this said Leigh Hunt may write some very
quaint articles--and to many perhaps objectionable articles--
in his Examiner; but no man can pretend to assert with
truth that he is devoid of talent. To be sure, there may
be some little follies chargeable on the master and his
disciple--they may have be-praised each other a little over-
much; and the purity of their taste in composition generally
may be made a matter of question; but with these trivial
subtractions from their fame, we have no doubt of their
obtaining an exalted place in the temple of our literary
benefactors.

It is known to our readers, that Mr. Keats belongs
to the Cockney School of Poetry--a school, we suppose,
so denominated, from the fact of its writers having been
educated in the city, and taking their pictures of rural life
from its immediate environs. This school, like others,
has its opponents and admirers: amongst the former, the
Quarterly Review, is the most able and the most unjust;
amongst the latter, and more amiable, is Baldwin's Maga-

zine. Mr. Keats, however, has suffered from both; less
perhaps, from the malicious hostility of his open opponent,
than from the perverted, strange, and affected friendship of
his admirer. Every one who has read "the review," as it
is termed, of _Endymion,_ in the Quarterly Journal, must
be satisfied of the truth of our remark; and no less so, if
they have had patience to peruse a notice of the same work
in the pseudo London Magazine. The foul injustice of the
one needs no comment; but the vicious tone of incongruous
remark in the other demands especial censure. When a
critic avows determined enmity--when he avows he has not
read the work he condemns[50] --the reputation of an author
cannot be much endangered. But when we find such a character of a man's work as the following presents, we can
scarcely hesitate to pronounce it as damning to the last
degree:--

> "Endymion is totally unlike all these, and all
> other poems. --(Alluding to Southey's and Camp-
> bell's.)--As we said, before, it is not a poem at
> all. It is an ecstatic dream of poetry--a flush
> --a fever--a burning light--an involuntary out-
> pouring of the spirit of poetry--that will not be
> controlled. Its movements are the starts and
> boundings of the young horse before it has felt the
> bitt--the first flights of the young bird, feeling
> and exulting in the powers with which it is gifted,
> but not yet acquainted with their use or their ex-
> tent. It is the wanderings of the butterfly in the
> first hour of its birth; not as yet knowing one
> flower from another, but only that all are flowers.
> Its similitudes come crowding upon us from all
> delightful things. It is the May-day of poetry--
> the flush of blossoms and weeds that start up at
> the first voice of spring. It is the sky-lark's
> hymn to the day-break, involuntary gushing forth
> as he mounts upward to look for the fountain of
> that light which has awakened him. It is as if the
> muses had steeped their child in the waters of
> Castaly, and we beheld him emerging from them,
> with his eyes sparkling and his limbs quivering
> with the delicious intoxication, and the precious
> drops scattered from him into the air at every
> motion, glittering in the sunshine, and casting the
> colours of the rainbow on all things around. "[51]

We are ready to believe all this was sincerely meant,

but nothing short of lunacy could have dictated such expressions.   Here we have a poem, styled a <u>dream--a fever--a burning light--not a poem at all</u>--Its movements are likened to those of a <u>young horse--a roving bird--a butterfly.</u>   It is called the <u>May-day of poetry--the sky lark's hymn--a child steeped in the waters of Castaly</u>!!!   Now in the name of common sense was ever such a farrago heaped together before?   The virulent condemnation of the Quarterly is at all events intelligible; but this is beyond the power of censure, and, what is worse, of cure.   Mr. Keats between these reviewers has been sadly abused, and treated with a cruelty more mad than ever was inflicted on the vilest heretic by the Spanish Inquisition.   Stephen, [52] when stoning to death, or Laurence, [53] broiling on the gridiron, had not half so much reason to complain, as our young and gifted author.

We shall endeavour to act differently by Mr. Keats; we shall not, with a dash of a pen, consign his labours to contempt; or, with an idiot's praise, make him a subject fit for laughter or for pity.   We shall allow him to speak in his own person, and enable the public to decide more correctly on his powers and pretensions.   We frankly confess our dislike of his rhythm, and his intolerable affectation, and mistaken stringing-together of compound epithets.   But still we feel he often <u>thinks</u> like a poet.   His knowledge of Greek and mythology seems to mystify him on every occasion; and his mode of expression is seldom natural.   He does not trust himself to his naturally strong and vivid impressions: he says nothing like other men, and appears always on the stretch for words to shew his thoughts are of a different texture from all other writers.   He looks as if he mistook affectation for originality--as some men do dirty linen and unreaped chins as proofs of genius.   Mr. Keats, however, is young, and may in time learn the folly of so misjudging.   His Endymion led us, with all its blemishes, to expect from him higher things; and though disappointed, on this occasion, we are still sanguine of his success.   We are sure Leigh Hunt never corrected his exercises in Lamia or the Basil Pot, or else they would have appeared to more advantage.   We shall now proceed to give some account of the work before us; and shall be the more extended, inasmuch as we wish to deal fairly by a clever young man, to whom we would recommend a little country air, to strengthen his nerves; and a change of diet, as necessary to the preservation of his health. [54]   The waters of Lymington might prove of essential benefit towards the re-establishment of his constitution; or, if these failed,

he might be able to procure a letter of introduction to the
retreat at York, which would be much more certain, though
more tedious and expensive.

The first of the poems in this volume, which is a fair
specimen of the whole, is a misti-mithological Fantasie,
whose story, if we understand it rightly, is as follows:

> "The ever-smitten Hermes empty left
> His golden throne, bent warm on amorous theft:"
> [Lamia, I. ll. 7-8.]

and made a retreat into a forest on the shores of Crete,
to look after a nymph, at whose feet we are told was a
world of love; at least--

> "So Hermes thought, and a celestial heat
> Burnt from his winged heels to either ear!"
> [I. ll. 22-23.]

In search for this beauty, who caused his very ears to burn,
he meets with

> "--a palpitating snake,
> Bright, and cirque couchant in a dusky brake."
> [I. ll. 45-46.]

She was besides

> "So rainbow-sided, touch'd with-miseries,
> She seem'd, at times, 55 some penanced lady elf,
> Some demon's mistress, or the demon's self!["]
> [I. ll. 54-57.]

This snake addresses herself to Hermes, and tells him,
that she has had a "splendid dream"56 of him the night before, in which she saw him among the gods: the only sad
one, as he neither heard the "lute-fingered muses,"

> "Nor even Apollo when he sang alone,
> Deaf to his throbbing throat's long, long melodious
>   moan."
> [I. ll. 74-75.]

She then proceeds to ask him, with rather a coquetish air,
what she knew well herself; if he had found the maid.

> "Whereat the <u>star</u> of Lethe not delay'd
> His <u>rosy eloquence,</u> and thus inquired: ["]
> [I. ll. 81-82.]

And when he had finished his speech, we are told,

> "<u>Light flew his earnest words, among the blos-
> soms blown.</u>
>
> *   *   *   *   *
>
> Then thus again the <u>brilliance feminine:</u>57
> [I. ll. 91-92.]

Who in this new capacity hath condescended to inform him
that she has rendered the Nymph invisible--

> "To keep her58 unaffronted, unassailed
> By the love-glances of unlovely eyes,
> Of Satyrs, Fauns, and blear'd <u>Silenus'</u> sighs.
> <u>Pale grew her immortality, for woe</u>
> <u>Of all these lovers.</u> "--
> [I. ll. 101-105.]

The tenure by which she held her immortality must indeed
be curious, and its nature not less so, when all at once she
could render it invisible. She however requires Hermes to
swear he will grant her a boon, if she allows him to behold
his Nymph; to which of course he assents, as in duty bound,
and

> "--Once again the charmed God began
> An oath, and through the serpent's ears it ran
> <u>Warm, tremulous, devout, psalterian.</u> "
> [I. ll. 112-114.]

With an air of pathetic gravity she says she was a woman
once, and wishes to be so again; and as if "wishing and the
deed were one,"59 she breathes on the brow of Hermes,
and swift was seen

> "Of both the <u>guarded</u> nymph <u>near-smiling</u> on the
> green. "
> [I. l. 125.]

A very singular effect, indeed: but the transformation
seems still incomplete. But in consequence of this,

[Quotes ll. 129-141, lines which continue the
description of the serpent's transformation.]

There seems something of the incomprehensible in this passage: we must not, however, stop at trifles. The serpent
now changes, but not before

> "Her mouth foam'd, and the grass therewith besprent,
> Wither'd at dew so sweet and virulent;" (!!!)
>   [I. ll. 148-149.]

while, strange to say,

> "Her eyes in torture fix'd, and anguish drear,
> Hot, glaz'd, and wide, with lid-lashes all sear,
> Flash'd phosphor and sharp sparks, without one cooling
>   tear."
>   [I. ll. 150-152.]

This is Epic sublimed, but nothing in point of grandeur to
the continued effect of the change thus heroically described--

> "--Convuls'd with scarlet pain:
> A deep volcanian yellow took the place
> Of all her milder-mooned body's grace;"
>   [I. ll. 154-156.]

Still unsatisfied with this usurpation, its daring not only

> --"lick'd up her stars:" (!!!)
>   [I. l. 160.]

but also undrest her of her "rubious argent."

> [Quotes I. ll. 165-170.]

Lamia "now a lady bright," does not change her character
without some reason; and we suppose, in order to wash her
clean of her snake-ship, fled to

> "--a clear pool wherein she passioned
> To see herself escap'd from so sore ills,
> While her robes flaunted with the daffodils."
>   [I. ll. 182-184.]

Lycius it appears was a happy fellow, or we will suppose
him to be, for his own sake; and she was

> "A virgin purest lipp'd, yet in the lore
> Of love deep learned to the red heart's core:
> Not one hour old, yet of sciential brain
> To unperplex bliss from its neighbour pain. "
> [I. 11. 189-192.]

She must indeed have a very vivid imagination to effect the
purpose of the last line, and not less so to "intrigue" effectually with "the specious chaos. " One deduction, however, we must make from her amiable qualities, for she
was a loiterer; but being newly converted, we must wonder
the less at her retaining some of her old propensities.

> [Quotes I. 11. 202-205, 215-216.]

Her object for lingering by "the way side" is now explained
to us, for

> "--on the moth-time of that evening dim
> He would return that way, "--
> [I. 11. 220-221.]

on his road to Corinth.   Jove inspires him to leave his companions,

> "--and set forth to walk
> Perhaps grown wearied of their Corinth talk:"
> [I. 11. 231-232.]

He now takes a turn or two over some solitary hills; on
which occasion,

> "His phantasy was lost where reason fades;"
> [I. 1. 235.]

and certainly but for the author's kindness in pointing out
where it escaped, few would have been able to discover; it
was

> "In the calm'd twilight of Platonic shades. " ! ! !
> [I. 1. 236.]

In despite, however, of this Lycius was not doomed to be
invisible; and

> [Quotes I. 11. 237-239, 242-247, lines which
> describe Lamia's meeting with Lycius and the
> first words she addresses to him.]

For in fact his eyes

> "--had drunk her beauty up,
> Leaving no drop in the bewildering cup. "
> [I. ll. 251-252.]

And with

> "Due adoration, thus began to adore;--
> Her soft look growing coy, she saw his chain so
> sure. " [qy. so sore.]60
> [I. ll. 255-256.]

His adoration, however, appeared to have but little effect; for, after stating her reasons for not yielding to his passion,

> "--she rose
> Tiptoe with white arms spread. He, sick to lose
> The amorous promise of her lone complain,
> Swoon'd, murmuring of love, and pale with pain. "
> [I. ll. 286-289.]

And how did the cruel lady then treat "the life" she "tangled in her mesh, " seeking

> "With brighter eyes and slow amenity,
> Put her new lips to his, and gave afresh
> The life she had entangled in her mesh. "
> [I. ll. 293-295.]

And then she began to sing to such a tune, that

> "--like held breath, the stars drew in their
> panting fires. "
> [I. l. 300.]

But still, to relieve his apprehensions of her "melting, " she tells him a plumper61--

> "--That the self-same pains
> Inhabited her frail-strung heart as his. "
> [I. ll. 308-309.]

and that she saw him first

"-- 'mid baskets heap'd
Of amorous herbs and flowers."--
[I. ll. 317-318.]

Pity she did not put him in her pocket, but perhaps she
then wore none: however, she entices him on

"To unperlex'd delight, and pleasure known."
[I. l. 327.]

For Lamia judged,
"--and judg'd aright
That Lycius could not love in half a fright
[I. ll. 334-335.]

*   *   *   *   *

Lycius to all made eloquent reply,
Marrying to every word a twinborn sigh."
[I. ll. 340-341.]

In fine, this notable matrimony induces the lady to go to
Corinth, but she, in her "eagerness,"

"Made, by a spell, the triple league decrease
To a few paces; not at all surmised
By blinded Lycius, so in her comprized."
[I. ll. 345-347.]

Entering Corinth, they met an old man, "slow-stepp'd," at
whose approach "Lycius shrank closer,"

"Into his mantle, adding wings to haste,
While hurried Lamia trembled: 'Ah,' said he,
'Why do you shudder, love, so ruefully?'
[I. ll. 367-369.]

*   *   *   *   *

While ye he spake they had arrived before
--a place unknown
[I. ll. 378, 388.]

(Yet having a gate whose hinges breathed "AEolian Sounds.")

Some time to any, but those two alone,
And a few Persian mutes, who that same year

> Were seen about the markets."--
>   [I. ll. 389-391.]

The most curious could not find out their place of retreat;
but the "flitter-wing'd verse" is not likely to keep the
secret; and we shall ascertain the fact by and by.

    The Second Part of this exquisite Poem thus very
sublimely opens:--

> "Love in a hut, with water and a crust,
> Is--Love, forgive us!--cinders, ashes, dust; (The
> Love in a palace is perhaps at last   deuce it is.)
> More grievous torment than a hermit's fast."
>   [II. ll. 1-4.]

And in the following lines the author truly says:

> "That is a doubtful tale from faery land,
> Hard for the non-elect to understand. 62 (!!!)

Bliss is but transitory, for it seems,

> "Love, jealous grown of so complete a pair,
> Hover'd and buzz'd his wings, with <u>fearful roar</u>,
> Above the lintel of their chamber door,
> And down the passage <u>cast a glow upon the floor</u>."
>   [II. ll. 12-15.]

They were reposing (not <u>withering</u> from the "fearful roar"
and buzzing of love's wings) in this chamber, when

> "Deafening the swallow's twitter, came a thrill
> Of trumpets--Lycius started--the sounds fled.
> But left a thought, a buzzing in his head. (!!!)
>   [II. ll. 27-29.]

       *   *   *   *   *

> The lady, ever watchful, penetrant,
> Saw this with pain, so arguing a want
> Of something more, more than her empery
> Of joys;"--
>   [II. ll. 34-37.]

> "Began to moan and sigh."
>   [II. l. 37.]

> "'Why do you sigh, fair creature?' whispered he:
> 'Why do you think?' returned she tenderly."
>
> [II. 11. 40-41.]

He then tells her he wishes his neighbours and friends to see
what bliss he enjoys, and that it is his determination to wed
her publicly.   This does not appear to have suited the lady's
taste; and so much did she feel, --that, in beseeching him to
change his purpose, she

> "--wept a rain
> Of sorrows at his words."--
>   [II. 11. 66-67.]

But it was of no avail (barbarous man); and

> "His passion, cruel grown, took on a hue
> Fierce and sanguineous as 'twas possible
> In one whose brow had no dark veins to swell."!!
>   [II. 11. 75-77.]

She reluctantly consented; when a very natural inquiry is
made by the lover, namely, what she was called, and where
were her relations.   This inquiry the lady contrives to
elude; and requests him, if his "vision rests with any
pleasure on her," not to bid old Apollonius to the feast:
for what reason we know not.

> "Lycius, perplex'd at words so blind and blank,
> Made close inquiry; from whose touch she shrank,
> Feigning a sleep and he to the dull shade
> Of deep sleep in a moment was betray'd."
>   [II. 11. 102-105.]

and thus we see how much the snake was an over-
match for the lover.   After an account of Lamia's prepara-
tion for the bridal feast, in which she was assisted by
"subtle servitors," but it is doubtful how and whence they
came, "the day arrived," and "the herd approached," and
"entered marvelling,"

> "Save one, who look'd thereon with eye severe,
> And with calm-planted steps walk'd in austere;
> 'Twas Apollonious: something too he laughed,
> As though some knotty problem, that had daft
> His patient thought, had now begun to thaw,
> And solve and melt:--'twas just as he foresaw."
>   [II. 11. 157-162.]

This is a description of a philosopher perhaps unequalled
in our language: but we cannot refrain from saying, that
the passage, though possessing considerable poetical beauty,
is not entirely new; for we remember the Baron Munchausen's
trumpet also played an admirably fine flourish when the thaw
came on. [63] The author perhaps had a "perplexed" recollection of the circumstance, and thus unintentionally subjected
himself to the charge of plagiarism. Apollonius, however,
after apologizing for coming uninvited to the feast, is led
into the house by Lycius, who went,

> "With reconciling words and courteous mien
> Turning into sweet milk the sophist's spleen."
> [II. ll. 171-172.]

We hope in a second edition of this work to learn by what
chemical process this was effected. After sundry preparations, the guests are seated, and

> [Quotes II. ll. 199-201, 209-210, lines which
> describe Lycius' guests listening to music, con-
> versing, and drinking wine.]

the company felt themselves quite at home. Garlands of
flowers were then brought in, that every guest

> "--as he did please
> Might fancy-fit his brow, silk-pillow'd at his ease."
> [II. ll. 219-220.]

Lycius was in the mean time sitting by Lamia, and wishing
to take wine with Apollonius, when he found

> "--The bald-headed philosopher
> Had fix'd his eye, without a twinkle or stir
> Full on the alarmed beauty of the bride,
> Brow-beating her fair form, and troubling her
> sweet pride."
> [II. ll. 245-248.]

Rather ungenerous treatment every one will admit. But
this look has the effect of taking recognition from "the
orbs" of Lamia; the loud revelry grew hushed--

> [Quotes II. ll. 266-268.]

Lycius upbraids Apollonius for his impoliteness in staring

his wife to death--

> [Quotes II. ll. 291-294, 299-306, lines in which
> Apollonius informs Lycius that Lamia is a ser-
> pent.]

The least that Lycius could do after this disappointment was
to die, which he accordingly does, and the Poem concludes.

It is impossible to have perused the interesting tale
we have just concluded, without admitting ourselves much
indebted to Mr. Keats. The precision of his remark, the
depth of his foresight, the imagery which abounds throughout the whole narrative, and the intensity of feeling which
he throws into the catastrophe are unequalled by any thing
ever written by Mr. Coleridge, or Mr. Fitzgerald, 64 or
Monk Lewis. We had determined after the perusal of Lamia,
to have left the remainder of the volume untouched, and not
rifle it of those jewels--fevered flushes--hawthorn blooms,
butterfly colorings, and young birds' wanderings into the
sky (as the writer in Baldwin's publication would have
described them), but yet we could not resist taking advantage
of the last opportunity that might possibly be afforded us of
ever seeing this Bijou again, and giving to our reader such
a feast, as Endymion never found on the brow of Latmos.

The Second Tale in this Volume is called "Isabella,
or the Pot of Basil." The story is told in about two
hundred and fifty lines;65 but as many of our readers may
fear to undertake the task of wading through it, we shall
epitomize it for their edification. "Lorenzo, a young
palmer in Love's eye," "would not in the self-same man-
sions dwell" with Isabel, "without some stir of heart,
some malady";

> "They could not, sure, beneath the same roof sleep
> But to each other dream, and nightly weep."
>   [St. I. ll. 7-8.]

Their love encreased--

> [Quotes Sts. IV. ll. 7-8; V. ll. 1, 3, 5-8. The last
> two lines read: "If looks speak love-laws, I will
> drink her tears, /And at the least 'twill startle
> off her cares."]

This is in truth a fine vein of poetry. That "looks" should,
however, "speak <u>love-laws,</u>" is not very original; but that
their influence <u>should have</u> prompted Lorenzo to "drink her
tears," which as yet had not reached farther than her pillow, is a discovery reserved for the ingenuity of our author.
But again, how could drinking "<u>her</u> tears" "<u>startle</u> off her
cares"? Mr. Keats leaves us <u>not</u> altogether in <u>doubt</u> as to
the fact; for he informs us, that this was said "one fair
morning," and, as we must suppose, when his head suffered
a little after the applications to his lips of the night before
--<u>Quem non fecundi calices fecere disertum</u>!66   But to proceed: the lover "anguished" out

<blockquote>
"A dreary night of love and misery,"
[St. VII. 1. 2.]
</blockquote>

and matters would have been a good deal worse,

<blockquote>
"If Isabel's quick eye had not been wed
To every symbol on his forehead high;
And ____ so, lisped tenderly,
'Lorenzo!'"--
[St. VII. ll. 3-4, 6-7.]
</blockquote>

This acted like a talisman upon the "palmer"; and after
telling his love he would not "grieve" her hand by "unwelcome pressing," or "<u>fear</u> her eyes by gazing on them,"
adds, in a strain of the most moving pathos,

<blockquote>
"--but I cannot live
Another night, and not my passion shrive.
[St. VIII. ll. 7-8.]
</blockquote>

*   *   *   *   *

<blockquote>
So said, his erewhile timid lips grew bold.
And <u>poesied</u> with hers in dewy rhyme:"
[St. IX. ll. 5-6.]
</blockquote>

No wonder then that

<blockquote>
"Great bliss was with them, and great happiness
Grew like a lusty flower in June's caress."
[St. IX. ll. 7-8.]
</blockquote>

Happiness, however, in this world is but very short lived,
and the "dewy rhyme" did not prevent their parting.   But

the manner in which they so parted is told us in happier lines
than we elsewhere recollect so heart-rending a scene to have
been described:--

> "Parting they seem'd to tread upon the air,
> Twin roses by the zephyr blown apart. "
>   [St. X. ll. 1-2.]

As soon as they reach home, they are once more in their
proper persons, and occupy themselves as befits those
over whom the zephyr had no more influence than is ascribed
to it by our poet.

> "She, to her chamber gone, a ditty fair
> Sang, of delicious love and honey'd dart;
> He with light steps went up a western hill,
> And bade the sun farewell, and joy'd his fill. "
>   [St. X. ll. 5-8.]

We presume the "sun" was the first object of his love, and
in gratitude for the past favours of the Diety, Lorenzo determined, as he was "blown apart" from "simple Isabel" not
only corporally but mentally, to give evidence of the distance
to which they were separated, by climbing up a "western
hill" where no doubt he very poetically "joy'd his fill. "
They soon met again--

> "--before the dusk
> Had taken from the stars its pleasant veil,
> Close in a bower of hyacinth and musk,
> Unknown of any, free from whispering tale. "
>   [St. XI. ll. 3-6.]

"At such a place as this, " we should have imagined the
lovers to be pleasantly, if not happily situated, if it were
not that our author starts a doubt upon the subject, and
asks,

> "Were they unhappy then?"--
>   [St. XII. l. 1.]

True, we have an immediate answer--

> "--It cannot be. "--
>   [St. XII. l. 1.]

But to us the reasons are not at all satisfactory.

"Too many tears for lovers have been shed,
Too many sighs give we to them in fee,
Too much of pity after they are dead,
Too many doleful stories do we see,
Whose matter in bright gold were best be read;
Except in such a page where Thesus' spouse
Over the pathless waves towards him bows."
[St. XII. ll. 2-8.]

Now with all due respect to Mr. Keats, we think, neither
"tears that have been shed," nor "sighs given in fee," nor
"pity after they are dead," nor all the "doleful stories" in
the world could prove the "Palmer," and his "simple Isabel"
were not unhappy. We may not be clear-sighted enough in
affairs of love to see the matter otherwise, and in differing
with our author, we feel the delicate ground on which we
tread, and offer our remarks with all that humility which
becomes us.

But the "fair Lady," we are informed, lived with her
two brothers, who were

"Enriched from ancestral merchandize;"
[St. XIV. 1. 2.]

and the verses in which we are told of the agents by which
they obtained their wealth, are amongst the most nervous
in the poem. Here and there we are a little at a loss to
comprehend their meaning, but our more intelligent readers
will no doubt at the first glance divine it:

"For them the Ceylon diver held his breath,
For them his ears gush'd blood; for them in death
The seal on the cold ice with piteous bark
Lay full of darts;"--
[St. XV. ll. 1, 3-5.]

The first line, and the half of the second line of the above
extract, are intelligible enough; but for the last line and a
half, we confess we are not such skilful naturalists as to
be able to discover their beauties.

We have next an apostrophe to Boccaccio, pp. 58-9
[Sts. XIX-XX]; and we afterwards find the brothers took it
in dudgeon that the "Palmer" should have won the sister--

> "When 'twas their plan to coax her by degrees
> To some high noble and his olive-trees.["]
>   [St. XXI. ll. 7-8.]

At last,

> "--with these men of cruel clay
> Cut mercy with a sharp knife to the bone;
> For they resolved"--
>   [St. XXII. ll. 5-7.]

Blush to hear it, ye virgins; hang down your heads and weep,
ye children of sentiment and love; shed the tear of pity over
the anticipated fate of the poor "Palmer."

> "For they resolved"--(what?)--"in some forest dim
> To kill Lorenzo, and"--(what? why)--"there bury
> him."!!!

They did not, however, choose the assassin-like time of midnight for this dreadful purpose; nor did Lorenzo seem at all
suspicious of their murderous intentions. They took a very
"pleasant morning" for the work; and of all times in the
world selected that hour when

> "--he leant
> Into the sun-rise;"--
>   [St. XXIII. ll. 1-2.]

and when

> "--towards him they bent
> Their footing through the dews."--
>   [St. XXIII. ll. 3-4.]

Thus we see how respectfully they approached their enemy;
and the language in which they addressed him was not less
so:

> "--and to him said,
> 'You seem there in the quiet of content,
> Lorenzo, and we are most loath to invade
> Calm speculation;"--
>   [St. XXIII. ll. 4-7.]

This might be rather enigmatical; but under all the circumstances, it must still be considered their notice to him to

quit was sufficient, couched as it was in these additional
terms:

> "'--but if you are wise
> Bestride your steed while <u>cold</u> is in the skies.'"
> [St. XXIII. ll. 7-8.]

But we forgot to state, that when they first saw Lorenzo,
he was leaning

> "--o'er the balustrade
> Of the garden terrace,"--
> [St. XXIII. ll. 2-3.]

and no wonder they should have politely requested him to

> "'Come down, we pray thee, ere the <u>hot sun</u> count
> His dewy rosary on the eglantine.'"
> [St. XXIV. ll. 3-4.]

These powerful entreaties of the <u>cold</u>, and the <u>hot sun</u>, had
their due effect, and

> "Lorenzo, courteously as he was wont,
> Bow'd a fair greeting to these serpents' whine;
> And went <u>in haste</u>, to get <u>in readiness</u>,
> With belt, and spur, and <u>bracing huntsman's dress.</u>"
> [St. XXIV. ll. 5-8.]

What an innocent soul must this Lorenzo have been; but
this is not all. He was exceedingly methodical in his pauses;
and though the "hot sun" was out, we find he still sighed
to hear his lady's matin song--

> [Quotes St. XXV, in which Lorenzo hears and sees
> Isabella singing.]

This happy event enables him

> "--to stifle all the heavy sorrow
> Of a poor three hours' absence;"--
> [St. XXVI. ll. 4-5.]

and to add--

> "'Good bye! I'll soon be back!'"--
> [St. XXVI. l. 7.]

to which,

>"--'Good bye!' said she;
>   [St. XXVI. 1. 7.]

and, in proof of her <u>ardent</u> affection,

>"--as he went, <u>she chanted merrily.</u>"
>   [St. XXVI. 1. 8.]

Well, Lorenzo, who thus went like a sheep to the slaughter, was, without much ceremony or remorse, very speedily slain, and buried in a forest. The brothers, on their return, tell their sister they have shipped off Lorenzo, adding, without much of affection,

>"To-day thou wilt not see him, nor to-morrow
>And the next day will be a day of sorrow."
>   [St. XXIX. 11. 7-8.]

The natural result ensued on this; and

>"Sorely she wept until the night came on,
>And then, instead of love, O misery!
><u>She brooded o'er the luxury alone</u>
>   [St. XXX. 11. 2-4.]

>   *   *   *   *   *

>But Selfishness, Love's cousin, held not long
>Its fiery vigil in her single breast;"
>   [St. XXI. 11. 1-2.]

>   *   *   *   *   *

And,

>"--So, sweet Isabel
>By gradual decay from beauty fell;"
>   [St. XXXII. 11. 7-8.]

like

>"--a roundelay
>Of death among the bushes and the leaves;"
>   [St. XXXII. 11. 4-5.]

and the worst of it was, all her uneasiness was excited

>"Because Lorenzo came not."--
> [St. XXXIII. l. 1.]

The brothers' consciences were not still callous to remorse, and

>"--their crimes
>Came on them, like a smoke from Hinmon's vale"
>   [St. XXXIII. ll. 5-6.]

Plague take it, that it did not suffocate them at once; but we presume that would be rather an unpoetical sort of death, and hence every night

>"--they groan'd aloud,
>To see their sister in her <u>snowy</u> shroud."
>   [St. XXXIII. ll. 7-8.]

The fact is, however, she was not yet dead, as our author informs us--

>"And she had died in <u>drowsy ignorance;</u>"
>   [St. XXXIV. l. 1.]

a singular sort of death by the war, if it were not

>"--for a thing more deadly dark than all;"

>"Like a fierce portion,"--"Like a lance,"--
>"It was a vision."--
>   [Sts. XXIV. ll. 2-3, 5; XXV. l. 1.]

And of course it was Lorenzo, who was sadly altered by his new habitation.

>"--The forest tomb
>Had marr'd his glossy hair, which once could shoot
>Lustre into the sun, and put cold doom
>Upon his lips, and taken the soft lute
>From his lorn voice, and past his loamed ears
>Had made a miry channel for his tears."
>   [St. XXXV. ll. 3-8.]

En passant, we may here remark, that never was hair so much endowed: not all we have ever heard or read

of Sampson, could half equal the powers ascribed by
Mr. Keats to his Lorenzo's "glossy hair"; let that, however,
pass.   He tells her he was murdered, and points out the
place of his interment; adding, that which she makes no
difficulty in believing, that

> "I am a shadow now, alas! alas!"
>   [St. XXXIX. 1. 1.]

"If spirits could go mad," he declares he "should rage" but
Isabel's "paleness warms" his "grave," and "makes" (him)
"glad"; and on sighing "adieu," he

> "--dissolv'd, and left
> The <u>atom</u> darkness in a slow turmoil;"
>   [St. XLI. 11. 1-2.]

All this, however, only

> "--made sad Isabella's eyelids ache,
> And in the dawn (of what?) she started up awake;"!!!
>   [St. XLI. 11. 7-8.]

But was this only for the moment; for with a simplicity worthy
of Lorenzo's love, she goes to visit his tomb, and takes

> "--with her an aged nurse,
> And went into that dismal forest-hearse."
>   [St. XLIII. 11. 7-8.]

Of course where he lay buried: she soon turned up one of
his soiled gloves,

> "--whereon
> Her silk had play'd in <u>purple phantasies</u>;[67]
>   [St. XLVII. 11. 1-2.]

and after laboring for three hours at very "travail sore,"

> "At last they felt the <u>kernel</u> of the grave,
> And Isabella did not <u>stamp</u> and rave."
>   [St. XLVIII. 11. 7-8.]

<u>Mirabile dictu</u>![68]   And then they found his head--

> "--and for its tomb did choose
> A garden-pot, wherein she laid it by,

> And cover'd it with mould, and o'er it set
> Sweet Basil, which her tears kept ever wet. "
> [St. LII. ll. 5-8.]

She now forgot the sun, moon, and stars, and thought only
of her "sweet Basil, " which she ever fed with "thin tears, "

[Quotes St. LIV. ll. 2, 7-8.]

But this did not reconcile her to the loss of her lover, whose
last relic she was apprehensive would have been stolen from
her by her envious brothers. Isabella, however, with all her
simplicity, was an over-match for them; for in order to
watch it,

> "--seldom did she go to chapel-shrift,
> And seldom felt she any hunger-pain. "
> [St. LIX. ll. 3-4.]

Excellent sentinels, no doubt--

> "And, patient as a hen-bird, sat her there
> Beside her Basil, weeping through her hair. "
> [St. LIX. ll. 7-8.]

Unfortunately, however, with all her watching, the Basil was
stolen; her brothers went away,

> "With blood upon their heads, to banishment. "
> [St. LX. l. 8.]

And we are told--

> "--Sweet Isabel will die
> Will die a death too lone and incomplete,
> Now they have ta'en away her Basil sweet. "
> [St. LXI. ll. 6-8.]

In our simplicity we should have imagined her death to be
the more complete for the reason assigned in the last line;
but our author tells us otherwise; and as those can paint it
best who have felt it most, we differ from our author with
a proportionate degree of diffidence. The poor girl's senses
seemed at length to be exceedingly though strangely fatigued[69]--

[Quotes St. LXII. ll. 3-6.]

Her tragical fate is now wound up, and she pays the debt
of nature--

>"Imploring for her Basil to the last."
>[St. LXIII. 1. 2.]

We have devoted an unusual portion of our Journal
to the consideration of Mr. Keats's new work, with the
hope, that his uncharitable enemies may learn from our
extracts to repent them of their enmity, and set that value
on his labours, which the perusal of our extracts may induce
them to form. To Mr. Keats's admirers we have nothing
to say; they need no recommendation to peruse his works.
On Primrose Hill, [70] as in the Blue Coat School; [71] in the
druggist's shop, [72] or by the Paddington Canel, [73] they must
guile the reader of many an hour, and often lead him to
pause on the extraordinary powers of the human mind, on
the wonderful destinies of man, and yet think there exists
such gross stupidity, nay so deplorable a want of taste,
amongst the bulk of English readers, as not to discover in
Mr. Keats powers and acquirements that dazzle while they
instruct, and astonish while they delight.

10.   A short review of the Lamia volume
       in the Monthly Magazine

> (This short but essentially friendly review ap-
> peared in the Monthly Magazine for September 1,
> 1820 [L, 166]. More than three years before,
> this same magazine had printed some favorable
> comments on Keats's first volume. [See Chapter
> II, item 4.]
> In his bibliography of Keats, MacGillivray lists
> this article in the Monthly after the review of the
> British Critic (see item 12 below), but he may
> not have known that the September number of the
> Monthly Magazine carried the exact date as well
> the month of issue. This commentary in the
> Monthly has been reprinted by Marsh and White,
> "Keats and the Periodicals of His Time," MP,
> XXXII [August 1934], 46-47.)

We have read with pleasure a volume of Poems,
lately published by Mr. Keats, the author of Endymion.
There is a boldness of fancy and a classical expression of

language in the poetry of this gentleman, which, we think,
entitle him to stand equally high in the estimation of poetic
opinion as the author of Rimini, or as he (Barry Cornwall)
of the Dramatic Scenes. Our pleasure, however, was not
unmingled with sentiments of strong disapprobation. The
faults characteristic of his school, [74] are still held up to
view with as much affectation, by Mr. K. as if he were
fearful of not coming in for his due share of singularity,
obscurity, and conceit. But though of the same genus, his
poetic labours are specifically different from those of his
fellow labourers in the same vineyard. --There is much more
reach of poetic capacity, more depth and intenseness of
thought and feeling, with more classical power and expression, than what we discover in the writings of his master,
or of his fellow pupil Mr. Cornwall. It is likewise more
original poetry than theirs. Mr. C. is compounded of imi-
tation--of Shakespeare and of Mr. Leigh Hunt. Mr. H. is
a familiar copier of Dryden, with the manner, only a more
sparkling one, but without the pathos, of Crabbe. Mr. K.,
on the contrary, is always himself, and as long as <u>fair</u> originality shall be thought superior to good imitation, he will
always be preferred. The Poems consist of various Tales,
<u>Lamia, Isabella, The Eve of St. Agnes,</u> of which we think
the first the best. <u>Hyperion,</u> however, is the most powerful.

11. A review of the Lamia volume in the <u>New Monthly</u>
     <u>Magazine</u>

          (This favorable review appeared on September 1,
          1820 in the <u>New Monthly Magazine</u> [XIV, 245-248],
          a conservative journal organized in 1814 by Henry
          Colburn as a rival to the <u>Monthly Magazine.</u> The
          author is not known, but his comments are gen-
          erally perceptive. Much of the review is com-
          prised of excerpts and plot summary from the title
          poems of Keats's 1820 volume: the odes are not
          mentioned. Nevertheless, the author recognizes
          the "gigantic stride" Keats has made since the
          publication of <u>Endymion</u> in 1818. His praise of
          <u>Lamia</u> and <u>Hyperion</u> is brief, but enthusiastic.
          The review has been noted before, but it is repro-
          duced here for the first time.)

     THESE poems are very far superior to any which the
author has previously committed to the press. They have

nothing showy, or extravagant, or eccentric about them; but
are pieces of calm beauty, or of lone and self-supported
grandeur.   There is a fine freeness of touch about them,
like that which is manifest in the old marbles, [75] as though
the poet played at will his fancies virginal, and produced his
most perfect works without toil. We have perused them with
the heartiest pleasure--for we feared that their youthful
author was suffering his genius to be enthralled in the meshes
of a sickly affectation--and we rejoice to find these his
latest works as free from all offensive peculiarities--as
pure, as genuine, and as lofty, as the severest critic could
desire.

    "Lamia," the first of these poems, is founded on the
following passage in Burton's Anatomy of Melancholy, which
is given as a note at its close:

        [Quotes Keats's note. (See paragraph three of
        Hunt's August 2, 1820 review in the Indicator.)]

    The poem commences with the descent of Mercury
to Crete, in search of a nymph of whom he is enamoured.
We give the opening passage, as it will enable the reader
to feel the airy spirit with which the young poet sets forth
on his career.

        [Quotes I. 11. 1-26.]

    After seeking the nymph with vain search through the
vales and woods, as he rests upon the ground pensively, he
hears a mournful voice, "such as once heard in gentle heart
destroys all pain but pity," [I. 11. 36-37] and perceives in
a dusky brake a magnificent serpent, with the lips of a woman,
who addresses him in human words, and promises to place the
nymph before him, if he will set her spirit free from her ser-
pent-form. He consents--his utmost wishes are granted--and
the brilliant snake, after a convulsive agony, vanishes, and
Lamia's soft voice is heard luting in the air. Having enjoyed
power during her degradation to send her spirit into distant
places, she had seen and loved Lycius, a youth of Corinth, whom
she now hastens to meet in her new, angelic beauty. He sees
and loves her: and is led by her to a beautiful place in the midst
of Corinth, which none ever remembered to have seen before,
where they live for some time in an unbroken dream of love.
But Lycius, at last, becomes restless in his happiness, and
longs to shew his beautiful mistress to the world. He resolves
to solemnize publicly his marriage festival, against which she
tremblingly remonstrates in vain. Finding she cannot win him
for her purpose,

> She sets herself high-thoughted how to dress
> Her[76] misery in fit magnificence:
>
> [II. ll. 115-116.]

And the following is the beautiful result of her art:

[Quotes II. ll. 119-145.]

The fatal day arrives--the guests assemble--Apollonius, the tutor of Lycius, comes an unbidden guest--but all, for a while, is luxury and delighted wonder. --

[Quotes II. ll. 199-220.]

The awful catastrophe is, however, at hand. In the midst of the festivities Apollonius fixes his eye upon the cold, pallid, beseeching bride--she vanishes with a frightful scream, and Lycius is found, on his high couch, lifeless! There is, in this poem, a mingling of Greek majesty with fairy luxuriance, which we have not elsewhere seen. The fair shapes stand clear in their antique beauty, encircled with the profuse magnificence of romance, and in the thick atmosphere of its golden lustre!

"Isabella" is the old and sweet tale of the Pot of Basil, from Boccaccio, which forms the groundwork of Barry Cornwall's delicious Sicilian story. It is here so differently told, that we need not undertake the invidious task of deciding which is the sweetest. The poem of Mr. Keats has not the luxury of description, nor the rich love-scenes, of Mr. Cornwall; but he tells the tale with a naked and affecting simplicity which goes irresistibly to the heart. The following description of Isabella's visit with her old nurse to her lover's grave, and their digging for the head, is as wildly intense as any thing which we can remember.

[Quotes sts. XLIV-XLVIII.]

"The Eve of St. Agnes" is a piece of consecrated fancy, which shews how a young lover, in the purity of heart, went to see his gentle mistress, the daughter of a baron, as she laid herself in her couch to dream in that holy season--and how she awoke and these lovers fled into the storm--while the father and his guests were oppressed with strange night-mare, and the old nurse died smitten with the palsy. A soft religious light is shed over the whole story. The following is part of the exquisite scene in the chamber:

[Quotes Sts. XXIV-XXVIII.]

"Hyperion, a fragment," is in a very different style.
It shews us old Saturn after the loss of his empire, and the
Titans in their horrid cave, meditating revenge on the
usurper, and young Apollo breathing in the dawn of his
joyous existence.   We do not think any thing exceeds in
silent grandeur the opening of the poem, which exhibits
Saturn in his solitude:

[Quotes I. ll. 1-21.]

The picture of the vast abode of Cybele and the
Titans--and of its gigantic inhabitants, is in the sublimest
style of Æschylus.   Lest this praise should be thought extravagant we will make room for the whole.

[Quotes II. ll. 5-81.]

We now take leave of Mr. Keats with wonder at the
gigantic stride which he has taken, and with the good hope
that, if he proceeds in the high and pure style which he has
now chosen, he will attain an exalted and a lasting station
among English poets.

12.   A review of the Lamia volume
        in the British Critic

(This mixed review appeared in the British
Critic for September 1820 [n. s. XIV, 257-264].
Although noted in several sources, it is now reproduced for the first time.   The author is not
known, but he admits that Keats's association with
Hunt was clearly an issue at stake in the Critic's
previous unfavorable review of Endymion [June
1818].   The significance of this admission should
not be underestimated.   The Critic found it difficult to reverse with consistency its former judgment on Keats.   It could hardly extoll the merits
of a poet whom it had damned in a most scathing
and ironic tone two years before.   In the review
under discussion, Hunt is still singled out, and
quite inaccurately so, as a damaging influence on
Keats's poetry.   The reviewer fatuously commends
himself on his impartiality, dismisses Isabella and

The Eve of St. Agnes in less than a sentence, and
says nothing about Keats's great odes; yet in his
own inadequate way, he attempts to be decent
about things.   This High Church review cannot
"approve of the morality of the principle poems,"
but in some cases they are "certainly deserving
of praise." _Lamia_ and, with some qualification,
Hyperion have the reviewer's general approval;
"Mr. Keats," we are told, "is really a person of
no ordinary genius." The review is a face-saving
attempt to correct a previous injustice against a
poet who was now receiving wider attention and
praise than had seemed possible in 1818.)

If there be one person in the present day, for whom we feel
an especial contempt, it is Mr. Examiner Hunt; and we confess that it is not easy for us to bring our minds to entertain respect for any whose taste, whether in morals, in
poetry, or politics, is so exceedingly corrupt as that person's must be supposed to be, who is willing to take such
a man for his model. It was for this reason that Mr. Keats
fell under our lash, so severely, upon the occasion of his
poem of Endymion. Upon recurring to the poem, we are
not unwilling to admit, that it possesses more merit, than
upon a first perusal of it we were able to perceive, or
rather than we were in a frame of mind to appreciate. We
can hardly doubt as to that poem having been corrected by
our modern Malvolio, and projected by his advice and under
his superintendence;--so full was it, of all the peculiarities
of that ingenious gentleman's ideas. The effect of this upon
Mr. Keats's poetry, was like an infusion of ipecacuanha
powder in a dish of marmalade. It created such a sickness
and nausea, that the mind felt little inclination to analyze
the mixture produced, and to consider, whether after all,
the dose might not have been mixed with some ingredients
that were in themselves agreeable. In the poems before us, the
same obstacle to a dispassionate judgment, is still to be en-
countered--not perhaps to so great a degree, as upon the former
occasion, but still in such a degree, as to reflect great praise,
we think, upon our impartiality for the commendation which we
feel willing to bestow.

        We cannot approve of the morality of the principal
poems in this little collection.   One of them is from Boccacio, [77] and the others upon exactly the same sort of subjects as the Florentine too generally choose. [78] However,
there is nothing in the details of either poem, that would
appear calculated to wound delicacy, and this, in cases

whether the temptation to the contrary may be supposed to
have existed, is certainly deserving of praise.

The first tale is in two parts, and called Lamia.
The subject of it is taken from the following passage in
Burton's "Anatomy of Melancholy;" and we extract it as
conveying a very agreeable fiction, and which loses none
of its merit in the hands of Mr. Keats.

> [Quotes Keats's note from Burton's <u>Anatomy of</u>
> <u>Melancholy.</u>]

We shall now present our readers with some specimens of the manner in which our poet has dressed up the
materials here afforded him; and we think those which we
shall give, will prove that Mr. Keats is really a person of
no ordinary genius; and that if he will only have the good
sense to take advice, making Spenser or Milton his model
of poetical diction, instead of Mr. Leigh Hunt, he need not
despair at attaining to a very high place in the public
esteem. --The poem opens with a description of Hermes
seeking a nymph, of whom he was enamoured. In the course
of his pursuit through the woods, he is addressed by a
voice which issues from a creature in the form of a serpent, who tells him that she is a woman in love with a
youth of Corinth, and that if he will restore her, as he is
able to do, to her natural shape, she will give him accounts
of the nymph whom he seeks. This being premised, the
reader will be able to enter into the beauty of the following
specimen of the manner in which this part of the poem is
managed, and from thence to form some judgment of the
whole.

> [Quotes I. ll. 1-37.]

After some explanation, the Lamia thus addresses
Hermes on the subject of his chase.

> [Quotes I. ll. 93-111.]

The god having agreed to the terms upon which his
assistance was asked, immediately destroys the spell, by
which the Lamia described herself as being bound.

> [Quotes I. ll. 134-145.]

Hermes and Lamia then depart different ways, and

soon the former meets the Corinthian youth, of whom she
was enamoured. Having changed a few looks and words,
the youth, of course, becomes entranced with admiration,
and addresses the Lamia.

[Quotes I. ll. 261-287.]

The Lamia then accompanies the youth to Corinth;
and the remainder of the story displays the same richness
of fancy, only as the scene becomes less peculiarly poetical,
the interest, in consequence, is not sustained. The next
tale is from Boccacio, and possesses less merit; nor is
there much to admire in the "Eve of St. Agnes;" but the
last poem, which is unfinished, and is called "Hyperion,"
contains some very beautiful poetry, although the greater
part of it appears not to have been executed with much success; nor do we think that Mr. Keats has evinced any want
of taste in leaving it incomplete; for it is plainly projected
upon principles that would infallibly lead to failure, [79] even
supposing the subject were not, which we think it is, somewhat above the pitch of Mr. Keat's peculiar genius,
which lies altogether in the region of fancy and description.
The fable of the poem seems to be, the wars of the Titans:
Saturn is described sitting alone, in despair for the loss
of his celestial dominions, and afterwards Thea and Coelus,
and others belonging to the Saturnian dynasty in heaven, are
severally introduced. The opening of the poem struck us
as very beautiful indeed.

[Quotes I. ll. 1-51.]

We pass over the speech which ensues; but the following lines, which come immediately after it, we think,
strikingly fine.

[Quotes I. ll. 72-92.]

We think that the specimens which we have now
given of Mr. Keats talents, are quite decisive as to
his poetical powers. That a man who can write so well,
should produce such absurd lines, and fall into such ridiculous modes of expression, as are to be met with in almost
every page, is really lamentable. An example or two will
be sufficient to convince our readers of the forbearance
which we have exerted, in giving these poems the praise
which is their due; for if we were to strike a balance between their beauties and absurdities, many would probably

be disposed to doubt as to which side the scale inclined.

Thus we are told that

"--charmed God
Began[80] an oath, and through the serpent's ears it ran
Warm, tremulous, devout, psalterian. " P. 10.
                                        [Lamia I. ll. 112-114.]

In another place the Lamia, as we are told,

"Writh'd about, convuls'd with scarlet pain:
A deep volcanian yellow took the place
Of all her milder-mooned body's grace. " P. 12.
                                        [I. ll. 154-156.]

We hear also of "a clear pool, wherein she passioned,
to see herself escaped. " P. 14. [I. ll. 182-183.] And likewise of this same person's pacing about "in a[81] pale contented
sort of discontent. " P. 35. [II. l. 135.] In another poem,
we have the following exquisite nonsense to describe a kiss:

"So said, his erewhile timid lips grew bold,
And poesied with her's in dewy rhymes. " P. 53.
                                        [Isabella, St. IX. ll. 5-6.]

Thus likewise we hear of pleasuring a thing, and
mirroring a thing; of doing a thing fearingly and fairly; of
leafits; of walking "silken, hush'd and chaste;" and innumerable other such follies, which are really too contemptible
to criticise. If all this nonsense is merely youthful affectation, perhaps as Mr. Keats gets more sense, he will
learn to see it in its true light; such innovations in language
are despicable in themselves, and disgusting to the imagination of every man of virtue and taste, from having been
originally conceited, as Mr. Keats would say, in the brain
of one of the most profligate and wretched scribblers that
we can remember to have ever either heard or read of.

13.   A review of the Lamia volume
      in the Eclectic Review

        (This unfavorable article, noted before but re-
      produced now for the first time, appeared in the
      Eclectic Review for September 1820 [s. 2. XIV,

158-171]. The identity of the author is not known,
but his low opinion of poetry in general is similar
to the viewpoint expressed in the Eclectic's September 1817 review of Poems; both reviews may
have been written by Josiah Conder. The present
article, however, is far more severe than the
previous one. The author seems to sanction the
Tory attacks of 1818 on Endymion. He disapproves
of Keats's use of language and mythology; and,
with only minimal exceptions, considers the poet's
third volume a failure.

Although a dissenting journal, the religious and
moral biases of the Eclectic are as discernible as
those of the British Critic. Throughout Keats's
1820 volume, the reviewer explains, there is not
"a single reference, even of the most general kind,
to the Supreme Being, or the Slenderest indication
that the Author is allied by any one tie to his
family, his country, or his kind." Moral posturing of this kind vitiated the critical objectivity
of more than one review of the period.)

It is just three years since we were called upon to
review Mr. Keats's first production. [82] We then gave it as
our opinion, that he was not incapable of writing good
poetry, that he possessed both the requisite fancy and skill;
but we regretted that a young man of his vivid imagination
and promising talents should have been flattered into the
resolution to publish verses of which he would probably be
glad a few years after to escape from the remembrance.
It is our practice, when a young writer appears for the
first time as a candidate for public favour, to look to the
indications of ability which are to be detected in his performance, rather than to its intrinsic merits. There is
a wasteful efflorescence that must be thrown off before the
intellect attains its maturity. The mind is then at a critical
period: there is equal danger of lavishing all its strength
in the abortive promise of excellence, and of its being
blighted by unjust discouragement. Such appeared to us to
be then the situation of Mr. Keats; and in the spirit of
candour and of kindness, we made those remarks on his
volume which were designed at once to guide and to excite
his future exertions, but for which he manfully disdained
to be the wiser. His next production had the good fortune
to fall into the hands of critics who rarely deal in either
half-praise or half-censure, and whose severity of censure
can at least confer notoriety upon the offender. [83] According

to his own account, the Author of Endymion must, while
smarting under the unsparing lash, have claimed pity almost equally on account of his mortified feelings and his
infidel creed; for, in the preface to that 'feverish attempt, '
he avows his conviction 'that there is not a fiercer hell
than the failure in a great object. ' How complete was his
failure in that matchless tissue of sparkling and delicious
nonsense, his Publishers frankly confess in an Advertisement prefixed to the present volume, wherein they take
upon themselves the responsibility of printing an unfinished
poem in the same strain, from proceeding with which the
Author was discouraged by the reception given to that poem.
And yet, under the sanction, we presume, of the same ad-
visers, Mr. Keats has ventured to proclaim himself in his
title-page as the unfortunate 'Author of Endymion. ' Are we
to gather from this, that he is vain and foolish enough to
wish that production not to be forgotten?

The present volume, however, we have been assured,
contains something much better. Startled as we were at the
appearance of the ghost of Endymion in the title, we endeavoured, on renewing our acquaintance with its Author,
to banish from our recollection the unpropitious circumstances under which we had last met, and, as it is now too
late to expect that he will exhibit any material change as
the result of further intellectual growth, to take a fresh
and final estimate of his talents and pretensions as they
may be judged of from the volume before us. The evidence
on which our opinion is formed, shall now be laid before
our readers. One naturally turns first to the shorter pieces,
in order to taste the flavour of the poetry. The following
ode to Autumn is no unfavorable specimen.

[Quotes "To Autumn. "]

Fancy has again and again been hymned in lays
Pindaric or Anacreontic, but not often in more pleasing
and spirited numbers than the following.

[Quotes "Fancy, " ll. 1-66.]

The lines addressed to a friend, 84 on Robin Hood,
are in the same light and sportive style.

[Quotes "Robin Hood. "]

Of the longer pieces, Lamia is decidedly the best.

The story on which it is built, is taken from the rich repository of old Burton, who cites from Philostratus the
memorable account of one Mennipus Lycius,

[Quotes Keats's note from Burton's Anatomy of
Melancholy.]

This sort of semi-allegorical legend is of the same family
of fictions as the Vampire. The plain matter of fact which
it envelops, would seem to be, the case of a young man of
good talents and respectable connexions, that falls in love
with a rich courtezan who has the address to persuade him
to marry her. The spell of her charms and her ill-gotten
wealth naturally enough dissolve together, and her victim at
last discovers her to be--a lamia. The story thus inter-
preted is not without a moral; though Mr. Keats does not
make use of it. 85   His account of the transaction is as follows. 'Upon a time,' or, as Mother Bunch has it with
stricter precision, once upon a time,

'before the faery broods
Drove Nymph and Satyr from the prosperous woods,
The ever-smitten Hermes'
[Lamia, I. ll. 1-2, 7.]

left Olympus for a forest in the isle of Crete, in search of
an invisible mistress who lived somewhere or other in that
neighbourhood; where, his god-ship could not tell. Here his
attention is arrested by a mournful voice that issues from
'a palpitating snake,' [I. l. 45]

[Quotes I. ll. 47-65.]

This feminine incarnation of the Evil Principle is
fortunately acquainted with what Hermes wants to know, and
a bargain is soon struck between them, by which, as a reward for her obligingly acting as a procuress, she is re-
stored, by virtue of 'the Caducean charm,' [I. l. 133] to
the shape of woman, according to the tenour of her demand:

'I love a youth of Corinth--O the bliss!
Give me my woman's form, and place me where he is. '
[I. ll. 119-120.]

All this, not being in Burton, we take it for granted
is out of Mr. Keats's own head, as the children say; except

so far as Mr. Coleridge may have helped him to the portrait
of the serpent-elf, in his Christabel.   The metamorphose is
thus described

[Quotes I. ll. 146-168.]

     Away she flies, to waylay the said Lycius, who, as
a matter of course, is deeply smitten with her, mistakes
her for a naiad, or a dryad, or a pleïad, he cannot tell
which, till she throws off the assumed goddess, and 'wins
his heart more pleasantly by playing woman's part'; [I. ll.
336-337] in short, he goes home with her.   In the enchanted
palace to which she conducts him, he lies, like most heroes
in similar toils, all dissolved in luxury, till he begins to
be tired of doing nothing but being happy, and is one day
roused by 'a thrill of trumpets,' [II. ll. 27-28] into the
desire to revisit the noisy world.   He wishes, in plain English, to drive his lady out through the streets of Corinth,
that his friends may see her beauty and envy him; and he
talks of a bridal feast.   His lady reluctantly consents, on
the condition that old Apollonius should not be invited; and
she proceeds to fit up the hall accordingly, by the help of
her demon-servitors, for the occasion.   The day arrives,
the gossip rout of guests enter, and among the rest, but
self-invited, the philosopher; the feast, however, goes forward, the music floats along the perfumed air, --but

          'Philosophy will clip an Angel's wings,
          Conquer all mysteries by rule and line,
          Empty the haunted air and gnomed mine--
          Unweave a rainbow, as it erewhile made
          The tender-person'd Lamia melt into a shade.'
                                        [II. 234-238.]

Lycius pledges his old master in a bumper; father bald-
head makes no answer, but fixes his eye 'without a twinkle'
[II. l. 246] on the alarmed beauty of the bride,

     'Browbeating her fair form and troubling her sweet pride.'
                                        [II. l. 248.]

Her lover, seeing her start and turn pale, asks her a very
silly and insulting question, considering the previous warn-
ing she had given him; to wit, whether she knew that man.

     [Quotes II. ll. 255-311.]

Isabella, or the Pot of Basil, is founded on a tale in
the Decameron. A poetical rival of Mr. Keats, whose
volumes are now on our table, has taken the same subject
in his 'Sicilian Story;' and in a future Number, we shall,
perhaps, afford our readers the opportunity of comparing
the different versions. 86   The Eve of St. Agnes, is the
story of a young damsel of high degree, who loves the son
of her father's foe. Having heard that upon St. Agnes'
eve, young virgins might, if they would go to bed supperless,
and perform certain other rites, enjoy a vision of their
lovers, she determines to try the spell; and Young Porphyro,
who learns her purpose from her Duenna, resolves to fulfill
the legend in propriâ personâ. 87   Every thing succeeds to
admiration; Madeline is quite delighted when she finds the
supposed vision is a palpable reality; and while all in the
castle are asleep, they elope together; the old nurse dies
in the night; and thus endeth the tale. A few stanzas must
suffice for further extracts:--

[Quotes sts. XXV, XXVII-XXVIII, XXXIII-XXXV,
XL-XLII.]

We have laid before our readers these copious extracts from Mr. Keats's present volume, without any comment, in order that he might have the full benefit of plead-
ing his own cause: there they are, and they can be made
to speak neither more nor less in his favour than they have
already testified.

Mr. Keats, it will be sufficiently evident, is a young
man--whatever be his age, we must consider him as still
but a young man, --possessed of an elegant fancy, a warm
and lively imagination, and something above the average
talents of persons who take to writing poetry. Poetry is
his mistress, --we were going to say, his Lamia, for we
suspect she has proved a syren, that her wine is drugged,
and that her treasures will be found to be like the gold of
Tantalus. 88   Mr. Keats has given his whole soul to 'plotting
and fitting himself for verses fit to live;"89 and the consequence is, that he has produced verses which, if we mistake not, will not live very long, though they will live as
long as they deserve. The exclusive cultivation of the
imagination is always attended by a dwindling or contraction
of the other powers of the mind. This effect has often been
remarked upon: it is the penalty which second-rate genius
pays for the distinction purchased by the exhaustion of its
whole strength in that one direction, or upon that one object,

that has seized upon the fancy; and it is the source of affection and eccentricity. In no other way can we account
for the imbecility of judgement, the want of sober calculation,
the intense enthusiasm about mean or trival objects, and
the real emptiness of mind, which are sometimes found
connected with distinguishing talents. Poetry, after all, if
pursued as an end, is but child's play; and no wonder that
those who seem not to have any higher object than to be
poets, should sometimes be very childish. What better
name can we bestow on the nonsense that Mr. Keats, and
Mr. Leigh Hunt, and Mr. Percy Bysshe Shelley, and some
other poets about town, have been talking of 'the beautiful
mythology of Greece?'[90] To some persons, although we
would by no means place Mr. Keats among the number,
that mythology comes recommended chiefly by its grossness
--its alliance to the sensitive pleasures which belong to the
animal. With our Author, this fondness for it proceeds, we
very believe, from nothing worse than a school boy taste for
the stories of the Pantheon [by J. H. Tooke] and Ovid's
Metamorphoses, and the fascination of the word classical.
Had he passed through the higher forms of a liberal education, he would have shed all these puerilities; his mind
would have received the rich alluvial deposite of such
studies, but this would only have formed the soil for its
native fancies; and he would have known that the last use
which a full-grown scholar thinks of making of his classical
acquirements, is to make a parade of them either in prose
or verse. There is nothing gives a greater richness to
poetry, we admit, than classical allusions, if they are not
of a common-place kind; but they will generally be found to
please in proportion to their slightness and remoteness: it
is as illustrations, sometimes highly picturesque illustrations
of the subject, not as distinct objects of thought, --it is as
metaphor, never in the broad and palpable shape of simile,
that they please. It was reserved for the Author of Endymion to beat out the gold of ancient fable into leaf thin
enough to cover four long cantos of incoherent verse. And
now, in the present volume, we have Hyperion, books one,
two, and three! We do not mean to deny that there is a
respectable degree of inventive skill and liveliness of fancy
displayed in this last poem, but they are most miserably
misapplied; nor should we have imagined that any person
would have thrown away his time in attempting such a theme,
unless it were some lad with his fancy half full of Homer
and half full of Milton, who might, as a school exercise,
try to frame something out of the compound ideas of the
Titan and the Demon, of Olympus and Pandemonium. But

Mr. Keats, seemingly, can think or write of scarcely any
thing else than the 'happy pieties' ["Ode to Psyche, " l. 41]
of Paganism.   A Grecian Urn throws him into an ecstasy:
its 'silent form' he says, 'doth tease us out of thought as
doth Eternity, ' [ll. 44-45]--a very happy description of the
bewildering effect which such subjects have at least had
upon his own mind; and his fancy having thus got the better
of his reason, we are the less surprised at the oracle which
the Urn is made to utter

> ' "Beauty is truth, truth beauty, "--that is all
> Ye know on earth, and all ye need to know. '
>   [ll. 49-50.]

That is all that Mr. Keats knows or cares to know. --But
till he knows much more than this, he will never write
verses fit to live.

We wish to say little of the affectation which still
frequently disfigures Mr. Keats's phraseology, because
there is very much less of it in the present volume than
in his former poems.   We are glad to notice this indication
of <u>growth</u>.   An imperfect acquaintance with the genuine resources of the language, or an impatience of its poverty
and weakness as a vehicle for his teeming fancies, is still
occasionally discernible in the violence he lays upon words
and syllables forced to become such: e. g. 'rubious-argent?'
'milder-moon'd;' 'frail-strung heart;' a 'tithe' of eye-sight, --

> '--With eye-lids closed,
> Saving a tythe which love still open kept. '
>   [<u>Lamia</u>, II. ll. 23-24.]

(N. B.   An American Keats would have said, 'a balance;')

'trembled blossoms;' 'honey'd middle of the night;' and
other splendid novelties.

We would, however, be the last persons to lay great
stress on such minutiäe, in estimating the merits of a
writer; but we feel it our duty to warn off all persons who
are for breaking down the fences which language interposes
between sense and nonsense.

The true cause of Mr. Keats's failure is, not the
want of talent, but the misdirection of it; and this circumstance presents the only chance there is that some day or

other he will produce something better: whether he ever
does or not, is a matter of extreme insignificance to the
public, for we have surely poets enough; but it would seem
to be not so to himself. At present, there is a sickliness
about his productions, which shews there is a mischief at
the core. He has with singular ingenuousness and correctness described his own case in the preface to Endymion:
'The imagination of a boy,' he says, 'is healthy, and 'the
mature imagination of a man is healthy; but there is a
'space of life between, in which the soul is in a ferment,
the 'character undecided, the way of life uncertain, the
ambition 'thick-sighted: thence proceeds mawkishness.'91
The diagnosis of the complaint is well laid down; his is a
diseased state of feeling, arising from the want of a sufficient and worthy object of hope and enterprise, and of the
regulating principle of religion. Can a more unequivocal
proof of this be given, than that there does not occur, if
our recollection serves us, throughout his present volume,
a single reference to any one object of real interest, a
single burst of virtuous affection or enlightened sentiment,
a single reference, even of the most general kind, to the
Supreme Being, or the slenderest indication that the Author
is allied by any one tie to his family, his country, or his
kind? Mr. Keats, we doubt not, has attachments and virtuous feelings, and we should fain hope, notwithstanding the
silly expressions which would justify a presumption to the
contrary, that he is a Christian: if he is not, it will matter
very little to him in a few years what else he may or may
not be. We will, however, take it for granted that he is
an amiable and well principled young man; and then we have
but one piece of advice to offer him on parting, namely, to
let it appear in his future productions.

14.   John Scott's review of the Lamia volume
       in Baldwin's London Magazine

              (This friendly review appeared in Baldwin's
       London Magazine for September 1820 [II, 315-321].
       Among existing reprints there is one by the For-
       mans in their Hampstead Edition of Keats [III,
       312-323].   Edmund Blunden [Leigh Hunt and His
       Circle (London, 1930), p. 153] has identified the
       reviewer as John Scott, editor of the London
       Magazine, and the Formans agree that the review
       is "probably" by Scott.   Internal evidence tends to

substantiate this claim. The author in Baldwin's
emphasizes the "vindictive" attacks on _Endymion_
by the _Quarterly_ and _Blackwood's_. _Blackwood's_
attack was to occupy Scott's attention in November
and December 1820 [II, 509-521, 666-685] when
he wrote two articles exposing that magazine's
excesses against Keats and other victims. In
each of these articles, the author's disgust with
Blackwood's is substantially the same as in the
review under discussion; and in both the September review and the December article, John Wilson
is singled out for criticism. The hand of John
Scott is evident in all three instances.

Although Scott criticizes Keats for "his frequent
obscurity and confusion of language" and his
"quaint strangeness of phrase," he grasps the
poet's essential abilities. _Hyperion_, he observes,
is "one of the most extraordinary creations of
any modern imagination." His criticism of _Isa-
bella_ is justified. One might wish that an editor
of Scott's abilities had voiced his opinion of Keats's
last volume with somewhat less qualification, but
he was attempting to disassociate the _London Mag-
azine_ from what he considered the extravagant
praise of Hunt in the _Examiner._ In general,
Soctt's viewpoint was both favorable and intelligent.)

We opened this volume with very considerable anxiety:
--an anxiety partly occasioned by the unqualified praises of
which the author has been the object, --but more owing to
the abuse by which he has been assailed. Perhaps from
the whole history of criticism, real and pretended, nothing
more truly unprincipled than that abuse can be quoted;
nothing more heartless, more vindictive, --more nefarious
in design, more pitiful and paltry in spirit. [92] We consider
it one of the worst signs of these, the worst times which
England, we are afraid, has ever seen, that the miserable
selfishness of political party has erected itself into a literary authority, and established, by means of popular chan-
nels, the most direct and easy access to the public ear on literary questions. The provocation, we allow, is reciprocal:
the vanity of the Examiner manifests just as great a defi-
ciency in real candour as is apparent in the bitter spite of
the Quarterly, or the merry ruffianism of Blackwood. [93]
But the distinct consciousness of depravity in the two latter,
which must accompany them in many of the lucubrations,
gives a blacker feature to their conduct. It would be well

worthy, we think, of the great talents and lofty principles
of the new Edinburgh Professor of Moral Philosophy, 94 to
discuss ethically from his comfortable chair, --where he sits,
the honour of Scotland, and fit substitute for Dugald Stewart
--the specific difference in moral guilt and personal degre-
dation, which distinguishes the misrepresentations of a blind
overweening vanity from those of a sordid and cunning
wordly greediness. The young Scotchmen would listen at-
tentively to the arguments of one so well-qualified to handle
this point; and the lecture might have blessed effects on
their future lives and fortunes. --But to the subject before
us, from whence we are wandering.

   Mr. Keats, though not a political writer, plunged
at once, with what we shall take the liberty of calling a
boyish petulance, and with an air of rather insulting bravado,
into some very delicate subjects;--subjects on which, we
have no hesitation to say, those very qualities of his mind
which confer on his poetry its most characteristic beauties,
incapacitate him fairly to pronounce. There have been, and
it is possible there may be even now, great comprehensive
intellects, which, to wealthy and voluptuous imaginations,
add a far-sightedness sufficient to discern, and a magnanimity
inducing them to acknowledge, the deep, internal, and in-
extricable connection between the pains and penalties of
human nature, and its hopes and enjoyments: whose spirits
dwell and play in "the plighted clouds, "95--but who understand enough of the philosophy of earthly existence to know,
that, as man must cultivate the ground by the sweat of his
brow, so he must cultivate his faculties by self-denials and
struggles of soul: --who perceive lurking in the common
restraints of society, eternal principles of human nature--
mysterious instincts, which, through the mortification of
desire, the humiliation of feeling, and often in the absence
of an active sense of justice or clear view of utility, conduct to the average maximum, such as it is, of human good
and moral beauty. Such intellects are scornful of none of
our necessities while they provide for our delights: in
stimulating the strength of human nature, they do not mis-
lead or neglect its weakness: they are impartial in their
judgments, because their views are commanding, and their
motives issue from lofty dispositions. They will not palter,
or play false with what they see daily before them, because
the conclusions it suggests may chance to reproach some of
their own actions. They will have learnt, by degrees, to
correct the unfavorable decisions which we are all naturally
inclined to found on dissimilarity of habits, and opposition

of tastes; and they will at length have been induced to con-
vert these into reasons for self-suspicion, rather than
grounds for accusing others. 96 Following human life into
its various walks; contemplating it fairly and kindly in all
its aspects, they will have been compelled to conclude,
that it is not self-abandonment to the favourite themes of
touching description, and to those pursuits which seem to
lead most directly to the indulgence and excitement of a
reflective sensibility, that exclusively proves the fine construction and delicate movements of the mind. In the
labyrinth of the world they will have found that appearances
are not guides;--that a face cast up towards the moon does
not more certainly infer an amiable or susceptible disposition, than a contracted brow cast down over a ledger of
bad debts. Selfishness, it will have struck them, is often
most active in the whirlwind of passion; and it will have
occurred to them that, in the estimation of intelligences altogether superior to this wordly turmoil, fainting away over
a fair bosom does not, unless accompanied by other symptoms, prove much more in favour of the refinement of the
transported person than clasping a money-bag, or ogling a
haunch of venison. A man may smell to a rose, or walk
out to admire an effect of sun-set, and yet not have half
the complication of the warmer affections stirring within
him, which shall move a tradesman of the Strand, seated
with his wife, children, and shopman, in his back parlour;
--and the said tradesman may take out a writ against a
dilatory customer, in no worse spirit than that in which
one author pursues another for literary defalcation. It is
well to let the imagination contemplate splendours hanging
over past times; the soul must stretch itself somehow out
of its cramps: but this may be done without committing
crying, positive injustice towards the present. It may be
allowable in poetry to treat ancient thieves with the respect
due to true men; but the poet has no business, more than
the police officer, to treat true men, his neighbours, as
thieves. If Maid Marian were to come back, and complain
in our hearing, as she does in Mr. Keats's poetry--

> --Strange! that honey
> Can't be got without hard money--
> ["Robin Hood, " ll. 47-48.]

we would ask her what there is strange in this? and whether
it is not quite as well to get things by hard money as by
hard blows? and whether more injustice be included in the
inequality of purses--a consequence of society--than in the

inequality of arms, which is an effect of nature? Of course,
we would not have thus selected, for the purpose of argument, a passage bearing an air of pleasantry, if we did not
think that Mr. Keats's sensibility is diseased in this re-
spect--that his spirit is impregnated with a flippant impatience, (irritated and justified by a false philosophy) of the
great phenomena of society, and the varieties of human nature, which hurts his poetry quite as much as it corrupts
his sentiments--and which is altogether unworthy of the
grandeur of his powers. There are some stanzas introduced into his delicious tale of "Isabel--poor simple Isabel, " [St. I. l. 1] in this volume, which, we think, dread-
fully mar the musical tenderness of its general strain.
They are no better than extravagant school-boy vituperation
of trade and traders; just as if lovers did not trade, --and
that, often in stolen goods--or had in general any higher
object than a barter of enjoyment! These stanzas in Mr.
Keats's poem, when contrasted with the larger philosophy
of Boccacio, and his more genial spirit, as exemplified
with reference to the very circumstances in question, are
additionally offensive. Instead of tirading against the
brothers as "money-bags, " [St. XVIII. l. 6] "Baalities of
pelf, " [St. LVII. l. 3] "ledger-men, " [St. XVIII. l. 1]--
and asking, "why, in the name of glory, were they proud?"
[St. XVI. l. 8] Boccacio describes the honour of the family
as actually injured by Lorenzo, whom they employed--he
shows us the elder brother, on discovering his sister's dis-
honour, afflicted with grief and perplexity, and passing a
sleepness night on his bed--he even compliments the discretion of this member of the family--and it is thus naturally, and faithfully, and feelingly introduced, that he leads
up the dreadful catastrophe to its consumation in Italian
revenge, and the broken-heartedness of widowed love.
Does the pathos of the tale suffer by thus looking fairly
into the face of human nature? Do we pity the lovers less;
do we sympathize less with Isabel's bitter tears, because
we have both sides of the case thus placed before us? No
--our sympathies, being more fairly excited, are more
keenly so: the story is in fine keeping, as a painter would
say: the effect of truth overpowers us: we weep the more
because we feel that human frailty provides for human suffering, and that the best impulses of the heart are not removed from the liability of producing the extremities of
agony and of crime. Mr. Keats, we are sure, has a sensibility sufficiently delicate to feel this beauty in Boccacio:
why then has he substituted for it, in his own composition,
a boisterous rhapsody, which interrupts the harmony of the

sorrowful tale, --repels sympathy by the introduction of caricature, --and suggests all sorts of dissenting, and altercating
prejudices and opinions? His device is a clumsy one:
Bocaccio's delicate and true. That most beautiful
Paper, (by a correspondent of course) in our last number,
on the "ledger-men," of the South Sea House, 97 is an elegant reproof of such short-sighted views of character; such
idle hostilities against the realities of life. How free from
intolerance of every sort must the spirit be, that conceived
that paper, --or took off so fair and clear an impression
from facts! It would not be prone to find suggestion of invective in the sound of Sabbath bells, as Mr. Keats has
done in a former work. 98 The author of Endymion and
Hyperion must delight in that Paper;--and, to give another
example of what we mean, he must surely feel the gentle
poetical beauty which is infused into the star-light tale of
Rosamund Grey, 99 through its vein of "natural piety. "100
What would that tale be without the Grandmother's Bible?101
How eclipsed would be the gleaming light of such a character as Rosamund's, in a re-modelled state of society,
where it should be the fashion for wives to be considered
as dainties at a pic-nic party, each man bringing his own
with him--but ready to give and take with those about him!
Creeds here are out of the question altogether;--we only
speak with reference to the wants and instincts of the human soul. We mention these things, not because we desire
to see Mr. Keats playing the hypocrite, or enlisted as a
florid declaimer on the profitable side of things; but because,
with our admiration of his powers, we are loath to see him
irrecoverably committed to a flippant and false system of
reasoning on human nature;--because to his picturesque
imagination, we wish that he would add a more pliable, and,
at the same time, a more magnanimous sensibility. Nor
need his philosophy be a whit more condescending to what
is grovelling and base. Let him write, as much as he
pleases, in the bold indignant style of Wordsworth's glorious Sonnet!

                The world is too much with us!

    Here the poet speaks--not the malcontent;--it is not
mortification, but inspiration he feels;--it is not classes of
men, but crawling minds he anathematizes. We must positively give this magnificent Sonnet entire, now we have ac-
cidently been brought to it by the current of our writing.
It cannot be deemed out of place any where--for it is a
high animation to noble thoughts.

[Quotes the sonnet.]

From what we have said, in the way of objection to
the fashion of Mr. Keats's thinking, on certain important
questions, it will easily be seen that he has very much,
and very incautiously exposed himself to attack;--and his
chivalry, as it will be guessed, has done him little service
in his contest with the windmills in Albemarle-street. 102
These things, that go furiously with the breeze of the time,
have beaten his lance out of its rest, battered his helmet,
and overturned in the dirt himself and his steed. It is
impossible,--however we may regret the extravagant course
his Knight-errantry has taken,--not to feel our wishes and
sympathies on the side of the knight of the Sorrowful countenance in this encounter. His spirit is a gallant one; his
brain is full of high feats; his heart beats in real devotion
to a Dulcinea whom he has clad with fine attributes in his
imagination, though, certainly, we believe her to be much
less a lady than he imagines her. His delusion, however,
is the offspring of a romantic temperament; whereas his
maulers are but things of brute matter, machines for grind-
ing grist;--"plates hung on pins to turn with the wind,"103
--acquiring a murderous power from their specific levity.

The injustice which has been done to our author's
works, in estimating their poetical merit, rendered us
double anxious, on opening his last volume, to find it likely
to seize fast hold of general sympathy, and thus turn an
overwhelming power against the paltry traducers of a talent,
more eminently promising in many respects, than any that
the present age has been called upon to encourage. We have
not found it to be quite all that we wished in this respect--
and it would have been very extraordinary if we had, for
our wishes went far beyond reasonable expectations. But
we have found it of a nature to present to common under-
standings the poetical power with which the author's mind
is gifted, in a more tangible and intelligible shape than
that in which it has appeared in any of his former compositions. It is, therefore, calculated to throw shame on
the lying, vulgar spirit, in which this young worshipper in
the temple of the Muses has been cried-down; whatever
questions it may still leave to be settled as to the kind
and degree of his poetical merits. Take for instance, as
a proof of the justice of our praise, the following passage
from an Ode to the Nightingale:--it is distinct, noble,
pathetic, and true: the thoughts have all chords of direct
communication with naturally-constituted hearts: the echoes

of the strain linger about the depth of human bosoms.

> [Quotes the last two stanzas of the "Ode to a
> Nightingale. "]

Let us take also a passage of another sort alto-
gether--the description of a young beauty preparing for her
nightly rest, overlooked by a concealed lover, in which we
know not whether most to admire the magical delicacy of
the hazardous picture, or its consummate, irresistible attraction. "How sweet the moonlight sleeps upon this
bank, "[104] says Shakespeare; and sweetly indeed does it fall
on the half undressed form of Madeline:--it has an exquisite
moral influence, corresponding with the picturesque effect.

> [Quotes sts. XXIII, XXV, XXVI, XXVII-XXVIII
> of The Eve of St. Agnes.]

One more extract, --again varying entirely the style
of the composition. It shall be taken from a piece called
Hyperion; one of the most extraordinary creations of any
modern imagination. Its "woods are ruthless, dreadful,
deaf, and dull:"[105] the soul of dim antiquity hovers, like a
mountain-cloud, over its vast and gloomy grandeur: it
carries us back in spirit beyond the classical age; earlier
than "the gods of the Greeks;"[106] when the powers of
creation were to be met with visible about the young earth,
shouldering the mountains, and with their huge forms filling
the vallies. The sorrows of this place are "huge;" its
utterance "large;" its tears "big."--Alas, centuries have
brought littleness since then--otherwise a crawling, reptile
of office, with just strength enough to leave its slimy
traces on the page of a fashionable Review, [107] could never
have done a real mischief to the poet of the Titans! It is
but a fragment we have of Hyperion: an advertisement tells
us that "the poem was intended to have been of equal length
with Endymion, but the reception given to that work discouraged the author from proceeding."[108]   Let Mr. Croker
read the following sublime and gorgeous personification of
Asia, and be proud of the information thus given--and of
that superior encouragement to which it is owing that we
have his Talavera in a complete state![109]

> [Quotes Hyperion, II. ll. 52-63.]

This is not the extract, however, which we were
about to make: it was the opening of the poem we thought

of. The dethronement of Saturn by Jupiter, and the later
gods taking the places of the early powers of heaven and
earth, form its subject. We seem entering the awful
demesne of primeval solitude as the poet commences:

[Quotes I. ll. 1-71.]

Will not our readers feel it as a disgrace attaching
to the character of the period, that a dastardly attempt
should have been made to assassinate a poet of power equal
to those passages: that one should come like a thief to
steal his "precious diadem;"[110]--a murder and a robbery
"most foul and horrible?"[111] Cold-blooded conscious dis-
honesty, we have no hesitation to say, must have directed
the pen of the critic of Endymion in the Quarterly Review:
making every allowance for the callousness of a worldly
spirit, it is impossible to conceive a total insensibility to
the vast beauties scattered profusely over that disordered,
ill-digested work. The author provokes opposition, as we
have already fully said: not unfrequently he even suggests
angry censure. We cannot help applying the word insolent,
in a literary sense, to some instances of his neglectfulness,
to the random swagger of occasional expressions, to the
bravado style of many of his sentiments. But, coupling
these great faults with his still greater poetical merits,
what a fine, what an interesting subject did he offer for
perspicacious, honourable criticism! But he was beset by
a very dog-kennel; and he must be more than human if he
has not had his erroneous tendencies hardened in him in
consequence.

What strike us as the principal faults of his poetry,
impeding his popularity, we would venture thus to specify.

1. His frequent obscurity and confusion of language.
As an instance of the latter, we may mention that he at-
taches the epithet of "leaden-eyed," to despair, considered
as a quality of sentiment.[112] Were it a personification of
despair, the compound would be as finely applied, as, under
the actual circumstances, it is erroneously so. There are
many, many passages too, in his last volume, as well as
in his earlier ones, from which we are not able, after
taking some pains to understand them, to derive any distinct notion or meaning whatever.

2. He is too fond of running out glimmerings of
thought, and indicating distant shadowy fancies: he shows,

also, a fondness for dwelling on features which are not
naturally the most important or prominent. His imagination
coquets with, and mocks the reader in this respect; and
plain earnest minds turn away from such tricks with disgust.
The greatest poets have always chiefly availed themselves of
the plainest and most palpable materials.

   3. He affects, in bad taste, a quaint strangeness of
phrase; as some folks affect an odd manner of arranging
their neckcloths, &c. This "shows a most pitiful ambition."113 We wish Mr. Keats would not talk of cutting
mercy with a sharp knife to the bone; [Isabella, st. XXII.
l. 6] we cannot contemplate the skeleton of mercy. Nor
can we familiarize ourselves pleasantly with the dainties
made to still an infant's cries:114 [Isabella, st. XLVII. l. 6]
--the latter is indeed a very round about way of expression,
and not very complimentary either, we think. Young ladies,
who know, of course, little or nothing of the economy of
the nursery, will be apt, we imagine, to pout at this
periphrasis, which puts their charms on a level with baby-
corals!

   But we are by this time tired of criticism; as we
hope our readers are:--let us then all turn together to the
book itself. We have said here what we have deemed it
our duty to say: we shall there find what it will be our
delight to enjoy.

Notes

1. A group of late eighteenth century sentimentalists and
  poetasters, of whom Robert Merry was the head.

2. The Cockney School.

3. Keats's "youth" is mentioned for the second time. The
  poet referred to this in his Preface to Endymion,
  but the reviewer may have also fallen prey to
  Reynolds' artifice in the Alfred. (See n. 88 of the
  previous chapter.)

4. Written at Diodati in July 1816.

5. Published in 1820, almost at the same time as the
  Lamia volume, Cornwall's poem on the tale of
  Isabella was frequently compared with Keats's ver-
  sion of the same story.

6. This phrase appears in Gray's letter of April 8, 1742
   to Richard West (Correspondence, eds. Paget Toyn-
   bee and Leonard Whibley [Oxford, 1935], I, 192).
   "Now as the paradisaical pleasures of the Mahome-
   tans consist in playing upon the flute and lying with
   Houris, be mine to read eternal new romances of
   Marivaux and Crebillion."

7. The complete "Advertisement" reads: "If any apology
   be thought necessary for the appearance of the unfinished poem of HYPERION, the publishers beg to
   state that they alone are responsible, as it was
   printed at their particular request, and contrary to
   the wish of the author. The poem was intended to
   have been of equal length with ENDYMION, but the
   reception given to that work discouraged the author
   from proceeding." As indicated by Hyder Rollins
   (Keats Circle [Cambridge, Mass., 1965], I, 115),
   Woodhouse was the author of this advertisement.
   In the fall of 1818 Keats told him in a less than
   candid moment that he never intended to write
   again; and Woodhouse, at first, took him quite
   seriously. Despite assurances to the contrary,
   the idea must have remained in Woodhouse's mind;
   thus, Keats himself planted the seed for the announcement that appears at the head of Hyperion,
   an announcement that Woodhouse cites again in this
   review (an additional reason for attributing authorship of the review to him). Keats, without realizing
   that he, himself, was the indirect source of the
   announcement, disavowed its import. "Crossing
   out this page in one of the gift copies, he [Keats]
   wrote above it: 'This is none of my doing--I was
   ill at the time,' and then beneath the last sentence,
   'This is a lie'" (Bate, p. 651). (The gift copy
   was sent to Burridge Davenport, a Hampstead neigh-
   bor. Amy Lowell reproduces Keats's note in John
   Keats [New York, 1925], II, 424.) Woodhouse
   probably heard of Keats's dissatisfaction, but not
   before his review in the Sun was published. Realizing that he had erred not once, but twice, he felt
   it was best to keep silent about this anonymous review. This would explain why the review is not
   mentioned either in the letters of Keats or of his
   friends.

8. Shakespeare's Sonnet CVI, l. 3.

9. Lucas (I, 471) calls this a recollection of Shakespeare's "And weep afresh love's long-since cancell'd woe" in Sonnet **XXX**, l. 7.

10. For "a" read "thou."

11. Hunt and the Cockneys.

12. Keats omits the indefinite article.

13. For "filled" read "fed."

14. Hunt is alluding to _Lamia_, II. ll. 234-237:
    "Philosophy will clip an Angel's wings,
    Conquer all mysteries by rule and line
    Empty the haunted air, and gnomed mine--
    Unweave a rainbow...."
    At Haydon's "immortal dinner" on December 28, 1817, attended by Wordsworth, Thomas Monkhouse, Lamb, and Keats, a discussion began concerning the host's still-to-be completed painting, "Christ's Entry into Jerusalem." One of the heads in Haydon's painting was modeled after the face of Newton, and Lamb jokingly attacked his host "for putting Newton, 'a Fellow who believed nothing unless it was clear as the three sides of a triangle.' And then he and Keats agreed he [Newton] had destroyed all the Poetry of the rainbow, by reducing it to a prism. It was impossible to resist them, and we drank 'Newton's health, and confusion to mathematics!'" (The Diary of Benjamin Robert Haydon, ed. Willard Bissell Pope [Cambridge, Mass., 1960], II, 173.) Hunt, of whom Haydon disapproved, was not at the dinner; but Keats probably expressed a similar opinion to his older friend. The accuracy of Hunt's ensuing comments has been questioned by Claude L. Finney, The Evolution of Keats's Poetry (Cambridge, Mass., 1936), II, 702: "Hunt understood the meaning of Lamia but he misunderstood the meaning of Apollonius. He thought that Keats was making a sweeping censure of natural philosophy or experimental science." Finney contends that it is not natural philosophy but Apollonius' "misapplication of the principles of natural philosophy" (p. 703) that Keats condemns. It is clear from his poems and letters of 1818 and 1819 that Keats admired natural philosophy. (His decision to study medicine indicates an early interest in science.)

It is equally clear that Hunt has overstated his case.
Nevertheless, it is far-fetched to suggest, as Finney
does, that Apollonius represents "the reviewers who
judged Keats's poems by the standard of fact and
reason" (p. 703). Keats was not writing an alle-
gory, and these lines are a direct echo of Lamb's
toast to Newton. As Bate suggests (John Keats
[New York, 1966], p. 559), Apollonius may represent a false, analytic philosophy; but Keats's attitude toward science is more complex and sometimes
confusingly ambivalent. In "God of the Meridian, "
for instance, he appeals to philosophy to "temper"
his scepticism, his "terrible division, " and yet the
image of a "young infant child ... in an eagle's
claws" suggests a terror which is incapable of such
reconciliation. In "To J. H. Reynolds, Esq. " Keats
writes that imagination
  "Cannot refer to any standard law
  Of either earth or heaven? It is a flaw
  In happiness, to see beyond our bourn, --
  It forces us in summer skies to mourn,
  It spoils the singing of the Nightingale. "
Keats's view of "standard law" conflicts with his
concept of the imagination, just as Apollonius'
analytical philosophy destroys the illusionary world
created by Lamia. Apollonius' function in the poem
may well reflect Keats's own ambiguity about the
conflict of science and art, of "truth and beauty. "

15.   For "him" read "thee. "

16.   Lamb, in the New Times of July 19, 1820, had cited
      the word and the quote that follows.

17.   Hunt alludes to Marino in the June 1, 1817 installment
      of his review of Poems in the Examiner. In the
      July 6, 1817 installment of the same review, Hunt
      also mentioned that Keats's faults "arise from a
      passion for beauties, " a phrase quite similar in
      meaning to the "exuberance of ideas" which he has
      just claimed in the previous sentence is the reason
      for Keats's only poetical weakness. Obviously,
      then, Hunt is silently drawing from his 1817 re-
      view as the source for these observations.

18.   Had Keats wished to reply, he might have observed
      that Shakespeare put equally exquisite metaphor into
      the mouth of Shylock.

19. "The expression the core of the story," the Formans
    observe in a footnote to their reprint, "not alto-
    gether a commonplace phrase, is to be found in
    Shelley's paper on Mandeville, which had appeared
    in The Examiner for the 28th of December 1817"
    (III, 298).

20. Hunt is incorrect. Lorenzo is never referred to as a
    Pilgrim. Isabella "would cry/After the Pilgrim in
    his wanderings, /To ask him where her Basil was
    ...." (St. LXII. ll. 4-6.) The Pilgrim is a pas-
    serby of whom Isabella makes inquiry.

21. Comus, l. 51.

22. "The wind bloweth where it listeth." (John iii. 8.)

23. Almost one year before Adonais was written, Hunt
    makes the charge here that the Tory attacks of
    1818 aggravated Keats's illness. In fairness to
    Hunt, however, it should be mentioned that he
    never countenanced Shelley's more extreme indict-
    ment that the Quarterly Review caused Keats's
    death. Of Lord Byron, who believed and repeated
    Shelley's charge, Hunt says "I told him he was
    mistaken in attributing Keats's death to the critics,
    though they had perhaps hastened and embittered
    it...." (Lord Byron and Some of His Contem-
    poraries [London, 1828], p. 266.) For a discus-
    sion of the charge of Shelley and others as it re-
    lates to Keats's reputation, see the introductory
    chapter.

24. A slightly inaccurate quote from Pope's Epistle to
    Augustus, l. 102.

25. Hunt is incorrect. Keats composed many of the poems
    that appeared in his 1820 volume in 1819. When
    Lamia was completed around September 1, 1819,
    Keats was not twenty, but almost twenty-four.
    Like Reynolds, who had exaggerated Keats's youth
    in a letter of July 13, 1820 to Jeffrey, Hunt may
    have deliberately misrepresented in order to im-
    press his reader with Keats's youthful ability.
    Hunt's subsequent comment concerning the privi-
    lege of "great faculties" to transcend time, tends
    to substantiate this conjecture.

26. The play was probably running at the time of the re-
    view. The author is not known. Allardyce Nicoll
    (A History of Early Nineteenth Century Drama
    [Cambridge, 1930], II, 546) refers to Woman's
    Will in his handlist of plays of the period, but he
    concludes it is a misprint for A Woman's Word;
    or, Imaginary Evils. The reviewer's reference to
    Woman's Will, however, contradicts Nicoll's asser-
    tion. Nicoll's December 15, 1820 date of produc-
    tion is much too late: the Guardian's review ap-
    peared on August 6. Woman's Will and A Woman's
    World are not the same play.

27. An aphorism.

28. Not the editor of the New Times, but Lamb, whose re-
    view of the Lamia volume appeared in the July 19,
    1820 issue of that newspaper. (See item 4 of this
    chapter.)

29. Hunt reprinted Lamb's review in the Examiner of July
    30, 1820, pp. 494-495. In addition, Hunt reviewed
    Keats's last volume in the August 2 and August 9,
    1820 issues of the Indicator. (See item 6 of this
    chapter.)

30. A line from Cornelius Webb's poem, reprinted at the
    head of Lockhart's review of Endymion in the
    August 1818 issue of Blackwood's. (See Chapter
    Three, item 4 and n. 34.)

31. Hunt uses the phrase "true poet" in the August 2 in-
    stallment of his review in the Indicator.

32. A paraphrase of Lamb's concluding remarks in the
    New Times.

33. In point of fact, this recreation is very similar to
    the concluding paragraphs of the Monthly's July
    1820 review of the Lamia volume.

34. The extant issues of the Morning Post for 1820 are
    very imperfect. No extracts from Keats's 1820
    volume appear in the issues which now exist.

35. Woodhouse's review of the Lamia volume appeared in

the July 10, 1820 issue of the Sun, a tri-weekly
newspaper.

36. These are all titles of contemporary publications.
"Londoners" is a reference to both Baldwin's and
Gold's Magazines. If they had not done so already,
they were, along with the Indicator (August 2 and 9,
1820), the Honeycomb (August 12, 1820), and the
British Critic (September 1820), to either review
Keats's 1820 volume or reprint poetry from it.
The other serials did not publish any Keats material.

37. Othello, II. i. l. 120.

38. "Whence we see spiders, flies, or ants entombed and
preserved forever in amber, a more than royal
tomb." Francis Bacon's Historia Vitae et Mortis,
Sylva Sylvarum, Cent. I. Exper. 100.

39. "There is a measure in things." Horace's Satires,
Bk. I. Ep. I. l. 106.

40. Ladies Diary (1704-1840) was the title of a London
annual. This was one of half a dozen magazines
with similar titles that had been or were now in
existence by 1820. Other ladies magazines continued to be published after this date.

41. A pun on the subtitle of Isabella.

42. Joseph Justin Scaliger (1540-1609) and Christian
Gottlob Heyne (1729-1812) were renowned scholars
of their time.

43. Obviously, the brand name of a hair dye.

44. Cf. with Wordsworth's "to adopt the very language of
men" in the Preface to Lyrical Ballads and "The
still sad music of humanity" in "Tintern Abbey,"
l. 91. It is ironic that Wordsworth's Lyrical
Ballads, subjected to conservative literary reaction
in its own generation, should now be alluded to in
this reactionary attack on Keats's originality.

45. "See our Number for last August. VOL. VII." (Reviewer's note.)

46. Thomas Stothard (1755-1834), the English illustrator
     and painter.

47. Sackville's Induction to the second part of the 1563
     edition, ll. 281-282.

48. "And sette her doun as stille as any stoon...."
     Troilus and Criseyde, II. l. 600.

49. Publius Syrus (ca. 42 B.C.), at one time a Roman
     slave, was a writer of mimes and maxims. This
     maxim may be translated, "He hurts the good who
     spares the bad." After the quote, the reviewer
     lists the complete title of Keats's 1820 volume.

50. See Croker's review in the Quarterly of April 1818.

51. Quoted from the review of April 1820 in Baldwin's
     London Magazine.

52. St. Stephen, the first Christian martyr, who was ac-
     cused of blasphemy and stoned to death (Acts vi.
     5-vii. 60.)

53. St. Lawrence, the third century Christian martyr, who,
     according to tradition, was burned alive on a grid-
     iron.

54. In the Indicator of August 9, 1820, Hunt had referred
     to Keats's poor health, and this was probably the
     source of the present reviewer's information. (If
     this assumption is correct, Gold's did not publish
     its August number until after the 9th.) Neverthe-
     less, his reference to a rest cure to strengthen
     the poet's nerves suggests something totally dif-
     ferent from Hunt's sympathetic remark. The im-
     plication here is that Keats's poetry, as well as
     his health, may suffer from hypersensitivity.

55. For "at times" read "at once."

56. Unless otherwise noted, phrases and short quotes of
     this type are from the poem under discussion.
     They occur too frequently in this review to make
     line references practical.

57. Despite the reviewer's asterisks, these lines run con-

secutively. The closing quotation mark is omitted.

58. For "her" read "it."

59. An aphorism.

60. Reviewer's query.

61. A slang term, the <u>OED</u> tells us, for a downright lie.

62. The quote should be closed here.

63. Rudolph Erich Raspe (1737-1794) was the author of <u>Baron Munchausen's Narrative of His Marvellous Travels and Campaigns in Russia</u> (1785), a collection of exaggerated adventures and exploits purporting to be the work of a German nobleman who did, in fact, exist. The book was popular in the period, and sequels by other authors followed.

64. William Thomas Fitzgerald (1759?-1829), a second-rate versifier to whom Byron refers in <u>English Bards and Scotch Reviewers</u>: "Still must I hear?-- shall hoarse Fitzgerald bawl/His creaking couplets in a tavern hall...." (ll. 1-2.) From Byron's lines it is clear that the reviewer's praise of Keats is ironic. Coleridge is also ironically grouped on the same level with Fitzgerald and Lewis as a writer of tales of horror.

65. An inaccurate count. The poem is slightly over 500 lines.

66. Horace, <u>Epistles</u>, I. v. l. 19: "The flowing bowl-- whom has it not made eloquent?", trans., H. Rushton Fairclough in the Loeb Classical Library series of Horace's <u>Satires, Epistles, Ars Poetical</u> (London, 1929), <u>p. 283.</u> This dual language text quotes the Latin as "fecundi calices quem non fecere disertum?"

67. The closing quotation mark is omitted.

68. "Wonderful to say."

69. In the context of the previous sentence, an ironic reflection on the "fatigued sense" of Keats's poetry (cf. with note 54.).

70. Located in the borough of Hampstead where Keats and
     Hunt lived.

71. Christ's Hospital, the school attended by Coleridge,
     Lamb, and Hunt. Coleridge never made any public
     profession of admiration for Keats; Hunt, of course,
     did. The reviewer also may have had Lamb in
     mind. Lamb's "Recollections of Christ's Hospital"
     appeared in the Gentleman's Magazine for June 1813.
     (The essay was reprinted in his Works of 1818.)
     Moreover, Lamb had written a review of the Lamia
     volume that appeared in the New Times for July 19,
     1820. Although the review was unsigned, the
     writer of this article in Gold's Magazine may have
     known in some way of Lamb's authorship.

72. From 1811-1815 Keats was apprenticed to Thomas Ham-
     mond, an apothecary.

73. The Paddington Canal, 13-1/2 miles in length, is lo-
     cated in the borough of Paddington in the west end
     of London. (Henry B. Wheatley, London Past and
     Present [London, 1891], III, 1, 3.) Unlike the pre-
     ceding references, however, it has no specific
     association with Keats.

74. The Cockney School.

75. A reference to the Elgin Marbles, housed in the British
     Museum. Haydon had fought eight years until the
     authenticity of these Parthenon scupltures was re-
     cognized.

76. For "her" read "the."

77. Isabella, or The Pot of Basil is taken from a story by
     Boccaccio.

78. Lamia and The Eve of St. Agnes, like many of Boc-
     caccio's stories, deal with the subject of sexual
     love. The British Critic, a guardian of morality,
     finds this subject distasteful.

79. A reference to the mythological basis of Hyperion.
     As a spokesman for the Established Church, the
     British Critic could not countenance a poem that
     dealt seriously with the Greek dieties.

80. This word belongs to the previous line.

81. The indefinite article does not appear in Keats's line.

82. See Chapter Two, item 9 for the _Eclectic's_ review of
     Poems.

83. The offender, according to the reviewer, was Keats;
     not the Tory critics. The suggestion here is that
     the _Eclectic_ was not sufficiently severe in its
     former review. The censure of _Blackwood's,_ the
     Quarterly, and the _British Critic,_ however, could
     have been a stroke of "good fortune, " had it re-
     sulted in a salutary curb on Keats's poetic excesses.

84. John Hamilton Reynolds.

85. The reviewer's interpretation is totally opposed to
     Keats's purpose. _Lamia_ is clearly the most sym-
     pathetic character in the poem. For a discussion
     of the moral of Lamia, see Hunt's comments on
     p. 220 and n. 14.

86. In a review of Barry Cornwall's _Dramatic Scenes, A
     Sicilian Story,_ and _Marcian Colonna,_ appearing in
     the _Eclectic_ for November 1820 (s. 2. XIV, 323-
     333), a brief comparison is drawn between the two
     authors.

87. In his own person.

88. That is, elusive, unattainable.

89. From Keats's Preface to _Endymion._ Keats's reference
     is taken from Milton's letter to Diodati. (See
     Chapter Three, n. 7.)

90. From Keats's Preface to _Endymion._

91. Single quotes have been used indiscriminately at this
     point.

92. Scott is referring to the Tory attack of 1818, and
     specifically to the reviews of _Endymion_ in _Black-
     wood's_ and the _Quarterly._

93. The _Examiner_ was certainly an anti-Tory newspaper,

but it was an independent, liberal publication rather
than a Whig organ like the Edinburgh. The Quarterly
and Blackwood's were, of course, Tory.

94. John Wilson, who participated in the Cockney School
series in Blackwood's, was elected to this post in
1820. He substituted for Dugald Stewart (1753-1828),
a distinguished scholar who still held his appoint-
ment to the Chair of Moral Philosophy but who no
longer gave lectures.

95. Comus, 1. 301.

96. This description is an anticipation of Arnold's standard to which Scott generally held in his own criticism.

97. "Recollections of The South Sea House," one of Lamb's
"Elia" essays, was published in the London Magazine, II (August 1820), 142-146.

98. This reference is not clear. "The Eve of St. Mark"
mentions a Sabbath-bell, but there is no suggestion
of invective, nor is it likely that in 1820 Scott was
familiar with this fragment which, although written
in 1819, was not published until 1848 in Milnes'
Life, Letters, and Literary Remains of Keats.

99. Lamb's prose romance, published in 1798.

100. From the last line of Wordsworth's "My Heart Leaps
Up." Also found at the head of the Immortality
Ode.

101. Rosamund frequently read the Bible to her blind
grandmother, Margaret.

102. The house of John Murray, publisher of the Quarterly,
was at 50 Albemarle Street. The parallel is drawn
between Keats and Don Quixote for the remainder
of the paragraph.

103. Probably an English translation from Don Quixote's
"Adventure of the Windmills." (Part I, Chapter
VIII.)

104. The Merchant of Venice, V. i. 1. 54.

105. Titus Andronicus, II. i. 1. 128.

106. Unidentified.

107. An allusion to Croker's review of Endymion in the
     Quarterly (April 1818). Croker held the office of
     Secretary to the Admiralty.

108. From Woodhouse's headnote to Hyperion. (See n. 7
     above.)

109. Croker's inferior poem, The Battles of Talavera
     (1809), was frequently reprinted in the period.

110. Hamlet, III. iv. 1. 100.

111. A paraphrase of Hamlet, I. v. 11. 27-28.

112. "Ode to a Nightingale," 1. 28.

113. Hamlet, III. ii. 1. 49.

114. An allusion to Isabella's breasts.

Chapter V

GENERAL AND MISCELLANEOUS COMMENTARIES,
1820-1821

(This chapter is a miscellaneous gathering of
references and allusions to Keats for the years
1820-1821. The passage on Keats in the New Bon
Ton Magazine is a new discovery. All other items
have been noted by MacGillivray in Keats: A
Bibliography and Reference Guide, but those in the
Retrospective Review and the New Monthly Magazine are reproduced for the first time. The excerpts from Blackwood's and Gold's London Magazine are more detailed than those that were reprinted by Marsh and White in "Keats and the
Periodicals of His Time," pp. 48-49, and by
MacGillivray, p. 71.
The materials introduced here, with the exception of two references in Blackwood's and one
in the New Bon Ton Magazine, are favorable to
Keats.)

1.   From a review of Wallace's Prospects of
     Mankind, etc. in the Retrospective Review

(The following brief reference to Keats appeared in the Retrospective Review of August 1820
[II, 204]. It was reprinted in the Weekly Entertainer, and West of England Miscellany on August
21, 1820 [n. s. II, 151]. The author is not known.)

Keats, whose Endymion was so cruelly treated by the
critics, has just put forth a volume of poems which must
effectually silence his deriders.   The rich romance of his
Lamia--the holy beauty of his St. Agnes' Eve--the pure and
simple diction and intense feeling of his Isabella--and the
rough sublimity of his Hyperion--cannot be laughed down,
though all the periodical critics in England and Scotland
were to assail them with sneers....

2. From an article on "Modern Periodical Literature"
    in the New Monthly Magazine

> (This excerpt appeared in the New Monthly
> Magazine of September 1820 [XIV, 306]. A head-
> note describes the author as "an esteemed Cor-
> respondent"; but it was not Hazlitt, who only be-
> gan to contribute to the New Monthly in 1822. In
> the article, the author refers to the Quarterly's
> attack on Lady Morgan and to Keats's friendship
> with Hunt [the motive for that review's attack on
> Endymion]. In his defense of Keats in the October
> 6, 1818 issue of the Alfred, John Hamilton Rey-
> nolds had made the same allusions [see Chapter
> III, item 8]. Although this evidence is
> not conclusive in itself, and no direct connection
> has ever been established between Reynolds and
> the New Monthly, the services of Keats's friend
> were frequently sought by serials. He could have
> been the author of this article.)

Its attack [the Quarterly's] on Lady Morgan, whatever were the merits of her work, was one of the coarsest
insults ever offered in print by man to woman.[1] But perhaps its worst piece of injustice was its laborious attempt
to torture and ruin Mr. Keats, a poet then of extreme youth,
whose work was wholly unobjectionable in its tendencies,
and whose sole offence was a friendship for one of the objects of the Reviewer's hatred,[2] and his courage to avow it.
We can form but a faint idea of what the heart of a young
poet is when he first begins to exercise his celestial facul-
ties--how eager and tremulous are his hopes--how strange
and tumultuous are his joys--how arduous is his difficulty
of embodying his rich imaginings in mortal language--how
sensibly alive are all his feelings to the touches of this
rough world! Yet we can guess enough of these to estimate,
in some degree, the enormity of a cool attack on a soul
so delicately strung--with such aspirations and such fears--
in the beginning of its high career. Mr. Keats--who now
happily has attained the vantage-ground whence he may defy
criticism--was cruelly or wantonly held up to ridicule in
the Quarterly Review--to his transitory pain, we fear, but
to the lasting disgrace of his traducer. Shelley has less
ground of complaining--for he who attacks established insti-
tutions with a martyr's spirit, must not be surprised if he
is visited with a martyr's doom. All ridicule of Keats was
unprovoked insult and injury--an attack on Shelley was open

and honest warfare, in which there is nothing to censure
but the mode in which it was conducted....

3. From an article "On the present State of
    Poetical Talent" in the New Bon Ton Magazine

        (The New Bon Ton Magazine was an undistin-
        guished general miscellany of tales, gossip, and
        occasional reviews. The "Address to the Public"
        in its first issue stresses the moral tone of the
        magazine: its avowed object, we are told, is to
        expose vice in high life [I (May 1, 1818), iv].
        The following excerpts from an unsigned article
        "On the present State of Poetical Talent" appeared
        in the September 1820 issue [V, 282-284].)

    With the works of Messrs. Coleridge, Hunt, Keats,
and Co. the world is now tolerably inundated; these worthies
belong to a separate school, and, to give them their due,
they are equally entitled to our notice and animadversion.
What, in the name of common sense, can induce these persons to be so ridiculous and unnatural? Is it the desire of
singularity, the love of insipidity, or the pleasure of being
dissimilar to every body else? It is almost impossible to
read half a dozen pages of their penning, without becoming
sick and disgusted; they are perpetually aiming to be nice,
and, therefore, are always sure of becoming contemptible;
they are always full of little conceits, half-fledged conceptions, and puerile affectations; gardens, flowers, bees,
gentle showers, tiny insects, 3 wreathing of grass, and such
like trumpery, constitute their poetic vocabulary, and to
describe a swallow's nest, a rainbow, or a row of garden-pots,
seems the acmé of their taste and ambition. Hence they flatter
and review the works of each other, hence they are always
bringing each other's stupidity before the public, 4 and hence,
in fact, the world gets tired with their reciprocal emptiness
and dormitory propensities....

                    *   *   *

If we look into the volumes of Messrs. Hunt and Keats, we
shall find the same puerilities, the same affectations, the
same absence of real genius and poetical inspirations [as
in Coleridge].   They foolishly suppose that their descriptions
of rural scenery must be POETRY, and poetry of the first

order too. Hence Mr. Hunt denominates Mr. Keats the first
poet of the day, and hence Mr. Keats bespatters his tutor
with sensible eulogies.   As in their verse they reflect the
folly and deformity of each other, so in their prose effusions their praises are reciprocally reflected: thus it is
that

> Birds of a feather
> Flock together!... 5

4. Three references to Keats in Blackwood's
    Edinburgh Magazine for September 1820

a. From "Mr. Wastle's Diary. No. III."

(The following extract [VII, 665] shows a soften-
ing in Blackwood's attitude toward Keats.   Joseph
W. Reed, Jr. [Selected Prose and Poetry of the
Romantic Period (New York, 1964), p. 258]
assigns Wastle's Diary to Lockhart.)

Aug. 16.   It is a pity that this young man, John
Keats, author of Endymion, and some other poems, should
have belonged to the Cockney school--for he is evidently
possessed of talents that, under better direction, might
have done very considerable things.   As it is, he bids fair
to sink himself entirely beneath such a mass of affectation,
conceit, and Cockney pedantry, as I never expected to see
heaped together by any body, except the Great Founder of
the School. 6   What in the name of wonder tempts all these
fellows to write on Greek fables.   A man might as well
attempt to write a second Anastasius without going into
the east. 7   There is much merit in some of the stanzas of
Mr Keats' last volume, which I have just seen; no doubt he
is a fine, feeling lad--and I hope he will live to despise
Leigh Hunt, and be a poet--

"After the fashion of the elder men of England. "8

If he wants to see the story of the Lamia, which he has
spoiled in one sense, and adorned in another--told with real
truth and beauty, and explained at once with good sense and
imagination, let him look to Weiland's life of Peregrinus
Proteus, vol. first, I think.

b.   From "Horae Scandicae. No. II."

("The Building of the Palace of the Lamp," a
satiric poem on the Cockneys, appeared in Horae
Scandicae [VII, 675-679]. William Maginn and
John Wilson frequently wrote such verses for
Blackwood's, and it is likely that one or both had
a hand in this poem. If it was Maginn, he came
to regret it upon hearing of Keats's death. In a
letter of April 10, 1821 to William Blackwood, he
states "when I heard that the poor devil was in a
consumption, I was something sorry that I annoyed
him at all of late. If I were able I should write a
dirge over him, as a kind of amende honorable;
but my Muse, I am afraid, does not run in the
mournful." [Margaret Oliphant, Annals of a Publishing House: William Blackwood and His Sons
(London, 1897), I, 375.] The attack on Keats that
follows, as John Scott was to point out [see item
6 of this chapter], is obviously inconsistent with
the grudging words of praise for the poet that appeared in this same issue of Blackwood's.)

Here they are, master, here they are plenty,
We can supply them twenty on twenty;
Hither we waft, on our high-soaring pinion,
The very best blocks of the Cockney dominion.

*   *   *

Here's Corny Webb, and this other, an please ye,
Is Johnny Keats;--how it smells of magnesia. 9

*   *   *

We, in the shape of reviewers went rooting,
And here have brought up, from the modern Parnassus,
The principle flowers of its principle asses;
False figures, false tropes, false language, false reason,
True venom, true blasphemy, very true treason,
Mixed with true affectation, true mimini pimini,
In fact, what you find in Endymion and Rimini.

*   *   *

We, from the hands of a cockney apothecary, 10
Brought off this pestle, with which he was capering,

Swearing and swaggering, rhyming and vapouring;
Seized with a fit of poetical fury,
(I thought he was drunk, my good sir, I assure ye)
With this he was scattering, all through the whole house,
Gallipot, glisterbag, cataplasm, bolus;
While the poor 'prentices at him were staring,
Or perhaps in their minds a strait waistcoat preparing,
Loud he exclaimed, "Behold here's my truncheon;
I'm the Marshal of poets--I'll flatten your nuncheon. 11
Pitch physic to hell, you rascals, for damn ye, a--
I'll physic you all with a clyster of Lamia."
Scared at the name, in a moment we darted,
Whipt the pestle away, and from cockney-land parted....

      c.   From a review of Prometheus Unbound

> (According to Newman I. White [The Unextin-
> guished Hearth, p. 378] either or both Wilson and
> Lockhart were the authors of this review. The
> passages relevant to Keats [VII, 686-687] are far
> more sympathetic than the previous verses, but
> Blackwood's new found liberality was only skin-
> deep. In 1821, particularly after Shelley published
> Adonais, the magazine reverted to its more famil-
> iar pattern of attack.)

We cannot conclude without saying a word or two in
regard to an accusation which we have lately seen brought
against ourselves in some one of the London Magazines; we
forget which at the moment. 12 We are pretty sure we know
who the author of that most false accusation is--of which more
hereafter. He has the audacious insolence to say, that we
praise Mr Shelley, although we dislike his principles, just
because we know that he is not in a situation of life to be in
any danger of suffering pecuniary inconvenience from being
run down by critics; and, vice versa, abuse Hunt, Keats,
and Hazlitt, and so forth, because we know that they are
poor men; a fouler imputation could not be thrown on any
writer than this creature has dared to throw on us; nor a
more utterly false one; we repeat the word again--than this
is when thrown upon us.

We have no personal acquaintance with any of these
men, and no personal feelings in regard to any one of them,
good or bad. We never even saw any one of their faces.
As for Mr Keats, we are informed that he is in a
very bad state of health, and that his friends attribute

a great deal of it to the pain he has suffered from the
critical castigation his Endymion drew down on him in this
magazine. If it be so, we are most heartily sorry for it,
and have no hesitation in saying, that had we suspected that
young author, of being so delicately nerved, we should have
administered our reproof in a much more lenient shape and
style. The truth is, we from the beginning saw marks of
feeling and power in Mr Keats' verses, which made us think
it very likely, he might become a real poet of England, [13]
provided he could be persuaded to give up all the tricks of
Cockneyism, and forswear for ever the thin potations of Mr
Leigh Hunt. We, therefore, rated him as roundly as we
decently could do, for these flagrant affectations of those
early productions of his. In the last volume he has published, we find more beauties than in the former, both of
language and of thought, but we are sorry to say, we find
abundance of the same absurd affectations also, and super-
ficial conceits, which first displeased us in his writings;--
and which we are again very sorry to say, must in our
opinion, if persisted in, utterly and entirely prevent Mr
Keats from ever taking his place among the pure and
classical poets of his mother tongue.... Mr Keats we have
often heard spoken of in terms of great kindness, and we
have no doubt his manners and feelings are calculated to
make his friends love him. But what has all this to do with
our opinion of ... [his] poetry.... What is the spell that
must seal our lips, from uttering an opinion ... plain and
perspicuous concerning Mr John Keats, viz. that nature
possibly meant him to be a much better poet than Mr Leigh
Hunt ever could have been, but that, if he persists in imi-
tating the faults of that writer, he must be contented to
share his fate, and be like him forgotten? Last of all,
what should forbid us to announce our opinion, that Mr
Shelley, as a man of genius, is not merely superior, either
to Mr Hunt, or to Mr Keats, but altogether out of their
sphere, and totally incapable of ever being brought into the
most distant comparison with either of them.... [14]

5.   Hunt's farewell to Keats in the Indicator

        (The following paragraph, addressed to Keats
     on his departure for Italy, appeared in the Indi-
     cator of September 20, 1820, pp. 399-400. It
     was reprinted and attributed to Hunt by Edmund
     Blunden in Leigh Hunt's "Examiner" Examined,
     1808-1825 New York, 1928, p. 158.)

Ah, dear friend, as valued a one as thou art a poet, --John Keats, --we cannot, after all, find it in our hearts to be glad, now thou art gone away with the swallows to seek a kindlier clime. The rains began to fall heavily, the moment thou wast to go;--we do not say, poet-like, for thy departure. One tear in an honest eye is more precious to thy sight, than all the metaphorical weepings in the universe; and thou didst leave many starting to think how many months it would be till they saw thee again. And yet thou didst love metaphorical tears too, in their way; and couldst always liken every thing in nature to something great or small; and the rains that beat against thy cabin-window will set, we fear, thy over-working wits upon many comparisons that ought to be much more painful to others than thyself; --Heaven mend their envious and ignorant numskulls. But thou hast "a mighty soul in a little body;"[15] and the kind cares of the former for all about thee shall no longer subject the latter to the chance of impressions which it scorns; and the soft skies of Italy shall breathe balm upon it; and thou shalt return with thy friend the nightingale, and make all thy other friends as happy with thy voice as they are sorrowful to miss it. The little cage thou didst sometimes share with us, looks as deficient without thee, as thy present one may do without us; but--farewell for awhile: thy heart is in our fields: and thou will soon be back to rejoin it.

6. A reply to Blackwood's in Baldwin's London Magazine

(It is well-known that John Scott's attacks on Blackwood's eventually resulted in his death in a duel with John Christie. In his article on "Blackwood's Magazine" [Baldwin's II (November 1820), 520], Scott referred to that Tory magazine's defense of itself in its September 1820 review of Prometheus Unbound: "We shall very soon allude to the treatment which Hunt, Haydon, Keats, &c. &c. &c. have experienced from Blackwood's Magazine ... we shall ... expose the excessive falsehood of what we see is now attempted to be maintained by Sir Walter Scott's Friends[16]--viz. that their attacks on these persons just named, have been restrained within the limits of fair criticism --that they have not manifested any 'personal feelings towards them, good or bad'--that they have

only 'expressed simple, undisguised, and impartial
opinions concerning the merits and demerits of
men they never saw; nor thought of for one moment, otherwise than as in their capacity of authors.'" John Scott continued his attack in "The Mohock Magazine." [Baldwin's, II (December 1820),
666-85.] The following excerpt from this article
[681-3] is a reply to Blackwood's September 1820
references to Keats.)
In the Number of Blackwood containing the Horāē Scandicāē,
we find the following very candid and amiable declaration:

> [Quotes from Blackwood's review of Prometheus
> Unbound, beginning with "We have no personal ac-
> quaintance" through a reference to Keats's
> "flagrant affectations." (See pp. 301-302)]

They have no "personal feelings," then, it seems, in
regard to Mr. Keats: they are sorry to have unnecessarily
hurt his feelings: but they have only "rated him as roundly
as they decently could do for his flagrant affectations:"--
and they afterwards ask, very reasonably, no doubt, "what
is there should prevent us from expressing a simple, undisguised, impartial opinion on the merits and demerits of men we
never saw, or thought of for one moment, otherwise than
as in their capacities of authors?"[17] --What, indeed?
Horāē Scandicāē is in the same Number with this moderate,
fair, gentlemanly appeal;--let us turn to it, and observe
how decently, as well as roundly, they rate Mr. Keats for
his affectations; how carefully they avoid trespassing on any
thing belonging to the man, but his capacity of author; how
obvious they make it, that they are actuated by no personal
feelings towards him: in short, how strictly legitimate is
their criticism on his writings, --"how pure a thing, --how
free from mortal taint," as Mr. Keats says of his Beauty
of St. Agnes. [St. XXV. 1. 9.]

> Here's Corny Webb, and this other, an please ye,
> Is Johnny Keats--how it smells of magnesia!
>   Horāē Scandicāē

A fine specimen this of their round and decent manner! Magnesia has much to do with "Hyperion," and the
"Ode to the Nightingale!"

> [Quotes from Horāē Scandicāē, beginning "We
> from the hands of a cockney apothecary," through

"I'll physic you all with a clyster of Lamia!"
(See pp. 300-301)]

This is their mode of expressing their "undisguised
and impartial opinion," " &c. &c. of Mr. Keats in his capacity
of author! This is to prove that "they are most heartily
sorry" for having hurt his feelings, and they sympathise, as
they conscientiously declare, with his friends who deplore his
bad health!...

*   *   *

The brutal blasphemy included in the above passage,
be it particularly observed, has no application whatever to
the private manners or published compositions of Mr. Keats:
Lamia is a gentle and graceful tale of a classical metamorphosis:--the disposition of Mr. Keats' mind, as evinced
in his works, is susceptible and romantic: the prevailing
strain of his poetry is characterised in the following exquisite verse of his "Isabella,"--which we would challenge
attention to, --as one of the very finest passages that can
be quoted from poetical literature.

> Moan hither, all ye syllables of woe,
>   From the deep throat of sad Melpomene!
> Through bronzed lyre in tragic order go,
>   And touch the strings into a mystery;
> Sound mournfully upon the winds and low;
>   For simple Isabel is soon to be
> Among the dead:--She whithers like a palm
>   Cut by an Indian for its juicy balm.
>   [St. LVI.]

Is the reader inclined, immediately after this, to go
back to Horaê Scandicaê--(misprint for Horaê Scandalaê)?
He will therefore find the following lines to match against
the above.

> Pitch physic to hell, you rascals, for damn ye, a--
> I'll physic you all with a clyster of Lamia!

Of Mr. Keats, as a private character, the Mohocks[18]
themselves are obliged to say--"we have often heard him
spoken of in terms of great kindness; and we have no doubt,
his manners and feelings are calculated to make his friends
love him." This is a reputation which a man would rather
have, than that of the Editor of the Mohock Magazine. Can

any traveller from Edinburgh to London report of him, "we have often heard him spoken of in terms of great kindness?" But, setting that aside, where then is the apology for the boisterous blasphemy of the above? It conveys no satire, either against the man or his writings: it has no application whatever to him: it is therefore sheerly wicked and disgusting: a spontaneous emanation from a naturally coarse and profligate mind....

7. From an "ESSAY ON POETRY" in Gold's London Magazine

> (The following reference to Keats appeared in Gold's for December 1820 [II, 559-561]. The author, who signs himself "D. N. ," is not known, but his remarks are generally more sympathetic than those in Gold's review of August 1820.)

There is a young man of the name of John Keats, whom it has lately become the fashion to abuse, because he has been bepraised by Leigh Hunt and abused by the Quarterly Review. He is a poet of excessive imagination; perhaps as much so as any writer of the present day; but abounds in errors both of taste and sentiment. His fragment of Hyperion, wild and unconnected as it is, is a giant in ruins, -- grand, vast, and sublime, and a fine specimen of original thinking, that is at no great lapse of time destined to achieve wonders in the poetical world. The prevailing foibles of Mr. Keats' system are, first, a strained inversion of sentiment; and, secondly, an intense, earnest affectation, that is intimately linked with the poetry, and cannot without injury be eradicated. But he has a happy facility of expressing apt images by individual expression, and of hitching the faculty of imagination on a single word; such as that exquisitely imaginative line--

> "She stood in tears amid the alien corn. "
> ["Ode to a Nightingale, " l. 67.]

For those who have hitherto treated the writings of Keats with scorn, and discovered nothing in his poetry but endless affectation and inverted sentiment, we shall extract the following lines; not because we consider them as the happiest effusions of the Author's muse, but because they abound less in the peculiarities of his style than almost any other of his

writings, and come forcibly home to the imaginations of the
thoughtful and the romantic:--

[Quotes "Robin Hood"]

8. Two references to Keats by Hazlitt

a. From "On Living To One's-Self" in Table Talk

(Hazlitt's first volume of Table Talk was published in January 1821. The following excerpt from
that volume [pp. 228-230] clearly links Hazlitt's
defense of Keats to the attack of the Quarterly on
his own Characters of Shakespear's Plays. The
extension to his old enemy, Blackwood's, was not
difficult for Hazlitt.)

The public is pusillanimous and cowardly, because it is weak.
It knows itself to be a great dunce, and that it has no
opinions but upon suggestion.... It is generally divided into
two strong parties, each of which will allow neither common sense nor common honesty to the other side. It reads
the Edinburgh and Quarterly Reviews, and believes them
both--or if there is a doubt, malice turns the scale. Taylor and Hessey told me that they had sold nearly two editions of the Characters of Shakespear's Plays in about three
months, but that after the Quarterly Review of them came
out, 19 they never sold another copy. The public, enlightened as they are, must have known the meaning of
that attack as well as those who made it. It was not ignorance then but cowardice that led them to give up their
own opinion. A crew of mischievous critics at Edinburgh
having affixed the epithet of the Cockney School to one or
two writers born in the metropolis, all the people in London became afraid of looking into their works, lest they
too should be convicted of cockneyism. Oh brave public!--
This epithet proved too much for one of the writers in
question, and stuck like a barbed arrow in his heart. Poor
Keats! What was sport to the town, was death to him.
Young, sensitive, delicate, he was like

"A bud bit by an envious worm,
Ere he could spread his sweet leaves to the air,
Or dedicate his beauty to the sun"--20

and unable to endure the miscreant cry and idiot laugh, withdrew to sigh his last breath in foreign climes.... [21]

b. From "Table Talk. No. VII., On Reading Old Books"
    in Baldwin's London Magazine

        (The brief reference to Keats that follows ap-
    peared in Baldwin's for February 1821 [III, 132].
    It was acknowledged by Hazlitt when it was in-
    cluded in the Galignani Edition of Table Talk [Paris,
    1825].)

        Books have in a great measure lost their power over
me; nor can I revive the same interest in them as formerly.
I perceive when a thing is good, rather than feel it. It is
true,

        Marcian Colonna is a dainty book;[22]

and the reading of Mr. Keats's Eve of St. Agnes lately
made me regret that I was not young again. The beautiful
and tender images there conjured up "come like shadows--
so depart."[23] "The tiger-moth's wings,"[24] which he has
spread over his rich poetic blazonry, just flit across my
fancy; the gorgeous twilight window which he has painted
over again in his verse, to me "blushes" almost in vain
"with blood of queens and kings."[25] I know how I should
have felt at one time in reading such authors; and that is
all....

                         Notes

1. See Chapter III, n. 92.

2. The reference is to Keats's friendship with Hunt.

3. An allusion to the sonnets by Keats and Hunt "On the
    Grasshopper and Cricket" published in the Examiner
    of September 21, 1817, p. 599.

4. Coleridge does not belong in this comparison. He
    never published any evaluations of either Hunt or
    Keats. Hunt probably reviewed Christabel, Kubla
    Kahn, a vision; The Pains of Sleep in the Examiner
    of June 2, 1816, pp. 348-349, and he also briefly

referred to Coleridge in his Preface to Foliage
(1818), but in both instances his praise was not
without serious qualifications. (His opinion of
Coleridge after 1820 is not relevant.) Keats published nothing pertaining to Coleridge, although his
debt to Christabel is obvious in Lamia and may
well be one of the reasons why these two poets are
linked together. Hunt and Keats, of course, exchanged many compliments in their publications.

5. Don Quixote, trans. Peter Motteux (Modern Library
   Edition), p. 474. Motteux's translation is indebted
   to Burton's "Birds of a feather will gather together." (Anatomy of Melancholy, Part III, Sect.
   1, Memb. 1, Subsect. 2.)

6. According to Blackwood's, Hunt was the founder of
   the Cockney School.

7. "Thomas Hope (c. 1770-1831), a wealthy art collector
   and connoisseur who had traveled extensively in the
   Near East, was the author of Anastasius, or Mem-
   oirs of a Greek (1819)." (Samuel Chew, "The
   Nineteenth Century and After" in Baugh's Literary
   History of England [New York, 1948], p. 1272.)

8. Unidentified.

9. As an apothecary, Keats would have sold magnesia as
   a laxative.

10. "I would not insult my readers by insinuating, that
    this means Johnny Keats, who, like Apollo, prac-
    tises poetry and pharmacy. The blasphemous
    language of the Cockney school is, with reluctance,
    imitated here." (Author's note.)

11. "Only Marshal. Hunt being king." (Author's note.)

12. In Baldwin's London Magazine for June 1820 (I, 646-
    654), an article "On The Qualifications Necessary
    To Success in Life" appeared in "Table Talk. No.
    I." The article was signed "T." and was acknowl-
    edged by Hazlitt when he reprinted it in The Plain
    Speaker (London, 1826). Speaking of why Black-
    wood's praises Percy Shelley, and villifies 'Johnny
    Keates:', Hazlitt observes, "they know very well

they cannot ruin the one in fortune as well as fame,
but they may ruin the other in both, deprive him of
a livelihood together with his good name, send him
to Coventry [i. e., to isolation], and into the Rules of
a prison; and this is a double incitement to the exercise of their laudable and legitimate vocation" (p.
654).

13. One might simply observe editorially here that Blackwood's August 1819 attack on Endymion does not
show a shred of such awareness.

14. Blackwood's opinion of Shelley was to change radically
when it reviewed Adonais in December 1821.

15. A recollection of "little body with a mighty heart" in
King Henry V, Part II, Prologue, l. 17.

16. Scott's son-in-law, John Gibson Lockhart, was on the
editorial staff of Blackwood's. Scott was also acquainted with John Wilson and others in the Blackwood's group, but he was not on close terms with
them.

17. Slightly misquoted from Blackwood's review of Prometheus Unbound.

18. "The Mohocks, of whom we read in the Spectator,"
Scott tells us in an earlier part of his article, "...
ludicrously insulted the women in the streets,
crippled children, and maimed the defenceless generally:--their 'irregularities,' were as popular as
those of Blackwood's Magazine, and were excused
in much the same way, till at length it was hinted
to the public that these merry fellows were malignant scoundrels, without either honour or courage;
that their jokes were the outrages of ruffians, and
their attempt to laugh it off an insult to decency.
The public quickly took the hint, and the Mohocks
soon fell into disrepute" (p. 667). Their modern
day successor, Scott goes on to explain, is Blackwood's Edinburgh Magazine.

19. XVIII (January 1818), 458-466.

20. Romeo and Juliet, I. i. ll. 156-158.

21. These last lines were written before word of Keats's
     death reached England.

22. Lamb's sonnet "To the Author of Poems Published
     under the name of Barry Cornwall," 1. 5.   In turn,
     Lamb's line is an allusion to Shakespeare's "He
     hath not fed of the dainties that are bred in a
     book...." (<u>Love's Labour's Lost</u>, IV. ii. 1. 25.)

23. <u>Macbeth</u>, IV. i. 1. 111.

24. <u>The Eve of St. Agnes</u>, st. XXIV, 1. 6.

25. <u>Ibid.</u>, 1. 9.

Chapter VI

KEATS'S DEATH, AFTERMATH, AND THE RECEPTION OF <u>ADONAIS</u> THROUGH 1821

(Keats died in Rome on February 23, 1821, but the news did not reach London until almost one month later. In March the <u>Gentleman's Magazine</u> and the <u>Monthly Repository</u> carried obituaries of one or two lines. From March 22-30 obituaries of the same type began to appear in a wide variety of London and Provincial newspapers. To be sure, Keats's friends informed and inserted notices in the larger London newspapers such as the <u>Times,</u> but obituaries also appeared in the <u>British Freeholder and Saturday Evening Journal, Military Register and Weekly Gazette, Caledonian Mercury, Liverpool Mercury,</u> and more than a score of similar journals. The response was widespread: tributes, obituaries, and notices of longer substance totalled over fifty for the year.

Of the poems and articles relating to Keats's death that are included in this chapter, exclusive of Reynolds, Clare, Shelley, and the reviews of <u>Adonais,</u> the sonnet in the <u>Kaleidoscope; or, Literary and Scientific Mirror</u> was first reprinted in "Keats's Reception in Newspapers of His Day." All other material has been noted before, but the items in the <u>Literary Chronicle and Weekly Review, Pocket Magazine of Classic and Polite Literature, Gossip</u> [April 14, 1821], and <u>New Monthly Magazine</u> are reproduced for the first time. The poems in Baldwin's <u>London Magazine</u> and the <u>Gossip</u> [May 19, 1821] have appeared only in William Hines's unpublished dissertation, "The Reception of John Keats by English Critics: 1816-1821" [Fordham, 1951], pp. 170-171.

Almost all the tributes to Keats included here recognize the worth of the <u>Lamia</u> volume, but many of them also return to the Tory attack of 1818 on <u>Endymion.</u> The theme of neglected genius,

popularized by the early deaths of Chatterton,
White and, now, Keats created a popular sentiment in which the idea of martyrdom took root,
even before Shelley published _Adonais_ in July 1821.
   Shelley's charges in _Adonais_ still further dis-
torted the situation. Despite the greatness of the
poem and the essential sincerity of the tribute
[regardless of Shelley's personal motives], the
poem and the Preface polarized critical opinion
once more. Some of Keats's friends accepted
Shelley's far-fetched charge that the reviewer of
Endymion in the _Quarterly_ was guilty of murder;
other friends rejected this accusation. Nevertheless, they all agreed that Keats was neglected
throughout his lifetime, notwithstanding evidence
to the contrary in the reviews of 1820. After a
favorable review of _Adonais_ in the _Literary Chron-
icle_, two attacks followed. The _Literary Gazette_
and _Blackwood's_ rejected Shelley's claims for
Keats and dismissed the charge against the _Quar-
terly_ as absurd. _Adonais_ was favorably reviewed
in 1822 by Hunt in the _Examiner_ and in 1825 by
the _European Magazine_, but both reviews are beyond the scope of this collection. At the close of
1821, Keats's name was known to many, and he
was recognized by some of the best critical minds
of his day as a poet of exceptional merit. He
had survived his earlier association with Hunt;
but, unwittingly, Shelley had mired the dead poet
in the center of critical controversy.)

1.   Verses to Keats by "P." in the _Literary_
     Chronicle and Weekly Review

     (This poem appeared in the _Literary Chronicle_ of
     March 31, 1821, p. 206. The author's identity
     is not known.)

VERSES
TO THE MEMORY OF
JOHN KEATS, THE POET

Who died at Rome, 23 Feb. 1821. ÆEtat. 25.

'O drop the briny tear with me!'--Chatterton.

If many kings and senators had died,
My heart could not have given mine eyes a tide
So strong and deep as that which drowns my breath,
Departed spirit of Keats! to bathe thy death!
Like an etheral minstrel, born for love--
To give a foretaste of the joys above,
O! thou wert wond'rous in thy gentle youth,
Giving delicious songs in lovely truth!
Nature thy guide--Simplicity thy aim,
Thou sang'st thy passage to the heaven of fame.
Like White, thy hallow'd ecstacies were zoned,
Celestial for the beauty which they toned;
Terrestrial ears were charm'd to hear thee sing,
And drank thy music from thy wells and spring.
Erewhile the fleeting pageantries of earth
Inspire Laureates to give Vision[1] birth,
Thou, on the blossoms of thine own sweet leaves,
'Borne with the very sigh that silence heaves,'[2]
Hast soon ascended to receive thy crown
Of fadeless bays eternal and renown.
Not like the mermaid that enchants the sea,
Then leaves the tar in hopeless destiny;
Not like the lark that goes to heavenly skies
And comes to earth again and songless dies;
Nor like the bird of night in thorns, that sings
To silent moonlight, from'd by Shadow's wings;
Not yet the cuckoo heralding the air
To love's companionship the lives that bear:--
--Thou in the worm's own mansion for mankind,
Thou risen to rest, thy works are left behind, --
These transcripts of thy fancy and thy heart,
With life will live, immortal as thou art!
The flatt'ring and the vain will drop unwept,
And millions sleep with those who've centuries slept;
Ages will roll and empires sink to dust--
Ruins be traceless, though by victory nurst, --
But thy descriptive and pathetic page
Shall yield delight to each succeeding age,
Like thy lov'd Chaucer and thy Spenser, be
Time's choice memorial to eternity!

Islington Green,[3] March 26, 1821   P.

2.   "Death of Mr. John Keats" by "L." (B.W. Procter?)
     in Baldwin's London Magazine

          (This death notice appeared under "Town Con-

versation. No. IV." in Baldwin's for April 1821
[III, 426-427]. It has been reprinted by Bertram
Dobell in Sidelights on Charles Lamb [London,
1903], pp. 192-196. It is clear from the author's
knowledge of Keats's last weeks in Rome with
Severn, that he either knew or was one of the
poet's circle of friends. Dobell dismisses Lamb
as a possibility and suggests that the author was
B. W. Procter [Barry Cornwall], who was a friend
of Hunt. Procter, Dobell tells us, used the signature "L." on more than one occasion.)

We commence our article this month with but a melancholy subject--the death of Mr. John Keats.--It is, perhaps, an unfit topic to be discussed under this head, but we
knew not where else to place it, and we could not reconcile
ourselves to the idea of letting a poet's death pass by in
the common obituary. He died on the 23rd of February,
1821, at Rome, whither he had gone for the benefit of his
health. His complaint was a consumption, under which he
had languished for some time, but his death was acceler-
ated by a cold caught in his voyage to Italy.

Mr. Keats was, in the truest sense of the word, A
Poet.--There is but a small portion of the public acquainted
with the writings of this young man; yet they were full of
high imagination and delicate fancy, and his images were
beautiful and more entirely his own, perhaps, than those of
any living writer whatever. He had a fine ear, a tender
heart, and at times great force and originality of expression;
and notwithstanding all this, he has been suffered to rise and
pass away almost without a notice:[4] the laurel has been
awarded (for the present) to other brows: the bolder aspirants have been allowed to take their station on the slippery steps of the temple of fame, while he has been nearly
hidden among the crowd during his life, and has at last died,
solitary and in sorrow, in a foreign land.

It is, at all times difficult, if not impossible, to
argue others into a love of poets and poetry: it is altogether a matter of feeling, and we must leave to time
(while it hallows his memory) to do justice to the reputation
of Keats. There were many, however, even among the
critics living, who held his powers in high estimation; and
it was well observed by the Editor of the Edinburgh Review,
that there was no Author whatever, whose writings would
form so good a test by which to try the love which any one

professed to bear towards poetry.

When Keats left England, he had a presentiment that
he should not return: that this has been too sadly realized
the reader already knows. --After his arrival in Italy, he
revived for a brief period, but soon afterwards declined,
and sunk gradually into his grave. He was one of three
English poets who had been compelled by circumstances to
adopt a foreign country as their own. 5 He was the youngest,
but the first to leave us. His sad and beautiful wish is at
last accomplished: It was that he might drink "of the warm
south, " and "leave the world unseen, " ["Ode to a Nightingale, "
ll. 15, 19]--and--(he is addressing the nightingale)--

[Quotes ll. 20-30.]

A few weeks before he died, a gentleman who was
sitting by his bed-side, 6 spoke of an inscription to his
memory, but he declined this altogether, --desiring that
there should be no mention of his name or country; "or if
any, " said he "let it be Here lies the body of7 one whose
name was writ in water!"--There is something in this to
us most painfully affecting; indeed the whole story of his
later days is well calculated to make a deep impression. --
It is to be hoped that his biography will be given to the
world, and also whatever he may have left (whether in
poetry or prose) behind him. The public is fond of patron-
izing poets: they are considered in the light of an almost
helpless race: they are bright as stars, but like meteors

"Short-lived and self-consuming. "8

We do not claim the patronage of the public for Mr.
Keats, but we hope that it will now cast aside every little
and unworthy prejudice, and do justice to the high memory
of a young but undoubted poet. L.

3.   J. W. Dalby's "Remarks on Keats" in the
     Pocket Magazine of Classic and Polite Literature

(This article is dated April 4, 1821 and probably appeared in the April issue of the Pocket
Magazine [VII, 333-338], a monthly miscellany
of occasional reviews, light essays, stories, and
poems. The author, J. W. Dalby, is identified

by John Foster Kirk [Supplement to S. Austin Alli-
bone's Critical Dictionary of English Literature
(Philadelphia, 1892), I, p. 440 b] as John Watson
Dalby, a poet and author of Poems (1822) and
Tales, Songs, and Sonnets (1866). During the
early 1820's, Dalby was a frequent contributor of
both verse and prose to the Pocket Magazine.)

REMARKS ON THE
CHARACTER AND WRITINGS OF THE LATE
JOHN KEATS, THE POET

——

"Thou indeed
Art not the first, and wilt not be the last
Whom an ungrateful native land has scorned.
But thy lays will survive thee; and thy name
Will live immortal,--Albion's maidens too
Will cherish thy sweet songs!--

"Hast thou been wafted to Elysian bowers,
    In some blest star where thou has pre-existed,
Inhaled the ecstatic fragrancy of flowers,
    Around the golden harps of seraphs twisted."9

——

POOR Keats left England10 in September, 1820, and
died at Rome on the 23d February, 1821, at the premature
age of twenty-five. Many of Mr. S. Skinner's very just
and eloquent observations on Henry Kirk White are extremely
applicable to the interesting subject of the present article.
It cannot be denied that there exists in all the productions
of the young poet we have just lost a beautiful spirit of
melancholy gentleness, which may be easily traced to the
disposition and temperament of the suffering author. The
nature of the first poem he published, his "Endymion, " did
not admit of an universal exhibition of this sort of feeling,
but even in that wildly beautiful and "singularly original"11
romance a constitutional pensiveness on the part of its
writer was visible. This work has been well described as
"flushed all over with the rich lights of fancy, and so
coloured and bestrewn with the flowers of poetry, that even
while perplexed and bewildered in their labyrinths, it is
impossible to resist the intoxication of their sweetness, or

to shut our eyes to the enchantments they so lavishly present. "12 Like White, regardless of personal and pecuniary
considerations, Keats early relinquished an eminently lucra-
tive, but rather unpoetical profession, 13 in order that he
might devote his time entirely to the luxurious passion that
engrossed his soul. Like White, he was exposed to the
attacks of grovelling and merciless critics, to whom his
honesty and sincerity had given offence. It has been said
that White's early death was attributable to the wounds his
spirit received from the envenomed shafts of those self-
constituted literary censors, who neglect the duties of an
office, which might be rendered at once honourable and useful, if they would only act towards authors with candour
and liberality, and with honesty and justice towards the
public; but who, failing to act in this manner, pander for
profit to the base appetites of a portion of the public, and
degrade themselves to a level with the merest personal
libellers. The truth of the above statement has been
doubted; and it may be that White's conscious superiority
enabled him to sustain such attacks without injury; but this
was not the case with his partner in talent and in misfortune: the mind of Keats (a fact which may be gathered
from his writings) was peculiarly susceptible of the impressions which are generally made on poets by censure and
neglect. He wanted a portion of that innate confidence which
enables a contemporary bard to continue writings and printing
on, awaiting with philosophic composure the time when his
talents shall be justly appreciated, and his labours honour-
ably rewarded;14 he ought also to have been a sharer in
that proud spirit, influenced by which another and more
popular writer is taught to smile at the puny efforts of his
revilers, or at once to silence and expose them with his
satire. 15 The heart of Keats was peculiarly formed for
the endearments of love and the gentle solaces of friendship. He was not bold or brave enough to encounter the
struggles of life, and he shrunk instinctively from the conflict. The purity and refinement of his manners, and the
general tenderness of his heart, fitted him rather to be an
inhabitant of his own beautiful regions of romance, a denizen
of the bright realms created by his own fine and original
imagination, than a wanderer in this lower world--a par-
taker in a scene of stir and bustle, quite uncongenial to his
delicate taste and retired inclinations. 16 His uncontroulable
and unlimited sympathy with all kinds of suffering, injured
at once his state of health, which was never good, and his
purse, which was never heavy. His last works, Lamia, the
Eve of St. Agnes, &c. went a great way towards enabling

the public to form a just opinion of his genius; they succeeded
in a great degree in exhibiting to the world the beauty and
the value of a treasure which it seemed to be unconscious of possessing. Some of his most unreasonable and implacable
enemies have been obliged reluctantly to confess the purity
of his private life; and now some of the most liberal among
them began to do tardy justice to his eminent abilities.
The Edinburgh Review, which had heretofore neglected him,
now stepped forward, and made ample amends for its offence,
by an eloquent and manly critique upon his works in general.
Among other complimentary remarks, the Reviewer, speaking of the imitation of our older authors having brought in,
as it were, "a second spring in our poetry, " says that "few
of its blossoms are either more profuse of sweetness, or
richer in promise, than that which is now before us."[17]
He then goes on to say, "there is no author whatever whose
writings will form so good a test by which to try the love
which any one professes to bear towards poetry."[18] Other
critics spoke of these poems, (which, through their publication had been thus long delayed, were all written when the
author was but twenty,)[19] in scarcely less flattering terms,
and one in particular, characterized them as follows:--
"The author's versification is now perfected, the exuberances of his imagination restrained, and a calm power, the
surest and loftiest of all power, takes place of the impatient
workings of the younger god within him. The character of
his genius is that of energy and voluptuousness, each able
at will to take leave of the other, and possessing, in their
union, a high feeling of humanity, not common to the best
authors who can less command them."[20] These concurring
testimonies appeared to promise much in favour of the
young aspirant's future fame and fortune; but alas! he has
not been allowed to remain among us to realize the bright
hopes in which they perhaps induced him to indulge. I
shall conclude these desultory remarks, so unworthy of the
illustrious spirit who is the subject of them, with a re-
statement of some particulars of the latter days of Mr.
Keats, communicated to the public by an intimate friend of
the departed poet.[21]

[Quotes the last three paragraphs of L.'s article
in Baldwin's London Magazine.]

April 4, 1821   J.W. Dalby

4. A reference to Keats in a "Posthumous Epistle
    From The Author of Tristram Shandy" in the Gossip

> (The following excerpt from a letter purporting to
> be by Sterne appeared in the Gossip of April 14,
> 1821, p. 54. It links Keats with Chatterton and
> White as an example of neglected genius.)

It was a glorious night.... Presently we perceived
three handsome youths coming to meet us, on nearer observation we recognised two of them, Chatterton and Kirke
White; but the third was a stranger, yet not an unwelcome
one; for there was an intellectual glory about his countenance,
which clearly indicated the possessor of lofty endowments.
Kirke White introduced him to our party; it was John Keats,
the author of Endymion. Your Reading Public, or rather
the savages they employ to weild [sic] the scalping knife and
tomahawk, in the character of reviewers, have treated this
young man with a wantonness of barbarity, which I trust,
will ultimately be its own punishment. These assassins of
reputation, have committed high treason against the suprem-
acy of genius, "may their pernicious souls rot half a grain
a day," may the ten plagues of Egypt pursue them; may
they--but I leave Dr. Slop to complete the anathema.... 22

5. A sonnet on Keats's death in the Kaleidoscope;
    or, Literary and Scientific Mirror

> (This unsigned poem appeared in the Kaleido-
> scope [n. s. I (May 1, 1821), 348], a Liverpool
> weekly. Almost a year before, on August 29,
> 1820 n. s. I, 69, Keats's "To Autumn" had been
> reprinted from the Lamia volume.)

SONNET,

ON THE DEATH OF JOHN KEATS, THE POET,
Who died at Rome, aged twenty-five years.

Thus fleet, so soon, young spirits, whose gentle love
    And rich affections, breathed in sad wild tone,
    And exquisite thoughts and fancies of days gone,

Revive old Greece and Italy; where grove,
Vine hill, and shady dells, and bowers bright-wove
  Of rose and myrtle flowers, poured songs that won
  The ear of Pan; and, from their sports, upon
Green wood or fountain side, could Dian move
With her chaste huntress train, nearer to list.
Such thy loud harpings of heroic deeds,
Of younger Rome, or Greece, whose pride of heart
Dreamed that the Gods their mother's lips had kist[23]
  Such bright unearthly fancies theirs!--Yet speeds,
Like them, thy life away; but fame doth not so part.

6. A sonnet on Keats's death in
    Baldwin's _London Magazine_

        (This poem, which Edmund Blunden suggests
        may have been written by John Taylor [Keats's
        Publisher: A Memoir of John Taylor (London,
        1936), p. 125], appeared in Baldwin's for May
        1821 [III, 526].)

                    SONNET,
        ON THE DEATH OF THE POET J. KEATS

                Sic pereunt Violae[24]

And art thou dead? Thou very sweetest bird
  That ever made a moonlight forest ring,
  Its wild unearthly music mellowing:
Shall thy rich notes no more, no more be heard?
Never! Thy beautiful romantic themes,
  That made it mental Heav'n to hear thee sing,
Lapping th' enchanted soul in golden dreams,
  Are mute! Ah vainly did Italia fling
  Her healing ray around thee--blossoming
With flushing flow'rs long wedded to thy verse:
Those flow'rs, those sunbeams, but adorn thy hearse;
  And the warm gales that faintly rise and fall
  In music's clime--themselves so musical--
Shall chaunt the Minstrel's dirge far from his father's hall.

1821.

7. Keats's death is reported in the
    New Monthly Magazine

> (This article on Keats's death appeared in the
> New Monthly for May 1821 [XV, 256-257]. Al-
> though no positive attribution of authorship can
> be made, the writer's knowledge of the cold Keats
> caught on his journey to Italy indicates that he had
> access to private information. Thomas Campbell,
> who became editor of the New Monthly in 1821,
> was well-known in literary circles and may have
> had access to such information. In any case, the
> article drew enough attention to be reprinted in
> the New Annual Register for 1821 [XLI, 267-268].)

MR. JOHN KEATS

Died at Rome, on the 23d of February last, Mr.
John Keats, well known for his poetical productions. He
left England for the benefit of his health, having exhibited
marks of a consumptive disorder, which appeared to be
rapidly increasing. A cold, caught on his journey to Italy,
hurried him still faster to the tomb: and though for a short
time after his arrival there he seemed to revive, it was
only to confirm the fallacy of hope too often indulged in
similar disorders; for he soon languished into an untimely
grave. He often talked of his approaching death, with the
resignation of one who contemplated its certainty without
anxiety, and seemed to wish to "steal from the world"[25]
into silence and repose. From a contemporary writer[26]
we learn that when a friend was sitting by his bed, and
talking of an inscription to his memory, he desired there
might be no notice taken of him, "or if any," to be "Here
lies the body of one whose name was writ in water." The
temperament and feeling of the poet which is always "much
nearer allied to melancholy than to jollity or mirth,"[27]
seem to have been the heritage of Keats: the deep susceptibility to external beauty, the intense vividness of
mental impressions, and the rich colouring of thought, which
are seen in genius, were all his. Though young, and his
taste leaning toward an extravagance which maturer years
would have no doubt corrected, his poetry displays throughout those breathing thoughts which so peculiarly identify
the presence of the poetical spirit. He was an original
writer, his productions were his own; and no pen of the
present age can lay claim to the epithet of poetical, on the
ground of a powerful fancy, freshness of colouring, and

force of expression, if Keats be not allowed a claim far
from humble, on those distinguishing characteristics of
the sons of song. A name richer in promise England did
not possess, and the mind insensible to the sweetness of
his productions must indeed be a miserable one--the very
climax of heartlessness. The subject of Endymion, his
principal poem, is perhaps less attractive than one more
natural and more agreeable to the general taste: mythological fictions do not now interest mankind; yet it does not
follow therefrom that they should not be told in strains of
exquisite poetry. His other poems possess sufficient attraction to interest every class of readers, and they will
still be read when the sneers of ephemeral critics shall
have long expired on the gross lips which impudently ar-
rayed themselves against acknowledged truth, and the whole
suffrage of the literary world. The base attack made with
the hope of crushing the rising genius of young Keats,
can never be forgotten: it was made against a youthful,
friendless, virtuous, highly-gifted character, by a pen,
equally reckless of veracity and justice, from the mean
motive of a dislike to his political tenets. It appears that
Keats had a presentiment he should never return to England,
and that he communicated it to more than one person. [28]
He is said to have wished to drink "of the warm South, "
and "leave the world unseen;" and his wish was accordingly
fulfilled. There is something very impressive about the
death of a genius, and particularly of youthful genius.
Poets, perhaps, have shared most of this feeling from
mankind; indeed their labours which survive themselves
are for ever creating it. Not only

> "By fairy hands <u>their</u> knell is rung,
> By forms unseen <u>their</u> dirge is sung, "[29]

but the beautiful, the tender, and the wise, are perpetual
sorrowers over their obsequies.

8.   G. V. D. 's "ON READING LAMIA, AND OTHER POEMS,
     BY JOHN KEATS" in the <u>Gossip</u>

> (This poem was published in the <u>Gossip</u> on
> May 19, 1821, p. 96. The initials with which
> the author signs himself give no hint of his
> identity. Other friendly references to Keats ap-
> peared in the <u>Gossip</u> on May 19, p. 92; July 7,

p. 145; and August 4, 1821, p. 182.

Young, warm aspirant! thy mellifluous song
   Is as thine own "full-throated" nightingale,
Breathing her moon-light melody among
   Close-tufted trees, and sleeping larks, whose tale
Is hush'd until the orient sky be stained
   With barred chrysolite and jasper deep,
   And sweeter amethyst of purpling dye,
      All softly rainbow-grained--
Blended like trickling tears, when spirits weep
   In unison for earthly misery.

Lamia, and Isabel, oh! what a fate
   Were yours! so opposite, yet both so sad!--
Gladly we turn from Apollonius' hate,
   To gentle Madeline, in vestments clad
Of "rustling" silks, beneath the prism-like moon;--
   From choruses of woodland melody
   We turn, to where thy "light-wing'd Dryad" sings
      Her warm love-flushed tune,
What time the gentle Fays assiduously,
   To load the chaliced flowers, ambrosia brings;

Soft, dewy drops! making an odorus bath,
   Where her sweet limbs Titania might enlave,
While lilies 'broidering the hedge-row path,
   Shook by attendent elves, fresh music gave!--
But now, alas! their mirth is turn'd to woe!
   For thou, who wert the muse's gifted child
   Hath passed away e'en like a favourite flower,
      Too sweet to thrive below;
And now thy inspiration deep and mild,
   No more will soothe us in our summer bower!

                                        G. V. D.

9.   J. H. Reynolds alludes to Keats in his
     Preface to The Garden of Florence

        (The Garden of Florence was published some-
     time shortly before July 1821. In the Preface
     [pp. xi-xii], Reynolds alludes to his dead friend,
     Keats, although he does not mention him by name.

In a favorable review of Reynolds' volume in Baldwin's London Magazine for July 1821, "the late Mr. John Keats" is identified as the friend. "We feel tempted to say something on that point;" the reviewer continues, "but it will, perhaps, afford us matter for a future paper;30 and it is altogether of too melancholy a nature to be mixed up with the consideration of any living writer" [IV, 59]. In addition to alluding to Keats in his Preface, Reynolds also includes three Robin Hood sonnets to his friend [pp. 122-127].)

The stories from Boccacio (The Garden of Florence, and The Ladye of Provence) were to have been associated with tales from the same source, intended to have been written by a friend;--but illness on his part, and distracting engagements on mine, prevented us from accomplishing our plan at the time; and Death now, to my deep sorrow, has frustrated it for ever!

He, who is gone, was one of the very kindest friends I possessed, and yet he was not kinder to me, than to others. His intense mind and powerful feeling would, I truly believe, have done the world some service, 31 had his life been spared--but he was of too sensitive a nature--and thus he was destroyed! One story he completed [Isabella], and that is to me now the most pathetic poem in existence!

10.   Shelley's Preface to Adonais

(Adonais was privately printed at Pisa on or before July 13, 1821. In his Preface to the poem, Shelley specifically indicts the Quarterly Review for its treatment of Keats. At the head of his Preface, the poet quotes from Moschus' Lament for Bion, ll. 111-114. Andrew Lang has translated these lines into prose: "Poison came, Bion to thy mouth, thou didst know poison. To such lips as thine did it come and was not sweetened? What mortal was so cruel that could mix poison for thee, or who could give thee the venom that heard thy voice? Surely, he had no music in his soul." [Theocritus, Bion, and Moschus (London, 1889), p. 202.] By December, Adonais and its inflammatory Preface had created a critical controversy around Shelley and the elegized Keats.)

It is my intention to subjoin to the London edition of
this poem a criticism upon the claims of its lamented object to be classed among the writers of the highest genius
who have adorned our age. [32] My known repugnance to the
narrow principles of taste on which several of his earlier
compositions were modelled prove, at least, that I am an
impartial judge. I consider the fragment of Hyperion as
second to nothing that was ever produced by a writer of the
same years.

John Keats died at Rome of a consumption, in his
twenty-fourth year, [33] on the---of---1821; and was buried in
the romantic and lonely cemetery of the Protestants in that
city, under the pyramid which is in the tomb of Cestius and
the massy walls and towers, now mouldering and desolate,
which formed the circuit of ancient Rome. The cemetery is
an open space among the ruins, covered in the winter with
violets and daisies. It might make one in love with death
to think that one should be buried in so sweet a place.

The genius of the lamented person to whose memory
I have dedicated these unworthy verses was not less delicate
and fragile than it was beautiful; and where cankerworms
abound what wonder if its young flower was blighted in the
bud? The savage criticism on his Endymion, which appeared
in the Quarterly Review, produced the most violent effect on
his susceptible mind; the agitation thus originated ended in
the rupture of a blood-vessel in the lungs; a rapid consumption ensued, and the succeeding acknowledgments from
more candid critics of the true greatness of his powers were
ineffectual to heal the wound thus wantonly inflicted.

It may be well said that these wretched men know not
what they do. They scatter their insults and their slanders
without heed as to whether the poisoned shaft lights on a
heart made callous by many blows, or one like Keats's composed of more penetrable stuff. One of their associates is,
to my knowledge, a most base and unprincipled calumina-
tor. [34] As to Endymion, was it a poem, whatever might
be its defects, to be treated contemptuously by those who
have celebrated with various degrees of complacency and
panegyric Paris and Woman and a Syrian Tale, [35] and Mrs.
Lefanu[36] and Mr. Barrett[37] and Mr. Howard Payne[38] and
a long list of the illustrious obscure? Are these the men
who in their venal good nature presumed to draw a parallel

between the Rev. Mr. Milman[39] and Lord Byron? What
gnat did they strain at here after having swallowed all
those camels? Against what woman taken in adultery dares
the foremost of these literary prostitutes to cast his op-
probious stone? Miserable man! you, one of the meanest,
have wantonly defaced one of the most noble specimens of
the workmanship of God. Nor shall it be your excuse that,
murderer as you are, you have spoken daggers but used
none. [40]

  The circumstances of the closing scene of poor Keats's
life were not made known to me until the Elegy was ready
for the press. [41] I am given to understand that the wound
his sensitive spirit had received from the criticism of
Endymion was exasperated by the bitter sense of unrequited
benefits; the poor fellow seems to have been hooted from
the stage of life no less by those on whom he had wasted the
promise of his genius than those on whom he had lavished
his fortune and his care. He was accompanied to Rome and
attended in his last illness by Mr. Severn, a young artist of
the highest promise, who, I have been informed, 'almost
risked his own life, and sacrificed every prospect to unwearied attendance upon his dying friend.'[42] Had I known
these circumstances before the completion of my poem, I
should have been tempted to add my feeble tribute of applause to the more solid recompense which the virtuous
man finds in the recollection of his own motives. Mr.
Severn can dispense with a reward from 'such stuff as
dreams are made of.'[43] His conduct is a golden augury of
the success of his future career--may the unextinguished
Spirit of his illustrious friend animate the creations of his
pencil, and plead against Oblivion for his name!

11. Charles Cowden Clarke's letter to the
  Morning Chronicle on "JOHN KEATS, THE POET"

  (This letter on Keats's death appeared in the
  Morning Chronicle of July 27, 1821. It is signed
  "Y.," but references to Keats as a "school-fellow and Friend" make it more than likely that the
  author was Clarke. Edmund Blunde, who quotes
  the letter in Shelley and Keats As they struck their
  Contemporaries [London, 1925], pp. 69-71, was
  the first to make this attribution, and all subsequent authorities have confirmed it. In his letter,

Clarke puts major emphasis upon the Tory attacks
of 1818.)

To the EDITOR of the MORNING CHRONICLE

Sir,

I find by the Daily Papers, that the young Poet, John
Keats, is dead. I shall feel gratified if you will allow a
few remarks from his School-fellow[44] and Friend, a place
in your Paper.

It appears that Mr. Keats died of a decline[45] at
Rome, whither he had retired to repair the inroads which
the rupturing of a blood vessel had made upon his constitution.

It is not impossible that his premature death may
have been brought on by his performing the office of nurse
to a younger brother, [46] who also died of a decline; for his
attention to the invalid was so anxious and unwearied, that
his friends could see distinctly that his own health had suffered in the exertion. This may have been one cause, but
I do not believe it was the sole cause. It will be remembered that Keats received some rough and brutal usage from
the Reviews about two years since; particularly from the
Quarterly, and from a Northern one;[47] which, in the opinion
of every gentlemanly and feeling mind, has rendered itself
infamous from its course [sic] pandarism to the depraved
appetites of gossips and scandal-mongers. To what extent
the treatment he received from those writers operated upon
his mind, I cannot say; for Keats had a noble--a proud--
and an undaunted heart; but he was very young, only one
and twenty. [48] He had all the enthusiasm of the youthful
poet burning in him--he thought to take the great world by
the hand, and hold its attention while he unburthened the
over-flowings of an aspiring and ardent imagination; and
his beautiful recasting of "The Pot of Basil," proves that
he would have done so had he lived. But his ardour was
met by the torpedo touch of one, whose "Blood is very
snow-broth;"[49] and the exuberant fancies of a young and
almost ungovernable fancy were dragged forward by another,
and exhibited in gross and wanton caricature. It is truly
painful to see the yearnings of an eager and trusting mind
thus held up to the fiend-like laugh of a brutal mob, upon
the pikes and bayonets of literary mercenaries. If it will

be any consolation to Mr. Gifford to know how much he contributed to the discomfort of a generous mind, I can so far
satisfy it by informing him, that Keats has lain awake
through the whole night talking with sensative [sic] bitterness of the unfair treatment he had experienced; and with
becoming scorn of the information which was afterwards
suggested to him; "That as it was considered he had been
rather roughly handled, his future productions should be
reviewed with less harshness." So much for the integrity
and impartiality of criticism! This charge would no doubt
be denied with high and flouncing indignation; but he told me
he had been given to understand as much, and I believe him.
If the object of this hint was to induce the young Poet to
quit the society of those whom he had chosen for his friends,
and who had helped him in pushing off his boat from shore,
it shows how little his character was known to his assailants.
He had a "little body," but he too had a "mighty heart,"[50]
as any one of them would have discovered, had the same
impertinences been offered to him personally which were
put forth in their anonymous scandal-rolls. Keats's great
crime was his having dedicated his first production to Mr.
Leigh Hunt. He should have cowered under the wings of
Mr. Croker, and he would have been fostered into "a pretty
chicken."[51]

I remember his first introduction to Mr. Hunt, and
the pleasure each seemed to derive from the interview. I
remember with adirmation, all that Gentleman's friendship
and disinterestedness[52] towards him--disinterestedness,
which would surprise those only who do not know him.[53]
I remember too, his first introduction to Mr. Haydon; and
when in the course of conversation that great artist asked
him "if he did not love his country," how the blood rushed
to his cheeks and the tears to his eyes, at his energetic
reply. His love of freedom was ardent and grand. He once
said, that if he should live a few years, he would go over
to South America, and write a Poem on Liberty, and now
he lies in the land where liberty once flourished, and where
it is regenerating.[54]

I hope his friends and admirers (for he had both,
and warm ones) will raise a monument to his memory on
the classical spot where he died; and that Canova,[55] the
Roman, will contribute the respect, so amply in his power,
to the memory of the young Englishman, who possessed a
kindred mind with, and who restamped the loveliest of all
the stories of his great countryman, --Boccaccio.

And now farewel [sic], noble spirit! You have for-
saken us, and taken the long and dark journey towards "that
bourne from whence no traveller returns;"56 but you have
left a memorial of your genius which "posterity will not
willingly let die."57 You have plunged into the gulf, but
your golden sandals remain. The storm of life has over-
blown, and, "the rest is silence."58

> "Fear no more the heat of the sun,
> Nor the furious winter's rages;
> Thou thy worldly task hast done,
> Home art gone, and ta'en thy wages.
> *   *   *   *   *   *   *   *
> Quiet consummation have,
> And renowned be thy Grave."59   Y.

12.   John Clare's sonnet to Keats in
       the Village Minstrel

> (In addition to Keats, Taylor and Hessey were
> the publishers of John Clare, the ploughman poet.
> In letters exchanged between Taylor and Clare,
> passing references of respect are made to Keats.
> Then, toward the end of September 1821, Clare's
> Village Minstrel was published. Sonnet LIX of
> that collection is addressed to Keats [II, 207].)

To The Memory of John Keats

The world, its hopes, and fears, have pass'd away;
    No more its trifling thou shalt feel or see;
Thy hopes are ripening in a brighter day,
    While these left buds thy monument shall be.
When Rancour's aims have past in naught away,
    Enlarging specks discern'd in more than thee,
And beauties minishing which few display--
    When these are past, true child of Poesy,
Thou shalt survive. Ah, while a being dwells,
    With soul, in nature's joys, to warm like thine,
With eye to view her fascinating spells,
    And dream entranced o'er each form devine,
Thy worth, Enthusiast, shall be cherish'd here,
Thy name with him shall linger, and be dear.

13. From a review of Adonais in the
        Literary Chronicle and Weekly Review

(A favorable review of Adonais appeared in the
Literary Chronicle of December 1, 1821, pp. 751-
754. The author is not known. This review and
the two that follow in the Literary Gazette and
Blackwood's have been reprinted by Newman I.
White in The Unextinguished Hearth [Durham,
1938], pp. 285-298. 60 Working from the original
articles, both here and in the succeeding two reviews of Shelley's poem, I have reproduced only
those passages relevant to Keats.)

Through the kindness of a friend, we have been
favoured with the latest production of a gentleman of no
ordinary genius, Mr. Bysshe Shelley. 61 It is an elegy on
the death of a youthful poet of considerable promise, Mr.
Keats, and was printed at Pisa.   As the copy now before
us is, perhaps, the only one that has reached England, and
the subject is one that will excite much interest, we shall
print the whole of it. 62

It has been often said, and Mr. Shelley repeats the
assertion, that Mr. Keats fell a victim to his too great
susceptibility of a severe criticism of one of his poems.
How far this may have been the case we know not.   Cumberland used to say, that authors should not be thin skinned,
but shelled like the rhinoceros; but poor Keats was of too
gentle a disposition for severity, and to a mind of such
exquisite sensibility; we do not wonder that he felt keenly
the harsh and ungenerous attack that was made upon him.
Besides, we are not without instances of the effects of
criticism on some minds. --Hawkesworth63 died of criticism:
when he published his account of the voyages in the South
Seas, for which he received £6000, an innumerable host of
enemies attacked it in the newspapers and magazines; some
pointed out blunders in matters of science, and some
exercised their wit in poetical translations and epigrams.
'It was, ' says Dr. Kippis, 64 'a fatal undertaking, and which,
in its consequences, deprived him of presence of mind and
of life itself. '

Tasso was driven mad by criticism; his susceptibility and tenderness of feeling were so great, that when
his sublime work, 'Jerusalem Delivered, ' met with unexpected opposition, the fortitude of the poet was not proof
against the keenness of disappointment....

Even the mild Newton, with all his philosophy, was
so sensible to critical remarks, that Whiston[65] tells us he
lost favour, which he enjoyed for twenty years, for contradicting Newton in his old age....

We have never been among the very enthusiastic admirers of Mr. Keats's poetry,[66] though we allow that he
possessed considerable genius; but we are decidedly averse
to that species of literary condemnation, which is often
practised by men of wit and arrogance, without feeling and
without discrimination.

Mr. Shelley is an ardent admirer of Keats; and
though he declares his repugnance to the principles of taste
on which several of his earlier compositions were modelled,
he says that he considers 'the fragment of Hyperion as
second to nothing that was ever produced by a writer of the
same years.' Mr. Shelley, in the preface, gives some details respecting the poet:--

> [Quotes all but the first paragraph of Shelley's
> Preface. (The preceding citation to Hyperion is
> from the first paragraph.) Of Shelley's reference
> "to those on whom he [Keats] wasted the promise
> of his genius," the editor observes in a footnote,
> "We do not know to whom Mr. Shelley alludes;
> but we believe we may say that the city of London
> does not boast a bookseller more honourable in
> his dealings, or more liberal to rising genius or
> indigent merit than the publishers of Mr. Keats's
> poems. --Ed."]

14. From a review of Adonais in the Literary
     Gazette and Journal of Belles Lettres

> (The excerpts that follow begin with the fourth
> sentence of an unfavorable review of Adonais in the
> Literary Gazette [December 8, 1821, pp. 772-773].
> Although a generally liberal weekly, the Gazette
> had, on previous occasions, attacked the "atheisti-
> cal" and "radical" sentiments of Shelley. Its only
> previous reference to Keats appeared on July 1,
> 1820 [pp. 423-424] when the Gazette reprinted
> "Ode to a Nightingale," "To Autumn," and "Lines
> on the Mermaid Tavern" from the Lamia volume,

        prefacing these pieces with the following brief,
        noncommittal comment: "Having received a copy
        of Mr. Keats' new volume of poetry, which is on
        the eve of publication, too late in the week for a
        regular review, we merely present by way of
        novelty, the following specimens from the minor
        productions. " Now, with Shelley's outspoken de-
        fense of Keats in Adonais, the Gazette found it
        necessary to attack Keats also. The author of the
        review is not identified by White.)

Adonais is an elegy after the manner of Moschus, on a
foolish young man, who, after writing some volumes of very
weak, and, in the greater part, of very indecent poetry,
died some time since of a consumption: the breaking down
of an infirm constitution having, in all probability, been ac-
celerated by the discarding of his neckcloth, a practice of
the cockney poets, who look upon it as essential to genius,
inasmuch as neither Michael Angelo, Raphael nor Tasso are
supposed to have worn those antispiritual incumbrances.   In
short, as the vigour of Sampson lay in his hair, the secret
of talent with these persons lies in the neck; and what
aspirations can be expected from a mind enveloped in mus-
lin.   Keats caught cold in training for a genius, and, after
a lingering illness, died, to the great loss of the Independents
of South America, whom he had intended to visit with an English
epic poem, for the purpose of exciting them to liberty. 67
But death, even the death of the radically presumptuous profligate, is a serious thing; and as we believe that Keats was
made presumptuous chiefly by the treacherous puffing of his
cockney fellow gossips, and profligate in his poems merely
to make them saleable, we regret that he did not live long
enough to acquire common sense, and abjure the pestilent
and perfidious gang who betrayed his weakness to the grave,
and are now panegyrising his memory into contempt.   For
what is the praise of the cockneys' but disgrace, or
what honourable inscription can be placed over the dead by
the hands of the notorious libellers, exiled adulterers, and
avowed atheists. 68

*   *   *

        Mr. Shelley summons all kinds of visions round the
grave of this young man, who, if he has now any feeling
of the earth, must shrink with shame and disgust from the
touch of the hand that could have written that impious sentence [in st. IV of Adonais, where the reviewer claims

Shelley has blasphemed God by attributing "crime to the
Great Author of all virtue!"]....

*   *   *

The poetry of the work is contemptible--a mere collection
of bloated words heaped on each other without order, harmony, or meaning; the refuse of a schoolboy's common-place
book, full of vulgarisms of pastoral poetry, yellow gems
and blue stars, bright Phoebus and rosy-fingered Aurora;
and of this stuff is Keats's wretched Elegy compiled.

*   *   *

The copy in our hands is one of some score sent to the
Author's intimates from Pisa, where it has been printed
in a quarto form "with the types of Didot,"69 and two
learned Epigrams from Plato70 and Moschus.   Solemn as
the subject is, (for in truth we must grieve for the early
death of any youth of literary ambition," it is hardly possible to help laughing at the mock solemnity with which
Shelley charges the Quarterly Review for having murdered
his friend with--a critique!71   If Criticism killed the dis-
ciples of that school, Shelley would not have been alive to
write an Elegy on another:--but the whole is most farcical
from a pen which, on other occasions, has treated of the
soul, the body, life and death agreeably to the opinions, the
principles, and the practice of Percy Bysshe Shelley.

15.   From William Maginn's "REMARKS ON SHELLEY'S
      ADONAIS" in Blackwood's Edinburgh Magazine

          (The excerpts that follow begin with the third
      paragraph of an unfavorable review of Adonais
      which appeared in Blackwood's for December 1821
      [X, 696-700].   The author of the review is William
      Maginn.   [See his Miscellanies (London, 1885),
      II, 310.]   Until this time, Blackwood's had seen
      merit in Shelley's poetry, but the editors may
      have feared that the charges in Adonais against
      the Quarterly could also be leveled against them.
      Indeed, the ad hominem attacks on Keats by Black-
      wood's had been far more vicious than Croker's
      review in the Quarterly.)

The present story is thus:--A Mr John Keats, a
young man who had left a decent calling for the melancholy
trade of Cockney-poetry, has lately died of a consumption,
after having written two or three little books of verses,
much neglected by the public. His vanity was probably
wrung not less than his purse; for he had it upon the authority of the Cockney Homers and Virgils, that he might become a light to their region at a future time. But all this
is not necessary to help a consumption to the death of a
poor sedentary man, with an unhealthy aspect, and a mind
harassed by the first troubles of versemaking. The New
School, however, will have it that he was slaughtered by a
criticism of the Quarterly Review. --"O flesh, how art thou
fishified!"[72]--There is even an aggravation in this cruelty
of the Review--for it had taken three or four years to slay
its victim, the deadly blow having been inflicted at least as
long since. We are not now to defend a publication so well
able to defend itself. But the fact is, that the Quarterly
finding before it a work at once silly and presumptuous, full
of the servile slang that Cockaigne dictates to its servitors,
and the vulgar indecorums which that Grub Street Empire
rejoiceth to applaud, told the truth of the volume, and
recommended a change of manners and of masters to the
scribbler. Keats wrote on; but he wrote indecently, probably in the indulgence of his social propensities. He selected from Boccacio, and, at the feet of the Italian
Priapus, supplicated for fame and farthings.

"Both halves the winds dispersed in empty air. "[73]

Mr P. B. Shelly having been the person appointed
by the Pisan triumvirate[74] to canonize the name of this apprentice, "nipt in the bud,"[75] as he fondly tells us, has
accordingly produced an Elegy, in which he weeps "after
the manner of Moschus for Bion. "[76] The canonizer is
worthy of the saint. --"Et tu, Vitula!"[77]--Locke says, that
the most resolute liar cannot lie more than once in every
three sentences. Folly is more engrossing; for we could
prove, from the present Elegy, that it is possible to write
two sentences of pure nonsense out of every three. A
more faithful calculation would bring us to ninety-nine out
of every hundred, or, --as the present consists of only
fifty-five stanzas, --leaving about five readable lines in the
entire. It thus commences:--

"O weep for Adonais--he is dead!
O, weep for Adonais! though our tears

Thaw not the frost which binds so dear a head!
And thou, sad hour! select from all years
To mourn our loss, rouse thy obscure compeers,
And teach them thine own sorrow, say with me
Died Adonais! till the future does
Forget the past. His fate and fame shall be
An echo and a light!! unto eternity. "

[St. I.]

Now, of this unintelligible stuff the whole fifty-five stanzas
are composed. Here an hour--a dead hour to--is to say
that Mr J. Keats died along with it! yet this hour has the
heavy business on its hands of mourning the loss of its
fellow-defunct, and of rousing all its obscure compeers to
be taught its own sorrow, &c....

On these principles [absurd epithets and rhymes;
excessive use of flowers, smells, and tastes], a hundred
or a hundred thousand verses might be made, equal to the
best in Adonais, without taking the pen off the paper. The
subject is indifferent to us, let it be the "Golden age, " or
"Mother Goose, "--"Waterloo, " or the "Wit of the Watch-
house, "--"Tom Thumb, " or "Thistlewood. " We will undertake to furnish the requisite supply of blue and crimson
daisies and dandelions, not with the toilsome and tardy
lutulence of the puling master of verbiage in question, but
with a burst and torrent that will sweep away all his weedy
trophies. For example-- Wontner, the city marshal, a very
decent person, who campaigns it once a year, from the
Mansion-house to Blackfriars bridge, truncheoned and uni-
formed as becomes a man of his military habits, had the
misfortune to fracture his leg on the last Lord Mayor's
day. The subject is among the most unpromising. We
will undertake it, however, (premising that we have no idea
of turning the accident of this respectable man into any
degree of ridicule.)

O WEEP FOR ADONAIS, &c.

O weep for Wontner, for his leg is broke,
O weep for Wontner, though our pearly tear
Can never cure him. Dark and dimly broke
The thunder cloud o'er Paul's enamelled sphere,
When his black barb, with lion-like career.
Scatter'd the crowd. --Coqetting Mignionet,
Thou Hyacinth fond, thou Myrtle without fear,
Haughty Geranium, in your beaupots set,
Were then your soft and starry eyes unwet?

> The pigeons saw it, and on silver wings
> Hunt in white flutterings, for they could not fly,
> Hoar-headed Thames checked all his crystal springs,
> Day closed above his pale, imperial eye,
> The silken Zephyrs breathed a vermeil sigh.
> High Heavens! ye Hours! and thou Ura-ni-a!
> Where were ye then? Reclining languidly
> Upon some green Isle in the empurpled Sea,
> Where laurel-wreathen spirits love eternally.

Come to my arms, &c.

*   *   *   *   *

... Percy Byshe feels his hopelessness of poetic reputation, and therefore lifts himself on the stilts of blasphemy. He is the only verseman of the day, who has dared, in a Christian country, to work out for himself the character of direct Atheism! In his present poem, he talks with impious folly of "the envious wrath of man or God!" [St. V. l. 6.] Of a

> "Branded and ensanguined brow,
> Which was like Cain's or Christs."
>   [St. XXXIV. ll. 8-9.]

Offences like these naturally come before a more effective tribunal than that of criticism. We have heard it mentioned as the only apology for the predominant irreligion and nonsense of this person's works, that his understanding is unsettled. But in his Preface, there is none of the exuberance of insanity; there is a great deal of folly, and a great deal of bitterness, but nothing of the wildness of his poetic fustian. The Bombastes Furioso[78] of these stanzas cools into sneering in the preface; and his language against the death-dealing Quarterly Review, which has made such havoc in the Empire of Cockaigne, [79] is merely malignant, mean, and peevishly personal. We give a few stanzas of this performance, taken as they occur.

[Quotes st. III.]

The seasons and a whole host of personages, ideal and otherwise, come to lament over Adonais. They act in the following manner:

"Grief made the young Spring wild, and she threw down
Her kindling buds, as if the Autumn were,
Or they dead leaves, since her delight is flown,
For whom should she have wak'd the sullen year?
To Phoebus was not Hyacinth so dear,
Not to himself Narcissus, as to both,
Thou, Adonais; wan thy stand, and sere,
Amid the drooping comrades of their youth,
With dew all turn'd to tears, odour to sighing ruth. "
                                                                [St. XVI.]

Here is left, to those whom it may concern, the
pleasant perplexity, whether the lament for Mr J. Keats is
shared between Phoebus and Narcissus, or Summer and
Autumn....

                    *   *   *

... we will proceed to the more gratifying office of giving
a whole, unbroken specimen of the Poet's powers, exercised
on a subject rather more within their sphere.   The following Poem has been sent to us as written by Percy Byshe,
and we think it contains all the essence of his odoriferous,
colorific, and daisy-enamoured style.   The motto is from
"Adonais. "   [St. XIII. ll. 1-7.]

ELEGY ON MY TOM CAT

"And others came. --Desires and Adorations,
Wing'd Persuasions, and veil'd Destinies,
Splendours, and Glooms, and glimmering Incantations
Of hopes and fears, and twilight Phantasies;
And Sorrow, with her family of Sighs;
And Pleasure, blind with tears, led by the gleam
Of her own dying smile instead of eyes!"

ELEGY

Weep for my Tomcat! all ye Tabbies weep,
    For he is gone at last!   Not dead alone,
In flowery beauty sleepeth he no sleep
    Like that bewitching youth, Endymion!
My love is dead, alas, as any stone,
    That by some violet-sided smiling river
Weepeth too fondly!   He is dead and gone,
    And fair Aurora, o'er her young believer,
With fingers gloved with roses, doth make moan.

And every bud its petal green doth sever,
And Phoebus sets in night for ever, and for ever!
And others come! ye Splendours! and ye Beauties!
Ye Raptures! with your robes of pearl and blue;
Ye blushing Wonders! with your scarlet shoe-ties;
Ye Horrors bold! with breasts of lily hue;
Ye Hope's stern flatterers! He would trust to you,
Whene'er he saw you with your chestnut hair
Dropping and daffodils; and rosepinks true!
Ye Passions proud! with lips of bright despair;
Ye Sympathies! with eyes like evening star,
When on the glowing east she rolls her crimson car.

Oh, bard-like spirit! beautiful and swift!
Sweet lover of pale night; when Luna's lamp
Shakes sapphire dew-drops through a cloudy rift;
Purple as woman's mouth, o'er ocean damp;
Thy quivering rose-tinged tongue--thy stealing tramp;
The dazzling glory of thy gold-tinged tail;
Thy whisker-waving lips, as o'er the swamp
Rises the meteor, when the year doth fail,
Like beauty in decay, all, all are flat and stale. "

This poem strikes us as an evidence of the improvement that an appropriate subject makes in a writer's style. It is incomparably less nonsensical, verbose, and inflated, than Adonais; while it retains all its knowledge of nature, vigour of colouring, and felicity of language. Adonais has been published by the author in Italy, the fitting soil for the poem, sent over to his honoured correspondents throughout the realm of Cockaigne, with a delightful mysteriousness worthy of the dignity of the subject and the writer.

Notes

1.   Southey, the poet laureate, had just written his
      panegyric upon George III entitled The Vision
      of Judgment.

2.   Slightly misquoted from "I Stood Tiptoe Upon a Little
      Hill, " 1. 12.

3.   Islington Green is located in London, approximately
      2-1/2 miles north of St. Paul's Cathedral.

4.   This contention is not substantiated by the reviews of
      1820.

5. Byron and Shelley were the other two poets.

6. Joseph Severn.

7. The words "the body of" are L.'s, not Keats's.

8. Unidentified.

9. Probably the verses of S. Skinner, to whom Dalby
    refers in the second sentence of his article.
    Henry Kirke White is the subject of the poem.

10. "The following little tribute addressed to him on his
    departure, " Dalby tells us in a footnote, "is ex-
    tracted from 'The Indicator'; as it shews the high
    sense of his private virtues which was entertained
    by his friend, Mr. Leigh Hunt, who was the first
    to introduce his talents to the notice of the public.
    I trust its insertion will not be considered mis-
    placed. --[Quotes Hunt's farewell to Keats in the
    Indicator of September 20, 1820, pp. 399-400.]
    How sadly have the above fond hopes been disap-
    pointed!"

11. Possibly a recollection of a phrase from Jeffrey's
    review in the Edinburgh of August 1820.

12. Jeffrey's review in the Edinburgh, XXXIV (August 1820),
    204.

13. Before turning to poetry, White was articled to a
    lawyer. Keats, of course, was a licensed surgeon.

14. Woodhouse's advertisement to Hyperion, which stated
    that the unfavorable reception of Endymion had
    discouraged Keats from completing the later poem,
    may have led Dalby to this conclusion. Keats's
    letter of October 9, 1818 to Hessey, already
    quoted in part in the headnote to item 3 of the
    fourth chapter, flatly contradicts Dalby's conten-
    tion: "Praise or blame has but a momentary effect
    on the man whose love of beauty in the abstract
    makes him a severe critic on his own Works....
    when I feel I am right, no external praise can give
    me such a glow as my own solitary reperception of
    what is fine.... In Endymion, I leaped headlong
    into the sea.... I was never afraid of failure; for
    I would sooner fail than not be among the greatest. "

(The Letters of John Keats, ed. Hyder E. Rollins
[Cambridge, Mass., 1958], I, 373-374.)

15. This reference is to Byron, who lashed out at his
critics in English Bards and Scotch Reviewers
and Don Juan, as well as in other works.

16. The idea of an effeminate Keats, which Hunt, Milnes,
and others later tried to combat, is clearly im-
plied in these remarks.

17. Jeffrey's review, p. 203.

18. Ibid., p. 205.

19. An error repeated from the August 9, 1820 installment of Hunt's review in the Indicator.

20. A quote from Hunt's review in the Indicator.

21. Dalby's assumption that L.'s article in Baldwin's was
the work of "an intimate friend of the departed
poet" was a guess rather than an established fact.

22. Slop damns Obadiah for knotting his surgical bag in
Vol. III, Chapter Eleven of Tristram Shandy. The
clause in quotation marks is not a direct quotation, but a reconstruction of the general tenor of
Slop's curses throughout the chapter.

23. "We need scarcely allude to their fabulous origin," the
poet or an editor observes in a footnote. Both
the Romans and the Greeks believed they were
descended from the gods, but moral prudence of
the time forbade specific mention of the sexual
escapades of the Olympians.

24. Thus, the violet perishes.

25. Pope, "Ode on Solitude," l. 19.

26. L.'s "Death of Mr. John Keats" in Baldwin's London
Magazine for April 1821.

27. Unidentified.

28. L.'s "Death of Keats," p. 426. The quote that fol-

lows from "Ode to a Nightingale" is also taken
from L.

29. Collins, "Ode Written in the Year 1746," ll. 7-8.

30. No such paper ever appeared in Baldwin's London
Magazine.

31. An allusion to Othello, V. ii. l. 342.

32. No London edition of Adonais was forthcoming during
Shelley's lifetime, although part of the Pisa impression was sent to the Ollier brothers for sale
in London.

33. Keats was past twenty-five when he died. As Shelley
is incorrect about Keats's age, it is evident in
what immediately follows that he does not know the
month or day of Keats's death.

34. Many authorities have assumed that Shelley had Milman
(see n. 39 below) in mind here, but Kenneth N.
Cameron makes a far more persuasive case for
Southey. ("Shelley vs. Southey: New Light on an
Old Quarrel," PMLA, LVII [1942], 489-512.) In
any event, Shelley was wrong. According to Roger
Ingpen (The Complete Works of Percy Bysshe
Shelley [New York, 1926], X, 95), John Taylor
Coleridge attacked Laon and Cythna, an earlier
version of The Revolt of Islam, in the Quarterly
Review for April 1819 (XXI, 460-471). Obviously,
Shelley had a personal motive for his attack on
the Quarterly and his defense of Keats.

35. Paris and a Syrian Tale are not mentioned by Walter
Graham, although he does list Charles Maturin's
Woman, A Tale as being reviewed by Croker in
the Quarterly of July 1818. (Tory Criticism in
the Quarterly Review [New York, 1921], p. 48.)

36. Alicia Le Fanu (1753-1817), the sister of Richard
Brinsley Sheridan. She was the author of Sons
of Erin, or Modern Sentiment, a patriotic comedy
which failed after its first performance on April
13, 1812 at the Lyceum Theatre.

37. Eaton Stannard Barrett (1786-1820), an Irish poet.

38. John Howard Payne (1791-1852), an American actor, playwright, and theater owner who was working in London at the time.

39. Henry Hart Milman (1791-1868), a churchman, historian, poet, and playwright.

40. An allusion to _Hamlet_, III. iii. 1. 414.

41. The information that follows originated in a letter by Robert Finch to John Gisborne. Gisborne, a friend of Shelley, wrote to the poet on June 16, 1821, enclosing Finch's letter under the same cover. (See _The Letters of Percy Bysshe Shelley_, ed. F. L. Jones [Oxford, 1964], II, 299-300.)

42. From Finch's letter to John Gisborne.

43. _The Tempest_, IV. i. ll. 156-157. The quote differs slightly in modern editions of Shakespeare but was given this way in Shelley's own day.

44. Keats attended Enfield Academy, where Charles Cowden Clarke's father, John Clarke, was headmaster. The younger Clarke was eight years Keats's senior and performed teaching duties at the school.

45. The decline mentioned here was, in fact, tuberculosis.

46. Thomas Keats.

47. _Blackwood's Edinburgh Magazine._

48. Keats was past twenty-two at the time _Endymion_ was published. When Croker's attack in the _Quarterly_ appeared in October 1818 (the April issue of the _Quarterly_ was delayed six months), Keats was almost twenty-three.

49. _Measure for Measure_, I. iv. ll. 34-35.

50. _King Henry the Fifth_, II. Prologue, l. 17.

51. A well-known phrase, a variation of which appears in _Macbeth_, IV. iii. 1. 218.

52. Used in the sense of unselfishness rather than impartiality.

53. This defense of Hunt was long past due. Despite Hunt's
     unfortunate influence on Keats's early style and the
     attacks on the poet that resulted from his associa-
     tion with Hunt, Keats found no loyaler friend or
     admirer. In the Examiner and the Indicator, Hunt
     was responsible for publishing more poems by and
     articles and reviews relating to Keats than any
     contemporary of the time.

54. Clarke is referring to Italy and, more specifically,
     to the uprising in 1820 when Naples unsuccessfully
     attempted to break away from the yoke of Austria
     and Metternich.

55. Antonio Canova (1757-1822), a sculptor.

56. A paraphrase of Hamlet, III. i. ll. 79-80.

57. Unidentified.

58. Hamlet, V. ii. l. 369.

59. Cymbeline, IV. ii. ll. 335-338, 357-358.

60. In his text, White Americanizes some British spellings
     and makes one or two very negligible textual
     errors which are not worth pointing out, although
     they have been silently corrected here.

61. According to White, " Shelley sent copies of Adonais
     to the Olliers and to Thomas Love Peacock by his
     friend John Gisborne, whose arrival in London
     probably preceded the edition sent by freight. It
     is probably to one of these men that The Literary
     Chronicle refers in the first sentence" (p. 285.)

62. In a later section of this review, not included in my
     excerpts, the author quotes all but stanzas XIX-
     XXIV of Adonais.

63. John Hawkesworth (1715?-1773), a miscellaneous
     writer whose Account of the Voyages of Captain
     Cook and others was harshly received in 1773.
     He died that same year.

64. Andrew Kippis (1725-1795), a nonconformist divine,
     a biographer, and a former teacher of William

Godwin, was one of the compilers of the Biographia Brittanica. The source of the quote that follows from Kippis is not known.

65. William Whiston (1667-1752), English theologian and mathematician who succeeded Newton as Lucasian Professor of Mathematics at Cambridge (1701). He was expelled in 1710 for his Arian views.

66. Despite P.'s tribute to Keats in the Literary Chronicle of March 31, 1821, this same journal had unfavorably reviewed Keats's Lamia volume on July 29, 1820. (See Chapter IV, item 5.)

67. In his letter of July 27, 1821 to the Morning Chronicle, Clarke mentioned that Keats proposed to "go over to South America, and write a Poem on Liberty...."

68. These references are to Hunt's libel on the Prince Regent, Byron's sexual liaisons in Italy, and Shelley's frequent professions of atheism. Although no Cockney, Byron was then on friendly terms with Hunt (with whom he later feuded) and Shelley. He was probably grouped with the Cockneys for this reason.

69. From the title page of Adonais.

70. Plato's epigram on Aster appears as the motto of Adonais. It was later translated by Shelley and published by his wife, Mary, in her 1839 collected edition of her husband's poem under the title "To Stella."
    "Thou wert the morning star among the living,
        Ere thy fair light had fled;
    Now, having died, thou art as Hesperus, giving
        New splendour to the dead."

71. "This would have done excellently for a coroner's inquest like that on Honey, which lasted thirty days, and was facetiously called the 'Honey-moon'." (Reviewer's note.)

72. Romeo and Juliet, II. iv. 1. 41.

73. An allusion to the Rape of the Lock, II. ll. 45-46.

74. The triumvirate included Byron and Hunt, as well as Shelley. At the time this review was written, the three men were finalizing plans for the Liberal, a literary journal to be established at Pisa.

75. Shelley uses the phrase "blighted in the bud" in his Preface to Adonais.

76. Not a direct quote, but an allusion to the lines at the head of Shelley's Preface. (See headnote to item 10 of this chapter.)

77. Vitula, bullock.

78. A burlesque by William Barnes Rhodes (1772-1826).

79. An imaginary land of luxurious and idle living.

SUMMARY OF ENGLISH PUBLICATIONS IN WHICH KEATS IS MENTIONED, 1816-1821

1. Public notices of Keats in serials and annuals, including Keats's individual poems and reviews.

> Where the attribution of authorship of anonymous reviews has been generally established, it has been indicated. Likely but less definite attributions are indicated by a parenthetical question mark. All unattributed reviews have been checked against Halkett and Laing's Dictionary of Anonymous and Pseudonymous English Literature [London, 1928].
> Notices labeled "obituaries" are a sentence or two at most. The phrasing, almost always the same, runs "Died. At Rome, of a decline, John Keats, the poet, aged 25 years." February 22 or February 23 is listed as the date of death. Less frequently, Endymion and the Lamia volume are mentioned. "Death notices," on the other hand, are longer in length, running in certain instances to several pages.
> Places of publication are only given when they are outside of London and not apparent from the title of the serial.
> An asterisk indicates a new discovery; two asterisks, first publication of a Keats poem.)

Alfred, West of England Journal and General Advertiser (Exeter):
> Reynolds, John H. "The Quarterly review--Mr. Keats," October 6, 1818. Reproduced, Chap. III, item 8.

> *Hunt, Leigh. "On Receiving A Crown of Ivy" from John Keats, October 13, 1818.

Annals of the Fine Arts:
> Keats, John. "To Haydon" and "On Seeing the Elgin Marbles," III (March 1818), 171-172; **"Ode to a

Nightingale, " IV (July 1819), 354-356, and ** "Ode
on a Grecian Urn, " IV (December 1819), 638-639,
both signed "+. "

Annual Register:
Obituary of Keats, "Appendix to Chronicle, " LXIII
(February 1821), 232. Keats is mentioned as "a
young man of distinguished genius as a poet. " His
three volumes are listed with years of publication.

Anti-Gallican Monitor:
*Two letters by Wilson on Keats and Poems, June 8
and July 6, 1817. Reproduced, Chap. II, item 7.

Baldwin's London Weekly Journal:
*Publication notice of Lamia, etc., July 8, 1820.

Bell's Weekly Messenger:
*Obituary of Keats, March 25, 1821, p. 96.

Blackwood's Edinburgh Magazine:
Lockhart, John G. "Cockney School of Poetry. No.
IV. , " III (August 1818), 519-524. Reproduced,
Chap. III, item 4.

Wilson, John and/or Lockhart, J. G.   From the
"Cockney School of Poetry. No. VI. , " VI (October
1819), 75-76. Reproduced, Chap. III, item 13.

Wilson, John. From a review of Hunt's Literary
Pocketbook, VI (December 1819), 239-240. Reproduced, Chap. III, item 14.

Lockhart, J. G. (?) "Mr. Wastle's Diary: No. III. , "
VII (September 1820), 665. Reproduced, Chap. V,
item 4a.

Maginn, William(?) of Wilson, John(?). "Horae
Scandicae. No. II. , The Building of the Palace of
the Lamp, " VII (September 1820), 675-679. Reproduced, Chap. V, item 4b.

Wilson, John and/or Lockhart, J. G.   From a review
of Prometheus Unbound, VII (September 1820), 686-
687. Reproduced, Chap. V, item 4c.

Maginn, William. From a review of Adonais, X
(December 1821), 696-700. Reproduced, Chap. VI,
item 15.

References and allusions to Keats in prose and verse:
II (October 1817), 38; II (November 1817), 194; II
(January 1818), 415; III (May 1818), 196-201; III
(June 1818), 249; III (July 1818), 455; III (August
1818), 533; IV (January 1819), 476; IV (February
1819), 568; V (April 1819), 97; VI (November 1819),
194; VI (December 1819), 243; VI (March 1820),
629; VIII (February 1821), 541; VIII (March 1821),
673-675.

British Critic:
Review of Endymion, IX (June 1818), 649-654. Reproduced, Chap. III, item 6.

Review of Lamia, etc. , XIV (September 1820), 257-
264. Reproduced, Chap. IV, item 12.

Reference to Keats:
X (July 1818), 94-95.

British Freeholder and Saturday Evening Journal:
*Obituary of Keats, March 24, 1821.

British Lady's Magazine:
*Publication notice of Poems, V (April 1817), 262.

British Mercury; or Wednesday Evening Post:
*Obituary of Keats, March 28, 1821, p. 104.

British Neptune:
*Obituary of Keats, March 25, 1821, p. 96.

British Register and London Critical Journal:
*Publication notice of Endymion, XII (August 1818), 279.

*Publication notice of Lamia, etc. , XIV (September
1820), 246.

Reference to Keats:
XV (March 1820), 34.

British Stage and Literary Cabinet:
*Publication notice of Lamia, etc. , IV (July 1820), 225.

*Obituary of Keats, V (May 1821), 150.

*Reference to Keats in a publication notice of Adonais,
V (November 1821), 374.

Brunswick:
    *Obituary of Keats, April 1, 1821, p. 262.

Caledonian Mercury (Edinburgh):
    *Obituary of Keats, March 29, 1821.

Champion:
    Reynolds, John H. Review of Poems, March 9, 1817,
      p. 78. Reproduced, Chap. II, item 3.

    Letter signed "Pierre," August 3, 1817, p. 245.
      Reply by John H. Reynolds(?) with Keats's sonnet
      **"On the Sea," August 17, 1817, p. 261. Repro-
      duced, Chap. II, item 8.

    Keats, John. "Mr. Kean," December 21, 1817, p.
      405. Review of Retribution and Harlequin's Vision
      (mistitled Don Giovanni), January 4, 1818, pp. 10-
      11.

    *Publication notice of Endymion, April 26, 1818, p. 271.

    Review of Endymion, June 7, 1818, pp. 362-364. Re-
      produced, Chap. III, item 3.

Chester Guardian:
    Defense of "Mr. Keats's Endymion," 1818. (Unavail-
      able--see Examiner, November 1, 1818, p. 696.)
      Reproduced, Chap. III, item 10.

Christian Remembrancer:
    *Publication notice of Lamia, etc., II (June 1820), 384.

Comet; or, Literary Wanderer:
    *Keats, John. "The Human Seasons" (Winter [?] 1820),
      p. 127.

Constitution:
    *Obituary of Keats, March 25, 1821.

Déjeuné:
    From "The Literary Assise Court," by "G.," I (Oc-
      tober 27, 1820), 45-47.

Dublin Magazine:
    From a review of Cornwall's A Sicilian Story, etc.,
      I (March 1820), 228.

Eclectic Review:
　　Review of Poems, s. 2., VIII (September 1817), 267-
　　275. Reproduced, Chap. II, item 9.

　　Review of Lamia, etc., s. 2., XIV (September 1820),
　　158-171. Reproduced, Chap. IV, item 13.

　　From a review of Cornwall's A Sicilian Story, etc.,
　　s. 2., XIV (November 1820), 323, 333.

　　Reference to Keats:
　　s. 2., XIII (January 1820), 85.

Edinburgh Annual Register:
　　*Publication notice of Endymion (1818), p. 347.

　　*Publication notice of Lamia, etc., (1821), p. 330.

Edinburgh Magazine and Literary Miscellany (formerly the
　Scot's Magazine):
　　Review of Poems, n. s. I (October 1817), 254-257.
　　Reproduced, Chap. II, item 10.

　　Review of Endymion, n. s. VII (August 1821), 107-110.
　　Reproduced, Chap. III, item 17.

　　Review of Lamia, etc., n. s. VII (October 1821), 313-
　　316. Reproduced, Chap. IV, item 8.

Edinburgh Monthly Review:
　　*Publication notice of Lamia, etc., IV (August 1820),
　　244.

　　Reference to Keats:
　　*II (December 1819), 673, 675.

Edinburgh Review:
　　Jeffrey, Francis. Review of Endymion, XXXIV (August
　　1820), 203-213. Reproduced, Chap. III, item 16.

Edinburgh Weekly Journal:
　　*Obituary of Keats, March 28, 1821, p. 102.

European Magazine:
　　Mathew, George F. "To A Poetical Friend," LXX
　　(October 1816), 365. Reproduced, Chap. II, item
　　1. Review of Poems, LXXI (May 1817), 434-437.

Reproduced, Chap. II, item 5. Sonnet beginning "Art thou a Poet?", LXXI (October 1817), 360.

Evening Mail:
  *Obituary of Keats, March 23-26, 1821.

Examiner:
  Keats, John. **"To Solitude," May 5, 1816, p. 282.

  Hunt, Leigh. "Young Poets" (including Keats's sonnet **"On First Looking into Chapman's Homer"), December 1, 1816, pp. 761-762. Reproduced, Chap. II, item 2.

  Keats, John. **"To Kosciusko," February 16, 1817, p. 107; **"After dark vapours," February 23, 1817, p. 124; **"To Haydon" and **"On Seeing the Elgin Marbles," March 9, 1817, p. 155; On **"The Floure and the Lefe" (with an introductory note by Leigh Hunt), March 16, 1817, p. 173.

  Hunt, Leigh. Review of Poems, June 1, 1817, p. 345; July 6, 1817, pp. 428-429; July 13, 1817, pp. 443-444. Reproduced, Chap. II, item 6.

  Keats, John. **"On the Grasshopper and the Cricket," September 21, 1817, p. 599.

  Reynolds, John H. "The Quarterly review--Mr. Keats," October 12, 1818, pp. 648-649, reprinted from the Alfred, October 6, 1818. Reproduced, Chap. III, item 8.

  "Mr. Keats's Endymion," November 1, 1818, p. 696, reprinted from an unavailable copy of the Chester Guardian, 1818. Reproduced, Chap. III, item 10.

  Keats, John. Review of Reynolds' Peter Bell, a Lyrical Ballad, April 25, 1819, p. 270.

  Lamb, Charles. Review of Lamia, etc., July 30, 1820, pp. 494-495, reprinted from the New Times of July 19, 1820. Reproduced, Chap. IV, item 4.

  Obituary of Keats, March 25, 1821, p. 184.

  References and allusions to Keats:
    October 11, 1818, p. 648; October 21, 1821, p. 665.

General Evening Post:
    *Keats, John. "Stanzas To Autumn," September 14-16,
    1820.

    *Obituary of Keats, March 20-22, 1821.

Gentleman's Magazine; or Monthly Intelligencer:
    Obituary of Keats, XCI (March 1821), 282.

Gossip (Kentish Town):
    From "A Posthumous Epistle From The Author of
    Tristram Shandy," April 14, 1821, p. 54. Repro-
    duced, Chap. VI, item 4.

    "On Reading Lamia, and Other Poems, by John Keats,"
    by "G. V. D.," May 19, 1821, p. 96. Reproduced,
    Chap. VI, item 8.

    References and allusions to Keats:
    May 19, 1821, p. 92; July 7, 1821, p. 145; August
    4, 1821, p. 182.

Guardian; or, Historical and Literary Recorder:
    Review of Lamia, etc., August 6, 1820. Reproduced,
    Chap. IV, item 7.

    *Obituary of Keats, March 25, 1821.

Honeycomb:
    Reference to Keats, August 12, 1820, p. 67.

Imperial Magazine (Liverpool):
    From "On the Neglect of Genius," by "M. M.," III
    (December 1821), cols. 1077-1078.

Indicator:
    Keats, John. **"La Belle Dame sans Merci," signed
    "Caviare," May 10, 1820, p. 248.

    Hunt, Leigh and Keats, John. **"A Now, Descriptive
    of a Hot Day" and Keats's **"A Dream, after
    Reading Dante's Episode of Paolo and Francesca,"
    signed "Caviare," June 28, 1820, pp. 300-303,
    304.

    Hunt, Leigh. Review of Lamia, etc., August 2 and
    August 9, 1820, pp. 337-344, 345-352. Reproduced,
    Chap. IV, item 6.

Keats, John. Four and one-half stanzas from **"The
Cap and Bells," signed "Lucy V___ L___ ," in an
article by Hunt on "Coaches," August 23, 1820, pp.
367-368.

Hunt, Leigh. Farewell to Keats on his departure for
Italy, September 20, 1820, pp. 399-400. Reproduced, Chap. V, item 5.

Investigator:
    *Publication notice of Lamia, etc., I (September 1820),
    452.

    *Obituary of Keats, III (July 1821), 212.

Kaleidoscope; or, Literary and Scientific Mirror (Liverpool):
    Keats, John. "To Autumn," n.s. I (August 29, 1820),
    p. 69.

    *"Sonnet on the Death of John Keats, the Poet," n.s.
    I (May 1, 1821), p. 348. Reproduced, Chap. VI,
    item 5.

Literary Chronicle and Weekly Review:
    Review of Lamia, etc., July 29, 1820, pp. 484-485.
    Reproduced, Chap. IV, item 5.

    "Verses to the Memory of John Keats the Poet," by
    "P.," March 31, 1821, p. 206. Reproduced,
    Chap. VI, item 1.

    From a review of Adonais, December 1, 1821, pp.
    751-754. Reproduced, Chap. VI, item. 13.

    Reference to Keats:
    August 26, 1820, pp. 554-555.

Literary Gazette and Journal of Belles Lettres:
    Keats, John. "Ode to a Nightingale," "To Autumn,"
    and "Lines on the Mermaid Tavern," with a brief
    reference to Lamia, etc., July 1, 1820, pp. 423-
    424.

    From a review of Adonais, December 8, 1821, pp.
    772-773. Reproduced, Chap. VI, item 14.

Literary Journal, and General Miscellany of Science, Arts,
   History, Politics, etc.:
      Review of Endymion, May 17 and 24, 1818, pp. 114-
      115, 131. Reproduced, Chap. III, item 1.

      "Pleasant Walks; A Cockney Pastoral," by "Beppo,"
      March 20, 1819, p. 192. Reproduced, Chap. III,
      item 12.

Literary Panorama:
      *Publication notice of Endymion, n. s. VIII (April 1818),
      73.

Literary Pocketbook (An annual by Leigh Hunt):
      *Publication notice of Endymion (1819), p. 205.

      Keats, John.   **"The Human Seasons" and **"To Ailsa
      Rock" (1819), p. 225.

      *Keats's name is included under "Living Authors,"
      (1820), p. 162.

      *Publication notice of Lamia, etc., (1821), p. 199.

      *Keats's name is included under "Living Authors"
      (1821).

Liverpool Mercury:
      *Obituary of Keats, March 30, 1821, p. 327.

London and Provincial Sunday Gazette:
      *Obituary of Keats, March 25, 1821.

London Chronicle:
      Keats, John.   "To Autumn," July 21, 1820, p. 70.

      *Obituary of Keats, March 26, 1821, p. 287.

London Magazine (Baldwin's; Taylor and Hessey's):
      Review of Endymion, I (April 1820), 380-389. Repro-
      duced, Chap. III, item 15.

      Hazlitt, William.   From "Table Talk. No. I., On The
      Qualifications Necessary to Success in Life," signed
      "T.," I (June 1820), 654.

      Scott, John.   Review of Lamia, etc., II (September

1820), 315-321. Reproduced, Chap. IV, item 14.
From "Blackwood's Magazine," II (November 1820),
520. From "The Mohock Magazine," II (December
1820), 681-683. Reproduced, Chap. V, item 6.

Hazlitt, William. From "The Drama. No. XI.," II
(December 1820), 686. From "Table Talk. No.
VII., On Reading Old Books," III (February 1821),
132. Reproduced, Chap. V, item 8.

Procter, B. W. (?). "Death of Mr. John Keats," signed
"L.," III (April 1821), 426-427. Reproduced, Chap.
VI, item 2.

Taylor, John(?). "Sonnet on the Death of the Poet J.
Keats," III (May 1821), 526. Reproduced, Chap.
VI, item 6.

Keats, John. Three and one-half stanzas from The
Eve of St. Agnes, IV (September 1821), 288-289;
"A Dream, after Reading Dante's Episode...," IV
(November 1821), 526.

References and allusions to Keats:
II (December 1820), 628; *III (January 1821), 69-
73; IV (July 1821), 58-59; IV (August 1821), 177;
*IV (September 1821), 285; IV (December 1821),
641.

London Magazine (Gold's):
Review of Lamia, etc., II (August 1820), 160-173.
Reproduced, Chap. IV, item 9.

From an "Essay on Poetry," II (December 1820),
559-561. Reproduced, Chap. V, item 7.

References and allusions to Keats:
London Magazine and Theatrical Inquisitor, III
(February 1821), 132; III (March 1821), 276-278.

London Moderator and National Adviser:
*Obituary of Keats, March 28, 1821.

London Packet:
*Obituary of Keats, March 21-23, 1821.

Military Register and Weekly Gazette:
*Obituary of Keats, March 28, 1821.

Mirror of the Times:
    *Obituary of Keats, March 17-24, 1821.

Monthly Literary Advertiser:
    *Publication notice of Endymion, May 9, 1818, p. 35.

Monthly Magazine:
    Review of Poems, XLIII (April 1817), 248. Repro-
    duced, Chap. II, item 4.

    Review of Lamia, etc., L (September 1820), 166.
    Reproduced, Chap. IV, item 10.

    Obituary of Keats, LI (May 1821), p. 396.

    References and allusions to Keats:
    XLIX (June 1820), 439, 447; XLIX (July 1820),
    549, 559.

Monthly Repository:
    Keats, John. "On the Grasshopper and Cricket," XII
    (October 1817), 623.

    Obituary of Keats, XV (March 1821). 181.

Monthly Review:
    Review of Lamia, etc., XCII (July 1820), 305-310.
    Reproduced, Chap. IV, item 1.

Morning Chronicle:
    Scott, John(?). Letter of "J. S." in defense of Keats,
    October 3, 1818. Reproduced, Chap. III, item 7.

    Letter of "R. B." in defense of Keats, October 8, 1818.
    Reproduced, Chap. III, item 7.

    Obituary of Keats, March 22, 1821.

    Clarke, Charles C. "Defense of John Keats, the
    Poet," by "his School-fellow and friend," signed
    "Y.," July 27, 1821. Reproduced, Chap. VI,
    item 11.

Morning Herald:
    *Keats, John.   "Stanzas to Autumn," September 16,
    1820.

*Obituary of Keats, March 23, 1821.

Morning Post:
    Reference to Keats's attendance at a private showing
    of Haydon's "Christ Entry into Jerusalem, " ca.
    March 27, 1820.

National Register:
    *Obituary of Keats, March 25, 1821.

New Annual Register:
    *Death notice of Keats, XLI (1821), 267-268. (Re-
    printed from the New Monthly Magazine, XV [May
    1821], 256-257.) Reproduced, Chap. VI, item 7.

New Bon Ton Magazine:
    *From "On the present State of Poetical Talent, " V
    (September 1820), 282-284. Reproduced, Chap. V,
    item 3.

New Monthly Magazine:
    Review of Lamia, etc. , XIV (September 1, 1820), 245-
    248. Reproduced, Chap. IV, item 11.

    From "Modern Periodical Literature, " XIV (Septem-
    ber 1, 1820), 306. Reproduced, Chap. V, item 2.

    Death notice of Keats, XV (May 1821), 256-257. Re-
    produced, Chap. VI, item 7.

New Observer:
    *Obituary of Keats, March 25, 1821.

New Times:
    *Publication notice of Lamia, etc. , June 30, 1820.

    Lamb, Charles. Review of Lamia, etc. , July 19,
    1821. Reproduced, Chap. IV, item 4.

    Keats, John. "To Autumn"; excerpts from "Ode to a
    Nightingale" and Hyperion, July 21, 1820.

    *Obituary of Keats, March 22, 1821.

    Advertisements for a projected edition of "Memoirs
    and Remains of John Keats, " March 29 and April
    9, 1821.

Newcastle Magazine:
    *Publication notice of Lamia, etc., I (September 1820),
      100.

    *Obituary of Keats, II (May 1821), 754.

News:
    *Obituary of Keats, March 26, 1821.

Observer:
    *Obituary of Keats, March 26, 1821.

Observer of the Times:
    *Obituary of Keats, March 25, 1821.

Oxford University and City Herald:
    Bailey, Benjamin. Two letters on Endymion, May
      20 and June 6, 1818. Reproduced, Chap. III,
      item 2.

Pocket Magazine of Classic and Polite Literature:
    Dalby, J. W. "Remarks on the Character and Writings
      of the late John Keats, the Poet," VII (April 1821),
      333-338. Reproduced, Chap. VI, item 3.

Public Ledger and Daily Advertiser:
    *Keats, John. "Stanzas to Autumn," September 19,
      1820.

    *Obituary of Keats, March 26, 1821.

Quarterly Review:
    Croker, John W. Review of Endymion, XIX (April
      1818), 204-208. Reproduced, Chap. III, item 5.

Retrospective Review:
    From a review of Wallace's Prospects of Mankind,
      etc., II (August 1820), 204. Reproduced, Chap. V,
      item 1.

St. James's Chronicle:
    *Keats, John. On "The Floure and the Lefe," March
      15-18, 1817.

    *Review of Lamia, etc., July 1-4, 1820. Reproduced,
      Chap. IV, item 2.

*Publication notice of <u>Lamia,</u> etc., July 4-6, 1820.

*Keats, John. "A Dream, after Reading Dante's Episode...," October 30-November 1, 1821.

Star:
‾‾‾‾
    *Keats, John. On "The Floure and the Lefe," April 4, 1817.

    *Publication notice of <u>Lamia,</u> etc., July 1, 1820.

    *Keats, John. Sts. II and III of "To Autumn," with introductory comment, July 22, 1820; "Ode to a Nightingale," with introductory comment, July 27, 1820.

    *Obituary of Keats, March 22, 1821.

    *Advertisement for a projected edition of "Memoirs and Remains of John Keats," with an excerpt from Jeffrey's August 1820 review in the <u>Edinburgh,</u> April 7, 1821.

Statesman:
‾‾‾‾‾‾‾‾‾
    *Obituary of Keats, March 23, 1821.

Sun:
‾‾‾
    *Publication notice of <u>Endymion,</u> September 15, 1818.

    *Keats, John. "The Triumph of Bacchus" from <u>Endymion</u> (IV. ll. 182-272), October 5, 1818.

    *Review of <u>Endymion,</u> October 21, 1818. Reproduced, Chap. III, item 9.

    *Publication notices of <u>Lamia,</u> etc., June 30, 1820 and September 25, 1820.

    Woodhouse, Richard. Review of <u>Lamia,</u> etc., "From A Correspondent," July 10, 1820. Reproduced, Chap. IV, item 3.

    *Obituary of Keats, March 22, 1821.

    *Advertisement for a projected edition of "Memoirs and Remains of John Keats," April 6, 1821.

Sunday Advertiser:
    *Obituary of Keats, March 25, 1821.

Tickler:
    Keats, John. "On the Grasshopper and Cricket," III
        (February 1821), 37; "To Solitude," III (August
        1821), 162.

Times:
    *Obituary of Keats, March 23, 1821.

Traveller:
    *Obituary of Keats, March 23, 1821.

True Briton:
    *Obituary of Keats, March 23, 1821.

Weekly Entertainer, and West of England Miscellany (Sher-
    borne):
        From a review of Wallace's Prospects of Mankind,
            etc., n. s. II (August 21, 1820), 151. (Reprinted
            from the Retrospective Review, II [August 1820],
            204.) Reproduced, Chap. V, item 1.

Weekly Intelligencer and British Luminary:
    *Obituary of Keats, March 25, 1821.

Yellow Dwarf:
    Keats, John. "Hymn to Pan" from Endymion (I. 11.
        232-306), May 9, 1818, p. 151.

2. Public notices of Keats in books, including the poet's
    three volumes of verse

Clare, John. The Village Minstrel. 2 vols. London, 1821.

        (Sonnet "To The Memory of John Keats," II,
        207. Reproduced, Chap. VI, item 12.)

Hazlitt, William. Table Talk. London, 1821.

        (From "On Living To One's-Self," pp. 229-230.
        Reproduced, Chap. V, item 8.)

Hunt, Leigh. Foliage. London, 1818.

> ("To John Keats, " "On Receiving a Crown of Ivy
> from the Same, " and "On the Same, " pp. cxxv-
> cxxvii. Reproduced, Chap. III, item 11.)

_____ . Amyntas, A Tale of the Woods. London, 1820.

> (Dedication to Keats.)

_____ . The Months. London, 1821.

> (Quotations from Keats's "On the Grasshopper and
> the Cricket" and "To Autumn, " pp. 79, 103-104,
> 107-108.)

Keats, John. Poems. London, 1817.

_____ . Endymion. London, 1818.

_____ . Lamia, Isabella, The Eve of St. Agnes, and
Other Poems. London, 1820.

Moore, Francis. The Age of Intellect. London, 1819.

> (A reference to Keats in "Letter VI. , From Jack
> Jingle in the Country to Bob Blazon in London, "
> p. 106.)

Reynolds, John H. The Garden of Florence. London, 1821.

> (A reference by Reynolds to his plan of collabora-
> tion with Keats, pp. xi-xii. Reproduced, Chap. VI,
> item 9. Three Robin Hood sonnets to Keats, pp.
> 122-127.)

Shelley, Percy. B. Adonais. Pisa, 1821.

> (Preface on Keats. Reproduced, Chap. VI, item 10.)

Terrot, Charles. Common Sense. Edinburgh, 1819.

> (Allusions to Keats, pp. 1, 13, 15.)